MW01090018

THE GRADUATE SCHOOL

Conflicting Worlds

New Dimensions of the American Civil War

T. MICHAEL PARRISH, EDITOR

From Property to Person

SLAVERY AND THE CONFISCATION ACTS,
1861–1862

Silvana R. Siddali

LOUISIANA STATE UNIVERSITY PRESS
Baton Rouge

Designer: Amanda McDonald Scallan
Typeface: Minion
Typesetter: G&S Typesetters, Inc.
Printer and binder: Thomson-Shore, Inc.

Library of Congress Cataloging-in-Publication Data

Siddali, Silvana R.
　From property to person : slavery and the Confiscation Acts, 1861–1862 / Silvana R. Siddali.
　　p. cm. — (Conflicting worlds)
　Includes bibliographical references and index.
　ISBN 0-8071-3042-7 (hardcover : alk. paper)
　1. United States—History—Civil War, 1861–1865—Confiscations and contributions.   I. Title.   II. Series.
　E480.S53 2005
　973.7′1—dc22

2004017497

Material from chapters 1 and 2 appeared previously in slightly different form as "The Sport of Folly and the Prize of Treason: Confederate Property Seizures and the Northern Home Front during the Secession Crisis," *Civil War History* 47 (2001): 310–33. Used with permission of Kent State University Press. Material from chapter 5 appeared previously as "'*Refined,* Highfalutin' Principles': The Northern Public and the Constitution in 1861–1862," *American Nineteenth Century History* 2 (2001): 60–81. Used by permission.

In grateful memory of
William E. Gienapp

Contents

Acknowledgments

The greatest debt I owe, not only in the completion of this work but also in my development as a scholar, is to William Gienapp, who advised the dissertation that eventually became this book. My original research topic was on the promise of land for the freed people after the Civil War, and Bill Gienapp always encouraged me to get back to the basics, to "think about property ownership." In the long run, of course, I discovered that he was right. These were the important questions: who had the right to own, what constituted legitimate property, and what did it mean to be owned as property? Bill Gienapp was an outstanding advisor: immensely conscientious, caring, precise, warm, supportive, wise, demanding, unfailingly loyal and generous to his students, and always scrupulously fair to all of us. I often credit him with the fact that I was able to find and keep such good friends from my graduate school experience. Serving as a Teaching Fellow in his Civil War course with my friends was one of the greatest experiences of my life because he allowed us to form a cohesive, supportive, loyal "company" under his leadership. Bill Gienapp taught me whatever I know about scholarly writing; I became a historian under his guidance; he was my good friend and mentor, and I will miss him immensely.

I was very fortunate in my graduate mentors and advisors. Heather Cox Richardson read and commented extensively on the dissertation. Her insightful critiques have improved the work beyond measure. I would also like to thank Joel Perlmann, my advisor at the Graduate School of Education, who inspired me to enter a Ph.D. program in the first place. He taught me the meaning and method of scholarly research, for which I will always be grateful.

There are many other friends and colleagues who deserve thanks for their advice and encouragement throughout the exigent process of turning a dissertation into a book. Michael Vorenberg has always been a kind and patient guide. Adam Smith and Martin Crawford have also commented on chapters and papers drawn from the dissertation. Mike Parrish, the series editor, was an especially valuable resource to me, and deserves much of the credit for imbuing this work with clarity and logic, as well as for helping me to contextualize my arguments and research in the broader scholarship. I am especially grateful to Sylvia Frank Rodrigue and to Greg Peters for their constant patience, encouragement, and good will as I struggled with the revisions.

My dear friends from graduate school days also deserve thanks, both for their willingness to read endless drafts, and for their kindness and love: Jody Bresnahan, Al Brophy, Tom Brown, Deborah Chmielewski, Andy Coopersmith, Nancy Davis, Christine Dee, Brett Flehinger, Susan Hunt, Libra Hilde-Jones, Marianne Lepp, Chandra Manning, Christine McFadden, Rowena Olegario, Pearl Ponce, Carole Stern, Susan Wyly, and Eva Sheppard-Wolf.

I would like to thank my friends and colleagues at Illinois State University, who read and commented on the early manuscript drafts, especially Lucinda Beier, Kyle Ciani, Ray Clemens, Linda Clemmons, Tony Crubaugh, John Freed, Paul Holsinger, Alan Lessoff, Lou Perez, Susan Westbury, and Mark Wyman. I am grateful to Michal Ditzian for her excellent editing help and priceless friendship. With love and hugs to Benjamin, Sophie, and Reuben. I would also like to thank my colleagues at Saint Louis University for their support and encouragement, especially Bentley Anderson, S.J.

This project was funded by several grants and fellowships while I was a graduate student, including grants from the Charles Warren Center at Harvard University, a grant from the Committee on Degrees in the History of American Civilization, the Emma Gildersleeve Lane Foundation, a Radcliffe Grant for Graduate Women, and several scholarship grants through the Harvard University Graduate School of Arts and Sciences. Two generous research grants from Illinois State University also enabled me to complete the book manuscript.

I am also grateful to the many research librarians who helped me throughout the research process, especially the archivists in the Manuscripts Division at the Library of Congress and the librarians at the Houghton, Lamont, and Widener Libraries at Harvard University, at the New York Public Library, and at the Boston Public Library.

From Property to Person

Introduction

In 1854, Abraham Lincoln told a Peoria, Illinois, audience that he trusted he understood, and truly estimated, the "right of self-government." He defined self-government as the proposition that "each man should do precisely as he pleases with all which is exclusively his own." But there were limits to this definition of self-government. The purpose of his speech was to condemn the recently enacted Kansas-Nebraska law, which permitted the extension of slavery north of the Missouri Compromise line. In his criticism of the law, Lincoln declared unequivocally that although the doctrine of self-government was "right—absolutely and eternally right," it could not justly be applied to the principle of extending slavery northward. Or rather, he asserted, the justice of the Kansas-Nebraska Act depended upon "whether a negro is *not* or *is* a man." For Lincoln, the legitimacy of property rights in human beings—and the right to spread the institution of slavery into free territories—revolved around the simple question of the humanity of black people. Clearly, for a white man, self-government simply meant that he could govern himself. Therefore, "if a negro is a man," Lincoln asked, then would it not be a "total destruction of self-government, to say that he too shall not govern himself?" Lincoln was making a radical statement not only about the nature of self-government and of property rights, but also about the survival of the nation. He called the government of one human being by another "despotism," and implied, through his use of the phrase "total destruction," that the extension of that despotism into free territories threatened democracy for all.[1]

In this speech Lincoln distilled the essential contradiction inherent in the American conception of self-government to just this: that there existed an irreconcilable conflict between the liberty to "do as one pleases with one's possessions" on the one hand, and the right of all human beings to liberty from

---

1. Basler, ed., *Collected Works*, 2:266; Paludan, *Presidency*.

"despotism," on the other. Lincoln was defining "self-government" in two ways—first, as the right to decide for oneself what constituted legitimate property, and second, as the right to govern oneself. There was some overlap between those two meanings, but they were not synonymous. In 1854, Lincoln already articulated a prophetic vision of the menace posed by the battle between private property rights, as protected by the Constitution, and individual rights, as defined by the principles expressed in the Declaration of Independence. This book argues that the era of the Civil War set in motion a reconsideration of property rights and individual liberties, and examines the origin of that transformation in the public and political debates over the confiscation of rebel property and the liberation of slaves.[2]

Initially most northerners believed that the war could, and indeed should, be fought conservatively. Their war aims were straightforward; they wanted to vindicate the Constitution and to reunite the nation "as it was," with property rights (even property in slaves) protected. But the goals of the war, and its progress, developed in an unexpected way. True, the southern rebellion threatened the Republic and implied the failure of the Constitution and of democratic government, which endangered the liberties of all Americans. But aside from the issues of sovereignty and the rule of law, there were also immediate practical problems that had to be considered. When they clamored for secession, few southerners had foreseen the chaos engendered by separating the mutually "owned" and "purchased" territories and federal possessions. There were federal properties (such as forts, customs houses, arsenals, and post offices) in all of the southern states. Moreover, southern planters owed millions of dollars to northern bankers and merchants. The separation of the states, therefore, was not only a question of ideological or philosophical differences: it also, on a more urgent and pragmatic level, forced a profound reexamination of the mutual rights (especially property rights) and obligations of the states. In fact, the first battle of the Civil War began over a contested piece of property, in the dispute over the possession of Fort Sumter. The fact that southerners had seized property that belonged mutually to all the states, and had repudiated debts they owed to northern merchants, enraged many northerners—even many of those who might otherwise have been willing to compromise with the rebels. North-

2. McCrary, "The Party of Revolution," 330–50; Huston, *Securing the Fruits of Labor;* Huston, *Calculating the Value of the Union.*

erners demanded reparations for the seized federal properties as well as for the threatened disruption to the economy and the potential cost of the war. They insisted that the rebels be forced to pay for their rebellion. Republicans, and even many War Democrats, communicated their anger over the property seizures to their representatives in Washington. Strident newspaper editorials called for the immediate repossession of federal properties and the enforcement of the laws. After Congress reopened in July 1861, many newspapers also re-printed, often verbatim, the congressional proceedings and speeches. Northern voters followed the debates carefully and wanted to weigh in on them; they de-manded a say in the conduct of the war. They flooded Washington with corre-spondence and with hundreds of petitions aimed at reminding congressmen and senators of their duty to prosecute a vigorous war effort. The representa-tives in Washington, in their turn, read and responded to the letters and often referred to their mail, and the petitions, in their speeches. Public opinion was of primary concern to those who were devising policy. During the special sum-mer session (July–August 1861) of the 37th Congress, and again later in the long session (December 1861–July 1862), Republicans in Congress proposed a great deal of punitive legislation, including many versions of confiscation acts, which were a direct response to vengeful northern public opinion.[3]

This book examines the political and public debates concerning the confis-cation of rebel private property, including human property. The First Confis-cation Act, debated during the special summer session in 1861, confiscated the property of rebels that was being used to aid the rebellion and discharged slaves from any service they owed to their rebellious owners. The property was to be considered the "lawful prize or capture," and taken for the "benefit of the United States." Anyone using slave labor to promote the rebellion was to forfeit all claim to such labor, and the slaves were to be immediately freed from their labors. Lincoln signed the First Confiscation Act into law on August 6, 1861. The Second Confiscation Act, debated in the longer session, and passed on July 17, 1862, was much more sweeping. This law provided for a fine, a prison sentence, possible execution, property confiscation (whether or not that property was ex-plicitly used to aid the rebellion), and the immediate emancipation of the slaves of anyone committing "the crime of treason" against the United States. Slaves

3. Nevins, *War for the Union*, especially vol. 2, *War Becomes Revolution, 1862–1863*. See also Grimsley, *The Hard Hand of War*.

who escaped from their bondage and fled to the Union Army would be considered "captives of war" and freed. The law also authorized the president to employ "persons of African descent" to put down the rebellion.

The two Confiscation Acts were not the only possible form of retribution against the rebels. In their demand for punishment, restitution, and justice, militant northerners proposed many and various efforts at confiscation, ranging from taxation, debt repudiation, foraging, plunder, outright theft, and various more legal attempts at taking private property. But because the two congressional confiscation laws involved a wide-ranging public response from many political and social groups, they remain the best way to study the changing attitudes toward property rights in the North. These two laws gave rise to a vigorous public debate precisely because they were an attempt at legitimizing an assault on constitutionally protected rights, and also because the proposed confiscation bills forced northerners to confront their own ideas about *human* property. The other efforts at property seizure (including, for example, direct taxation or punitive fines) required fewer legal and political justifications, because they were based on traditional congressional powers. Similarly, wartime property seizures, such as foraging or the capture of enemy property by the federal armies, provoked less discussion because such actions were within the domain of accepted military procedures. Although conservative northerners certainly expressed their opinions on taxation and forage, the debates over the two Confiscation Acts more clearly reveal the struggle of northerners to come to terms with shifting ideas about property rights, the rights of citizens in rebellion against a democratic republic, and the destiny of chattel slavery in a nation founded on the principle that all human beings were created equal.

The era of the Civil War, then, brought about a crisis in American ideas regarding property rights. But that crisis was founded on long-term, deeply rooted conflicts that had plagued Americans since the ratification of the Constitution, and had steadily grown more contentious in the first half of the nineteenth century. First, antebellum Americans had argued with one another over the sanctity and transcendence of private property rights against other deeply held values, such as Christian ethics and the right of all human beings to liberty. Second, early nineteenth-century Americans struggled with the competing claims of the interests of the individual over the community. Although southern Democrats had for generations relied on biblical, political, and constitu-

tional justifications for slavery, northern Whigs had grown increasingly reluctant to surrender their consciences to those rationalizations. Furthermore,
before the Civil War, nineteenth-century Americans looked to state constitutions for protection of their private property rights, especially the right to own
human beings. But those rights were not infinite; the local, state, and federal
governments claimed the right to condemn private property or to uphold the
claims of corporations against individual property owners, in the interests of
the welfare of the community. These changing ideas concerning property rights,
already in motion during the Jacksonian era, would become more sharply
marked during the Civil War when Americans sought more effective ways of
prosecuting warfare against their countrymen.[4]

According to antebellum Whigs and later Republicans, property rights in
human beings conflicted with Christian morality. Therefore, slave property in
particular had been perceived as a threat to the American political and moral
community. Still, in spite of the growing anger over issues such as the Fugitive
Slave Law, the Kansas-Nebraska Act, and the Dred Scott decision, few Americans were willing to contemplate widespread emancipation. Before the outbreak of the Civil War, only abolitionists, as yet a tiny minority in the North,
advocated interference with slavery where it already existed. Because they had
sworn to uphold the Constitution, with all its guarantees of property rights and
its compromises with slavery, the members of the 37th Congress could not
make laws that attacked the property rights in human beings. As a result of the
perceived need to attack enemy private property (including property in slaves)
during the war, Americans reluctantly had to make the shift from honoring private property rights to respecting the rights of all human beings to be free and
to enjoy the fruits of their labor. This process conflicted with northerners' in-
grained race prejudice, which always limited the ethical reach and fulfillment of
those ideological shifts. In the end, Americans came to a realization—albeit
halting and incomplete—that they had to reinterpret property rights in order
to ensure the survival of the Republic, with its foundation in popular government, majority rule, and the inherent liberties of all Americans left intact. By
the end of the war, the liberties of all Americans—even those who were the vic-

---

4. Friedman, *History,* 235–6; Hall, *The Magic Mirror,* 99, 114; Novak, *The People's Welfare;* Fox-
Genovese and Genovese, *Fruits of Merchant Capital,* chapter 13.

tims of severe prejudice—would have to take precedence over the property rights of people in rebellion against the government.[5]

In the long run, the First and Second Confiscation Acts were of dubious efficacy. They were complicated, vague, and so softened and meliorated by the congressional committees that they were nearly useless. Moreover, they were rarely enforced. But no one could have predicted that outcome while the laws were being debated in the halls of Congress and in northern newspapers and correspondence in 1861 and 1862. The laws seemed to strike at the very foundations of the Republic. Conservatives in Congress and at home feared that any assault on Confederate private property—even human property—would bring down the structure of the Constitution. The debates for and against confiscation quickly became a forum for a far-reaching discussion of property rights, civil liberties, wartime powers, executive authority, civilian control over the military, and slavery.

These debates laid the groundwork for the Reconstruction Amendments because they broadened the reach of the federal government into the private property of American citizens and envisioned a new interpretation of the limits of states' authority over people in bondage. Prior to the war, most Americans had believed that any emancipation policy would be not only unconstitutional but also tyrannical. A combination of rising hard war sentiment in the North, increasing critiques of the constitutional compromises with slavery, and a growing, though reluctant, awareness that human property no longer deserved the same constitutional protections as "ordinary property," brought about an important revolution in American attitudes that allowed Congress to revise the Constitution to widen the scope of freedom for all Americans. But like all revolutions, the change went much farther than most northerners had intended. Before the outbreak of war, only utopian visionaries would have contemplated meddling with private property rights; only radicals would have advocated the emancipation of slaves.

And like most of his compatriots, Lincoln was no radical. Throughout his inaugural address, Lincoln stressed the rule of law, the will of the majority, the absence of any need for violent or revolutionary action in a democratic republic, and the responsiveness of representative government to the popular will. So

---

5. For antebellum attitudes toward the proslavery compromises in the Constitution, see Vorenberg, *Final Freedom*, especially chapter 1.

long as Americans remained obedient to constitutional law, they possessed power and authority over their government. The Constitution would protect even property rights in human beings. But was the Constitution strong enough to save the life of the nation while still expressing the will of the people? It was the will of the southern people, after all, that had driven their rebellion forward; it would be the will of the northern people that prosecuted the war against the rebellion.

There was a further problem in placing unswerving faith in the nation's founding document. If it was true that the will of the people impelled social and political changes, then it stood to reason that those changes could extend to fundamental organic law. Even within the first year of the war, it was becoming clear to many that the old compromises and accommodations were no longer justified. Nor had they been particularly effective. In 1861, few northerners believed that the Constitution itself would have to be rewritten or even that fundamental American social arrangements would suffer a profound transformations. Early in the crisis, Lincoln and many other moderate northerners still believed that the Constitution could and should be upheld "as it was," and that with a military victory, the nation could be reconstructed with slavery intact, guaranteed, and contained. Antebellum Americans still conceived of the federal Constitution as the divinely inspired product of their revolutionary heritage. But just as southerners had underestimated the problems associated with separating from the Union, northerners had overestimated their ability to control the long-term effects of their assault on the very definition of property. Their anger against the rebels overwhelmed their moderation on the Constitution and on time-honored civil rights. They wanted revenge for the southern attack on the Union and the Constitution, as well as on their federal and private possessions. The only way to do that, many felt, would be to launch a personal assault on Confederate property. War-minded northerners conceptualized the conflict in highly personal terms, against individuals and their personal possessions, not against a southern nation. In order to reconstruct the Union and reestablish the Constitution as the law of the land, northerners believed that they would not only have to take back the federal possessions that had been seized but also assault Confederate private property. Moreover, there was no doubt among prowar northerners that they had a perfect right to do so. Most Civil War historians agree that hard war sentiments developed slowly over a period of more than two years. It is also true, however, that within a few weeks of the secession crisis, northern Republican voters already expressed vengeful sentiments specifically aimed at taking rebel property. Radicalism on property rights, however, was not necessarily linked to radicalism on slavery. War Democrats, for example, advocated attacks on private rebel property, but expressed little interest in emancipating slaves. Even many Republicans wanted to maintain some form of control over the freed slaves after they were confiscated from their rebel owners.[6]

At the same time, by the summer of 1861, many northerners had become aware that slaves were an important resource for the Confederate war effort, and believed that it would be proper to take them along with other war matériel. Anyone who favored the war effort understood that Confederates would have to be deprived of the means to prosecute the rebellion. Only conservatives in Congress (like Peace Democrats and border state politicians) and on the home front opposed all confiscation measures. Most moderates therefore tried to argue *for* confiscation but *against* emancipation. The fact that men in Congress thought they could deliberate carefully about the property status of slaves, or contemplate taking them from their owners without releasing them from their bondage, strikes the modern reader as callous in the extreme. But a confiscation policy that included emancipation, many believed, brought with it threats of race wars, widespread black emigration to the North, and the destruction of the southern plantation economy.

The congressional debates over the confiscation bills quickly derailed over the definition of slave property. Democrats—especially those hailing from the border states—demanded that human property be treated, as they put it, "like ordinary property." In other words, the law should allow the confiscation of slaves, but permit the Union armies or the federal government to retain ownership over them and their labor, in much the same way as the armies retained ownership over captured horses or artillery. But in 1861 this was not only an anachronism, it was a refutation of established legal principles on slave property dating back to the pre-Revolutionary era. Colonial courts, and later the Constitution, had always recognized the special status of human property. The Constitution referred to slaves as "persons held to labor," and state laws still recognized the dual nature of human property—for example, through their protection of the lives of slaves. Conservatives were forced to make this anachronistic and even irrational argument (one that would have received no serious

6. Kammen, *Machine.*

hearing in any American court of law) because they could not reasonably advocate against military confiscation without appearing to support the rebellion. At the same time, conservatives could not bring themselves to agree that slaves should be confiscated along with the rest of enemy property, and then simply liberated from the labor they "owed" to their owners.[7]

The debates over the constitutionality of confiscation and the status of slaves as property occupied a great deal of time in the 37th Congress. Enslaved southerners, however, did not wait on political deliberations or on shifts in northern public opinion. Taking matters into their own hands, they began to flee to the Union Army, a few dozen at first and then by the hundreds and thousands. Their actions overthrew the North's uneasy (and now increasingly doubtful) acquiescence to the legitimacy of human property. But because of their lifelong prejudices against black people, as well as their residual convictions about the sanctity of private property rights, many northerners were unwilling to relinquish entirely their ideas about the freedom of enslaved southerners. In the first year of the war, many expressed absolute bewilderment about the fate of slaves freed through confiscation. Within another year, however, as the likelihood of widespread emancipation grew more real, that confusion gave way to callous ideas about the desirability of maintaining possession of confiscated slave labor.

The debates over the confiscation of property, then, brought to light a series of crucial questions: first, what were the rights of rebellious citizens, especially if one hoped eventually to restore them to their former status? Second, in a democratic republic that protected the rights of all of its citizens equally (at least in theory), what kind of property were slaves? And finally, the question that most concerned conservatives and border state politicians: what would the assault on the private property rights of enemy civilians do to the property rights of loyal Unionists? Could the Constitution survive such an assault—even on such problematic property as the labor of a fellow American? Much of this debate centered on the fact that the Constitution still protected private property through its implicit compromises. Therefore, among Republicans these discussions led to a profound questioning, criticism, and erosion of reverence for the Constitution.

Conservative Democrats such as Kentucky senator (later congressman in the 37th Congress) John J. Crittenden and his congressional border state colleagues believed that the confiscation legislation posed as great a threat to the

7. Finkelman, *An Imperfect Union*.

Republic as the southern rebellion. As Republican voters and politicians drove their constitutional critique forward, the conservatives' rhetoric became steadily more entrenched in a reactionary, undemocratic interpretation of the Constitution that was rooted in proslavery ideology. They argued that the Constitution had to be preserved precisely as it stood in order to forestall any attacks on human property. The emergence of a constitutional critique forced conservatives into an intransigent position and denied them the life-saving strategy of flexibility. Conservatives resorted to the language of a fundamentalist religious faith, likening the Constitution to a sacred text that could be neither reinterpreted nor revised, in spite of the fact that the founders had certainly envisioned a document that was capable of amendment. In 1861, John J. Crittenden attempted to bind this militant, even ahistorical, definition to the Constitution by including, in his famous compromise, an "unamendable amendment" that guaranteed the security of slave property in perpetuity. The conservatives' fears were probably prophetic. The debates over property and white southerners' disputed rights made it possible for more adaptable, more pragmatic Americans to contemplate fundamental changes to the Constitution.[8]

Citing Lincoln's hope that the war would not degenerate into a "merciless struggle," as well as the limited war strategy of men like Generals George B. McClellan, Don Carlos Buell, and Henry Halleck, historians have assumed that hard war measures were primarily the handiwork of congressional radicals. But judging from congressional speeches and correspondence, their proposals for hard war policies were a reaction to changing attitudes on the home front. Indeed, Congress rather ameliorated and weakened the Confiscation Acts, primarily through the moderate, bipartisan Committees on the Judiciary in both houses that considered the legislation and softened its most punitive provisions. Moreover, although President Lincoln did sign both laws, he did not permit military officers to enforce them. For that reason the Confiscation Acts have been described as preliminary steps toward emancipation and Reconstruction. However, both the northern public and the members of the 37th Congress engaged in an intense, protracted debate over these two laws from early 1861 until late 1862. The proposed bills produced an immense outpouring of public opinion in newspapers, pamphlets, sermons, and letters to politicians

8. For northern home front ideas about the Constitution early in the war, see Hyman, "Reconstruction and Political-Constitutional Institutions," in *New Frontiers.*

in Washington. And in Congress there were so many speeches on confiscation that the *Congressional Globe* had to print an appendix volume to contain
them all.[9]

The debates over the confiscation of Confederate property stimulated a series of transformations in the public mind: first, that the federal government
could (and should) make laws that directed the war effort against rebellious citizens, rather than leaving the war effort to military authority; second, that the
Constitution ought to be amended to eliminate its compromises with the South
and its "peculiar institution"; and third, that under some circumstances, and to
a limited degree, enslaved black people should be released from their bondage.
The first two shifts in opinion could be more readily found among moderate
and radical Republicans, but the third was also increasingly evident among
some War Democrats. In the meantime, radicals in Congress dominated the
joint Committee of the Conduct of the War, whose purpose was to investigate
charges of fraud in military purchases and incompetence among military leaders. Although the congressional committee was primarily composed of radicals,
it did bring home to the Union Army the reality that civilians were committed
to maintaining some control over military affairs and tactics.[10]

During the Civil War, Americans were deeply engaged with congressional
politics; they felt they had a right to be heard on the legislative and military
conduct of the war. Growing skepticism about the political process before the
war undermined their faith in political compromises and influenced deeper
uncertainties about the federal Constitution. At the same time, Americans in
the Union, even radical Republicans, took constitutional issues seriously, which
is why many of them demanded that the document be amended or reframed,
rather than simply subverted or ignored. The impulse for constitutional reform
was more evident among voters than in Congress. Where radical politicians in
Congress believed that presidential and congressional war powers permitted a
wider (if merely temporary) interpretation of the Constitution, prowar northerners held that the Constitution required deeper, and more permanent, re-

9. Syrett, *The Confiscation Acts;* Franklin, *The Emancipation Proclamation,* 18–24; Trefousse,
Lincoln's Decision, 34–5; Holt, "An Elusive Synthesis: Northern Politics During the Civil War," in
McPherson and Cooper, eds., *Writing the Civil War.*

10. Benedict, "A Constitutional Crisis," in McPherson and Cooper, eds., *Writing the Civil
War;* 171.

form. It was their willingness to consider revising the Constitution during the war that made it easier to ratify the Reconstruction Amendments afterward.[11]

These two laws, then, created a forum for prowar, antislavery northerners (and even for many moderates and conservatives) to examine and debate fundamental shifts in their conceptions of the role of government, the nature of the Constitution and its protections of civil liberties and rights, and most important of all, the meaning of human bondage in America. In spite of ethical and moral oppositions to the institution, most Americans—all but the most ardent abolitionists—had still understood slavery as a property relationship in the early years of the war. Therefore, the confiscation bills were the arena in which Americans would have to work out this fundamental problem inherent in the structure of American society and politics. The congressional speeches for and against confiscation, taken together with editorials, pamphlets, manuscript letters, and other primary sources reveal a rather swift transformation in rhetoric concerning the Constitution and its protections of property rights, but a slower and incomplete change in attitudes about southern black people and their future in the reunited nation. This incomplete change persisted in the form of severe race prejudice against black people, even after the passage of the Thirteenth Amendment and throughout postwar Reconstruction.[12]

The Union victory in the Civil War ensured the triumph of the Constitution over the potentially destructive southern rebellion and over the constitutional compromises with slavery and the southern slave power. The reunion of the states and the liberation of millions of Americans from bondage stand as two of the most heroic themes of our nation's history. Lincoln's Gettysburg address placed momentous questions before Americans during the time of the nation's greatest calamity: could a nation conceived in liberty and dedicated to the proposition that all men are created equal survive a horrific civil war? Was the fratricidal conflict only a war against slaveholders, or was it also a war against slavery? Could a Constitution that guaranteed the freedom of individual citizens, and at the same time protected the right to hold human beings as property, be reformed of its fundamental contradiction without being destroyed in the process?[13]

11. Altschuler and Blumin, *Rude Republic.*

12. Foner, "Rights and the Constitution," 863–83; See also Bestor, "The American Civil War as a Constitutional Crisis," 327–52.

13. For black peoples' constitutional rights during and after the Civil War, see Foner, "Rights and the Constitution," 863–83.

Americans have inherited their larger view of the Civil War as a test of the Constitution and of the principles of the Declaration of Independence directly from Abraham Lincoln. Somewhat generously, they also now attribute Lincoln's grand vision to all Union citizens who were sacrificing their sons, brothers, and husbands to the struggle and who were pouring out their blood and treasure in an effort to maintain the "best government on the face of the earth." While it is certainly true that the northern home front made great sacrifices for the cause of the Union, their commitment also entailed a profound and often difficult struggle to come to terms with the Constitution's implied protections of the institution of slavery.[14]

Some historians of the Civil War and Reconstruction debate whether Lincoln's grand vision was realized at all. While I am persuaded that the Civil War did indeed represent a political, social, and economic revolution, I agree that the revolution was incomplete. The purpose of my book is not to add to the already voluminous debate over the revolutionary nature of the Civil War. My focus is on the process by which Americans achieved the transformation of a society based on a document that both enshrined liberty as a sacred right for all citizens and at the same time sanctioned human bondage and protected the rights of white southerners to coerce the labor of black southerners. A constitutional critique was necessary in order to discover which was primal: the right of all Americans to their personal liberty, the territorial integrity of the nation, and the preservation of popular government—or an inviolate Constitution that continued to allow people to be owned as slaves.[15]

That Lincoln's vision of a reunited America free from the stain of slavery was achieved—even partially and without the necessary guarantees and protections of the freed peoples' rights—should not blind us to the laborious process by which Americans living in the North arrived at that conclusion. They reached the end of slavery, by the beginning of 1863, over nearly insurmountable obstacles: northern race prejudice, constitutional guarantees for property ownership, a powerful commitment to federalism even among radical Republicans in Congress, and a frustratingly slow military campaign. In spite of the northern home front's insistence on the sweeping confiscation of private prop-

14. Paludan, *Covenant with Death*; Syrett, *Confiscation Acts*. See also Franklin, *The Emancipation Proclamation*, 18–24, and Trefousse, *Lincoln's Decision*, 34–5.

15. See, for example, Gerteis, *From Contraband to Freedman*; Gillette, *Retreat from Reconstruction*; McPherson, *Abraham Lincoln and the Second American Revolution*, 17.

erty, and in spite of its insistence that the government should maintain some level of control over black people's labor in the South, in the end the Constitution endured and slavery did not. The survival of the Constitution can be attributed in part to the 37th Congress's conservatism on the document and the Fifth Amendment's protections of private property ownership. Congress protected the Constitution by writing ineffective confiscation laws that could not achieve any of their stated ends, primarily because political compromises during committee deliberations had forced Republicans to soften the most punitive provisions. At the same time, the fact that thousands of slaves had already "confiscated" themselves by mid-1862 and thus forced a recognition of their ability to decide their own future made it impossible for moderates to cling to the institution of lifelong and inherited slavery.[16]

When President Lincoln issued the Preliminary Emancipation Proclamation in September 1862, radicals decried the document because it freed only slaves living in a few occupied areas, including northern Virginia, Tennessee, New Orleans, and the Sea Islands and Port Royal in South Carolina. The Proclamation freed only slaves who belonged to rebels still in arms against the government—and those slaves could not be reached by the Union armies. It did not liberate slaves living in the border states because many of them still belonged to loyal owners, and loyal citizens' property was still protected from seizure by the Fifth Amendment. But in spite of the provision that rebels could maintain ownership of slaves if they returned to the Union by the end of the year, Abraham Lincoln's proclamation did assail the notion that human beings could be held in legal possession. The final Emancipation Proclamation, issued on January 1, 1863, established the power of the federal government to interfere with constitutional protections of private property ownership in times of internal rebellion. Perhaps one of the more important results of the Emancipation Proclamation was that it forced the northern home front to relinquish any hope of permanent control over the people freed from bondage. The Emancipation Proclamation may have gone too far for more conservative northern voters in late 1862, but the Republican home front's willingness to question some of the nation's founding principles—including the constitutional guarantees of the sanctity of private property ownership of rebellious white southerners—may

16. Benedict, "Preserving the Constitution," 65–90. See also Kelly, "Comment on Harold M. Hyman's Paper," in Hyman, ed., *New Frontiers,* 55.

have made it easier for them to accept, however reluctantly, the liberation of millions of enslaved black southerners. The combination of militancy early in the war and the urgent debate over the Constitution, both in Congress and on the home front, brings into focus one of the most fundamental problems of the Union war effort: how to preserve the integrity of the Constitution while assailing constitutionally protected property rights in human beings.[17]

Note: All primary source quotations are reproduced exactly as in the original, except as noted.

17. Franklin, *The Emancipation Proclamation*, 90–3. For the immediate results of the Emancipation Proclamation, see Vorenberg, *Final Freedom*.

CHAPTER 1

Confederate Property Seizures and the Northern Home Front during the Secession Crisis

I<small>N THE WINTER OF</small> 1860–1861, a series of shocking events agitated the northern public. As each southern state declared itself out of the Union, its government seized federal properties located within its borders. From late December 1860 through May 1861, seceding southern states captured federal forts, arsenals, customs houses, and dockyards. Worse, the rebels repudiated all debts they owed to northern tradesmen and even launched privateers to prey against Yankee merchant ships. These actions enraged and frightened northerners of all political persuasions, even many conservative Democrats who might otherwise have sympathized with their southern brethren. Northern newspapers reported the rebels' aggressions on federal and private property in indignant detail. Editorials, private letters to congressmen and senators, diary entries, sermons, and pamphlets seethed with the notion that the southern states, as they seceded from the Union, were "stealing" themselves, along with valuable federal and private property, from their former fellow citizens. Secession was a direct attack on the Republic, the Union, and on the constitutionally protected rights of Americans in the North.

The northern public response to the rebels' property confiscations has received little attention in the narrative of the Civil War, perhaps because the seizures of forts, arsenals, and even private northern assets were later subsumed into the general turmoil of those troubled times. The seizure of federal properties—especially real estate—would appear to be a natural consequence of the political act of secession. But the aggressive and apparently unexpected nature of these actions provoked an immediate outburst among northerners of all political persuasions. The property seizures and the attacks on northern private assets forced an immediate recognition that secession was not simply an abstract or political question: it had concrete, long-term consequences for northern citizens who now confronted the reality of the destruction of their Union. Politicians and legal theorists focused on the threat to the Republic posed by the anarchical southern rebellion. Northern citizens, also deeply concerned about the safety of the Constitution and the Union, nevertheless concentrated their immediate anxieties on the tangible problem of mutually owned territories and federal possessions.[1]

Few northerners had expected an assault on federal and private property. Many of them had assumed, or hoped, that southerners' threats of secession were mostly empty posturing, that if some southern states did secede they could be quickly brought back to heel, or that their departure would not affect northern citizens in any material way. But the rebels' attack on federal and private property during the secession crisis proved that disunion directly threatened the rule of law and northern prosperity as well as national territorial unity. The property seizures were of immense importance to citizens in the free states; not only was their constitutional Union breaking apart, but their personal well-being was imperiled. Although the sectional conflict had been steadily worsening for some time, most northerners had never fully articulated their relationship to the citizens of the southern states. The rebels' aggressive actions early in the conflict now forced northerners to think hard about the reciprocal rights and obligations between the states. The public response to the property seizures reveals that northerners had for some time thought of the Union of the states as a kind of mutually beneficial partnership, bound together by a written agreement—the Constitution—but now threatened with destruction by one of the partners.[2]

There were, of course, deep divisions among the northern public on all aspects of the national crisis—including the right of secession, the desirability of emancipation, and the conduct of military operations. In spite of these internal divisions, the property confiscations made it clear to conservative Democrats and radical Republicans alike that a civil conflict would cost them materially

1. Paludan, "The American War Considered as a Crisis in Law and Order," 1013–34; Paludan, *Covenant with Death,* 19.

2. McPherson, *Battle Cry of Freedom;* Stampp, *And the War Came;* see also Nichols, *The Disruption of American Democracy,* and Potter, *Lincoln and His Party.*

and that their government was unable or unwilling to protect them. The combination of an unexpected personal attack on northern property and a weak, hesitant, lame-duck administration quickly ignited northern hostility toward their former fellow citizens in the South. The secession of the rebel states brought to the forefront of northern public opinion many serious problems, including the disruption of the American political process, the arming and training of rebel troops, and the right of navigation on the Mississippi River. Nevertheless, the confiscation of northern federal and private property is an indispensable element in understanding northern rancor toward the South during the secession crisis and later as the conflict developed into open warfare. These incidents, and the northern public's reaction to them, helped lay the foundation for future aggressive sentiments toward the rebel civilian population, for strong northern public support for punitive legislation against southern private property, and for a growing willingness to suspend—or even defy—constitutional protections of private property rights.

Several Deep South states had threatened to secede from the Union after Lincoln won the election in November 1860, but President James Buchanan had trusted that the worst could be kept at bay until he could leave office honorably. His fervent hope, that he could hand over the reins of an intact government to the president-elect, was now shattered. Buchanan now faced the worst political crisis of his life. Because of his long-standing sympathy for the southern states and his vacillating stance on the secession crisis, he quickly lost the support of the northern public. Although Buchanan opposed secession, he did nothing when rebel states began to seize federal and private assets located within their borders. Frustrated northerners, dismayed by what they perceived as Buchanan's treasonous weakness, began to wonder whether they had a government at all. The rebels' seizures, coupled with the government's weak response, seemed to indicate that their Republic was not strong enough to withstand an internal rebellion. Worse, many northerners began to worry that their administration could not protect them from the depredations of southern rebels. At the end of the month, one disgusted Brooklyn resident declared, "we have no one to represent us."[3]

3. B. F. Phillips to Henry L. Dawes, Henry L. Dawes Papers, Library of Congress, (hereafter LOC), January 31, 1861.

Buchanan's final address to the 36th Congress, given on December 3, 1860, took a weak, contradictory, querulous tone. The president blamed the crisis entirely on northern antislavery agitators. He stated, on the one hand, that secession was illegal and that the federal government would maintain its hold over any forts and arsenals located in the South. On the other hand, he also believed that because the government had no right to coerce the rebellious states, it could only act defensively. When northerners read Buchanan's message in their papers, they reacted with anger and contempt for its "weakness and imbecility." In the meantime, the 36th Congress refused to enact any measures empowering the president to take action against the seceding states, and voted down every proposal to increase the Army or reinforce the forts. The northern public, however, placed the blame directly on Buchanan. Over the next few weeks, his credit in the public eye plummeted. He was excoriated in the press as an imbecile, a coward, and a traitor who did nothing but "pray and cry" while the country was being torn in two. Republicans hated Buchanan because of his long record of sympathy for southerners and for slavery. He was hardly more popular with the members of his own party, however. Southern Democrats despised him for his unconditional Unionism, while northern Democrats blamed him for their defeat in the 1860 election and for his enmity to their candidate, Stephen A. Douglas. Many northern Democrats believed that Buchanan had been instrumental in splitting the Democratic Party by throwing his support to John C. Breckinridge in the 1860 presidential election, thus draining southern votes from Douglas.[4]

The northern public's disenchantment with the incumbent administration set the scene for an ongoing struggle between the people and their representatives in Washington. Northerners began to see themselves in an adversarial relationship with what they vaguely called the "Administration," by which they meant the president, his cabinet, and any politicians who happened to disagree with their views. As the crisis developed, northern citizens lost confidence in their government. After he had read Buchanan's message to Congress, Illinois

4. James Buchanan, final address to Congress, December 3, 1860, *Cong. Globe*, 36th Cong., 2nd sess., 1–7. For negative public opinion on James Buchanan during the secession crisis, see Stampp, *And the War Came*, 46–8; J. H. Wilson to John Logan, Logan Family Papers, LOC, January 9, 1861; Pryor, quoting Lewis Cass, in *Reminiscences of Peace and War*, 112. See also, Rev. B. F. Phillips to Henry L. Dawes, Dawes Papers, LOC, who thought Buchanan should have been indicted for treason for his "inability and neglect of duty," January 31, 1861.

congressman John Logan's friend J. H. Wilson commented that if indeed the federal government had "no power to coerce a rebellious state to obedience to the law[,]" then their forefathers "must have been fools." Although Buchanan remained loyal to the Union, and never wavered in his intention to hold the forts or support Major Robert Anderson at Fort Sumter, he lost credibility with Republicans and Democrats alike during the secession crisis.[5]

Events proceeded too quickly for the cautious Buchanan administration. Less than a week after South Carolina's secession, Major Anderson spiked the guns at Fort Moultrie on the Charleston shoreline and quietly moved his forces to Fort Sumter, which was built on a manmade granite island in Charleston Harbor. Anderson made this unauthorized move because Fort Sumter was more defensible than Fort Moultrie, but in so doing he considerably worsened the crisis. Several commissioners from South Carolina were already in Washington to negotiate a peaceful settlement with Buchanan; when they heard the news of Anderson's action, they angrily canceled their meeting with the president. The South Carolina Convention, which had issued the secession proclamation on December 20, had empowered these men to negotiate with President Buchanan for the "delivery" of the forts, magazines, lighthouses, arsenals, and "other real estate." The commissioners demanded a division of all other property held by the federal government, which they insolently claimed had been acting "as agent of the Confederated States of which South Carolina was recently a member." Clearly, the South Carolina rebels believed that when they seceded from the Union, they would be able to take the federal properties with them. They reckoned without their former fellow citizens' determination to maintain possession of the mutually owned properties, however.[6]

In the winter of 1860–1861, some conservative northerners were still willing to consider a peaceful separation of the states, while moderates proposed a series of compromises that would keep the Union intact. Widespread support for conciliatory proposals vanished, however, when southerners began to seize property belonging to the U.S. government. On December 27, 1860, South Carolina's Governor Francis Pickens, in accordance with the wishes of the South Carolina Convention, ordered the state militia to seize Fort Moultrie, recently abandoned by Major Anderson, and to occupy Castle Pinckney in Charleston

5. J. H. Wilson to John Logan, Logan Family Papers, LOC, January 9, 1861. For Buchanan's administration during the secession crisis, see Smith, *The Presidency of James Buchanan*, 143–92.

6. McPherson, *Political History*, 29; Smith, *The Presidency of James Buchanan*, 172.

Harbor. The same day, the schooner *William Aiken* surrendered to the South Carolina state militia. Over the next few weeks, events proceeded swiftly among the disaffected states of the South. On New Year's Eve, South Carolina took over the U.S. arsenal, post office, and customs house in Charleston. After that, as other states seceded, their governors ordered state militias to seize all federal properties within their borders. Georgia's Governor Joseph E. Brown ordered state troops to occupy Forts Pulaski and Jackson, as well as the U.S. Army arsenal, on January 2. By the end of the month, Georgia had seized brigantines, schooners, and steamers from New York, all carrying government goods and arms whose estimated worth was over fifty thousand dollars. Governor Brown also commanded the collector of the port of Savannah to retain "all moneys from customs in his possession, and make no payment on account of the Federal Government." In Texas, state militias seized over a million dollars' worth of Army property. In the first three months of 1861, similar scenes took place in seven other states; forts, arsenals, guns, mints, post offices, revenue cutters, and customs houses were seized swiftly and without much resistance from U.S. Army officers. By the end of January, there were only four pieces of federal real estate left in the seceded states—Forts Jefferson, Taylor, and Pickens in Florida, and Fort Sumter in South Carolina.[7]

Northerners reacted with helpless rage. Believing that Buchanan meant to betray their forts and arsenals into southern hands, many called him a traitor and a coward, and wanted him hanged alongside the rebels, or at least impeached. Some northerners were by now becoming painfully aware that Congress was refusing to take any decisive action against the seizures. A Brooklyn man denounced the inactive Congress as a group of "exhumed fossils," and warned ominously that "we do not any of us like to dwell too much on states rights now." Indiana banker Calvin Fletcher was horrified by the thought "of these 7 seceding states withdrawing & grabbing what they could lay their hands on belonging to the 33 states in common without giving notice or rea-

7. The *Cincinnati Daily Enquirer*, the *Albany Atlas and Argus*, the *Cincinnati Daily Press*, and the *Columbus Crisis* all supported peaceful separation during the secession crisis. Indeed, even Horace Greeley, the antislavery editor of the *New York Tribune*, briefly flirted with the idea that the "erring sisters" should be permitted to depart in peace. McPherson, *Political History*, 27. For the Confederate governors' actions, see John B. Edmunds Jr., "South Carolina," and Paul Escott, "Georgia," in Yearns, ed., *The Confederate Governors*. Bruce Catton gives a detailed account of some of the seizures in *The Coming Fury*, 1:233.

son," and declared that these actions were an outrage that could not "be laimly submitted to."[8]

Aghast at the rapid loss of the federal properties, northern citizens argued that secession was equivalent to theft. Recalling Frederick Douglass's comment that in running away from slavery, he had stolen himself, northerners said that the seceded states had stolen themselves from the Union. On January 29, for example, radical Republican congressman Thaddeus Stevens declared that the states who had gone out of the Union had "robbed the people of millions of money." Benjamin Brown French, a Washington, D.C., office-holder, confided his outrage to his diary: "Six States gone out of the Union! Immense amounts of property stolen by the Secessionists! They denominate it 'seized'—yes it has been *seized* just as I might thrust my hand into my neighbor's pocket and *seize* his money."[9]

Even pro-southern border state or Ohio River valley newspapers considered the seizures tantamount to a declaration of war. The *Baltimore Sun* said that the federal property in the South was the most "dangerous problem to which secession will give rise," and would undoubtedly cause a bloody conflict. The *Philadelphia Inquirer* ran a satirical editorial entitled, "If You Steal Any More, I'll Inquire Into It." The *Inquirer* was a Republican paper, and while it would remain generally supportive of Lincoln's policies throughout the war, it usually took a moderate stance on most political matters. However, the *Inquirer* railed against the do-nothing policy of Buchanan's administration. Reporting the seizure of the U.S. Mint and "Government treasures" in New Orleans, the paper was disgusted with the inactivity of the "functionaries who stand pledged before the country to enforce the laws" but who were doing nothing more than *inquiring* into the outrages committed by traitors. The protection of public and private property was seen, in the nineteenth century, as the fundamental basis

8. Fletcher, *Diary,* vol. 7, *1861–1862,* 50–1, entry dated February 21, 1861; Rev. P. K. Clark to Henry L. Dawes, Dawes Papers, LOC, January 10, 1861. In a letter dated January 21, 1861, to Senator John Sherman, David Maltby called Buchanan an "Old Tory"; and James K. Smith of Bellevue, Ohio, wrote to Sherman on January 1, 1861, calling Buchanan "a villin, consumate coward, knave, trator," and "Old Poltice." Fletcher, *Diary,* 50–1, entry dated February 21, 1861.

9. *Cong. Globe,* 36th Cong., 2nd sess., 621. Stevens was responding to President James Buchanan's final address to the 36th Congress on December 3, 1860. Cike and McDonough, eds., *Benjamin Brown French,* 341, entry dated February 10, 1861. French was subsequently appointed by Abraham Lincoln to the post of commissioner of public buildings.

for a republican form of government, and the Buchanan administration's inability to protect its possessions threatened the country's existence as much as the secession of the southern states.[10]

In an effort to calm the nation, President Buchanan declared January 4, 1861, a national day of fasting and prayer, but this action only provided fresh fuel for his critics. Unfortunately, the fast day proved to be a focal point for public disaffection and caused a great outpouring of criticism against the lame-duck administration. The public demanded action, not prayer. Calvin Fletcher, a staunch Unionist, contemptuously recorded in his diary that "very few people have respect [for] the man & couple that estimate with [the] day." He still thought it was his duty to observe the fast, but most other Republicans indignantly refused. Abolitionist Henry Ward Beecher's brother Charles publicly denounced the president from his pulpit in the South Congregational Church in Georgetown, Massachusetts, during a "red hot" antislavery sermon. Frederick Douglass, recalling the president's support of the Dred Scott decision and a proslavery constitution for the Kansas territory, thought that Buchanan had now thrown "around his character the very poetry of villainy, when he called upon the nation to join him in prayer and fasting."[11]

Many northern pastors seized on the president's fast day as a suitable occasion for calming their confused and upset flocks. Fast Days, Days of Humiliation and Prayer, and other national religious holidays were a common occurrence during the Civil War, in both sections of the country. Most Americans took such national days of prayer seriously and usually attended a church service. Buchanan's fast day yielded a torrent of clerical rhetoric throughout the North, much of it recorded for posterity in printed pamphlets. Although northern printers had been issuing pamphlets on slavery and other political questions for some time, the fast day sermons represented the first significant expression of public sentiment after the outbreak of the secession crisis. The ministers might reasonably be expected to honor the president's fast day and to urge their congregations to practice peace and Christian forbearance. Instead, they criticized Buchanan and his administration harshly. One of them condemned the entire government, asserting that there were now "incompetent, unreliable, and immoral men in office, all over the land, from the President

10. *Baltimore Sun*, January 5, 1861; *Philadelphia Inquirer*, February 15, January 30, 1861.

11. Fletcher, *Diary*, 8; *Baltimore Sun*, January 2, 1861; quoted from *Douglass' Monthly*, January 1861, in Foner, *Life and Writings*, 3:60.

down." Another declared, "The Union must be preserved. If the President is himself a traitor, *let him be impeached* & another man put in his place." Indeed, one New York City minister claimed that the Fast Day Proclamation was only *slightly* more moral than Buchanan's notorious support for a slave constitution in the Kansas territory.[12]

Still, as hard as the ministers were on Buchanan, they reserved their harshest criticisms for the rebels who had basely threatened the Union of the States and northern prosperity. At the same time, the ministers seemed to be uncomfortably aware that Americans had struck a bargain—Union for slavery—when they agreed to join as a nation. Many of the fast day sermons were preoccupied with the notion that Americans had somehow debased the idealistic principles of their forebears by reducing the Union to a mere commercial partnership. Many northerners viewed secession as a breach of contract. Others, of course, took a harder line and interpreted the states' rebellion as a blatant robbery. Although the parsons blamed the South more than the North, since the rebels themselves had "trample[d] all compromises and concessions under foot," they were not entirely pleased with this businesslike interpretation of the Union. For example, the Reverend William H. Lord lamented that there were so many people in the "North as well as South," who looked upon the Union as a simple contract that could be dissolved at the pleasure of the two parties. The Union, he felt, was seen as nothing better than a "partnership between traders, an agreement in a trade of spices and provisions, of cotton, tobacco and manufactures; that it can be constructed and broken and reconstructed at the whim of the parties." A Cincinnati preacher was more inclined to impute these materialistic ideas only to the rebel states. He demanded to know whether "our political system [was] an association of partners in a commercial firm any one of which may retire at pleasure?" However the ministers may have felt about this interpretation of the Union, nearly all fast day sermons stressed the "financial

12. For this study I examined twenty-one fast day sermons, and six other sermons preached before May 1861. All of them contained the businesslike language observed here. In these sermons the ministers' opinions on slavery, the South, and secession ranged from conservative to moderate. I did not find any examples of radical (e.g., pro-abolition) sermons, although I found references to such sermons in newspapers. The sermons in my sample came from Connecticut, Massachusetts, Missouri, New York, Pennsylvania, Ohio, Rhode Island, and Vermont. Aughey, *Renovation of Politics,* 8; P. F. Clark to Henry L. Dawes, in Dawes Papers, LOC, January 10, 1861; Thompson, *The President's Fast,* 7. For the importance of sermons during the secession crisis, see Chesebrough, *"God Ordained this War."*

embarrassments" that were likely to result from the destruction of the Union. One Missouri parson, deploring the standstill of industry and the "loss of value" to the tune of $8 million, declared that nothing could more clearly show that all parts of the nation would suffer from the results of the secession crisis.[13]

The sermons revealed poignantly that nineteenth-century Americans were struggling to understand the relationship between the states of the Union. They had always been able to compromise their differences in the past, but now they were in the midst of a national catastrophe. Northern citizens were forced to cobble together a hasty interpretation of the mutual rights and obligations of the Union's members. In order to arrive at a sensible conclusion, northerners and their pastors resorted to ideas that seemed familiar and rational to them. For example, a Reverend Eddy of Northampton, Massachusetts, recommended that in the event of permanent dissolution of the Union, the Confederacy should be recognized solely by a "commercial treaty and league," not as an independent republic. The ministers attempted to combine patriotic ideals with a modern, well-regulated, and just self-interest.[14]

A more poignant example of northerners' "contested property" metaphor for their Union was the notion that the land, heritage, and wealth of the nation had been bought and paid for by the revolutionary generation. Therefore, attempts to secede were nothing short of larceny. The northern men of God were indignant that the nation was now being "robbed of its property, after having, at vast expense, purchased her territory." In straightforwardly materialistic language, one minister said that secession would prove to be a "great financial embarrassment" to the nation, and that the restoration of peace would have to be bought and paid for. "We can never purchase a permanent settlement of the controversy between Freedom and Slavery but by firm resistance to its encroachments. That is the price which is to be paid, sooner or later."[15]

13. Thompson, *The President's Fast,* 20; Lord, *A Sermon on the Causes and Remedy of the National Troubles,* 10; Wilson, *A Nation Nonplussed,* 10; Clarke, *Secession, Concession, or Self-Possession: Which?* 4, 35; Anderson, *Dangers and Duties,* 2.

14. Eddy, *"Secession—Shall it be Peace or War?"* 20. See also, Goodale,*"Our Country's Peril and Our Duty,"* 1. In another example, in May 1861, an anonymous religious tract published for Union soldiers proclaimed boldly: "We never were partners. All Federal property always has been and will be exclusive. There can be no shares" (Dodge, *A Book for every Soldier's Knapsack,* 31).

15. Aughey, *Renovation of Politics,* 11; Lord, *A Sermon on the Causes and Remedy of the National Troubles,* 11; Wilson, *A Nation Nonplussed,* 15; Clarke, *Secession, Concession, or Self-Possession: Which?* 35.

Nineteenth-century Americans interpreted the idea of embattled property ownership rather broadly. For the past forty years there had been bitter fights about the right to extend either slavery or freedom into the new western territories. Now northerners were not only troubled about the seizure of federal and private property, but also about threats to their future prosperity and national greatness. The secession crisis endangered trade with the northern and midwestern states, because the rebels—upon seceding—would no doubt make it their business to gain control over the important waterways. Since late December 1860, northerners, especially those living in the West, had been vociferous in their demands that the government protect the mouth of the Mississippi River. Many northern merchants feared that the rebel states would hinder right of navigation, or that southern "mobs" would confiscate northern cargoes. Even before South Carolina had officially seceded, some papers had predicted a "tornado of indignation" if any rebel government attempted to cut off the Mississippi River from northern commerce. The *Cincinnati Daily Gazette,* a moderate Republican journal that had advocated peaceful secession in December, warned that interference with northern traffic on the Mississippi River would simply not be tolerated; moreover, any rebel forts built to hinder northern merchant ships would be leveled to the ground. Even an otherwise peace-minded minister preached that if Louisiana seceded, war would follow. "The people of the Valley of the Mississippi will never allow the mouth of that river to be held by a foreign power," and even the mildest man of God, he said, would be justified in "preach[ing] a Western crusade for the capture of New Orleans." [16]

This became an especially burning issue shortly after January 12, when rebels captured the customs house at New Orleans and placed artillery along the banks of the Mississippi River near Vicksburg. Midwesterners, whose trade was especially dependent upon the right of free navigation of the river, were outraged at reports that all steamboats were to be hailed and "overhauled" at the pleasure of the rebels. "The West will take its remedy into its own hands," the *New York Evening Post* declared, "President or no President." Some of the midwestern states, like Iowa and Illinois, had kept themselves carefully neutral in the early days of the secession crisis, but the threat to the river roused their wrath. The *Burlington* (Iowa) *Daily Hawk-Eye* claimed that its state had "stood

16. *Chicago Tribune,* December 18, 1860; *Buffalo Morning Express,* December 24, 1860; *Cincinnati Daily Gazette,* January 14, 1861; Clarke, *Secession, Concession, or Self-Possession: Which?* 38.

secession" with the "utmost equanimity," but that any interference with navigation of the Mississippi would be tantamount to a declaration of war.[17]

From mid-January through early February, delegates from all the seceded states were gathering in Montgomery, Alabama, to form their new government. Northerners waited anxiously to see what the Confederates would do about the Mississippi River. Some hoped that Louisiana would scarcely be so foolhardy as to interfere with northern trade on the Mississippi, but many newspaper editorials warned that the newly formed Confederate government would undoubtedly seize the most important waterway in the United States. The Montgomery Convention, in the end, decided not to interfere with the river trade, and asked Mississippi's Governor John Pettus to remove most of the cannon placed at Vicksburg. Much to the chagrin of midwestern newspapers, however, the customs house at New Orleans was still in the Louisiana rebels' hands, and would remain so until General Benjamin F. Butler captured the city in 1862. The editor of the *Chicago Tribune* fiercely recommended "blotting Louisiana out of the map," but even more conciliatory Democratic papers thought the rebels' continued control of the customs house and ports was an act of war.[18]

Around the same time the rebels were gathering in Montgomery, a few delegates from both southern and northern states met in Willard's Hotel in Washington, anxious to develop a plan for the settlement of the crisis. But the hopeful ideas of the "Old Gentlemen's Convention," as the Peace Convention was contemptuously called, sundered on the shoals of the territorial question. The question of contested property in the western territories had been plaguing Americans for forty years. Territory—with its promise of future wealth, land for white northern farmers, national progress, and above all, increased congressional representation—had been one of the central factors in the final breakdown between the sections. A minister writing to Massachusetts congressman Henry L. Dawes was outraged at the proposals to grant even more concessions to what he called "a few thousand insolent slaveholders." The very thought of ceding any territory to them was abhorrent. "No, No! A thousand times No! . . . *No more Free Territory given over to slavery!*" The Reverend Samuel J. Baird, who fervently exhorted his congregation to support concilia-

17. *New York Evening Post,* January 23, 1861, in Perkins, ed., *Northern Editorials,* 547; *Burlington* (Iowa) *Daily Hawk-Eye,* February 8, 1861, in Perkins, ed., *Northern Editorials,* 553.
18. *Chicago Tribune,* February 25, 1861.

tion and compromise, and who deplored all interference with slavery, thought that the rebels should be brought to justice for seizing federal forts and other properties.[19]

In the end, the peace proposals painfully hammered out by the Peace Convention failed specifically because of the territorial question. Compromise was impossible so long as the Republican Party maintained its position that slavery could not expand into the territories. The *Newark Daily Advertiser* explained that the Peace Convention would fail because it would enforce constitutional protection of slavery in territories south of 36°30'. What frightened the Republicans in Congress particularly, according to the *Advertiser,* was the phrase "and all territory hereafter to be acquired," which would "place the slave power forever in the ascendant." The fear that compromises over future territorial acquisitions would leave the slave power in control of Congress preyed on the minds of even the most conciliating Union men.[20]

Northerners saw southern demands for the protection of slavery—and, more important, of the right to expand the institution westward—as a direct threat to their own future dominance of the territories. Many newspaper editorials and letters, therefore, referred to the territories as a possession that was in danger of being wrested from them by the arrogant slave power. One of John Sherman's constituents from Ohio declared, "the Slave power have asked us to concede to them the right to carry Slaves in the territories. That we cannot do!" Another Ohioan urged Sherman to stand fast. Southern slaveowners must be prevented from spoiling the future inheritance of the nation's posterity. "[L]et us not be compelled to hear the clanking of their chains," he pleaded, "[and] witness the *curse,* of their *blighting footprints, upon our virgin soil.*"[21]

Many northerners believed that the Missouri Compromise line had been a terrible mistake because it had served to divide the "*common* Territory." Ac-

19. For northern public opinion on compromise, see Stampp, *And the War Came,* chapter 8; Rev. P. K. Clark to Henry L. Dawes, Dawes Papers, LOC, January 10, 1861; Baird, *Southern Rights and Northern Duties,* 7–9.

20. Bensel, *Yankee Leviathan,* 27; Gunderson, *Old Gentlemen's Convention; Newark Daily Advertiser,* January 22, 1861, in Perkins, ed., *Northern Editorials,* 252.

21. N. E. Prentice to John Sherman, John Sherman Papers, LOC, January 1, 1861. See also, the *Philadelphia Inquirer,* January 2, 1861. John Sherman served as congressman from Ohio during the 36th Congress, but he was about to be sworn in as senator in March 1861. Peleg Brinker to John Sherman, Sherman Papers, LOC, January 12, 1861.

cording to one New Yorker, such a division was unconstitutional because the territories belonged "to *all* the citizens" of the nation. The territories represented the future of the nation—not only the material wealth and political power, but also the future of the democratic ideals of liberty, the rule of law, and self-government. In a characteristic blending of pragmatic materialism and idealism, northerners talked about liberty as a kind of "property," which had to compete with the property peculiar to the South: slavery. For example, according to a Kentuckian named R. L. Dabney, northerners could carry into the territories "only *one* value, which is freedom," while the rebels claimed the "right to carry in *two* values—freedom and slavery." This was an injustice, Dabney felt, because the South deserved "no rights in the territories that the North do not have."[22]

Although many northerners disliked the institution of slavery, few of them were yet willing to cast their lots with abolitionists. Indeed, the vast majority of northerners were little troubled about the welfare and rights of slaves, and were mostly concerned that their own welfare and rights would suffer if slaveholders and their slaves continued to spread westward. Still, Dabney's odd analogy of "freedom" as a kind of material value led him to question the ethics of the right to hold human property. Freedom, he said, was the "*only unconflicting* property" that could move into the territories, because it was "*natural* property." A Connecticut minister agreed that slavery was an unnatural kind of property and should not be permitted to taint the western territories. "All may carry [into the territories] the property, which is regarded as property in the eyes of the world. None, either from the South or the North, shall carry there that artificial property which is only constituted such by local law." These references to "freedom" as a kind of property were not mere poetic fancies; in the coming years, such ideas would gain greater prominence as lawmakers in Washington struggled over the rebels' disputed right to dispose of their slaves' labor and liberty.[23]

Over the following weeks it became clear that no peaceful settlement could be hoped for. Thousands of letters poured in to Congress, expressing anger over the inactivity of the incumbent administration and demanding action. Many of the writers feared there was little hope of galvanizing an irresolute ad-

---

22. R. L. Dabney to Robert J. Breckinridge, Breckinridge Family Papers, LOC, April 29, 1861.
23. Ibid.; Abbott, *An Address Upon Our National Affairs*, 15.

ministration. They also called the rebels "plunderers," emphasizing the theft of property that free state citizens had paid for out of their taxes. Moreover, northerners were enraged that this jointly owned property would now be used to prosecute a rebellion against their own government. One Ohio resident warned John Sherman that "if the federal property falls into the Rebbels hands it will double their numbers in 24 hours." He only hoped that in that case there would be enough hardy northerners found willing to "lend the riffle, unsheath the soard and let loos the Bulldogs of war in all of its hedious forms." An indignant pamphleteer declared that "for a single State, one after another, . . . to seize forts, arsenals, custom-houses, post-offices, mints, and other valuable property of the Union, paid for by the treasure of the Union," was nothing but "rebellion, treason, and plunder." And a New Yorker told Sherman that nothing short of military action could enable the government to repossess federal properties. He was also tired of what he considered the rebels' self-pitying claims of abuse at the hands of northern abolitionists, and suggested that instead of redressing their grievances, the federal government ought to "supply them with an extra rag or two to dry up all their Crocodile Tears."[24]

Even the most conservative Democratic newspapers refused to back down on the seizures of government property. The *Cincinnati Daily Enquirer,* for example, had earlier supported a peaceful separation of the states, but was now outraged over the seizures. The paper reported that the news was being received everywhere with "mingled feelings of horror, amazement, indignation and alarm." Civil war was no longer a "threatening specter in the distance," but appeared "to be imminently close upon us!" Others thought the seizures merely capped what had been an ongoing process of southern war preparations. The property the two sections owned mutually was now being used to prosecute a civil war and to destroy the very government that northerners had helped to build. The seizures were not only theft, but they also abetted treason. A Louisville paper mistrusted the cotton states' repeated pleas for peaceable se-

---

24. Stampp, *And the War Came,* 87–9. *Battle Cry,* McPherson asserts that "thousands" of editorials and speeches expressed indignation over secession, 246; Stampp says that "thousands" of letters poured in to Congress (87). James S. Smith to John Sherman, Sherman Papers, LOC, January 15, 1861; John Lothrop Motley, quoted in Freidel, ed., *Union Pamphlets of the Civil War,* vol. 1, 41; David P. Smalley to John Sherman, Sherman Papers, LOC, January 1, 1861. He signed his letter "on behalf of tens of thousands." For a similar view, see also George P. May to John Sherman, Sherman Papers, LOC, January 19, 1861.

cession, because they were busy "purchasing arms, raising money, organizing the militia, seizing forts, and performing all the acts that characterize revolution." Such sentiments were evident even in the far west. Speaking in the California Senate, Judge Caleb Burbank claimed that arms and "implements of bloodshed" had been stealthily carried southward for at least six months prior to the November election. He heaped contempt on his conciliatory colleagues, saying that any effort to negotiate with the seceded states would make the forts, arsenals and ships, "but the sport of folly and the prize of treason."[25]

The seizures were a blow to national pride and proved that southerners were thumbing their noses at the laws and government of the United States. Indignant northerners demanded that the government retake the forts and raise arms to protect itself from further depredations. One Ohio man insisted that the government use armed force against the "seceders" and suggested a constitutional amendment that would "require an *express* relinquishment of the right of secession." Another said that if the president raised a force of volunteers to "man the forts and defend and preserve the public property," the southern states might recognize their error and return to the Union. Judge Burbank, in addressing this specific issue, wanted to make clear that southerners' complaints of northern coercion were inappropriate. In fact, the U.S. government need not even make war on the South to repossess her forts since the rebels were not foreign enemies but domestic criminals. It was simply a matter of holding the seceded states to strict account. Coercion and war, he explained, were terms that "should not be confounded with the terms of punishment and accountability." The question of whether rebels were to be treated as foreign enemies or as rebellious citizens would continue to plague both the northern public and politicians, but the dividing line between punishment and accountability was growing less distinct as the conflict wore on. The seizures of the forts, arsenals, and customs houses united the North as secession alone had failed to do. In laying their hands on federal property, the southern rebels had stepped outside the law and committed a criminal act. Therefore, northern citizens began to feel that an appropriate retaliatory action would have to include not only

25. *Cincinnati Daily Enquirer*, January 4, 5, 1861; *Louisville Daily Democrat*, January 15, 1861; Burbank, *Speech of Judge Burbank*, 5, 15. The California State Legislature was primarily Democratic and would remain so throughout the war. Burbank was referring to the fact that Buchanan's former secretary of war, John Floyd of Virginia, had been indicted for secretly shipping arms to the Confederacy. Floyd had resigned his position in January 1861.

the repossession of the forts, but also some sort of retribution against rebel assets. Almost everyone saw the seizures as a direct attack on northern prosperity and security; it was gradually becoming evident that the civil conflict would cost them dearly, and they wanted the rebels to bear the brunt of the financial burden.[26]

For that reason, most northerners appeared to be less concerned about the military value of the coastal forts than about their role in collecting customs revenues. Collecting the revenue was seen throughout the North as synonymous with enforcing the laws. The revenue was the property of the U.S. government, no less than the forts, arsenals, courts, and post offices. Failure to pay duties in the ports amounted to robbery of the U.S. Treasury. But what was worse, it now appeared that their government had lost authority. If the federal government could not collect revenues, then it followed that loyal citizens were no longer protected against criminal outrages by traitors. Even moderate newspapers agreed that the decision to come to blows was contingent on southern obedience to revenue laws. "If South Carolina does not obstruct the collection of the revenues at her ports nor violate another Federal law," said the *Springfield* (Illinois) *Journal,* "there will be no trouble and she will not be out of the union. If she violates the law then comes the tug of war."[27]

Union citizens distinctly saw the collection of duties as a test of the strength of the government. Southerners' refusal to pay revenue brought back the nightmare of tariff nullification, and northerners thought the president should take a leaf from Andrew Jackson's book in handling this new crisis. "It is not a question of *coercing* South Carolina but of *enforcing* the revenue laws," said the *Philadelphia Press.* "We cannot allow a sovereign State to nullify revenue laws." Some northerners took an even harder line. They thought the government should control not only the revenues, but also the cargoes upon which the revenues were due, and even the ships themselves. James A. Hamilton, a lawyer who had been a district attorney for New York, wrote to Salmon P. Chase that every vessel with "dutiable goods on board, as soon as she comes within the jurisdiction of the United States, . . . is held . . . to be in the actual possession of

26. H. F. Page to John Sherman, Sherman Papers, LOC, December 31, 1860; Augustus E. Noble to William Pitt Fessenden, William Pitt Fessenden Papers, LOC, January 24, 1861; Burbank, *Speech of Judge Burbank,* 6.

27. *Springfield* (Ill.) *Journal,* n.d., quoted in Victor, *Comprehensive History of the Southern Rebellion,* 1:100.

the Collector of such port." Therefore, the marshal in charge of the port had a
duty to seize such vessels if they attempted to defraud the government of its revenues. The *Philadelphia Press* agreed that if the United States could not maintain possession of the forts, then the revenue laws could not be enforced.
"Maintaining or retaking those forts, then, is . . . a convenient means of enforcing the revenue laws of the United States."[28]

Fears for the safety of federal property and anger over the southerners' refusal to turn over the revenues now propelled many northerners into an aggressive attitude toward southern private property. Northerners' lack of confidence in the strength of the government impelled them to urge violation of
the rebel citizens' private property rights. They were blaming southerners for
having started what would probably be a costly and bloody conflict, and wanted
revenge as swiftly as possible. That meant making the rebels sorry they had ever
dared to raise their hands against the Union. The *Chicago Tribune* made no
bones about the only way to dissuade southerners from their mad course. Declaring roundly that all government had its "ultimate base in force," the *Tribune*
demanded that the president attack the rebels' "lives, their wealth, their family comfort, their slaves, [and] the property of their children." Bringing the
war home to southern families would ensure that "this war would cease to be a
holiday business." The *Cincinnati Daily Press,* an extremely conservative, proslavery Democratic paper, advocated peaceful separation, but displayed a similarly hostile attitude toward the cradle of the rebellion. "The Government
should . . . not permit itself to be robbed of its property, driven out of its
forts by force, and bullied and disgraced by rebels. It has received insult and
injury enough at Charleston alone to justify it in laying that town level with
the ground." Even the conservative Democratic *New York World* cautioned its
"Friends at the South" that if they seceded, they would take nothing with them.
The "great mass" of the American people would never give "consent to the par-
tition of the possessions of this country for the ends of slavery."[29]

28. *Philadelphia Press,* January 15, 1861, in Perkins, ed., *Northern Editorials,* 219; Hamilton,
Reminiscences of James A. Hamilton, 474; *Philadelphia Press,* January 15, 1861, in Perkins, ed., *Northern Editorials,* 219.

29. *Chicago Tribune,* April 8, 1861; *Cincinnati Daily Press,* January 21, 1861; *New York World,*
January 5, 1861; see also, *Cleveland Daily Plain Dealer,* January 14, 1861; *New York World,* January 14,
1861, *Louisville Daily Democrat,* January 15, 1861.

Northerners who held investments south of the Mason-Dixon line were probably more concerned with the safety of their own private property (such as outstanding debts owed by planters, or even lost future profits) than with federal possessions and were enthusiastic about the use of force to protect or reclaim any confiscated belongings. One Philadelphian felt that the problem of the safety of *private* Union property in the South was far more urgent than the safety of the forts. He suggested that Confederate property be used to reimburse losses of loyal Union citizens. The federal government, he said, should force the southern states to respect northerners' property; if the administration were unwilling or unable to do so, then the rebels should be compelled to pay the damages to the U.S. government, which would in turn indemnify the "parties interested." Some newspapers thought this was an excellent notion, and even took it a step further. The radical Republican *New York Tribune,* for example, bitingly remarked that Virginia's property "in houses, in lands, in mines, in forests, in country, and in town" could now be confiscated. All this was perfectly fair because, according to the *Tribune,* the "worn-out and emasculated First Families must give place to a sturdier people, whose pioneers are now on their way to Washington at this moment in regiments." Certainly, an allotment of Virginia farmland would be a "fitting reward to the brave fellows who have gone to fight their country's battles."[30]

Such ideas would become increasingly popular in the North as the crisis worsened and would receive sustained attention in Congress during the special summer session. In the early months of the conflict, before the full reality of civil war had come home to northerners, many of them talked about the rebels as wrong-headed and selfish business partners who were attempting to break an established agreement. What was worse, southerners were trying to take property that did not belong to them. An attack on property rights—both the private property rights of fellow citizens and the property rights of the nation as a whole—meant a profound disregard of all the sacred principles of the rule of law and of the mutual responsibilities and duties of the citizens of a democratic republic. Northerners felt justified in demanding personal reparations from the rebels, which would certainly include a direct attack on southern private property. Most historians writing on the first few months after the firing on Fort

30. *New York Tribune,* quoted in the *Baltimore Sun* on April 26, 1861.

Sumter have described the northern public's patriotic fervor, the prodigious number of volunteers for the Union Army, and the bloodthirsty rhetoric heard everywhere in pro-Union rallies. While it would hardly be reasonable to argue that northerners wanted to go to war to attack southern property, their response to the rebel depredations do reveal a highly personal interpretation of the crisis, as well as their strong desire to visit retribution on the seceders.[31]

31. Alexander Browne to Edward McPherson, Edward McPherson Papers, LOC, January 7, 1861; Paludan, "The American Civil War Considered a Crisis in Law and Order," 1013–34.

CHAPTER 2

Privateers, Debt Repudiation,
and the "Contraband"

THE NORTHERN PUBLIC may have been spouting martial gasconades, but they had elected a president who was much more prudent in his rhetoric. By the time of Lincoln's inauguration on March 4, 1861, seven states had seceded from the Union and four others were threatening to do so. Moreover, the continued allegiance of the crucial border states—Maryland, Kentucky, Missouri, and Delaware—was in doubt. President Lincoln, who had upon his inauguration inherited the worst crisis in the nation's history, confronted the problem of somehow preventing a widening of the secession movement without surrendering additional federal properties into the hands of rebellious states. The Confederate property seizures proved to be a singularly troublesome issue for the new chief executive. During his railway journey to the nation's capital, Lincoln had made several speeches in which he promised faithfully that he would not use force against the rebels unless they openly took up arms against the government. But he was absolutely firm on the question of federal properties and the collection of revenues: the federal government could not yield its possessions and its revenues into the hands of the insurgents without risking the destruction of the Constitution and of the Republic. Lincoln had been saying privately for some time—since the day after South Carolina seceded, in fact—that upon taking office he intended to retake the federal forts. Before leaving for Washington, he had written to General Winfield Scott, as well as to future Secretary of State William Henry Seward, that the federal properties should not be allowed to remain in rebel hands. In fact, the original draft of Lincoln's inaugural address contained a statement that the president intended to "reclaim" the fallen forts, as well as to "hold, occupy and possess" all other federal properties. His conservative friend Orville Hickman Browning, however, persuaded Lincoln to take a more conciliatory tone in his first inaugural address to the American people. There were still the border slaveowning states to consider—and Virginia had not yet cast her lot with the Confederacy.[1]

Lincoln made the suggested modifications, but they did not reflect his real position. He had always intended to retake the forts and arsenals, and if that meant war, so be it; the tug had to come, sooner or later. Lincoln's position on the coastal forts and customs revenues revealed his deeply rooted commitment to the rule of law and the primacy of the federal government's sovereignty over the states. While he deplored the possibility of armed conflict with fellow Americans, his urgent desire to maintain the Union and the Constitution did not overshadow his immovable stance on his duty to the nation as a whole. With the appropriate reassurances, he hoped, the southern states would return to the Union and to an obedience of the laws. At the same time, as his first official act as president (aside from choosing his cabinet) his inaugural address revealed him as a political leader who—despite his inexperience—had already determined precisely where to draw the line between firmness and conciliation. American citizens could not simply seize American property and flout the federal government's authority. Lincoln was always considered conciliatory toward the South, especially by the more radical members of his party—indeed, he would later take measures to soften confiscation and other punitive acts. But there were several issues even at this early stage of the war that Lincoln simply did not consider negotiable. He did meet with border state delegates from the Peace Convention in early February, but he made it clear to them that he intended to collect the revenues, though he was careful to position the Coast Guard ships (which never actually collected any duties) offshore. The president may have softened his position for his inaugural address, but there was never any doubt that he considered the federal possessions and the customs revenues of crucial importance; to lose the one and to relinquish the other was tantamount to an admission of defeat. A government that could not maintain its possessions nor enforce its laws could never stand. Moreover, the Republican Party's legitimacy, indeed its survival, depended on Lincoln's resolve.[2]

1. Nicolay and Hay, eds., *Complete Works of Abraham Lincoln,* 3:249–51, 6:82; Abraham Lincoln's confidential letter to David Hunter, December 22, 1860, in Basler, ed., *Collected Works,* 6:159.

2. Thomas, *Abraham Lincoln: A Biography,* 246; Oates, *With Malice Toward None,* 214; Trefousse, "Unionism and Abolition," in Förster and Nagler, eds., *On the Road to Total War,* 103.

As a result of his modification of the inaugural address, the northern public understood Lincoln's attitude toward the forts to be somewhat more moderate than it was in reality. In the final version, the president stressed his duty to "hold, occupy and possess" the forts and arsenals and "to collect the duties and imposts." But he also hastened to reassure his listeners that "beyond what may be necessary for these objects, there will be no invasion—no using of force against, . . . the people anywhere." Lincoln's calm good sense placated those citizens who feared an armed conflict, while his unwillingness to compromise the basic principles of his party's platform reassured others that he intended to be more active than his predecessor. The president's moderate tone combined with his firm stance toward nonnegotiables would stand him in good stead with a majority of northerners, even those who had not voted for him in the 1860 election. Moreover, his stance on slavery harmonized well with northern public opinion, which was for the moment preoccupied with the safety of the Union and with federal property. During the early months of the secession crisis, only confirmed abolitionists linked the conflict with the extermination of slavery. In his inaugural address, Lincoln assured "his dissatisfied fellow countrymen" that he had no intention of interfering with the institution where it existed. For the moment, President Lincoln was far more concerned with the physical integrity of the Union and with the safety of government properties. A month after his inauguration, the question of federal forts took on extreme urgency when the Union government lost Fort Sumter to the South Carolina rebels in mid-April.[3]

On April 15, 1861, three days after the battle of Fort Sumter, President Lincoln acted on his earlier wish to retake the forts. He issued a proclamation calling up seventy-five thousand organized state militia volunteers and stated that their first service would "probably be to repossess the forts, places and property which have been seized from the Union." Lincoln also insisted, somewhat unrealistically, upon "the utmost care . . . to avoid any devastation, any destruction of, or interference with, property . . . in any part of the country." But when Virginians seized the Gosport Navy Yard in Norfolk on April 16, and the Harpers Ferry Arsenal three days later, northern newspapers reacted with fury. These events suddenly raised fears that Washington itself was in danger. Even the Democratic *New York Herald* railed against the seizure of the arsenal. The purpose of the war, the *Herald* insisted now, was the recovery of U.S. property.

3. Basler, *Collected Works*, 6:262–71.

The equally conservative *Cleveland Daily Plain Dealer* called the Virginians a "gang of pirates." The concern for government property in the South was one of the few issues that could cross party lines and probably the only one capable of bringing Democrats, both private citizens and politicians, to consider the confiscation of southern property as recompense.[4]

A few days after Harpers Ferry fell to the Virginians, the *New York Herald* stated again, even more explicitly, that the war against the revolted states was an "appeal to arms" for the recovery of U.S. "customs houses, forts, arsenals, navy yards, mints, marine hospitals, courts of justice, post offices and post roads." According to the *Herald,* the North was united against the rebellious states, even though the government lagged "far behind our public sentiment." Every last piece of federal property had to be recovered and "the utmost penalties due to treason" inflicted on the traitors. During the war years the *New York Herald*'s editorial policies were somewhat changeable and therefore difficult to gauge, but there is no mistaking the punitive sentiment of this editorial. The *Herald* declared that the rebels' property would be confiscated and, "wherever their lives are not forfeited, it will be exclusively owing to the Executive clemency."[5]

The northern public's use of expressions like "thieves," "robbers," and especially "pirates" became even more pronounced when the newly appointed Confederate president Jefferson Davis officially authorized privateering against northern merchant ships. Within a few days of the firing on Fort Sumter, Davis issued letters of marque and reprisal, triggering fresh outrages from the northern papers, this time equally vehement on both sides of the partisan press. Davis's message to the Provisional Confederate Congress in Montgomery made it clear that the letters were intended to protect the South from the invading hordes and that he still prayed for a "just and honorable peace." The purpose of Davis's proclamation, issued on April 17, 1861, was to recruit and deputize privately owned armed vessels to resist "so wanton and wicked an aggression," referring to Lincoln's April 15 proclamation calling for volunteers. By the middle of May, several schooners had been authorized to act as a militia on the high seas against the "ships, vessels [and] goods" of the United States of America. Nevertheless, Davis enjoined the owners of these private vessels to "pay the strictest regard to the rights of neutral powers and the usages of civilized na-

4. Ibid., 6:331; *New York Herald,* April 18, 24, 1861; *Cleveland Daily Plain Dealer,* April 20, 1861.
5. *New York Herald,* April 24, 1861.

tions . . . [and] toward the enemy . . . to proceed, in exercising the rights of war, with all the justice and humanity which characterize this Government and its citizens." Many northern editorials, however, called this mere rhetoric; letters of marque and reprisal, issued to privateers, had always been a euphemism for pure piracy. The *Cleveland Daily Plain Dealer* exposed the rebels' practical intentions, culled from an editorial printed in the *Mobile Advertiser:* "There is no sea upon which the ships of New England and New York do not cluster thickly, and each one a rich prize for the daring privateer. Let the note of war be sounded, and soon hundreds of craft, bearing letters of marque, from the Confederacy, would be scouring the ocean to prey upon the defenceless commerce of Lincoln's people." Echoing the general sentiment along the northern home front, the *New York Times* likened Davis's proclamation to the worst "despotisms of the old world," and unequivocally defined it as license for piracy.[6]

In the ensuing months, Republicans would use Davis's proclamation as a justification for confiscating rebel land and crops since they were now seen as a kind of "prize," similar to private property captured on the high seas. This argument would gain greater force in the Congressional debates in 1862 over the Second Confiscation Act, even though privateering had mostly died out by that time. The rebels' wanton attacks on northern merchant ships appeared to warrant harsh, punitive measures. In spite of the conservatives' sustained opposition to laws that confiscated land, slaves, and crops, congressional radicals would have very little trouble passing laws that attacked rebel ships and their cargoes. For the remainder of the war, the Republican voters would generally support sharp attacks on private enemy property (and on rebel citizens); even some moderate citizens favored punitive legislation. This sentiment arose not merely from a spirit of vengeance; it was considered simple justice in return for rebel depredations on northern assets.[7]

At the request of General-in-Chief Winfield Scott, James Hamilton prepared a naval plan of action in response to the privateering crisis. In a letter

---

6. Richardson, ed., *Messages and Papers of Jefferson Davis,* 60, 75, 103, 111; *Mobile Advertiser,* April 7, 1861, as quoted in the *Cleveland Daily Plain Dealer,* April 20, 1861; *New York Times,* May 21, 1861.

7. The first enthusiastic wave of privateering lasted only through the summer of 1861, at which time the much greater profits to be gained by blockade-running lured ship owners from privateering. Robinson, *The Confederate Privateers.*

dated April 16, 1861, he submitted a detailed series of steps to be undertaken by the Union forces, in retaliation against Confederate captures on the high seas. Since Jefferson Davis had called for privateers to attack private property, the U.S. government should retaliate by confiscating the South's slaves. He thought that Davis's example justified the government in "attacking private property of the enemy of every kind, whenever it can be reached." He also thought that it would be "judicious" to enlist the slaves in the Union Army, and "give them their freedom with their swords." Hamilton's ideas were too radical for his time, but in a little over a year, the second session of the 37th Congress would pass legislation that did precisely as he had suggested. The Second Confiscation Act, passed on August 6, 1862, freed slaves behind enemy lines and gave leave to the president to "employ them" as deemed necessary and proper "for the suppression of this rebellion."[8]

A more direct Confederate attack on northern private property occurred around the same time. On April 26, Georgia governor Joseph E. Brown issued an order repudiating all northern debts. Henceforward, no Georgian was to pay any debts owed to northern merchants, but instead was to deposit the funds in the Georgia state treasury. An enraged *New York Times* called Brown a "truculent knave" and denounced his action, as well as the dishonest propensities of Georgian citizens *en masse.* "The contracting of honest debts at the North was always a favorite amusement with the people of Georgia, while the maxim 'base is the slave who pays,' was cherished down there as a great fundamental truth." According to the *Times,* Georgians owed millions of dollars to northern bankers. Governor Brown ordered that the debts had to be paid into an escrow account, where the money would accrue 7 percent interest. However, the *Times* sneered that these debts would not be paid to northern creditors until the "crack of doom." The real crime, according to the *Times,* was not that the debts themselves had been repudiated, but that the money would be paid into a Confederate treasury. This shifted the problem of debt repudiation from mere default to outright theft. "To refuse to pay honest debts was one thing—to donate to the State, under pretence of a loan, was another." At the same time, the *Times* admitted freely that the money owed to northern creditors had originally been used to purchase slaves, supply plantations, and even furnish "whips to negro-

---

8. Hamilton, *Reminiscences of James A. Hamilton,* 523. Scott never implemented the emancipation part of Hamilton's plan, but the First Confiscation Act freed slaves unconditionally if they were being used to support the Confederate war effort.

drivers." Nevertheless, northern complicity in the institution of slavery did not exonerate the rebels' attacks on private property.[9]

From the beginning of April through early summer, similar actions occurred in the other seceded states. The governor of Tennessee ordered the seizure of money in the hands of the surveyor of the port of Nashville, to the amount of seventy-five thousand dollars. According to the *Chicago Tribune*, Florida and Mississippi had "repudiated long ago." A month later, on May 28, Arkansas passed a similar law, and Jefferson Davis would submit a resolution to the Confederate Congress asking for a nationwide law repudiating and sequestering debts owed to northern creditors. On May 21, 1861, the Confederate Congress passed a law that required southern debtors to pay all moneys due to northern creditors to the Confederate treasury. In an editorial entitled "Repudiation and its Profits," the *Tribune* called the rebels "Confederate Burglars." The paper issued an ominous warning to the "repudiating States," saying that the debts would have to be paid no matter what, and the only question that remained was whether there would be "anything valuable left in the rebel states" after the war was over. "They may repudiate fifty times a day. They may confiscate a hundred times a week. They have got to pay those debts, *though there be nothing but real estate left in the South after the rebellion is crushed.*" Although Brown and other southern politicians justified their actions by referring to European legal theorists, the repudiation of debts was in contravention of accepted international standards of civilized warfare, which decreed that upon the cessation of hostilities, debts to enemies were to be paid.[10]

Indeed, some northern merchants eyed southern real estate and crops as a way of balancing their accounts. The New York Chamber of Commerce would meet regularly throughout the war to discuss its probable effects upon northern merchants and bankers. The Chamber had avidly supported the Crittenden Compromise and now dreaded the coming news of unpaid debts, disrupted supplies, and cancelled orders. The British journalist William Howard Russell frequently remarked on the hesitant attitude among New York's financial class, at least in the early months of the war. But the northern public was beginning to grumble about the businessmen's cautious attitude and to equate caution with cowardice. Some went so far as to accuse businessmen of placing their

9. *New York Times*, May 12, 16, 17, 1861; see also *New York World*, January 18, 1861.

10. McPherson, *Political History*, 205; *Chicago Tribune*, May 15, 1861; Randall, *Constitutional Problems*, 304–5.

greed ahead of patriotism. Jacob Brinkerhoff, who was a prominent antislavery Ohio judge, told John Sherman that public sentiment was "growing stronger and stronger *against any Compromise whatsoever.*" He begged Sherman not to "regard the cowardly whiners and howls of Mammon-worshipping commercial cities." Similarly, a Pennsylvania minister prayed, "let patriots and statesmen see and feel that it is not commerce, power and wealth purchased by giving way to the exactions of the slave power, but righteousness which exalteth a nation." Businessmen, he feared, would only support the war effort if they could be certain of a fair rate of return.[11]

Businessmen feared that they would bear the brunt of war because they stood to lose the most, and because they no doubt would have to pay the costs by shouldering higher taxes. During one of the fast day sermons at the beginning of the crisis, Rhode Island's Reverend Leonard Swain had stressed the idea that the real heroes in the ensuing battle would be the merchants and men of business, who "loved their native land better than they loved their wealth." Swain declared optimistically that northern merchants would be ready "to pour out their treasures and to take joyfully the spoiling of their goods." In the meantime, Lincoln's election caused several panics on the New York Stock Exchange. Prominent businessmen, who had grown fearful during the secession crisis, strongly supported compromise measures. As time would show, early in the war northern merchants did lose considerable sums when the rebels refused to honor their debts, which eventually pushed the normally cautious business community to take a harsher view of the enemy. Later, of course, wartime industrial production more than compensated northern businessmen for their losses in 1861–1862. In the meantime, their political leaders were ineffectual in their attempts to smooth over the differences between the warring sections, or to take any decisive stand that would resolve the looming disaster. The administration was hobbled by a weak, lame-duck executive, a divided Congress, and a paralyzing uncertainty about how to cope with the worst calamity that had ever befallen the nation.[12]

11. Jacob Brinkerhoff to John Sherman, Sherman Papers, LOC, January 1, 1861; Aughey, *Renovation*, 15; see, for example, the diary entry for March 25, 1861, in Russell, *My Diary North and South*, 36; Anderson, *Dangers and Duties*, 4.

12. Swain, *Our Banners Set Up*, 4; Potter, *Lincoln and His Party*, 121–3. In *Duty and Interest Identical in the Present Crisis*, Henry W. Bellows assured New Yorkers that "what is most in the interest of piety and virtue is most for the interest of trade and commerce" (5).

More principled northerners were troubled by the merchants' view of the war in terms of property ownership and profits. A few northern clerics, for example, were deeply critical of the business community's avarice and acquisitiveness, and they nearly always linked their greed to the institution of southern slavery. Such men of God were disgusted with what they perceived as the materialistic perversion of democratic ideals that had corrupted the North, which had now become a "nation of idolaters." Yankee businessmen, in pursuing profits (especially profits associated with cotton) were praying only to the God of Mammon. Some ministers even thought that pride and materialism were pervasive "American characteristics."[13]

One New York preacher thought that northern merchants and businessmen were greatly to blame for their complicity with cotton planters and slavery. There were those, he said, who "put trade above every thing; who count it as a sufficient argument for or against any measure of public policy," and all to appease slavery and save business profits. A Cincinnati sermon denounced the "brokers who sell cotton, Northern shipmasters who seek it as freight; the Northern merchants and manufacturers who are anxious to secure southern trade." The preacher, a Reverend Llewellyn Evans, said that the influence of greed and profits, engendered by slavery, had become so powerful that the "men in public office could no longer consult their consciences, and were no longer dedicated to acting purely in the name of republican principles." Politicians now looked at everything in the "yellow light of the dollar." Even when businessmen finally supported a vigorous prosecution of the war effort, they did so with an eye on the main chance. Within a year, the New York Chamber of Commerce began petitioning Congress for harsh legislation that would confiscate southern cotton and transfer its ownership to northern merchants who had been bankrupted by debt repudiations.[14]

In the meantime, the unsettled state of the northern economy was raising real fears. It had been hit hard during the 1857 panic, and the financial reverses suffered as a result of that panic were felt more severely in the North than in the South, which had been protected by the international cotton trade. Therefore,

13. Goodale, *"Our Country's Peril,"* 12. See also Thompson, *The President's Fast,* 19, and Dorr, *The American Vine,* 17.

14. Thompson, *The President's Fast,* 9, 10, 17; Abbott, *An Address Upon Our National Affairs,* 6; Evans, *Duty of the Christian Citizen;* New York Chamber of Commerce, *Report.* See also Elder, *Debt and Resources.*

in 1861 and 1862, the southern debt repudiations endangered the foundations of northern financial stability, which threatened to disrupt trade everywhere. In the border states, some newspapers voiced alarm about northern creditors' unwillingness to continue to extend loans even to loyal planters. Trade was paralyzed in all regions of the nation, proclaimed the *Louisville Daily Democrat,* and "never before has Mr. Cash been so popular in this section." Now that public confidence had been "destroyed," according to the *Democrat,* the warring sections had become "chary" of each other. Merchants would soon cease to sell their goods on credit. "They cannot trust their merchandize in the chances of trade, when law and order are disregarded." The rule of law and the safety of private property had always been closely linked in the minds of American citizens—a notion that was not lost on the northern business community.[15]

In some ways northern merchants and financiers had only themselves to blame. They had been falling over each other to grant credit to southern planters. New York publisher Orville J. Victor commented on debt repudiation in his postwar memoirs. He thought that the South's callous disavowal of northern debts argued a "demoralized sentiment of probity, which equally alarmed and angered the Northern people." He illuminated the antebellum financial climate that had made repudiation particularly distressing for northern merchants and bankers. Before secession, according to Victor, southerners had been able to obtain almost unlimited credit from northern businessmen. This remained true even during the dark days of financial losses after the 1857 panic. A southern merchant or planter had only to say, "I am from the Cotton States," to get as much credit as he desired. Nineteenth-century businessmen usually consulted credit reports, such as the Commercial Agency (which Victor called "that secret and powerful inquisition"), prior to advancing credit to their associates. But "so eager was the deluded merchant to secure a 'southern trade'" that he hardly bothered to do so when confronted with rich cotton, tobacco, and sugar planters. Victor said that in the matter of southern credits, the "wretched list of failures in the Winter and Spring of 1861" would long remain as a "monument of Northern commercial temerity."[16]

It is true that the northern stock market plummeted in the anxious days of the secession winter, but it is also true that when northern industry converted

15. *Louisville Daily Democrat,* February 3, 1861.

16. Victor, *Comprehensive History of the Southern Rebellion,* 1:497; Atherton, "The Problem of Credit Rating in the Ante-Bellum South," 534–56.

to wartime production the economy recovered. Still, the repudiations represented a deep violation of American business practices, which depended to a great extent on personal trust and the probity of a man's word. When southern planters repudiated their northern debts, they attacked a profound belief in the honor of private business obligations. Contemporary legal theorists, such as Francis Lieber, and even the much more conservative Joel Parker, took these attacks even more seriously. Both Lieber and Parker firmly believed in the need for law and order to safeguard the Republic, and both had a deep faith that the nation had its basis in the protection of (and respect for) private property. Although they would later part company on their interpretations of the constitutional right to confiscate rebel property, both men saw the Civil War as a fight to reestablish the rule of law, which was threatened by Confederate disregard for federal and private property rights. Northerners, however, took these actions more personally. Feeling themselves betrayed, they demanded reparations. Yankee merchants had no trouble linking debt repudiation with outright theft, which indeed it was. When it came time to discuss the confiscation of rebel property, many northern businessmen would state that it was nothing but justice to take back from the Confederates what they had stolen. Secession could not be accomplished without personal blows. Now northerners responded with wild talk of vengeance.[17]

In the meantime Maine senator William Pitt Fessenden wrote to former New York governor Hamilton Fish that he thought his business constituency could play an important role in the conflict. "One bugle note from the great Commercial Centre," he said, would be much more effective than "all that a thousand like me could say or do." Within a year, his wish was granted. The northern business community rallied around the cause, especially when it became clear that Army contracts could lead to quick wealth.[18]

While it would hardly be fair to argue that northerners went to war for material interests in the narrowest sense, in early 1861 they certainly talked about the civil conflict in terms of contested property. Both the *New York Times* and the *Chicago Tribune* called the Confederacy's policy of seizing Union property

17. Paludan, *Covenant with Death*, 22, 96, 128; O'Brien, *Economic Effects of the American Civil War*, 11–8; Hilkey, *Character Is Capital*.

18. William Pitt Fessenden to Hamilton Fish, Hamilton Fish Papers, LOC, December 15, 1860; Stampp, *And the War Came*, 223; New York Chamber of Commerce, *Report*; O'Connor, *Lords of the Loom*; Foner, *Business and Slavery*; and Abbott, *Cotton and Capital*.

a "gigantic robbery." Federal property, partially paid for by the taxes of all U.S. citizens, ought to remain within the Union. By late spring there were numerous examples of this attitude, even among fairly moderate men. In a speech to the ladies of Frederick, Maryland, Reverdy Johnson, who was one of America's foremost constitutional lawyers, defined secession as usurpation, which he said was "an unjust or illegal seizure and occupation of public power and property." Upon renouncing the true government, southerners had "defied and plundered the United States." Some Democratic papers echoed this sentiment as well. In a satirical editorial on Jefferson Davis's "modest desire to be let alone," the *Louisville Daily Democrat* scolded, "Now really, Jeff, you are a very unreasonable individual. You propose to rob us of eight States—think of that. We were talking of buying Cuba; giving two hundred million dollars for it; at the same rate, these eight States are worth to us sixteen hundred millions. Indeed, they are worth more; they are all on this Continent, and full of good fellows. Gold couldn't buy them." [19]

By the early summer of 1861, tens of thousands of raw recruits from New York, Pennsylvania, Massachusetts, and Illinois were massing near the nation's capital. Many Americans still hoped that the war would be over by harvest time and that, with judicious management, they would be able to minimize their potential losses. Union citizens rallied around the cause of Constitution and Union and were prepared to hammer the Confederates wherever they could— on the field of battle and at home. Northerners felt justified in this vengeful stance because the rebels' decision to seize both federal property and private northern assets had made it clear that whoever struck the hardest blow, without regard for the niceties of civilized warfare, would likely achieve military victory as well as maintain financial solvency. Their former president's irresolute handling of the crisis had further proved to northerners that they would have to push the current administration hard to take decisive action. As a result, the northern home front responded vindictively and often irrationally; for most northerners, a decisive military victory should also include a sharp attack on rebellious citizens' private property. In this they were far ahead of their political leaders and even many senior military officers, such as Generals George B. McClellan and Don Carlos Buell.

19. Reverdy Johnson, "Speech to the Ladies of Frederick upon Presentation of the National Flag to the Home Guard," as reported in the *New York Times*, May 21, 1861; *New York Times*, June 30, 1861; *Chicago Tribune*, May 15, 1861, *Louisville Daily Democrat*, May 5, 1861.

When the northern public's immediate wrath eroded with the passage of time and with continual news of defeats, its internal divisions came to the forefront again, especially over the explosive issue of slavery. Eventually northerners had to come to grips with the fact that war was, after all, a long, bloody, and costly business and that it would not be easy to make the rebels pay for their role in the conflict. Democrats and Republicans, however, would grow more divided on the issue of precisely how far to go in their desire for revenge, and what role slavery would play in the formulation of war aims. The home front's reaction early in the conflict had been an amalgam of abstract ideals and immediate material concerns; Union citizens had swung between eternal principles of democracy and their fears over their own—and their nation's—material well-being. While young men might have gone off to fight for the principles bequeathed to them by the revolutionary generation, northern businessmen and preachers worried about property "purchased" mutually by their revolutionary forebears. This meant that northerners would eventually have to sort out their own responsibility for their part in supporting the South's peculiar institution and the resultant tangle of their relationships with the southern states. Even men of God understood this dilemma and tried to make sense of the ethical muddle created by broken bargains, mutually owned property, and democratic ideals. In some sense, the business community would have the best of both worlds, once they fully understood that to support the cause of Union would prove profitable both in terms of ideals and to their counting houses. The Confederate property seizures during the secession crisis had thrust unexpectedly painful questions into the forefront of the northern public mind. Their complicity in profits earned from slavery, the difficulty of separating the possessions and inheritance of the North and South, and the destruction of nationhood based on shared responsibilities and rights would continue to trouble Union citizens for some years to come.

The problem of slavery had remained somewhat in the background during the early months of the conflict. While abolitionists continued to agitate the issue, as they had done for more than forty years, most northerners—including President Lincoln—worried about the immediate problem of the destruction of the Union. In the New England and Mid-Atlantic states, opposition to the institution was more pronounced than in the Ohio River Valley; most northerners opposed slavery on moral and political grounds, but few of them supported immediate or widespread emancipation. The Republican Party certainly opposed the extension of slavery into the territories, but President Lincoln had been elected with only 39 percent of the popular vote. In 1861, the majority of the northern public would have opposed any effort to emancipate southern slaves. According to most northerners, there were far more pressing issues at stake, and most Union Army officers fully agreed. During the first spring and summer of the Civil War, most military leaders refused to interfere with slave property and indeed made every effort to return runaway slaves to their owners. Because there was no set military policy, and because federal laws on fugitive slaves were still in force, officers could consult their political and personal views when deciding how to deal with people who fled to their marching lines or forts. Early in the war, soldiers usually followed their officers' orders regarding fugitives. Eventually, as the enlisted men gained more personal experience in dealing with former slaves who provided services and information, and told of their experiences in slavery, some soldiers protected fugitives in direct violation of their senior officers' commands. Although the Union soldiers' attitudes toward slaves varied—some inflicted cruelties on southern black people, and others protected them from their former owners—on the whole, their prejudices changed more rapidly than the attitudes of northerners who had remained at home. Although the problem remained manageable in 1861, the northern public would soon have to confront their long-held assumptions about slaves and about human property.[20]

The problem of fugitive slaves arose quite early in the conflict. From the moment southern states began to secede, some enslaved southerners took matters into their own hands, forcing the issue on the notice of the northern people—about a month before Fort Sumter fell to the rebels. In March 1861, eight black men asked for asylum in Fort Pickens off the coast of Florida. The officer in charge, a Lieutenant Adam J. Slemmer, summarily ordered that the men be returned to their masters. About a month later, General Benjamin F. Butler told Maryland's Governor Thomas H. Hicks that he had no intention of interfering with the institution of slavery and offered his aid in putting down any "servile insurrections" that might occur in Maryland. General William S. Harney issued a similar proclamation in Missouri on May 14, 1861, which would remain in effect until General John C. Frémont replaced him in June. General

20. James Marten, "A Feeling of Restless Anxiety: Loyalty and Race in the Peninsula Campaign and Beyond," in Gallagher, ed., *The Richmond Campaign of 1862*, 137–8.

George B. McClellan was particularly vocal about his intention to respect private property in western Virginia; he declared that it was the aim of the federal government to protect slave property "religiously." The conservative generals' refusal to interfere with the slave property of rebels pleased northern Democrats and incensed antislavery Republicans, but when some Union Army officers and soldiers began to shelter the runaways, it became clear that some kind of consistent policy was needed.[21]

In the spring and summer of 1861, there was no coherent legal or military policy toward fugitive slaves. Democratic newspapers, worried that some Union Army officers were refusing to return slaves to their former owners, demanded a fixed policy. Northerners might have approved of stern measures toward the rebels, but many of them expressed strong reservations about using slaves as the spoils of war. An editorial in the *Cleveland Daily Plain Dealer,* for example, asserted that such spoils "would spoil on our hands. It would be like the elephant won in a raffle—we should not know what to do with him." The *Albany Atlas and Argus,* an extremely conservative Democratic paper, did not want to be misunderstood as "at all tender about the property of our enemies at the South." It was clearly the duty of Union troops to assail the enemy both in property and in person. The country was in a state of war and should be no more careful of the enemy's private property than of their persons on the field of battle. What was perhaps more surprising was that the editor of the *Argus* thought that slave property had to "take its chance with the rest," in spite of the fact that this paper always inveighed loudly against any interference with slavery. The editorial ended with a prophetic question. If the nation were compelled to conquer a peace, it would undoubtedly have a right "to all the property we can take, slaves included." But what then? What should be done with such property? "Shall it remain *chattel,* or become *persons?* If chattels, how dispose of—if persons, whither sent?" In the coming months, precisely this question—whether slaves were primarily persons or property—would become a crucial touchstone for transformations in public opinion over slavery. The *New York Herald* suggested a characteristically northern Democratic solution. "The planters and slaveholders of the South . . . will see the 4 million of slaves, they now own, transferred to the possession of those loyal citizens of the South." The *Herald*'s plan perfectly captured the moderate home front's wishes: it would

21. Berlin, *Freedom,* 1:18–9.

take slaves from rebels, but it would also keep them in the South. More important, the slaves would not be emancipated, but simply transferred from a disloyal owner to a more worthy one. But such solutions hardly appealed to more thoughtful northerners, who understood that the federal government could not become a gigantic slaveowner and slave dealer.[22]

Prior to the outbreak of the Civil War, most northerners had acquiesced—however reluctantly—in the notion that human beings could be held as property. Americans had always considered slavery to be a local institution, primarily governed by state laws and immune to federal interference. The onset of armed conflict between the sections now forced to the forefront the constitutional protections of, and compromises with, the institution of slavery. In the meantime, however, beginning in the spring of 1861, military leaders had to cope with the problem of fugitive slaves entering their camps to request asylum. An incident in May 1861 revealed to anxious northerners a possible means of depriving southerners of slave labor, without necessarily altering the slaves' status as property. On May 24, 1861, three men escaping from bondage came to Fortress Monroe in Virginia, then under the command of General Benjamin F. Butler. The men told Butler that they had been laboring on artillery earthworks, and asked him to protect them from their former owner. Butler was interested in their plight, at least in part because he needed their labor and because he thought they might have useful information about the placement of rebel batteries. A few days later General Butler issued his famous "contraband" policy, declaring the fugitive slaves contraband of war, and thus subject to seizure by the federal armies. Historian Harold Hyman has called Butler's order a "constitutional evasion" that "denied with a wink" that emancipation was in any way involved. It was true that Butler's policy in no way interfered with the fugitives' status as property, but it did protect them from being forced back into bondage, and it did acknowledge that they had a valuable contribution to make. Union Army officers and soldiers recognized the potential usefulness of runaway slaves long before the northern home front came to this view. In the meantime, because Butler's action did not portend widespread emancipation, it was popular on the Union home front, and many northerners, even the "venerable gentle-

22. The *Boston Daily Evening Transcript*, November 11, 1861; *Cleveland Daily Plain Dealer*, September 24, 1861; *New York Herald*, September 30, 1861; *Cleveland Daily Plain Dealer*, May 8, 1861. The quotation from the *Albany Atlas and Argus* is from the May 8, 1861, issue.

man who wears gold spectacles and reads a conservative daily [paper]" cheerfully adopted the word "contraband" as a nickname for fugitive slaves.[23]

Butler had to wait through the summer for a definitive policy from the secretary of war, Simon Cameron. He would not get it until August, when the 37th Congress passed the First Confiscation Act, legitimizing Butler's contraband policy. In the meantime, Cameron told Butler that he had to obey federal legislation. After all, the Fugitive Slave Law was still in effect. Cameron thought Army officers should shelter the runaways, keep track of owners' names, and also of all the labor performed by the fugitives. In the following weeks, hundreds of fugitive families flocked to Fortress Monroe. Republicans gleefully declared that Butler had proposed a "better Fugitive Slave Law," but Democrats were much more critical, worrying that the government had now embarked on an emancipation policy.

The problem of the future of freed slaves became steadily more acute as the northern public heard that the wives and children of the fugitives were now joining their husbands and fathers. The New York Times, which had earlier called General Butler's contraband phrase a "happy fancy," began to worry whether the contraband policy would still be a "practical solution" when freed slaves numbered in the tens of thousands. Nevertheless, Republican newspapers were resolute about keeping the freed slaves out of the hands of their former owners until their owners' true unionist sentiments could be ascertained. However, even the Republican Times firmly believed that the government had no right to touch the slaves of loyal or peaceable citizens.[24]

Over the following months, more and more fugitives asked for sanctuary in every theater of war. On a daily basis throughout May and June, many northern newspapers reported the number of fugitives who joined U.S. Army marching lines, camps, and fortresses. There are no definitive figures available on the number of slaves who fled to Union Army lines in the first summer of the war, but some historians have suggested that even in mid-1861 they numbered in the thousands. Because Congress would not enact definitive legislation about fugitive slaves until March 1862, Union Army officers could follow their own

23. Hyman, "Reconstruction and Political-Constitutional Institutions," in New Frontiers, 20–1; Freehling, The South vs. the South; Atlantic Monthly 8 (November 1861), quoted in McCrary, Abraham Lincoln and Reconstruction, 72; Berlin, Freedom, 1:15–6.

24. New York Times, June 1, 1862.

political inclinations when confronted with runaway slaves who wished to join their camps or marching lines. As a result, military policies were confused and contradictory. Some of the officers, like General McClellan, continued to order the return of the slaves to their owners; others refused to allow them within their lines, and still others actively protected fugitive slaves. Moreover, soldiers who disagreed with their commanding officers on this issue did not always obey orders dealing with fugitives. In mid-1861, most northerners still viewed the issue of slavery as primarily a political problem; however northerners may have felt about the institution and its role in the conflict, the status of slaves was still essentially one of chattel property. As black families living in the Upper South fled to Union Army fortresses and marching lines, however, their status as property—at least in the eyes of white northerners—became increasingly doubtful.[25]

25. Berlin, *Freedom,* 1:61; Rose, *Rehearsal for Reconstruction;* for national policy regarding fugitive slaves, see McPherson, *Struggle for Equality,* 70; *OR,* ser. 2, vol. 1, 750–3.

CHAPTER 3

Congress Debates the Confiscation of Rebel Property in 1861

$\mathbf{I}$N ITS FINAL SESSION, the 36th Congress had proposed a constitutional amendment guaranteeing slavery in perpetuity, and in his inaugural address President Lincoln had promised his dissatisfied fellow countrymen that he had no intention of interfering with slavery where it already existed. Lincoln detested slavery, but he was not yet ready to subvert constitutional guarantees or to endanger northern public support for the war effort by moving precipitously against the institution. But the continued safety of slavery was now increasingly in doubt. The fugitives were already forcing a change in the goals of the war. Radical Republicans were rather pleased by this turn of events, but they as yet commanded little allegiance in the North. They had always maintained that punishment of the rebels and the emancipation of slaves served the same goals. The Army, they felt, should be the instrument of liberation, and antislavery activists looked forward to the time when "the advancing armies, or acts of Congress, would take a sterner hand in extinguishing the institution of slavery." In June 1861, former New York District Attorney James Hamilton, who had been instrumental in drafting the Navy's policies toward privateers, turned his hand to the Articles of Association for the Democratic Association of the Friends of Freedom, a pro-Union group in New York City. The association was a decidedly antislavery organization, and its members were cheered by the growing numbers of slaves who had already gained their freedom. Hamilton insisted, "Slaves who become practically freed by the advance of our armies, or by acts of confiscation, shall never be reduced to bondage." During the secession crisis, Hamilton had tried to include an emancipation clause in his antiprivateering plan. At the time his proposal had seemed too radical (although it appealed to Salmon Chase, who copied some of these ideas in a report he submitted to Congress in early July), but now seemed to be an auspicious moment to revive Hamilton's plan. Because Congress would be debating the confiscation of rebel property that summer, Hamilton chose this moment to reaffirm his belief that the war would (and should) strike a blow at the institution of slavery through the seizure of human property.[1]

For those northerners who did not subscribe to abolitionist principles, slave labor was still a question of contested property. One might confiscate slaves from the enemy as contraband war matériel, but that did not refute the idea that slaves were still a legitimate type of possession. Before the outbreak of armed conflict, few northerners seriously questioned the right of southerners to hold human property, and only Republicans had forcefully disputed their right to bring slavery into the territories. Even if one had read *Uncle Tom's Cabin* and wept over Eliza's tribulations, it would still be extremely difficult to question the notion that, right or wrong, slaves still belonged to someone, and any attack on even such questionable property meant an attack on deeply held beliefs about the sanctity of private property rights. Abolitionists such as Frederick Douglass understood this attitude quite well and frequently used it to support their arguments. In an editorial published in the June 1861 issue of his *Monthly,* entitled "The Position of the Government Toward Slavery," Douglass declared that slaves were property and ought to be treated as such. They were subject to seizure and confiscation, like any other property, in time of war. According to Douglass, the government did not have to respect this kind of property more than any other kind. Harvard law professor Theophilus Parsons, in supporting this position, agreed that the Army could legally "seize and use [the slaves] in its military labors." Why not? After all, they were property much like horses or oxen. In his view, there was no question that the Army had a right to confiscate slaves. It was precisely on the same footing as "a destruction of private property in an enemy's country," although even a radical like Parsons argued this should only be done as a military necessity.[2]

---

1. Paludan, *Presidency,* 124–5; Hans L. Trefousse, "Lincoln and Race Relations," in Greenberg and Waugh, *The Price of Freedom,* 2:319; Michael F. Holt, "Abraham Lincoln and the Politics of Union," in Thomas, ed., *Abraham Lincoln and the American Political Tradition,* 129; "Draft of Articles of Association, June 1861," in Hamilton, *Reminiscences of James A. Hamilton,* 484.

2. Quoted in Foner, *Life and Writings,* 105; Theophilus Parsons's speech was published in the *Chicago Tribune,* June 12, 1861. For antebellum ideas about property rights in slaves as the origin of the sectional conflict, see James L. Huston, *Calculating the Value of Union.*

Abolitionists knew that they had to frame their antislavery arguments in terms of property ownership to get anyone to listen to them. They used northern anger over rebel attacks against federal and private northern property to fan indignation against slavery. Earlier that year northern newspapers—even conservative ones—had been rife with fury over rebel property seizures during the secession crisis. Emancipationists now cleverly linked the northern anger over secession to the iniquitous institution of slavery. The *Anti-Slavery Advocate* declared, for example, that since secession had been nothing short of "robbery, insult, and outrage," immediate abolition was now the order of the day. "All title to property in slaves shall instantly cease; because their Creator has never relinquished his claim of ownership, and because none have a right to . . . buy those of their own species as cattle." In fact, the *Advocate* thought that immediate abolition was simply the "restoration of stolen property [the slaves' liberty and right to compensated labor] to its rightful owners." Similarly, a New York preacher also insisted that slavery was nothing more than "systematized robbery," implying that emancipating the slaves would restore to them their stolen birthright.[3]

The most outspoken northerners—generally, those with strong antislavery and prowar commitments—wrote to the politicians in Washington, both their own representatives as well as other well-known men whose speeches echoed their own sentiments. They had great hopes for the new Congress now gathering in Washington for the special emergency session, which had been called together by President Lincoln in his April 15 proclamation. Most of the southerners had left when their states seceded, and the remaining Democrats and southern sympathizers were clearly in a minority. Perhaps this new Congress, with its significant Republican majority, would be able to guide the nation toward a successful conclusion of the war effort and a timely end to the wicked institution that had caused the conflict. On July 1, 1861, a radical Republican named R. M. Strong from Coldwater, Michigan, wrote a blistering letter to the Republican senator from his state, Zachariah Chandler. Claiming to speak for his fellow state citizens, Strong demanded that the government conduct a military campaign that had as its ultimate end the destruction of slavery, and "*in addition thereto,* the defrayal of all the expenses incurred by the government." He assured Chandler that nothing less would satisfy Michigan and the North.

3. *The Anti-Slavery Advocate,* n.d., Breckinridge Family Papers, LOC. This undated newspaper clipping was filed in the 1861 correspondence folder. Thompson, *The President's Fast,* 25.

Moreover, since the rebellious southern states had voluntarily placed themselves in the relationship of belligerents to the government, and had "prostrated and deranged" the North's trade and industry, Congress need feel no scruples about attacking their private property. He demanded energetic action, and hoped that Chandler would act accordingly.[4]

Within a few days of their arrival in Washington, other Republican senators and congressmen received letters from their constituents urging them to them to enact punitive legislation as a measure of national self-defense. For example, one Ohioan believed that because the rebels had threatened to "destroy the public credit and deplete the public armorys," the innocent poorer people of the North were now "under the penalty of death and confiscation of property." He told Senator John Sherman that the first action Congress should undertake was to pass a law confiscating all slaves as enemy property. In a more bloodthirsty mood, the writer suggested that if any slaveowner tried to recapture his slaves, it ought to be "lawfull for another person, or persons to kill, or maltreat such person as they may see fit, without being punished for the same." And one of William Pitt Fessenden's constituents, acknowledging that the Constitution did not adequately provide for rigorous punishment of rebels, advised his senator simply to "amend the law of treason," so that rebel citizens could be punished more easily. Congressional Republicans would try to respond to the wishes of their constituents, whose expressions of rage and desire for vengeance were often so extreme that they left little room for interpretation. Consequently, over the following weeks and months, Republicans in the 37th Congress felt a greater freedom to propose punitive legislation that might, in its inclusion of emancipation clauses, have exceeded demands from the wider home front. Republican citizens wanted harsh measures, but they were far from ready to countenance widespread emancipation.[5]

In the meantime the 37th Congress faced a monumental task. They had to finance the enlargement of the Army and Navy, and legislate the conduct of the war. Because of the extreme urgency of the problems they were facing, they decided to limit their discussions strictly to military matters. The House passed William S. Holman's resolution to consider only bills and resolutions "concerning the military and naval operations of the Government, and the financial

4. R. M. Strong to Zachariah Chandler, Zachariah Chandler Papers, LOC, July 1, 1861.

5. Samuel Clark to John Sherman, Sherman Papers, LOC, July 4, 1861; J. H. Jordan, M.D., to William Pitt Fessenden, Fessenden Papers, LOC, July 6, 1861.

affairs therewith connected, and general questions of a judicial character." Moderates of both parties interpreted this to mean that they would not discuss slavery. As politicians of both parties understood it, however, legislating the war effort necessarily included punitive measures against the rebels. Both moderate and radical Republicans in Congress took the urgings of the home front seriously. Over the following six weeks, they proposed many measures punishing the rebels. Moderates supported legislation that constitutionally assailed southern property, such as tax laws and the seizures of ships and their cargoes, but they argued against laws that attacked property rights more broadly, such as sweeping confiscation legislation. Democrats, some of whom were deeply sympathetic to the South, found themselves in a beleaguered minority. They always tried to block punitive legislation, but without success. There was little they could do to stem the tide of belligerent feeling in Congress and in the North. The southern exodus left Republicans in control in the Senate by a 16-vote majority. Of 48 members of the Senate, 32 were Republicans, 13 were Democrats, and 3 were Unionists, most of whom were former Whigs. Only about half of the Republicans, and about a third of the Democrats, had prior state or national legislative experience. Most of them had some knowledge or background in the law (nearly two-thirds of the congressmen and more than three-fourths of the senators were lawyers); nevertheless, their participation in the 37th Congress, as one historian put it, would provide a "crash course in constitutional law." Most of the committee appointments, including half of the standing committee appointments, went to New Englanders. Vice President Hannibal Hamlin of Maine presided over the Senate, with John W. Forney acting as secretary. Of 176 members in the House, 106 were Republicans, 40 were Democrats, and 30 Unionists. The debates in the brief emergency session were often confused and hasty, but they clearly show the emergence of a hard war policy against southern civilians, and the alignment of Republican and Unionist moderates against extreme measures.[6]

On July 5, the day after Congress officially opened, and immediately after the reading of President Lincoln's address, Zachariah Chandler rose to introduce a punitive confiscation bill. The purpose of Chandler's bill was to warn south-

6. *Cong. Globe,* 37th Cong., 1st sess., 24; Holt, "Abraham Lincoln and the Politics of Union," in Thomas, ed., *Abraham Lincoln and the American Political Tradition,* 116; Paludan, *Presidency,* 125; Lucie, *Freedom and Federalism,* 6.

erners from taking up military commissions or important political offices, and to exact retribution for the loss of northern property in the South. Therefore, the bill provided for the seizure of the property of all "Governors of the [Confederate] States, members of the Legislatures, judges of courts, and all military officers above the rank of lieutenant" who either took up arms against the government, or in any way aided the rebellion. Chandler also proposed that these individuals should be "forever disqualified from holding any office of honor, emolument, or trust," presumably referring to both state and federal offices. Chandler's bill was one of the harshest confiscation bills to be introduced in the 37th Congress, and the notion that the federal government could pass a law that could interfere with state and local political appointments implies a significant widening of federal power. The bill was also one of the few that proposed to transfer rebel property into the hands of private Union citizens. Whatever property the government confiscated from the rebel leaders was to be used to restore to loyal Unionists living in the rebel states "any losses which may have resulted to them in consequence of the present rebellion."[7]

Chandler had always been a firebrand abolitionist, and his hotheaded rhetoric had created difficulties for him in the past. The radical Republicans from central and western Michigan had sent him to the Senate in 1857, in spite of criticism that as an uneducated, self-made man, his speeches lacked refinement. Standing squarely on his feet, given to wild facial contortions to emphasize a point, he gestured "with vigor rather than grace." Chandler had long detested southern power and its dominance in the Senate, and thought that no compromise should ever be entertained. During the secession winter he had written an indiscreet letter to Michigan governor Austin Blair concerning the state's delegates to the February Peace Convention. Fearing that the Peace Convention would compromise away the Union, Chandler told Blair that they must send antislavery men "or none." He commented sarcastically that "some of the Manufacturing States think that a fight would be awful." In the postscript, he warned that "without a little blood-letting this union would not be worth a rush." Somehow his letter was leaked to the press, and the postscript was to haunt him for the rest of his political life. Chandler came to be known to his political enemies as the "blood-letter." Indeed, for the next two years, whenever a Republi-

---

7. *Cong. Globe*, 37th Cong., 1st sess., 11. The bill was formally introduced a week later, on July 15, and referred to the Committee of the Judiciary for further debate.

can in Congress so much as mentioned confiscation or other punitive mea-sures, Democratic papers like the *Detroit Free Press* instantly denounced it as "blood-letting."[8]

Because Chandler's proposed confiscation legislation explicitly provided for the reimbursement of loyal Union citizens who had sustained losses as a result of the civil conflict, his bill marched well with the sentiments of the home front. Since January, northern newspapers, sermons, and pamphlets had been agitat-ing for a vigorous prosecution of the war. Enraged by southern seizures of fed-eral property, debt repudiation, and privateering, northerners demanded retal-iatory measures, the purpose of which would be to retake the forts, collect revenue, and secure northern private property. During the secession crisis the previous winter, Republicans and many Democrats had asserted that since the rebels had initiated the war, they should be forced to bear the resulting finan-cial burden.

More radical men, such as James A. Hamilton, had already proposed the confiscation of rebel property earlier that year. The Confederate Congress had already passed a confiscation law on May 21, 1861, and would pass another at the end of August. General Benjamin F. Butler's famous "contraband" order had opened the door for the confiscation of any rebel property—including human property—that was being used in the Confederate war effort. Now Secretary of the Treasury Salmon Chase gave the proposition of confiscation of rebel prop-erty high-level support in his annual report on the finances of the country. Chase suggested that the property of the rebels be used "to contribute to the expenditures made necessary by their criminal misconduct as a part of the punishment due to the guilt of involving the nation in the calamities of civil war." He thought that Congress could make a law authorizing the confiscation of the "estates of offenders . . . for the payment of the proceeds into the public Treasury." Commenting favorably on Chase's report, the *Chicago Tribune* re-minded its readers that the seceded states had begun the war by confiscating "all the Federal property they could lay their hands on." The rebels had also confiscated the property of citizens in the loyal states, refused to pay private debts, and conducted piratical expeditions on private steamers. The war was likely to cost the Union "a thousand millions" in the long run. Therefore, the

8. The Michigan legislature refused to send delegates to the Peace Convention. Detroit Post and Tribune, *Zachariah Chandler*, 42–3, 190.

editorial asked (somewhat irrationally) whether the government did not have the right to do "legally what the traitors have been and are constantly doing illegally," and recommended that Congress give "speedy effect" to Secretary Chase's suggestion to confiscate the property of rebels. Similarly, a *New York Times* editorial commented that the war would undoubtedly cost enormous sums of money, but there was no reason for loyal Union citizens to shoulder the burden. The law and usage of nations made it "entirely legitimate to make the property of the citizens of the rebel States, whose wickedness has provoked this war, pay the whole debt incurred by the Nation." These were both Republican newspapers, but even the more moderate *Newark Daily Advertiser* considered the confiscation of rebel property a "light penalty indeed," and nothing more than a righteous retribution for the rebellion.[9]

Persistent nagging from Republicans in newspapers as well as in letters and in dozens of weekly petitions steadily drove the question of confiscation into the forefront. Horace Greeley urged the fledgling Army onward to Richmond, and the home front groused about the administration's lack of action. In response, the Republicans in Congress inaugurated many attacks on southern property. By the middle of the session, both Houses were deluged with bills and resolutions (as well as hundreds of petitions from the home front) proposing to confiscate property and to punish the rebels. Some, but not all, included provisions for emancipating the slaves of rebels. Almost all of the bills went straight to the moderate Committees on the Judiciary, which diluted the most radical confiscation ideas before reporting the bills back to the House or the Senate. Of the eight confiscation bills proposed within the first two weeks of the session, only the most moderate survived, and would come up for serious discussion toward the end of the session. On July 8, Connecticut congressman Dwight Loomis proposed a confiscation bill in the House of Representatives; four days later, Senator Henry Wilson proposed a similar bill in the Senate. This was followed, on July 15, by Chandler's bill, and by similar bills by Lyman Trumbull, Charles Sumner, and freshman senator Samuel C. Pomeroy from Kansas. Pomeroy's bill (S. 28) contained a provision to emancipate all the slaves of

9. Randall, *Constitutional Problems,* 275; Report of the Secretary of the Treasury, Senate Executive Document 2, 37th Congress, 1st sess., serial 1112; *Chicago Tribune,* July 15, 1861. See also editorial, *Chicago Tribune,* July 18, 1861. *New York Times* editorials, July 8, 10, and 16, 1861; *Newark Daily Advertiser,* July 12, 1861.

rebels, while Sumner's (S. 29) and Trumbull's bills (S. 26) did not. Neither did Hickman's bill to punish the conspiracy through fines. All bills were referred to the respective Committees on the Judiciary.

The Committees on the Judiciary performed most of the substantive work on confiscation legislation and on other punitive bills. Although the legislators debated the merits of these bills at great length on the floors of both houses, and often offered substitutes, amendments, or entirely new confiscation bills, ultimately it was the committees that decided how severe the legislation was to be, how many safeguards were to be placed on enemy property, how slaves were to be treated, and how the procedure of confiscation was to be effected. Although it was true that radical Republicans in both houses of Congress pushed the agenda of punitive legislation and emancipation, their most severe proposals did not survive the committee deliberations. In the end, the bills that were reported from the Committees on the Judiciary reflected the moderate center of Congress, which acquiesced in the popular demand for the confiscation of rebel property, but balked at the prospect of widespread emancipation.

The Senate Committee on the Judiciary was composed primarily of moderates and border statesmen. It included no radicals. Lyman Trumbull, who had been a free-soil Democrat until the Kansas-Nebraska debacle, chaired the committee. Not an extremist, he prided himself on being a careful defender of the Constitution. The other members were Connecticut senator Lafayette S. Foster, a former Whig, now a moderate Republican, and John C. Ten Eyck of New Jersey, also a former Whig turned moderate Republican, hailing from one of the most southern-sympathetic states in the Union. The committee also included Pennsylvania's Edgar Cowan, a freshman senator who would consistently block confiscation legislation and all other radical Republican measures, and the only Republican to vote against the Second Confiscation Act. Moderate Republican Ira Harris of New York, James A. Bayard of Delaware, and Democrat Lazarus Powell of Kentucky also served on the committee. The House Committee on the Judiciary was chaired by John Hickman of Pennsylvania, who had served as a Democrat in the 34th and 35th Congresses, but was now a Republican. Among the committee members were antislavery Republican John A. Bingham of Ohio and George H. Pendleton, a Democrat, also of Ohio, but much more conservative than his colleague. The other members included moderate Republican Alexander S. Diven of New York, James F. Wilson of Iowa, William Kellogg of Illinois, Albert G. Porter from Indiana, and Benjamin F. Thomas of Massachu-

setts. The only border state representative was an outspoken critic of the administration, Henry May of Maryland.

During the six weeks of the special session, Congress debated many different ways of taking rebel property. The First Confiscation Act, passed at the end
of the special session, was certainly the most explicit legislation concerned with
the military seizure of rebel land, crops, and slaves—but the passage of a law
specifically confiscating enemy property was only one example of a far more
widespread impulse. The two most successful methods of confiscating southern
property were through the seizure of "contraband," similar to a customs officer's seizure of smuggled goods, and through exorbitant taxation, such as the
Direct Tax Act of 1861. Although most of these attacks on southern property
were far more effective than either of the two Confiscation Acts, they excited
far less debate, either among the public or in Congress. There may be several
possible answers to this conundrum. First, because some of these other modes
of taking property were historically sanctioned, such as the seizure of rebel
ships and cargoes, they did not appear to strike directly at the Constitution.
Also, Congress's power to impose taxes and tariffs was unquestioned, and it was
therefore much easier for radicals to pass even the most prohibitive taxes, especially if their purpose was to reimburse the loyal North for expenses incurred
by the traitorous South. Finally, even the most ardently pro-southern Democrats did not wish to appear reluctant to fight a vigorous war, and they may have
felt that a refusal to exercise their traditional duties would have branded them
as rebel sympathizers. Congress passed the Direct Tax Act on August 5, 1861, the
day before Lincoln signed the First Confiscation Act. The Direct Tax Act set
specific quotas on all the states of the Union (including the seceded states), ap-
portioned according to the population in each state, and provided that the
federal government could use force to collect taxes (and in lieu of taxes, real estate) from states who had not met their quota. This law raised about $2.3 mil-
lion from the southern states, nearly twice as much revenue as both Confiscation Acts combined.[10]

Therefore, although Chandler's bill had been the first to recommend confiscation explicitly, senators and congressmen submitted a multitude of bills
that attacked southern assets by other means. Some proposed taking private
property used in support of the war, with or without compensation (none of

10. Randall, *Constitutional Problems*, 423.

these bills included emancipation clauses). Others imposed monetary fines as punishment for participating in the insurrection. Most of these bills attempted to find a practical solution for the potentially crippling costs of the war; many of them also included provisions for punishing the rebels for treason. There were also several bills and resolutions that sought to force the seceded states to honor their financial obligations to the federal government. Chandler's was the only confiscation bill that explicitly mentioned reimbursing loyal Unionists, and it is significant that the bill did not survive the committee process. Like all the confiscation bills that would follow it swiftly in the next two weeks, Chandler's bill was submitted to the moderate Senate Committee on the Judiciary, where it disappeared in favor of a more moderate bill by Senator Lyman Trumbull. Other measures threatened to take southern ships and cargoes, and proposed to use the Navy to enforce the law. The first such legislation was H.R. 16, a bill to provide for the collection of revenue in ports belonging to the seceded states. Ostensibly the purpose of this bill was to strengthen the 1795 force bill. On July 9, Illinois congressman Elihu Washburne reported H.R. 16 from the House Committee on Commerce. It provided that wherever states were in rebellion, the president could close the ports and establish floating customs houses at sea. The bill authorized the president to seize merchandise, ships, and cargoes belonging to persons still in rebellion against the government fifteen days from the date on which the bill became law.[11]

But H.R. 16 was not simply a stronger version of the 1795 force bill. The radical element on the home front was fully alive to the ramifications of an attack on private property of rebellious southerners. According to a *Chicago Tribune* editorial, the best way to use this bill was to emancipate slaves. The *Tribune* applauded the provisions of the bill that gave it an apparently "permanent" char-

---

11. The Militia Act of 1795 provided that "whenever the Laws of the United States shall be opposed . . . the President may call the militia of such State." This law was intended to enforce collection of duties in ports (*Statutes at Large,* February 28, 1795, c.36, 1 Stat. 424). H.R.16, "An Act to further provide for the collection of duties on imports, and for other duties," was approved by President Lincoln on July 17, 1861. Besides S. 25, 26, 28, 29, the other bills that proposed confiscating rebel property included S. 33 and S. 35 (both punishment for insurrection bills that included confiscation clauses) and several House bills, including H.R. 45, 86, and 55, the latter a piracy bill that proposed seizing ships and cargoes. In addition, both houses passed H.R. 16, discussed above, S. 51, a Senate bill that provided for additional powers for H.R. 16, and the Direct Tax Act, H.R. 54. All of these bills became law.

acter, which augured well for the government's future (long-term) ability to seize southern property. The law was clearly not intended to serve only as a wartime stopgap. The editorial based its reinterpretation of the bill on the section that confiscated "all goods and chattels" (to which the *Tribune* added, in brackets and with an exclamation point, [negroes!]). This legislation would put the "contraband" out of the reach of the Fugitive Slave Law, so long as the U.S. government accepted the southern rendering of the word "chattel." That is, the federal government had to agree, at least for now, that a human being was a legitimate form of property. In this instance, as in many others to follow, the radicals on the home front outstripped the radicals in Congress—who had at this time not yet expressed their intention to emancipate the slaves, at least not explicitly in their speeches in the houses of Congress.[12]

But of course slaves were not the only kind of property to be found south of the Mason-Dixon line; many of the various proposed confiscation laws were not originally intended (except those by radical Republicans) to be emancipation bills. Even Chandler's harsh bill had not included an emancipation clause. Most Republicans were, for the moment, more concerned with hampering the enemy's ability to wage war than with destroying the institution of slavery. For example, Henry Wilson's July 12 confiscation bill focused on taking personal property, if it had been put to public use and if the owners were found in open rebellion. Even though Wilson had been a life-long antislavery man, his reference to "property" was widely interpreted to mean cotton. In an approving editorial, the *Chicago Tribune* said the bill was intended mainly to confiscate the cotton crop and "convert it into gold." No doubt the Army would take great pleasure in collecting the hundred thousand bales of cotton from the "arch traitors of the rattle-snake State." Further, the editorial pointed out that slaves, being considered property under the laws of the seceded states, would also be "legitimate subjects" and would be very useful to the Army as scouts and spies, and in collecting cotton from their former owners.[13]

Although the members of the special session were concentrating their efforts on the conduct of the war and on punitive measures against nonhuman property, the topic of slavery continually crept into their debates. Border state politicians, such as Congressman Henry C. Burnett and Senator John C. Breck-

12. *Chicago Tribune,* July 10, 1861.

13. *Cong. Globe,* 37th Cong., 1st sess., 78; *Chicago Tribune,* July 20, 1861; *New York Herald,* August 4, 1861.

inridge, both from Kentucky, always objected vociferously, claiming that the topic had no place in their deliberations. But on July 2, the House of Representatives voted to pass Owen Lovejoy's Resolution, that it was "no part of the duty of the soldiers of the United States to capture and return fugitive slaves." The Lovejoy Resolution was nonbinding—it merely recommended that Union Army officers and soldiers cease to play the part of "slave-catchers," but said nothing about permitting the fugitives to join Union bivouacs or marching lines. There was a difference between refusing to capture slaves and actively encouraging them to flee. The War Department was still telling generals to refuse the fugitives entry into Union camps, which became a divisive issue on the home front. Less than two weeks after the passage of the Lovejoy Resolution, General Joseph K. Mansfield issued an order not to allow any fugitive slaves to pass over the Potomac with his regiment. One incensed Ohioan, a man named M. J. Thomas, demanded to know by whose authority General Mansfield issued his decree refusing entry or shelter to fugitive slaves. The contrabands, he said, had "escaped from their traitorous masters, who employ them in all manner of military operations against our government and its loyal citizens." If these men came to Union troops seeking liberty and protection, then they deserved to be granted their freedom. Thomas wanted to know whether it was indeed by Lincoln's order that the fugitives be turned away. If that was indeed the case, then what had "humanity and justice gained by the election of Abraham Lincoln?" In contrast, the Democratic *New York World,* in an editorial on the "Advancing Army and the Slaves," praised Mansfield's decision not to allow fugitive slaves to follow army columns. There were too many logistical problems involved; the army could not feed the runaways, and the slaves would be a "chain and ball" on the ankle of Union soldiers. It is not surprising that Democratic papers were usually more aware of the pragmatic questions concerned with fugitive slaves, while Republican papers focused primarily on the moral and ethical issues of slavery. As a nonbinding House resolution, the Lovejoy Resolution did not carry a great deal of weight with conservative Army officers. Congress was in recess from August through December and would not legislate on this issue until the following spring. In March 1862, the 37th Congress finally passed an article of war that forbade officers, on penalty of dismissal, to aid in the capture or return of fugitive slaves.[14]

14. *New York World,* July 10, 30, 1861; M. J. Thomas to John Sherman, Sherman Papers, LOC, July 29, 1861.

Most northerners would, no doubt, have agreed with the *World* rather than with Thomas. There was a constant tension evident in public opinion between empathy for the fugitive slaves and fear that their presence in the Union Army camps would create a social problem of insurmountable magnitude. By the end of summer, Fortress Monroe had become home to nearly fifteen hundred fugitives, half of them women and children. Butler had a clear sign from the administration that the refugees at Fortress Monroe would not have to be returned to rebellious owners. But that did not help him with the problem of what to do with the wives and children of the runaways; nor did it address the problem of the slaves who had fled loyal border state owners. For most of the war, northerners were convinced that freed slaves would become a burden on the North, would refuse to work and thus destroy southern agriculture, or would commit atrocities against their former owners. Democratic papers, especially, regularly published editorials predicting horrific slave insurrections; one Maine newspaper foretold a bloody "reign of terror," and the *Racine* [Wisconsin] *Gazette* predicted that the end of slavery was certainly coming, and that it would come as a result of a bloody revolt "like in Haiti."[15]

Newspaper editorials, pamphlets, and sermons commented almost daily on the fact that slaves were escaping the moment they had somewhere to go—that is, from the moment the Union Army marched into southern territory. All through the summer Republican papers like the *Chicago Tribune* and the *New York Times* reported on the growing number of fugitive slaves who joined Union Army camps and marching lines. In 1861, most northerners still firmly believed that the Army should fight for no other goal than to restore the Union, but they also understood that the presence of bluecoated soldiers on southern soil would inspire slaves to seek their freedom. Some of the more conservative Democratic papers, like the *Detroit Free Press,* minimized the problem, saying that a "few thousand" fugitives could hardly affect the outcome of military movements, and thus opposed any change in policy. But most northerners now demanded a "declared policy on the subject." The situation had clearly become unpredictable and perhaps uncontrollable, and the fact that Army officers simply followed their own inclinations was highly unsatisfactory.[16]

15. Gerteis, *From Contraband to Freedman,* 19; Gerteis comments that Union lines included another ten thousand black people (22); Perkins, ed., *Northern Editorials,* 464; Paris (Maine) *Oxford Democrat,* April 26, 1861; Racine (Wisconsin) *Gazette,* September 12, 1861.

16. Sprague, *Glorifying God.* See, for example, *Chicago Tribune, New York Times, Detroit Free Press. Cleveland Daily Plain Dealer,* May 8, 1861.

There was no consensus on this issue. Even the political affiliations of newspapers are not a reliable guide to public opinion. Some Democratic papers, for example, supported the government's right to take all property, including human property; some Republican papers thought the government should stop short at the confiscation of slaves, or at least should distinguish carefully between the slaves of rebels and the slaves of loyal Unionists; and there was a vide variety of opinions between these two positions. Radical Republican papers like the *Chicago Tribune* applauded any military or governmental action that led to the emancipation of slaves. But the problem (especially for Democrats) always returned to the inescapable fact that there were 4 million persons enslaved in the South and that the exigencies of warfare might lead to their liberation. Many northerners were deeply prejudiced against black people and contemplated the prospect of widespread emancipation with foreboding. It had now become strikingly clear to most northerners, however, that fugitive slaves had minds of their own and were not going to wait on careful deliberations over their relative status as person or chattel. It was also evident that this was promising to become a social problem of unprecedented magnitude.

By mid-July the senators and congressmen had been laboring in the stifling heat for a little over two weeks. Some important bills and resolutions had already been passed, notably the Army appropriations bill and the new "force bill." The proposed confiscation bills were still in committee, however, and the resolution to approve the president's actions had not yet passed either house. The discussions had been wide-ranging and often confused, but there were hints that the members of Congress were ready to wrap up their business. Several senators and representatives proposed motions to adjourn on July 20. Although none of these motions were seconded, there was a general feeling that the hot, humid weather would soon bring an end to the political deliberations.

CHAPTER 4

The First Confiscation Act and the Emancipation of Slaves

O N SUNDAY AFTERNOON, July 21, the Union and Confederate armies clashed in the first significant battle of the war, about twenty-five miles south of the capital. At Manassas Junction, General Irvin McDowell's green Union troops, pushed into battle by the public's clamor for action, fought General P. G. T. Beauregard's green Confederates. Washington's politicians, clerks, ladies, and reporters had gone out, in a holiday atmosphere complete with picnics, to view what they thought would be a magnificent victory. Many of the members of the 37th Congress were prominently in evidence, either viewing the battle or (perhaps apocryphally) directly involved. Conspicuous among them was the "Jacobin Club" of Ohio senator Benjamin Franklin Wade, Lyman Trumbull, and Zachariah Chandler. Massachusetts senator Henry Wilson and Illinois congressman Elihu Washburne came in an open barouche, and brought an immense hamper of sandwiches that they distributed to soldiers. Iowa senator James Grimes and Trumbull rode on horseback from the capital to Manassas. On their way they stopped to visit a Union hospital, where they were horrified by their first sight of wounded and dying men. Losing their taste for battle scenes, they left quickly. On their way back to the capital, they met with California senator James McDougall, and the three men returned to Centreville, where they had a picnic lunch and waited for what would prove to be depressing news.[1]

---

1. John Hay called these three men the "Jacobin Club" in his diary, but he probably did not originate the nickname, since it was widely used throughout the early years of the war. See Dennett, ed., *Lincoln and the Civil War*, 31.

Sanguine predictions of victory had not borne fruit. McDowell's troops were three-month volunteers, some of whom were nearly at the end of their enlistments. Inadequate supplies and lack of information about the terrain caused delays and confusions; as a result, McDowell was never able to deploy all the men at his command. At first the raw volunteers on both sides fought well, but shortages in food and water had weakened the Union troops, who had been fighting for over fourteen hours. When Confederate general Joseph Johnston brought in six thousand fresh reinforcements by rail, part of the retreat turned into a rout. The engagement ended in a humiliating defeat for the Union forces. It was said that soldiers, officers, sightseers, and newspaper correspondents mingled and ran all the way back to Washington. *London Times* journalist William Howard Russell described the rout as disgraceful, and placed the entire blame for the defeat on the disorganization and cowardice of the Union troops. His reportage in the *Times* earned him no end of opprobrium in the northern press. The stories of a wholesale flight, however, are probably exaggerated. Historian James M. McPherson estimated that half of the Union forces had fought bravely and stood their ground.[2]

The defeat sharpened and focused northern attitudes toward the war and its aims. Although the home front and the politicians were concerned about different aspects of the battle and its overall significance, everyone now realized that the war no longer appeared to be a glorious summer adventure. When the politicians returned to their seats in Congress the following morning, many of them were exhausted and miserable. They had had little or no sleep the night before, and were now more fully alive to the realities confronting them. The ugly scenes they had witnessed left them with small inclination to boast of an imminent Union victory, and with much greater determination to make an end of the war. A few days after the battle Massachusetts representative Henry Dawes received a letter from his wife, Electa, telling him to take heart. She believed that even if the Army "shall fail once, or twice, they only fail, to the more surely in the end accomplish the deliverance of the captive." She believed that the defeat was God's punishment for the "national sin" of slavery, and now the nation must "bleed to atone for its iniquities." She still prayed for the liberation of all the slaves: "God grant that the day may be soon." The president was deeply

2. *National Daily Intelligencer*, July 22, 1861. Trefousse, *Benjamin Franklin Wade*, 150. McPherson, *Battle Cry*, 344–7. See also Detroit Post and Tribune, *Zachariah Chandler*, 150.

shocked, at least in part because he realized that he had been to blame for pushing the untried troops into battle. He now considered replacing McDowell with
General George B. McClellan, and began to plan an advance on the western theater of the war.[3]

The defeat horrified the northern public and forced a realization that the nation was embroiled in a long war that would require greater sacrifice and commitment than they had expected. Neatly summarizing the shift in the North's
attitudes as a response to the defeat, Charles Francis Adams observed that the
nation had now gone through three stages in their attitudes toward the civil
conflict. The first stage, he said, was "the cold fit, when it seemed as if nothing
would start the country. The second was the hot one, when it seemed almost in
the highest continual delirium. The third is the process of waking to the awful
reality before it." London correspondent William Howard Russell also commented that the defeat had let some of the "poison gas" out of the northern
pride.[4]

This event also revealed a marked contrast between the lawmakers' attitudes
and those of the public. People at home focused on the humiliation of the rout,
and on widespread rumors that rebel soldiers had committed atrocities against
the wounded and dead. They were also disturbed by rumors that the labor of
"thousands" of black men had been used in the fight to build entrenchments
and carry arms. As a result, the northern public was now more ready to punish
the South harshly, and to consider slaves as a suitable subject for confiscation.
Even conservative proslavery Democrats now realized that the rebels would use
whatever means they could to win independence—and that a slave could be
useful to both friend and foe. But the politicians in Washington were more concerned with the proof that an untrained, undisciplined three-month volunteer
army could not hope to win what promised to be a long war. Horace Greeley,
who was horribly aware that his own insistence on pushing the army toward
Richmond had been greatly responsible for the defeat, became profoundly depressed. The opinion leaders, therefore, were much less likely to advocate for
further depredations until the logistics of warfare could be worked out. Re-

3. Electa Dawes to Henry L. Dawes, Dawes Papers, LOC, July 25, 1861; Gienapp, *Abraham Lincoln and Civil War America,* 87; Donald, *Lincoln,* 308–9.

4. Charles Francis Adams to Charles Francis Adams Jr., August 16, 1861, in Ford, ed., *A Cycle
of Adams Letters,* 27; Russell, *My Diary North and South,* 234.

publican voters, always ahead of Congress in their desire for sharp measures, pressed the lawmakers to enact more radical legislation.[5]

The northern public, meanwhile, was also being regaled with horrific accounts of atrocities committed by rebel soldiers. The enemy, they were told, had cut wounded Union boys' throats, bayoneted them, or propped them up against trees and shot them. There were also ghoulish descriptions of desecrated or mutilated dead bodies. The stories were almost certainly false, but the scandal sharply altered home front opinion about the conduct of the war, whipping up the North's desire for revenge to a fever pitch. Although many northerners had been advocating a forceful prosecution of the war and an attack on southern property, they were now out for blood. An Illinoisan had heard the rumors and was outraged. "Shame Shame What cowardice[!]" he exclaimed. He thought the Union Army should immediately shoot all Confederate prisoners of war in retaliation. Northerners demanded revenge and relief for the mortification of defeat. One of Elihu Washburne's constituents declared that he hoped "measures will be put on foot at once to wipe out both the stain [of cowardice] and the Rebles." Even so moderate a lady as Sarah Wister called the rebels "savages" when she heard of the atrocities. When she had first heard of the defeat, she had written in her diary that it "at once ends all hope of crushing them singly & leaving nothing for it but to wait with set teeth for the issue," but the reports of the cold-blooded killings left her hoping for swift retribution.[6]

Many northerners linked the barbaric treatment of wounded Union soldiers with the barbarism of slavery. It appeared to them that the rebels were going to fight dirty, and that their own soft-hearted, "modern" notions of civilized warfare would simply put the North at a disadvantage. Throughout the war the northern public would link the idea of fighting a harsh war with taking rebel property, and now it appeared to them that the time had come to break loose from the tenderhearted constraints of a Constitution the rebels themselves had spurned. Calvin Fletcher had been so horrified by the news of the defeat that he

5. Greeley quoted in McPherson, *Battle Cry*, 347. For northern public opinion on the defeat at Bull Run, see Rawley, *Turning Points of the Civil War*, 57; see also Strong, *Diary*, July 22, 1861, 3:169; Royster, *Destructive War*, 79–81.

6. James F. Smith to John Sherman, Sherman Papers, July 31, 1861; J. R. Jones to Elihu Washburne, Elihu B. Washburne Papers, LOC, July 24, 1861; diary entry dated July 21, 1861, in Wister, ed., *That I May Tell You*, 57. The *Philadelphia Inquirer*, the *New York World*, and many other newspapers carried the reports of the atrocities.

had become paralyzed and depressed, unable even to get out of bed. He saw the rebels' cruelty toward Union soldiers as being roughly equivalent to the treatment of southern slaves. The country, which had "had tampered & lied to reconcile rebellion," could no longer delude itself that it could survive with the institution intact. He recognized that loyal Americans had not fully grasped "the horors of slav[e]ry, the real cause of the war till our prisoners fell into the slave holders hands & gave them temporary possession of our men . . . over whom they tyranized kill[ed], burned, hacked destroyed sick & well. Northern men their victims who will tell a tale that will not be forgotten on slav[e]ry— what they have practised on the slave, they practised on their captiv[e]s on whom they looked as being as degraded as the African." New York diarist George Templeton Strong also unleashed bitter invective on the rebels, and drew similar conclusions about the southern aristocracy and their penchant for brutality. "How the inherent barbarism of the chivalry crops out whenever it can safely kill or torture a defenseless enemy . . . [with] an elaboration of artistic fertility." There was nothing for it now but to "tune ourselves up to the same pitch, hang rebels, arm their niggers, burn their towns, expel all sympathizers with treason."[7]

One of the results of the defeat at Bull Run—and the atrocity stories—was that the militant northerners' impatience was now channeled into a willingness to fight a less restrained, less "gentlemanly" war. Frederick Douglass claimed that Bull Run made people more aware of the only sure way to end the war. Echoing the sentiments of many of his countrymen, Douglass thought the atrocities clearly exhibited the difference between southern and northern styles of fighting. "The South is in earnest," he claimed, "we are not." It was obvious that the Union Army and government would have to become harsher, and resort to much more drastic methods, in order to win against such an unscrupulous enemy. Deploring the continuing reluctance to enact an emancipation law, Douglass compared northern and southern methods of warfare. He observed that the North had been "very careful about the rights of property," while the South "fills the sea with pirates, and plunders the Government of every thing it can get its hand upon." Unitarian minister Henry Bellows made a similar comparison. He thought that in a street quarrel, a ruffian (who presumably would not be constrained by the finer points of civilized fisticuffs) would have a great

7. Strong, *Diary*, entries dated July 25, August 2, 13, 1861, 170–5.

advantage over a "Christian gentleman." Although, according to Bellows, the mark of a real gentleman was reluctance to quarrel at all, it was now time to let convictions be "sharpened into bayonets."[8]

Furthermore, Republicans now distinctly linked the first serious defeat in the war with a need to attack the institution of slavery. Former Rhode Island congressman Elisha R. Potter made this point in a speech shortly after the battle. It was the North's "miserable policy of self deception" that had cost them the battle at Bull Run. He was not only referring to northerners' grandiose rhetoric, but also to their inability to understand that slavery was the root of the civil conflict. Although Potter stated that he was not an abolitionist, he predicted that this war against slaveholders would soon become an antislavery war. "We may commence the war without meaning to interfere with slavery; but let us have one or two battles, and get our blood excited, and we shall not only not restore any more slaves, but shall proclaim freedom wherever we go." While it was true that so far the slaves had remained peaceably in bondage, that was only because they had "nowhere to flee." Once sure of an asylum and safety, "fire and poison and the bludgeon" would soon desolate the South. Many northerners agreed that the solution to the war would be to confiscate the slaves owned by the rebellious masters and make them "*work for* or *fight for* and not *against*" the Union.[9]

Soldiers returning from the fight at Manassas Junction told Congressman James G. Blaine that slaves "by the thousand" had been driving teams, cooking, building earthworks, and put to work on all forms of camp drudgery. Blaine realized that slaves were "adding four millions to the population from which the Confederates could draw their quotas of men for military service." It hardly mattered that the rebels never intended to put arms into the black men's hands. The slaves released white men from farm labor, who could at once be mustered into the ranks. The Confederate Army's use of slaves had "seriously increased the available force of fighting men at the first engagement." Individual slaves were now becoming, in the northern public eye, a potentially useful resource. Similarly, a *Chicago Tribune* editorial entitled "What the Slaves are Doing for

8. Frederick Douglass, "The War and Slavery," quoted in Foner, *Life and Writings,* 128, 131; Bellows, *Advantage,* 7.

9. Potter, *Speech of Hon. Elisha R. Potter,* 3, 11; William Reddick to Lyman Trumbull, Trumbull Papers, LOC, July 25, 1861; see also *New York Times,* July 22, 24, 1861. Both editorials asserted that the defeat at Bull Run now called for emancipation.

the Rebels" pointed out that when northerners crowed about superior numbers of men, they should understand that their "calculations are fallacious," because southern slaves were strengthening the Confederate fighting force. Another *Tribune* editorial hammered this point home. "War means quick destruction. . . . It means exhaustion of the resources of the parties engaged therein, in such a way that one or the other will confess their inability to carry it on." What better way, the paper suggested, than by striking at the main resource upon which the rebels relied for food and money. Their slaves produced "the bread that treason eats. They dig the trenches and throw up the embankments behind which traitors strut." [10]

The northern public and their representatives in Washington reacted rather differently to the Bull Run disaster. Northerners, already angry over the rebels' property seizures, secession, and the defeat, were now even more enraged over the atrocity stories, and politicians were forced to confront the immense problem of directing a civil war without adequate preparation. Still, the discussions about the conduct of the war and the treatment of rebel citizens had been ongoing for seven months, and the northern public had been angrily expressing punitive sentiments since December 1860. Historians frequently point out that Lincoln approved a bill for the enlistment of five hundred thousand three-year men on the day after Bull Run. But Congress had already passed that law on July 14, a week before the battle, and the bill had been debated since the beginning of the session. Similar claims are made about the Confiscation Act. However, by July 21, several confiscation bills had already been under consideration in committee, and occasionally debated on the floor, for three weeks. Indeed, many historians now assert that the defeat at Bull Run was the single most important motivating factor behind the inclusion of an emancipation clause in the Confiscation Act, pointing to the fact that Trumbull's emancipation amendment was discussed in the Senate on the day after the defeat. However, the facts of the story are somewhat more complicated. Acting as chairman of the Committee on the Judiciary, Trumbull reported the confiscation bill on July 20, 1861, the day before the battle, and it was also on that day that he added his emancipation amendment. The confiscation bill was taken up for consideration on July 22, the day after the battle, with the emancipation provision al-

10. James F. Smith to Lyman Trumbull, Trumbull Papers, LOC, July 31, 1861; Blaine, *Twenty Years of Congress*, 1:342; Chicago *Tribune*, June 13, August 22, 1861.

ready in place. Several members of the Senate Committee on the Judiciary were present at the morning session on July 22, so the committee was obviously already finished with its deliberations on the confiscation bill. The emancipation amendment would already have been in place, then, before the bill was reintroduced in the afternoon. The Bull Run defeat has long been viewed as a crucial touchstone for the development of punitive sentiment both on the home front and in Washington, but the home front and politicians had been engaged in an intense debate on this subject for some time, at least since the beginning of the secession crisis.[11]

It is true, though, that prior to the defeat at Bull Run, the congressional debates over slavery had not been primarily concerned with emancipation or the evils of the "peculiar institution." Instead, discussions about the propriety of confiscating slaves were usually linked to the constitutional protection of property rights, as well as to the practical difficulties of liberating 4 million human beings. Widespread confiscation of slaves was not discussed seriously until northerners woke to the gradual realization that slaves were human beings with a real future, and with a real use to the Confederacy and potentially to the North. The defeat at Bull Run, and the news that black men had been seen working on the Confederate side, now focused the discussion and kept it strictly on track, in marked contrast to the wide-ranging debates during the first two weeks of the special session.[12]

During the Monday afternoon session on July 22, the confiscation bill (S. 26) came back from the Senate Committee on the Judiciary to be considered in the Committee of the Whole. S. 26 was Trumbull's moderate confiscation bill that had superseded all the others referred to the Judiciary Committee, including Chandler's. Trumbull's bill provided for the seizure, confiscation, and condemnation of all property "knowingly used" to aid the rebellion. Trumbull's bill, however, was not entirely successful in surmounting the objections of conservatives, who said it violated the Bill of Rights. In order to obviate discussions about Fifth Amendment property rights, which the bill rather conveniently

11. For the effect of the Battle of Bull Run on Army enlistment bills, see McPherson, *Battle Cry*, 348; also Rawley, *Turning Points of the Civil War*, 62. For the effect on politicians' attitudes on the Confiscation Act, see Grimsley, *Hard Hand of War*, 32; Trefousse, *Lincoln's Decision*, 22; and Franklin, *Emancipation Proclamation*, 16. See *Cong. Globe*, 37th Cong., 2nd sess, 128–9, for the debate on Trumbull's amendment.

12. *Cong. Globe*, 37th Cong., 1st sess., July 22, 1861, 218.

skated over, confiscated property was "hereby declared to be lawful subject of prize and capture wherever found." The "prize and capture" phrase was a reference to maritime captures, and was probably intended to draw a parallel (if tenuous) analogy between rebel property found on land, and smuggled goods captured at sea.[13]

In defense against the accusation that confiscation violated the Constitution, Republicans argued that the rebels themselves had set aside the Constitution and therefore could not expect its protections. Normally, the government could not take the property of American citizens without a jury trial, or, in the case of eminent domain seizures, without fair compensation. But the courts were not in session behind enemy lines. The wording of the Confiscation Act acknowledged this fact by stating that the country was being threatened "by combinations too powerful to be suppressed by the ordinary course of judicial proceedings." Trumbull's bill proposed, therefore, that the attorney general, or any district attorney, could institute the proceedings of condemnation. Condemnation is simply the process of transferring the title of property from private ownership to public use, as in lands taken by the federal government for railroads or public buildings. The Fifth Amendment provides for such seizures, but guarantees a fair payment to the original owner. Naturally, the Confiscation Act provided no such payment, but instead transferred ownership directly to the federal government. This was to be accomplished through a legal stratagem known as *in rem* proceedings. Confiscating property *in rem* simply meant that the property itself was held to be guilty, and therefore liable to seizure. It was not necessary to adjudicate the guilt or innocence of the owner. Such proceedings were used in admiralty cases, for example, in judgments concerning Coast Guard seizures of smuggled goods.[14]

Federal district attorneys would be responsible for initiating such actions in individual cases, although loyal state officials or even neighbors might bring forward information about property used to aid the rebel armies. In that case, the informer would receive half of the value of confiscated property. The law did not specify the role of U. S. Army officers; neither did the bill explain how or

---

13. See Appendix 1 for the final wording of the First Confiscation Act.

14. Lucie, *Freedom and Federalism*, 24–6. The First Confiscation Act did not refer to *in rem* proceedings. The Second Confiscation Act, passed on July 17, 1862, did explicitly contain reference to *in rem* proceedings.

why U.S. attorneys would be present in areas controlled by Union forces. Because the lawmakers did not debate this point, it is difficult to reconstruct their reasoning; it might be assumed that Army officers or loyal Unionists living in the area would perhaps be best informed about the military uses of private property. The First Confiscation Act included a provision that anyone could file information about property to be confiscated with the attorney general or district attorney, in which case the informant and the United States would share the confiscated property equally. However, while officers and soldiers were empowered to "lay information" to the district attorney, under the Confiscation Act they did not have the authority to condemn the property itself. This specific point would later be unsuccessfully tested by several abolitionist officers, like Generals John C. Frémont and David Hunter. Since the law did not specify what was to be done with the property after it was condemned, it did not actually fulfill the public's demand for redress for their personal financial losses. The failure to do so would eventually cost the politicians some good will among their constituencies.[15]

The clauses dealing with the methods of taking property in the Confiscation Act were astonishingly spare and vague. The technical details were hammered out in the committee meetings, and were not debated in the halls of Congress. The politicians who crafted and debated this legislation may have assumed that it would be relatively easy to distinguish property that had been used either in battle or to support the Confederate war effort. Those senators and congressmen who opposed the Confiscation Act simply declared it to be unconstitutional, but did not enter into detailed discussions about its provisions. There may be several possible explanations for this, including the speed and urgency of the first session of the 37th Congress and the fact that for opponents to the confiscation bill, its unconstitutionality may have seemed the most glaring fault. Moreover, General Butler's famous "contraband" order had been a popular solution to the problem of enemy property used as war matériel, and may have placed the confiscation law on a sound legal footing, at least for moderates.

The law provided for the confiscation of "any property of whatsoever kind

---

15. The discussion on these pages refers to Trumbull's proposed S. 25, which was not substantially changed in the final version. Indeed, even after the bill was reported back from the Committees on the Judiciary of both houses, it was still essentially the same bill Trumbull had reported on July 20. See Appendix 1 for full text of the First Confiscation Act.

or description" that was "purchased or acquired . . . with intent to use or employ the same, or suffer the same to be used or employed, in aiding, abetting or
promoting such insurrection or resistance to the laws." Since the bill referred
explicitly to the confiscation of property "purchased or acquired" for the purpose of aiding and abetting the rebellion, the general inference was that the law
referred to guns, ammunition, livestock, provisions for soldiers, and the like.
On the other hand, the law was sufficiently vague as to what constituted "intent
to use or employ" such property, that it would probably have been impossible
to prove such intent in a court of law. Moreover, the phrase "any property" left
the field wide open for the capture of livestock, money, food, cotton, or any
other commodity that might conceivably be used to aid the rebellion.

The members of the Committee on the Judiciary made no provisions in the
enforcing clauses of the law to indicate who was supposed to be responsible for
making the determination whether property (including the labor of slaves) had
been used to aid the Confederate war effort. The law provided that "such prizes
and capture shall be condemned in the District or Circuit Court of the United
States," or in the "admiralty in any district in which the [property] may have
been seized . . . or taken." This clause assumed that District Courts were in session in the rebellious areas, or that it would be easy to assess the relative guilt
or innocence of the property. Because this law was not specifically intended
to punish rebels, but rather to deprive the Confederate Army of useful war
matériel, the guilt or innocence of the owner was not relevant in the court's determination. The property was simply to be confiscated without a jury trial. In
the following year, Congress would debate a harsher confiscation act that included punishment and fines (as well as the confiscation of contraband property), and the question of loyalty became more important to the decision to
seize private property.

During the summer session several members of the 37th Congress began to
occupy themselves with the problem of loyalty oaths. Until August 1861, however, only civil servants and office holders were required to take such oaths, and
the question of determining the allegiance of southern civilians was as yet un-
resolved. Therefore, a problem of considerable urgency arose during the special
session: there were loyal Unionists living in areas controlled by the Confederate
forces, whose property might presumably be captured by rebels and used to
support the insurrection. As a result, there was some debate in the Senate about
the exact wording of the phrase "suffer the [property] to be used or employed"

in battle. Obviously, loyal Unionists living in the South might not have much choice about whether the rebels would put their property to military use. After some haggling, the phrase was altered to "permit or suffer," but the essential problem remained unsolved. Neither of the two confiscation laws ever made it clear who was to take responsibility for distinguishing between the loyal and the disloyal, or even by what criteria their loyalty was to be judged. The Second Confiscation Act debated in the following session rather lamely forbade Army officers to adjudicate between rebels and Unionists, but never specified who was to do so. The First Confiscation Act simply ignored the question altogether, and in any case, the legislators did not debate this point.[16]

The fourth—and most controversial—section of the confiscation law was Trumbull's amendment setting free any slaves who had been used to aid the war effort. The wording of the fourth section was careful to avoid any hint of legitimizing property in human beings: "*And be it further enacted,* That whenever any person claiming to be entitled to the service or labor of any other person, under the laws of any State, shall employ such person in aiding or promoting any insurrection, or in resisting the laws of the United States, or shall permit or suffer him to be so employed, he shall forfeit all right to such service or labor, and the person whose service or labor is thus claimed shall thenceforth discharged therefrom, any law to the contrary notwithstanding."

In this small way, Republicans in Congress were attempting to change slaves' identity from chattel property to that of individual. Historians usually claim that the Confiscation Act freed no slaves because it did not explicitly emancipate them. In fact, however, the law interfered radically with the status of slaves as property because it proposed to discharge them from their labor—thus recognizing not only the slaves' innate right to be free of coerced labor, but also affirming the federal government's authority to make decisions about their status. Because nineteenth-century Americans had always acquiesced in the notion that black persons could legally be owned—body and soul—the mere recognition that the slave and his labor were two separate entities can be seen as revolutionary. Proponents of confiscation legislation—especially bills that emancipated slaves—first had to change the status of the slave as property, then declare that it was not the slave but rather his *labor* that was property (as opposed to the person). The law then declared the confiscated slave free, without

16. Belz, *Abraham Lincoln, Constitutionalism,* 101–3.

subjecting this species of property to the same "condemnation" procedures as other forms of property, such as land, crops, financial assets, or livestock.[17]

For these reasons, Trumbull simply called slaveowners persons "claiming to be entitled to the service or labor of another person," and was equally careful to avoid calling slaves by any name that might construe them as property. The section provided that whenever a rebel employed someone to whose labor they "claimed to be entitled," or whether the rebel permitted or suffered him "to be so employed," the purported owner would instantly forfeit all rights to such "service or labor." The wording of the section in no way admitted that the slave *himself* might be property, but simply acknowledged that the relationship between owner and slave was one of a putative "entitlement" to the slave's labor. The slave's *labor* was the property being confiscated, not the slave himself. The distinction was sufficiently important to merit considerable debate in the second session of the 37th Congress, since border state representatives did not care to have their right to own human beings diminished or questioned.

Radical Republicans saw Trumbull's amendment, and the entire confiscation bill, as a way of achieving one of their most cherished goals: the abolition of slavery. Still, the first consideration for Republicans, even radicals, was to take this potentially useful weapon away from the enemy. This was true even of dedicated abolitionists like Massachusetts senator Henry Wilson. Wilson was entirely in favor of the emancipation amendment, but at the moment he expounded on the practical—not the moral—aspects of emancipation. He thought that the slaves should be freed, either for military use or, at the very least, to deprive the Confederates of an important work force. All abolitionists, including Frederick Douglass, supported emancipation as a military measure because they knew that military necessity would be an irrefutable argument for liberating black people in the South. Eventually Wilson would become a strong supporter of bills arming former slaves and enrolling black men in the Union Army. Like many other Republicans, he also viewed slaves as potentially dangerous weapons in the hands of the Confederates. He was horrified at the idea that men who were in arms against their own country should be permitted to use others for that purpose; what was even more egregious was the suggestion

17. Berlin, Fields, Miller, Reidy, and Rowland, *Slaves No More*, 21. See also Gerteis, *From Contraband to Freedman*, 16–7; Franklin, *Emancipation Proclamation*, 16; Belz, *Abraham Lincoln, Constitutionalism*, 105.

that the government should stand by and issue orders to Union Army officers to return such men to their "traitorous masters." The only reasonable course to pursue was "that the Government shall at once convert those bondmen into men that cannot be used to destroy our country." One of Trumbull's constituents read this debate in the paper and agreed wholeheartedly. He declared in a vehement letter that he had "no faith in any sugar-plum policy," and proposed a novel form of retribution. Since rebel prisoners had forfeited their lives, "if not put to death at once [they] ought to work on our fortifications and entrenchments, and if refusing to work should be shot." He pointed out that black men were doing similar work for the rebels and yet, "strange to say our men are ordered to repel the blacks who flock to our Camps." Even such a conservative Democratic paper as the *Detroit Free Press* agreed that slaves should be taken from the enemy because they could be useful to Union armies. No distinction should be made, and if slaves were "wanted to dig, to throw up embankments, to cook, to do the menial services of the army, there is no reason why this kind of property should not be taken as quickly as any other." [18]

The more moderate Republicans in Congress—those who opposed slavery on ethical grounds but did not desire immediate abolition—now confronted a two-fold problem: not only did they have to countenance the confiscation of property, which was in and of itself a constitutional dilemma, but some of this property, once confiscated, suddenly changed its nature from chattel to person. Still, this did not necessitate conversion to abolitionism or even toward a more charitable disposition toward the slaves. Midway through the session, for example, New Jersey senator John C. Ten Eyck changed his mind about confiscation, largely in response to the news from Manassas. An old-line Whig from New Jersey, he had come into the Senate as one of the most conservative Republicans. As a member of the Judiciary Committee considering the bill, he had voted against the law, and especially against Trumbull's amendment. But he now felt that his earlier conservative votes were wrong. He claimed that had not believed that the rebels would make use of slaves in battle. He had also been worried about "what was to become of the poor wretches? God knows we do

---

18. *Cong. Globe,* 37th Cong., 1st sess., July 22, 1861, 219; Anson S. Millis to Lyman Trumbull, Trumbull Papers, LOC, August 2, 1861; *Detroit Free Press,* August 8, 1861. The *Free Press* was an extremely conservative Democratic paper that had supported the right to peaceful secession earlier that year, and would always inveigh strongly against all forms of emancipation.

not want them in our section of the Union." But now that he had learned that southern slaves were being used to shed the blood of the "Union-loving men of this country," he had begun to care much less what might become of "these people," meaning the slaves. Once again, a moderate politician was making it clear that emancipation had a specific pragmatic purpose apart from granting liberty to the bondspeople. Indeed, Ten Eyck, like many of his countrymen, believed that sudden emancipation would be harmful to the slaves; the fact that he was willing to set them free argued not only a fair degree of callousness toward their fate, but also an increasing hostility to the South.[19]

Ten Eyck's opinion closely reflected the majority of the home front's sentiments. All but the most radical northerners opposed emancipation, partly because they did not really want to overthrow the social institutions of the South on a sweeping scale, and also because they had no idea of what would become of the freed slaves. But their anger over the South's attack on the Union, and the growing awareness that slaves could be useful to both sides, did make northerners less squeamish about confiscating human property. At the same time, many conservative northerners held rather unrealistic ideas about the South's slave population. Believing that the region's 4 million slaves wanted (and would immediately be able) to migrate to the North *en masse,* northern Democrats opposed the idea that the slaves should be freed unconditionally. Trumbull's confiscation bill, however, solved none of the problems that were of such grave concern to the conservative and moderate North. For example, his bill simply "discharged" the slaves from their labors, "any law to the contrary notwithstanding," but did not say what would become of them or make any provision for their future. Nor did the bill transfer their ownership to the government after setting them free, thus assailing the slaves' status as property.

These and similar problems provoked sharp criticism from conservatives in Congress, and eventually from the president himself. Senator James A. Pearce of Maryland, for example, hoped that everyone in the Senate understood that the people he represented were "a little sensitive" to anything that looked like emancipation, no matter how "limited and qualified." Border state slave-owners were wary of anything that threatened to free any slaves, regardless of where those slaves resided or to whom they belonged. It was a well-known fact

---

19. *Cong. Globe,* 37th Cong., 1st sess., 219; Glover to Montgomery Blair, Trumbull Papers, LOC, July 22, 1861.

throughout the slaveowning areas of the country that if any slave gained his freedom all others in the neighborhood would become discontented with their lot. The problem, for Pearce, was not *confiscating* the slave, to which he "made no objection," but *emancipating* him. If there were some way of protecting the property status of the confiscated slaves, many of the law's obnoxious qualities would disappear. The difficulty lay in the fact that confiscating a slave automatically also meant turning him into a free man. Pearce predicted that nothing would come of the confiscation law but more "irritation," which was presumably a euphemism for civil warfare.[20]

Pearce pointed out two other essential difficulties inherent in the confiscation bill, both of which would continue to plague the framers of such legislation over the next four years. First, he thought the law would be *brutum fulmen*, meaning, harsh and impossible to enforce. How could they gather evidence? Where and by what court would these cases be heard? By what authority enforced? The proposed bill did not answer any of these questions. Further, the state courts would undoubtedly defy the law, and state laws would immediately rescind any order to free a slave. The confiscation law itself did not indicate who was to carry out its provisions. Although this may appear to be an egregious oversight, it was not corrected in the Second Confiscation Act, which simply forbade the Army to adjudicate the loyalty of any civilians, but did not indicate who was to do so. This presented an insoluble problem, since presumably the courts would be closed in any areas still in rebellion. The law therefore would be enforceable only in areas under U.S. Army control. By the summer of 1861, the Union armies had not yet advanced significantly into enemy territory, and it was difficult to predict, especially after the defeat at Bull Run, how much southern territory the federal armies would be able to reclaim in the near future. But no one pointed out (or sought to correct) this difficulty. The Senate agreed to Trumbull's amendment, 33 to 6, which essentially passed the bill, since all other provisions had been approved earlier. The bill was now ready to go to the House. Naturally, all of the border state senators, including John C. Breckinridge and Lazarus Powell of Kentucky, Trusten Polk and Waldo Johnson of Missouri, and Anthony Kennedy and James Pearce, both of Maryland, voted against it.[21]

20. *Cong. Globe,* 37th Cong., 1st sess., 219.

21. In spite of sustained opposition from Democrats, Republicans always carried these bills, because they had a numerical majority in both houses of Congress.

The home front usually read more into the bills and into congressional actions than was really there. For example, hearing the news of the Senate's approval, one of Charles Sumner's constituents rejoiced, "we are soon to get rid of these feudal lords, these insolent claimants of property in men." The confiscation bill, as approved by the Senate and sent to the House, was simply not strong enough to "rid" the nation of its southern "feudal lords." The House sent the confiscation bill to the Committee on the Judiciary on July 23. On August 2, 1861, Ohio congressman John A. Bingham reported it back from the Committee on the Judiciary, albeit unwillingly. He was unhappy with the House committee's proposed substitute to section four (Trumbull's amendment) of the Senate bill, which further snarled the already problematic issues of property ownership and slavery. The committee had substituted a paragraph that changed the meaning of the bill from forfeiting *all* property used to prosecute the war effort, to forfeiting only slaves. Further, as Rhode Island's William Sheffield pointed out, the bill only provided for a "forfeiture of all claim" of the slaves' labor, but did not say to whom the claim would be forfeited. This fault had been a problem in the earlier version as well, and would never be resolved, at least not until Lincoln issued the Emancipation Proclamation in 1863, which obviated the question of slave ownership. Bingham agreed with him, but explained the committee's reasoning that the service or labor would be forfeited to the slaves themselves, which is precisely what frightened most northerners. But Bingham did not care any longer to discuss the faulty substitute section. As far as he was concerned, the Constitution had provided that Congress has the power to make "rules concerning captures on land and water," and if there was ever a time to avail oneself of this power, that moment has arrived *now*. If the House consented to the substitute, they would only declare to the world that they were very tender about the property "of these rebels in arms, in their rifled cannon, in their bullets, in their powder, in their sabers, in their horses, in their mules, with which they blow out the brains, or cut out the hearts, or trample out the lives, of the loyal people of the United States." William Kellogg of Illinois, however, thought it was important to keep alive the distinction between slaves as confiscated property, and slaves as the object of emancipation. He wanted their labor "simply confiscated, not the slaves discharged therefrom." Although Kellogg's suggestion was ignored in the House, this was precisely what the northern public would demand in the coming months.[22]

---

22. *Cong. Globe,* 37th Cong., 1st sess., 410, August 2, 1861.

Bingham offered a much more comprehensive amendment in place of the one from the committee. His own substitute declared that "any property of whatsoever kind or description" was liable to be "seized, confiscated, and condemned" if there was evidence of any intent on the part of the owners to use it to aid the rebellion. Hardly pausing for breath, he once again called for the previous question. But the extremely conservative Kentucky congressman Henry C. Burnett—who would shortly leave Washington for the Confederacy—was, as always, unwilling to refrain from debate. He thought the bill amounted to "wholesale emancipation," but Bingham carefully placated him. No, only the slaves used in aid of the war effort would be liable to confiscation. Burnett was still dissatisfied. "This is what I object to: that when you pass a law in reference to property, you should take one species of property and put it upon a different footing from another."[23]

In this Burnett was quite right. This bill was attempting to put slave property on a different footing from all other property used to aid the rebellion, since slaves were simply being set free, rather than transferred to the federal government's ownership. If southerners contended that slaves were property, then antislavery minded northerners were quite willing to go along with this definition, especially if it justified confiscating the slaves as "contraband of war." At the same time, only congressional Republicans insisted that the slaves be liberated once confiscated. Moderate northerners, on the other hand, were less sure. While hardly anyone liked to advocate reenslavement, most northerners wanted to maintain some kind of control over the former bondspeople. The famous Maryland pamphleteer Anna Ella Carroll, for example, considered the question of slaves as property versus slaves as "persons held to labor" in a pamphlet she published later that year criticizing the First Confiscation Act. Carroll had made a name for herself as an able orator and a conservative defender of the civil liberties of border state residents. Her discussion of slave property reflected many of the sophistries and confusions rife on the home front. She argued that since the Constitution expressly forbade the taking of "private property for public use without just compensation," it was impossible to take private property unless when it was in "actual use as an instrument of war," at least, not without annulling the Fifth Amendment. Then, since the private property was no longer private in the strictest sense but had now become

---

23. *Cong. Globe,* 37th Cong., 1st sess., 409–10; Richardson, *The Greatest Nation of the Earth,* 213; remarks of Henry C. Burnett, *Cong. Globe,* 37th Cong., 1st sess., 411.

public, and thus belonged to the enemy, it was legally liable to capture. Therefore, Carroll explained, the Confiscation Act was unconstitutional and "repug-
nant," because the proposition was not to take the slaves and convert them to
"public use" at all, but to liberate them from subjection as property. This was
the desire expressed in many moderate newspapers—namely, to take Confederate property, as much of it as could be reached, including slaves, but to do so
without liberating the slaves. Their labor would be valuable to the whole nation,
North and South, and their freedom dangerous.[24]

Because of Fifth Amendment protections of private property rights, the legitimacy of human property was a crucial constitutional question that had to be
resolved before the slaves could be set free. Even a radical Republican newspaper like the *Chicago Tribune* claimed that a fugitive slave should be considered
not a criminal, but a debtor. In other words, the *Tribune* editorial appeared, at
least for the moment, to agree that the fugitive "owed" his labor to his owner,
even if the paper denied that the putative owner had a right to prosecute the
slave for "stealing himself." These questions about the nature of human property were not mere political quibbling—the debates over the confiscation of
rebel property revealed the complexities of shifting ideas about property rights
and human freedom.[25]

The question of slave property was now fully open to discussion in the halls
of Congress. For the first time since the outbreak of the sectional conflict, Republicans felt free to strike at, or at least undermine, the right to own human
beings. Although the Republicans were still careful to distinguish between the
slaves of loyal Unionists and the slaves of rebels, border state representatives
suspected them of attempting to institute an emancipation policy. The question
itself caused endless contention and hard words on the Senate floor. Henry Burnett and other border state politicians always returned to the point that the
confiscation bill would result in widespread confiscation and emancipation; but
the only conservative who focused on constitutional protections of slave property in his anticonfiscation arguments was Kentucky congressman John J. Crit-

24. *Cong. Globe*, 37th Cong., 1st sess., 219; William H. Furness to Charles Sumner, Charles
Sumner Papers, Houghton Library (hereafter HL), Harvard University, Cambridge, Mass., July 26,
1861; Thomas G. Shearman to Lyman Trumbull, Trumbull Papers, LOC, July 30, 1861. *Brutum fulmen* refers to a punitive law that cannot be enforced. *Cong. Globe*, 37th Cong., 1st sess., 411; Carroll,
War Powers of the General Government, 10.

25. *Chicago Tribune*, April 8, 1861.

tenden. In the middle of a vociferous debate about the nature of confiscable property, Crittenden silenced the House by pointing out to them that infringing on any constitutional rights, even in wartime, might have terrible long-term results. However, although everyone quieted down to listen to him, his words had almost no effect on his more radical brethren, who insisted that wartime permitted broader interpretation of the Constitution. In the emergency session of the 37th Congress, it was moderates who saw the problem most clearly: the fundamental dilemma for these men was simply that the federal Constitution guaranteed the property rights of all citizens, and American courts had always supported the notion that Americans possessed the right to own fellow human beings. In order to strike at the private property of American citizens—even of citizens in rebellion—the Constitution would have to be reformed or rewritten. Conservatives feared that such governmental interference with constitutionally protected property rights and with local institutions threatened the very fabric of federalism.[26]

But according to Republicans, the confiscation bill operated on the individual, not on the law, and not on the state. To support this point, William Kellogg pointed out that treason was a federal crime, and that the Constitution did provide for the forfeiture of property for treason. In fact, they could legally take the traitor's horses, houses, lands, mules, cannon, "yea, his right to service in another [person]." Kellogg was arguing that the bill did not have a "permanent" character, and once the rebellion was over, the country could return to the status quo ante. That is, it was the individual rebel's treasonous act that put the law into motion, and the confiscation law would not, therefore, constitute a general emancipation bill. Slavery had always been considered a municipal institution, immune to federal legislation. Therefore, when Republicans argued that confiscation bills operated on the individual and not on the states, they were attempting to place responsibility for secession (which they defined as treason) squarely on the shoulders of individual southerners.

Crittenden abandoned his argument on that point, and asserted that because the bill freed the slave for life, it was unconstitutional. The law would remove the slave property from the owner "beyond the lifetime of the offender." Indeed, Lincoln agreed with this position, and in the following year would force Congress to include an explanatory amendment to the Second Confiscation

---

26. *Cong. Globe*, 37th Cong., 1st sess., 411.

Act, carefully limiting the confiscation of property to the lifetime of the individual. Crittenden wearily concluded with the observation that if the law passed, "we shall have no peace." Conservatives were faced with a nearly insurmountable obstacle: the need to fight a war against fellow citizens, whose rights one had sworn to protect. It was extremely difficult to make a case for the protection of rebel property that was explicitly being used to wage war against the national government—and in the end, they were simply outnumbered. Men like Thaddeus Stevens, who were their most vehement opponents, had nothing but contempt for arguments that pleaded for the constitutional rights of rebels and traitors. Stevens sarcastically commented that he had been under the impression that "the laws of war governed them now." He could hardly believe that anyone was still citing the rebels' constitutional rights. According to Stevens, rebels had no right to constitutional protections. The government could, with impunity, take everything they had on earth. Further, as international law declared, an oppressed people freed by the enemy could not be returned to bondage, even if the enemy were vanquished. In the meantime, Stevens uttered harshly prophetic sentiments about the South. "If their whole country must be laid waste, and made a desert, in order to save this union from destruction, so let it be." But even with all these strikingly harsh sentiments, Thaddeus Stevens was careful to limit the emancipation of slaves to rebellious owners. He predicted that soon every slave "belonging to a rebel . . . I confine it to them—shall be called upon to aid us in war against their masters, and to restore this Union." [27]

All the fracas was for naught, however, since the bill was now briefly recommitted to the Committee on the Judiciary, and was reported back, stating that "whenever thereafter the person claiming such labor or service shall seek to enforce his claim, it shall be a full and sufficient answer to such claim, that the person whose service or labor is claimed has been employed in hostile service against the government of the United States." With this amendment to the original Senate bill there was almost no further debate in the House on the confiscation bill. On August 3, the bill passed in the House, sixty in favor and forty-eight against. The bill was reported back to the Senate on the same day, but Delaware senator James A. Bayard asked that it be postponed until the following Monday.

27. Ibid., 412. A year later, Abraham Lincoln would echo Crittenden's objections in his own criticisms of the second Confiscation Act. *Cong. Globe,* 37th Cong., 1st sess., 414–5.

Trumbull agreed readily, possibly because the Kentucky legislature was about to vote on the state's neutrality stance on that day, and he may have been hesitant to sway their vote by passing a punitive law. On Monday, August 5, the Senate briefly discussed the House amendment, which Trumbull felt was substantially the same as his own, and concurred in it. This vote on the amendment passed the bill in the Senate with twenty-four yeas, eleven nays. President Lincoln signed it on the following day.[28]

Despite the vehement rhetoric over the bill on both sides, the final version of the Confiscation Act did not meet with much fanfare, whether in Washington, in the White House, or among the northern public. James G. Blaine later recalled that Abraham Lincoln signed the law with reluctance, and that "it did not meet with his entire approval." According to Blaine, Lincoln did not object to the law in principle, but he thought it was ill-timed and premature. Further, the president thought it was *brutum fulmen,* and would only serve as a further source of rebellion in border states. But Lincoln also felt that he could not veto it, because that would be tantamount to saying that the Confederacy should have "full benefit of the slave population as a military force." According to Blaine, Lincoln wished Congress would wait on his recommendations.[29]

John B. Wood of Lawrence, Kansas, had read in a local paper that the president signed the bill reluctantly, and was moved to write a letter of protest to Trumbull. Wood claimed that according to the president, "instead of the non-extension of slavery it was to be the *Non Extension of Freedom.*" Wood was incensed that the president "*reluctantly* signs a bill to confiscate the horse and the sword of an officer taken prisoner and also his servant if found to have been engaged in the war." Wood warned the moderate, cautious Republicans in Congress that although the slaveholders were after them with bullets, antislavery men would soon be after them with ballots. Reluctance to confiscate rebel property and reluctance to free the rebels' slaves were tantamount, according to northern radicals, to surrender. Men such as Wood believed that there was little doubt now that emancipation would be a necessary military measure, and it

28. Ibid., 416; 426–7; 430–1, 434. See Appendix 1 for a record of the Senate and House votes, as well as the full text of the law.

29. Blaine, *Twenty Years of Congress,* 1:343. All the major Lincoln biographies make this contention, but none of them support it in any way. Nicolay and Hay do not refer to the circumstances surrounding Lincoln's approval of the First Confiscation Act. There is no evidence in any source indicating that Lincoln signed the First Confiscation Act *without* reluctance.

had become abundantly clear that the administration and the military were still hesitant to take decisive steps to ensure a swift victory.[30]

For six weeks in mid-summer 1861, Congress had labored over laws that would make it possible to confiscate the private property of rebellious southerners. Any property used to prosecute the war against the U.S. government would be subject to seizure—even human property. Recognizing that the government could hardly proclaim ownership in people, Congress skirted the moral aspects of this issue by confiscating only the labor of slaves, not their bodies and souls. The Confiscation Act did not technically emancipate slaves, but neither did it treat slaves like chattel property. The law simply provided that the owner "forfeit[ed] all right" to the slave's labor, and "discharged" the slave from their employment. In mid-1861, even the most radical Republicans—whatever their private views may have been—were not yet ready to advocate the general emancipation of southern slaves. True, their belligerent constituents had been demanding punitive measures against the rebels since early January, but few moderate northern citizens called for a direct attack on the institution of slavery. Indeed, within a week after the Battle of Bull Run, both houses of Congress passed a resolution declaring that the North had no intention of interfering with slavery in the South. In that resolution Congress probably closely reflected the opinion of the majority of the northern public, if not radicals on the home front.

Few newspapers bothered to report the passage of the Confiscation Act, and those that did notice the new law were rather critical. The bill did not actually do anything northerners had hoped it would do. It sanctioned only the confiscation of property that was explicitly being used to prosecute the war effort, and it would be difficult to prove that cotton, wheat-growing lands, livestock, and money were being used in this way, no matter how reasonable the northern public might have considered such a proposition. Many letter-writers thought the law was still too careful with the rebels' constitutional rights. One New Yorker mistakenly believed that the law insisted on proving the slaveowners' guilt, rather than simply confiscating the property outright. Without such a change, he feared that the Confiscation Act would be a "dead letter." He hoped that Congress would take "an even broader ground" in the next session, without "puling about the rights of our Southern *brethren*."[31]

30. John B. Wood to Lyman Trumbull, Trumbull Papers, LOC, August 25, 1861.
31. Thomas G. Shearman to Lyman Trumbull, Trumbull Papers, LOC, July 20, 1861.

In keeping with the generally punitive tone of northern public sentiment, the chief criticism that appeared in many Democratic newspapers was that the Confiscation Act was far too weak and would accomplish nothing. On August 1, the conservative *New York World* called it a "half measure," and feared that the government, including Congress, was "altogether too squeamish and tenderhearted." It might be a step in the right direction, but all those "refinements of constitutional objections" were unnecessary. This was war. The *World* reminded its readers that Congress passed an act confiscating property of British subjects on July 24, 1776, so why should the present administration limit themselves to confiscating only property used in aiding the insurrection? But the *World* did not "exactly fancy" the notion that slaves would be released from labor without being transferred, as property, to another owner. The *World* would rather have seen a general forfeiture of property that the government would sell to help reimburse war expenses. The government could not turn "slave-dealer." It would have been preferable to confiscate "something that would not cease to be property the moment we deprive rebels of it. . . . It would be better to confiscate their plantations, and then see what they will do with their slaves." Contrary to its frequently avowed sentiments, the *World* was apparently less concerned about constitutional guarantees of private property ownership than about the potentially remunerative qualities of the property to be confiscated. The *Albany Atlas and Argus,* another extremely conservative paper, was equally unimpressed because "Proclamations of Confiscation and Emancipation, even tho' backed by enactments of Congress, are nugatory, unless they come from a government which has power to enforce them." [32]

Judging from editorials in the partisan press in 1861, many Democrats, in fact, were quite willing to countenance harsh war measures, so long as they did not interfere with the institution of slavery. War Democrat papers supported the idea of confiscating rebel property when it was used to support the rebellion. But the majority of moderate northerners who supported confiscation flinched at the applying the law to human property. On July 13, 1861, the *Springfield* (Massachusetts) *Daily Republican* published a caustic editorial denouncing the widespread sentiment in the North that a slave was "more sacred as a piece of property than anything else. About the taking of a house or a ship-load of provisions from the enemy, we have no doubt; but we stop to question before taking a slave." In fact, they recalled that when General Butler declared

32. *New York World,* August 1, 1861; *Albany Atlas and Argus,* July 23, 1861.

slaves to be contraband of war, "we thought it a good joke rather than sound law." Those who supported the confiscation law thought of it as strictly a military measure, necessary for the country's self-preservation. Only the rebellious states' own persistence could or should destroy the institution. The *Cleveland Daily Plain Dealer* (which had endorsed Stephen A. Douglas in 1860) assured its readers that the U.S. Army was not fighting for "rapine and plunder," and that the purpose of the war was still to uphold the government and to recover property belonging "in common to the United States." The *New York Herald* stated that the Confiscation Act was nothing more nor less than a "necessary supplement, adapted to existing circumstances, of the laws that always have prevailed, against treason." [33]

Over the following months, debates over rebel property decisively raised the question of emancipation. No matter how unprepared the northern people might have been for the liberation of southern slaves, they now confronted the fact that both the accidents of war and the tenor of the times were bringing them to exactly that end. The members of Congress had argued fastidiously over what type of property slaves were, or how to go about confiscating their labor without liberating their persons. But these debates became futile now that so many black southerners had begun taking matters into their own hands. Indeed, the home front understood this situation much more clearly than Congress and frequently urged policies intended to solve what promised, to many northerners, to be a nearly impossible social problem.

33. *Springfield* (Mass.) *Daily Republican,* July 13, 1861; *New York Herald,* November 9, 1861.

CHAPTER 5

John C. Frémont and Simon Cameron
Attempt to Emancipate Slaves
and Punish Rebels

O N AUGUST 10, 1861, a few days after Congress adjourned, the Federal Army suffered a significant defeat in the Battle of Wilson's Creek in Missouri, which cost the Union the life of General Nathaniel Lyon. There had been riots in St. Louis the previous April, and now bitter violence between citizens wracked the state. Shortly after the disastrous defeat at Bull Run in July, Major General John C. Frémont had taken over the Western Department at St. Louis, where he experienced a great deal of trouble controlling guerrilla warfare. Missourians had elected Hamilton R. Gamble, a pro-Union governor, but the pro-Confederate faction was strong enough to elect a rival rebel government, which requested—and was granted—membership in the Confederacy. In spite of deep internal divisions, however, Missouri, Delaware, Maryland, and Kentucky never officially joined the Confederacy. But their allegiance to the Union created legal and political problems for loyal border state residents who owned slaves. Since these states had chosen to cast their lot with the Union, such citizens were now in the awkward position of being "northern" slaveowners. The notion that loyal Unionists could hold slave property might not have troubled conservative Democrats, but it certainly raised the suspicions of more militant northerners and Union soldiers. In any event, many Republicans—at home, in uniform, and in Congress—had begun to believe that the institution of slavery was doomed, and that its extinction would begin in the border states. The July 1861 issue of the *Christian Examiner* declared that "probably before the end of the war slavery will have been so weakened in the Border States" by the escape of fugitives to the North, by other slaves being carried farther South, and by General Butler's contraband policy, that "these Border States will enter the Union as free States."[1]

Border state slaveowners should probably have been paying closer attention to northern public opinion, which was not only turning toward the confiscation of human property, but also growing less interested in placating the touchy border states. Loyal slaveowners still refused to see the "signs of the times," as Lincoln would later phrase it. Union citizens had begun to doubt the border states' loyalty, especially after rioting Baltimoreans had fired on Union troops in April and Kentucky's governor, Beriah Magoffin, had flatly refused Lincoln's request for troops. Border state residents, painfully aware of their precarious position between the warring sections, were growing nervous. Although they still refused to consider emancipating their slaves, they were aware of shifts in northern public opinion regarding human property. Like their neighbors to the South, many border state slaveowners exaggerated northern antislavery sentiment, which had not yet embraced sweeping emancipation. At the same time, they were certainly aware of the increasing demands for the confiscation of rebel property. In an editorial bemoaning the North's growing reluctance to protect slave property, the *Baltimore Sun* warned that "*Property—insecurity* of property," was the real issue at hand, when "systematic robbery has been common to one section against the other, conducted by regular organization." The editor of the *Sun* was probably right to be nervous, because his neighbors to the North were growing intolerant of conciliatory government policies toward the border states. By the end of the summer, the *Boston Daily Evening Transcript*— hitherto a fairly moderate Republican paper—declared roundly that the administration's great blunder was to ask continually, "what will the border States do?" instead of "what *shall* the border states do?" In other words, perhaps it was time for Lincoln's administration to set policy, rather than to permit border state residents to dictate their terms.[2]

Could a citizen, in fact, be a slaveowner and remain loyal to the Union? Could a slaveowning Unionist support the war effort and the reunion of the states? Loyal border state residents certainly thought so, whether through sheer obtuseness or through their faith in the constitutional guarantees for slavery. Since slave property was still recognized by the laws of the land, border state

1. *Christian Examiner,* July 1861, 111.
2. *Baltimore Sun,* July 15, 1861; *Boston Daily Evening Transcript,* September 17, 1861.

slaveowners held fast to the idea that the Union government should (and would in perpetuity) guarantee the safety of their human property. This attitude would not stand them in good stead in the days to come; indeed, even after Lincoln implored them in the following spring to consider emancipating their slaves for due compensation, border state slaveowners stubbornly refused to recognize the changing climate. The Fugitive Slave Law was nominally still in force, but the Lovejoy Resolution and the Confiscation Act had now chipped away at the federal government's authority and willingness to protect slave property in the South. Congress was clearly making strides in the direction of emancipation, and where better to begin the process than in the border states, where federal authority was still in control? A Baltimorean named John H. Hugg sent a long letter on the subject (which he laboriously copied out by hand) to many senators and congressmen, pleading with them to hold in one hand the "Sword of Justice," while offering with the other the "Olive Branch of Peace." He told them that what border state citizens most earnestly hoped for was "the protection for their property," to which he carefully added, in parentheses, "slaves." Above all, he pleaded, border states now called for the repeal of personal liberty laws. His letter revealed the unrealistic attitudes of border state residents—in the midst of warfare, there was little chance that northern state legislatures would yield anything of the kind.[3]

Earlier that summer President Lincoln and Republicans in Congress had, in fact, tried repeatedly to reassure border state slaveowners with one resolution after another, declaring that the war would end the moment the rebellious states were conquered and that it was not the government's intention to interfere with the institution of slavery where it already existed. Lincoln's policy was to encourage the border states to emancipate their slaves themselves, not to force emancipation on them, but his pleas would always meet with obstinate resistance. Most border state residents, however, especially those who owned slaves or at least supported the institution of slavery, mistrusted the predominantly Republican Congress. They also deplored the signs that northern public opinion was turning against the protection of slave property. An inveterate

3. John H. Hugg to Edward McPherson, McPherson Papers, LOC, July 1, 1861. (Hugg sent this letter to several congressmen. Later that year, the letter was printed as a pamphlet, entitled *Compromise Will Not Save the Union* [New York, n.p., 1861]. I am indebted to Andy Coopersmith for calling my attention to this pamphlet.)

southern sympathizer from Maryland who later joined the Confederacy, Admiral Franklin Buchanan wrote to Admiral Samuel F. Du Pont and quoted extravagantly and probably apocryphally what he claimed were the headlines of many northern papers: "War to the death," "Slavery must be abolished," "Slavery is a sin," "Annihilation of all slaveholders," "Subjugation of the South," "Slaves must be set free, and the land divided out among northerners." Admiral Buchanan's allegiance to the Union vacillated with the fortunes of his state; he resigned his commission when he believed Maryland would secede, but attempted to withdraw his resignation when he realized his state would remain loyal. While Admiral Buchanan exaggerated the belligerent tone of northern headlines, there is no doubt that the northern public was losing patience with the government's eternal obeisance to border state interests. Some criticisms of border state slaveowners contained dangerous hints that the mere fact that a Union citizen owned slaves impugned his loyalty and laid him open to potential punitive action.[4]

The political climate was changing, and one important symptom of this was that people in the North were now much less interested in respecting border states' desires to hold on to their slaves. By August 1861, northerners had been agitating for a hard war against rebel civilians for six months; their increasing ire against the vacillating border states now strengthened their antislavery sentiment. Border state residents, anxious to maintain their slave property, were now seen as a liability to the Union cause. This had of course long been the attitude of outspoken abolitionists such as Frederick Douglass, but even more moderate antislavery northerners now believed that the time for conciliation of border states was coming to an end. In 1861 both Frederick Douglass and Unitarian minister Orestes Brownson argued that appeasing the border states would accomplish nothing. Brownson, who had only recently adopted antislavery views, now thought that if border state slaveowners were truly loyal to the Union, they would not insist on unreasonable conditions. Such men, he felt, ought to be willing to make sacrifices to preserve the Union. In any event, whether they were willing or not, it was hardly fair to expect the northern states

4. Paludan, *Presidency,* 127; Franklin Buchanan to Samuel Francis Du Pont, in Hayes, ed., *Samuel Francis Du Pont,* 1:95. I found no such headlines in any newspapers, including the radical *Chicago Tribune* and the *New York Tribune.* Du Pont was the admiral who had organized Lincoln's blockade of southern ports in 1861. Symonds, *Confederate Admiral.*

to pour out "blood and treasure" while the border states refused to help the cause by freeing their slaves. Still, Brownson believed that loyal border state slaveholders should be compensated for losing slaves, and that the slaves ought to be "freed on our own soil" and not forced to emigrate. Brownson's views were more representative of the northern public's attitude toward slavery than Douglass's, but it was clear that even moderate men were now looking askance at border state slaveowners. In fact, some northerners expressed rather callous sentiments about their hesitant neighbors. A letter to John J. Crittenden discussing southern sympathizers in Kentucky suggested that there was "nothing like human suffering to cure the distemper of rage & folly." The tears of widows and orphans, he felt, would be "very efficacious in extinguishing the flames of war."[5]

The border states were a thorn in the side of Union policymakers, who continually had to reassure and placate them. Naturally their property rights in human beings were still protected under the federal Constitution, but radical Republicans were largely unimpressed with arguments about the rights of slaveowners, loyal or otherwise. In fact, one of them urged Trumbull not to talk of "compensating masters for what they have no natural right to." For antislavery northerners, the institution could not be threatened so long as the border states had to be placated. If only the border states could be secured permanently to the Union, or else ignored or sent on their way to the Confederacy, then nothing would stand in the way of a Union victory. Regardless of harsh sentiments, however, many hitherto bellicose northerners were less than enthusiastic when a Union Army general put their ideas into practical application at the end of August.[6]

About three weeks after the president signed the Confiscation Act, some of its underlying principles received their first test at the hands of Major General John C. Frémont, who commanded the Western Department of the Union Army. Frémont had entered St. Louis on July 25, 1861, and found the city in the midst of guerrilla warfare and partisan uproar. He reported that his command

5. See Frederick Douglass's "Notes on the War," in Foner, *Life and Writings*, 3:115; Orestes Augustus Brownson, "Brownson on the Rebellion," St. Louis, 1861, in Freidel, *Union Pamphlets of the Civil War*, 1:157–9; J. B. Underwood to John J. Crittenden, John J. Crittenden Papers, LOC, July 13, 1861.

6. W. G. Snethen to Lyman Trumbull, Trumbull Papers, LOC, July 12, 1861.

was "in disorder, nearly every county in an insurrectionary condition, and the enemy advancing in force by different points of the southern frontier." He had no men, no ammunition, and no money to pay his ninety-day volunteers, who were threatening to leave as soon as their terms expired. Union soldiers were confiscating property and supplies from both loyal citizens and traitors, which only served to exacerbate guerrilla activity. Finally, on August 30, Frémont issued a far-reaching and punitive proclamation of martial law throughout Missouri. He declared that "anyone found with arms within Union lines would be shot upon being found guilty by a court-martial." But the most shocking provision of the proclamation was that it confiscated the property of all persons found in arms against the U.S. government and emancipated all their slaves.[7]

Frémont's proclamation was the first instance of a Union Army officer attempting to enforce congressional legislation on the conduct of the war. Union home front reaction to Frémont's edict, and to Lincoln's subsequent revocation, reveals both characteristic anger toward southern rebels as well as ambivalence toward human property. At the same time, even that ambivalence indicates a significant shift (especially among conservative northerners) toward the prospect of emancipation, since Democrats had previously always deplored any interference with slavery. Still, just because Democrats were growing ambivalent about (rather than explicitly in favor of) property rights in human beings did not mean that they favored widespread emancipation. Civil War historians have argued that the northern public was universally positive about Frémont's proclamation. Accordingly, most historians have interpreted the home front's reaction as approval of the emancipation edict it contained. Contemporary Republican memoirs emphasized the generally favorable notice most newspapers gave to Fremont's edict, and later generations have followed their lead. But a scrutiny of other sources, including Democratic letters and newspaper editorials, reveals that while many Republicans and Democrats indeed approved of the martial tone of Frémont's proclamation, they were not all equally enchanted with its sweeping emancipation clause. The first reactions by mainstream papers indicated relief that some action had finally been taken, but when northerners reflected more carefully they realized—contrary to their earlier militant rhetoric—that they really did not want the Army taking such liberties.[8]

7. Parrish, *Turbulent Partnership*, 60.

8. McPherson, *Struggle for Equality*, 69–74. McPherson quotes responses by abolitionists Frederick Douglass, Gerrit Smith, Thomas Wentworth Higginson, and William Lloyd Garrison. See

Frémont's action caused a sensation throughout the North. William Pitt Fessenden, writing to his friend James Pike, described the "electric effect" Frémont's proclamation had "upon all parts of the country. . . . Men now feel as if there was something tangible and real in this contest." In their biography of President Lincoln, his secretaries, John Nicolay and John Hay, commented that the "antislavery drift of public opinion throughout the North was unmistakably manifest," and that in their opinion, Frémont issued his proclamation primarily to appeal to the northern public. Republican editorials praised Frémont to the skies. The *Chicago Tribune,* for example, declared that "Frémont's proclamation metes out the extreme penalty to ruffians and traitors, death to themselves, confiscation of their property and *freedom to their slaves.*" Everything else had been tried and had failed. One could not fight a hard war while leaving the institution of slavery intact. The *Tribune* sneered at those Democrats who had been demanding a vigorous prosecution of the war effort while still condemning emancipation. Such men, the *Tribune* complained, demanded that the Army confiscate the rebels' houses, lands, and goods, "and if need be shoot them through the head, *but don't touch their niggers.*"[9]

It is true that the initial reaction even in moderate Republican papers, such as the *Boston Daily Evening Transcript,* and many conservative newspapers, such as the *New York World* and the *Cincinnati Daily Enquirer,* was positive. The most frequent point that newspapers praised was that someone had finally done *something.* Still, those editorials focused their approbation more on the clauses of the proclamation that specified harsh punishment for rebels; most criticized the emancipation clause. An editorial in the Democratic *New York World* thought Frémont's proclamation would have "fruitful" consequences. The paper's first reaction seemed to place greater trust in Frémont's proclamation than in the confiscation law, and hinted rather ominously that the Army was now stronger than the administration in Washington. "Martial law," the *World* declared, "transcends congressional enactments." The *World* was also now less kindly disposed toward the border states. Professed loyalists in those areas ought to "submit without chafing" to watching their treasonous neighbors punished. Although the *World* had never been in favor of emancipation,

---

also, Nevins, *Frémont,* chapter 30; Trefousse, *Lincoln's Decision,* chapter 2, and Parrish, *Turbulent Partnership,* chapter 7.

9. Quoted in Jellison, *Fessenden of Maine,* 138; Nicolay and Hay, *Abraham Lincoln,* 417; Nevins, *Frémont,* 503; Chicago *Tribune,* September 9, 1861.

the paper now maintained that "the slaves of a rebel are not more sacred than life." In another column, however, the editor still hotly denied that Frémont's proclamation was an emancipation policy. The *Cincinnati Daily Enquirer* was somewhat less approving. It declared that Frémont now "overtops Lincoln, Seward, and Chase." The editor of the *Enquirer* worried, as always, about the working men of the North, fearing that the "freeing of the slaves will work injury to the laboring man in the free States." However, the paper also conceded that the weight of public sentiment was decidedly in favor of the proclamation, and delivered an almost admiring assessment of the general's action. Frémont had "made his move, boldly and fearlessly, and we shall now see whether he will sink or swim." A week later the *Enquirer* was still praising Frémont's audacity in breaking through the "apparently don't know what to do" policy of the administration.[10]

The public heaved a sigh of relief that someone had finally taken vigorous action, but then most northerners (including the president himself, who unfortunately only learned of the proclamation after he read about it in a newspaper) compared Frémont's action to the Confiscation Act and found the proclamation to be in violation of the recently enacted law. These two reactions were not entirely contradictory. Even conservative northerners had been clamoring for some kind of definite policy and had been growing steadily more impatient with the administration's vacillating attempts to fight the war in a "gentlemanly" manner. Most people thought that such conciliatory policies —whether toward rebels or toward border state citizens—only encouraged treason. Lyman Trumbull wrote to James R. Doolittle on the day after Frémont issued his proclamation that the administration's delicate handling of the border states meant that wherever the rebels were able to muster any strength, they could bully or threaten loyal citizens without fear of reprisal. It was time, he declared, to fight the battle on the same terms as the traitors. Trumbull thoroughly approved of Frémont's proclamation, and praised the general as "active and efficient."[11]

Many northerners agreed with Trumbull on this precise point. Some form of punitive sentiment against the rebels was nearly universal, even if the more

10. *New York World,* September 2, 1861; *Cincinnati Daily Enquirer,* September 3, 17, 1861.
11. Trumbull to Doolittle, August 31, 1861, in Mowry, "A Statesman's Letters of the Civil War Period," 48.

moderate northerners still feared widespread emancipation. Judging from newspaper editorials, most citizens approved of the proclamation's provision to shoot traitors after convicting them in courts-martial. But they did not wholeheartedly applaud the emancipation of the slaves in Missouri. The *New York Herald*'s editorial on the subject displayed the common ambivalence. The *Herald* was a conservative Democratic newspaper, which had supported John C. Breckinridge's candidacy during the 1860 presidential race. The paper now generally praised Frémont, claiming that he had based his proclamation on the recently enacted confiscation law. But the *Herald* also had its doubts, fearing that the clauses dealing with slaves would only serve to protract the war. Any emancipation edict should be a last resort for self-preservation. As a military measure, however, the paper had no fault to find with the proclamation. Perhaps, the *Herald* suggested, the troops of the cotton states would all have to go home now, to look after their slaves. President Lincoln's decisive handling of the Frémont situation would not just save Missouri and Kentucky for the Union, it also would bring many northern Democrats behind him, at least for the moment.[12]

Editorials in Democratic and moderate Republican papers stated that punitive actions against rebel citizens properly belonged to the chief executive and to Congress, not to the military authorities. At the same time, even fairly conservative newspapers accepted the notion that Union Army officers could confiscate slaves so long as they were not enacting widespread emancipation. This represented a significant shift in home front opinion just six months after the firing on Fort Sumter, when conservative northerners would have condemned any interference with slavery. According to the *National Daily Intelligencer,* a Washington, D.C., paper with Democratic sympathies, an advancing army might have to "make what use it can of all property of rebels in arms," which would certainly include slaves. This would, of course, mean the virtual freedom of many slaves. How, the *Intelligencer* asked, could the South have expected any other result? But emancipation should be construed an "accidental effect of war," which would be a very different matter from the confiscation of property, for which "a legal proceeding is necessary, involving a conviction for treason . . . by a competent court." The *Intelligencer*'s reading of the recently enacted confiscation law was incorrect—confiscation did not require a conviction of treason. Nevertheless, this editorial raised a significant point: that mod-

12. *New York Herald,* September 1, 1861.

erate and conservative northerners were ready to let the institution of slavery take its chances with the accidents of war, where a mere six months ago they would have vehemently deplored all federal or military interference with human property. The *Intelligencer* now declared that after the war slaves would once again become subject to local laws, and those fugitives who had been used to aid the insurrection could have their case pleaded in court, presumably by a friendly white person. General emancipation would make the war drag on forever, and the *Intelligencer* was sure that humanity shrank "with horror" at the thought.[13]

Still, whatever they said about emancipation, most Democratic papers were almost unanimously in favor of parts of the proclamation dealing with the punishment of rebels. The *Cleveland Daily Plain Dealer* (which had supported Douglas in 1860), for example, was annoyed that "sundry white feather partisan papers are attempting to make party capital out of [the provision] . . . which emancipates the negroes of rebels." Since the southern army wanted to "destroy and sack and pillage" Washington, D.C., the *Plain Dealer*'s editors declared, "we are not very anxious to protect any property." The *National Daily Intelligencer* also approved of Frémont's actions. Martial law ought to have no terrors for good, law-abiding citizens. If the Missouri rebels had taken advantage of provisional Governor Hamilton Gamble's amnesty, their property and slaves would have been safe. This kind of proclamation could have been "long foreseen" as an inevitable result of the rebellion. "Those who take up arms for the overthrow of the [government] have surely . . . waived all right and title to the protection . . . either in their persons or property."[14]

Lincoln was exasperated by Frémont's actions because he deemed the provisions confiscating property and freeing the slaves premature and ill-considered. He feared that Frémont's proclamation would drive the two most important border states, Missouri and Kentucky, into the arms of the Confederacy. Kentucky still maintained its policy of neutrality, and a hasty emancipation action in Missouri might have the effect of pushing both states out of the Union. On September 2, he sent a gently worded request to the general, asking

13. *Cong. Globe*, 37th Cong., 1st sess., 189; *National Daily Intelligencer*, September 19, 1861. The *Intelligencer* had endorsed John Bell in the 1860 presidential election.

14. *Cleveland Daily Plain Dealer*, September 10, 1861; *National Daily Intelligencer*, quoting the *St. Louis Republican*, September 6, 7, 1861.

him to rephrase his proclamation to conform to the Confiscation Act. That act had confiscated only slaves specifically used to aid the rebellion, not *all* slaves of rebellious owners. Frémont refused to modify his proclamation, fearing it would make him appear foolish or indecisive. He asked his wife, Jessie, to travel to the capital to plead his cause with the president, but she only managed to alienate the president further by storming at him in defense of her husband. Lincoln finally lost patience with the obstreperous Frémonts and revoked the proclamation on September 11. When Orville Hickman Browning, who had always been a moderate, attempted to speak in Frémont's support, Lincoln told him that Frémont's actions in Missouri seriously jeopardized the cause of the Union in all the border states. Rebels in Kentucky would undoubtedly use the Frémont situation as an excuse to force secession. "To lose Kentucky," he told Browning, "is nearly the same as to lose the whole game. Kentucky gone, we cannot hold Missouri, nor, as I think, Maryland. These all against us, and the job on our hands is too large for us. We would as well consent to separation at once, including the surrender of this capital." [15]

Fremont's proclamation did in fact threaten the border states' continued allegiance to the Union, and it was not in accordance with the Confiscation Act. Thomas Ewing, a conservative judge who was also General William T. Sherman's father-in-law, considered Frémont a "vain pompous blatherskite, without military education or experience and without talent to stand as their substitute." Frémont's proclamation was "very wrong—unsupported by law and equally wrong in policy." Like many moderate northerners, Ewing thoroughly approved of Lincoln's handling of the situation. There were two distinct issues at stake in this situation. This was not just a matter of punishing rebels; it was also a question of attacking the fundamental guarantees of rights belonging to the American people, such as the right to due process. If military commanders could assume superiority over civil legislation, where did that leave the "priceless rights" protected by the Constitution? Ewing also thought that if Lincoln had not corrected Frémont's proclamation at once, the nation would have lost Kentucky, and the war would be raging on the banks of the Ohio. The loyal Unionists in those areas would have been abandoned because they could "not have maintained themselves for a month against the overwhelming tide of se-

15. Basler, *Collected Works,* 506, 517, 531; Nicolay and Hay, *Abraham Lincoln,* chapter 23. See also Volpe, "The Frémonts and Emancipation in Missouri," 339–54.

cession which it would have forced in upon them." Indeed, Frémont's action was shortsighted and impolitic, and nearly catapulted two of the most important border states into the Confederacy.[16]

Lincoln's rebuke to Frémont precipitated a sudden shift in conservative public opinion. Democratic papers now enthusiastically championed the president. It almost appeared as though the home front had finally seen a decisive policy that could overcome their ambivalence without pushing them too far on the explosive slavery issue. Northern newspapers, especially those with a strong Democratic readership, now stopped hedging their bets and placed their money firmly on the chief executive. In so doing, they also tacitly (and sometimes explicitly) approved of the congressional confiscation law, which had after all carefully avoided any hint at widespread emancipation. This represented considerable movement toward punitive sentiment, and, in a much smaller and more hesitant way, toward antislavery sentiment, among northern Democrats. The *Cleveland Daily Plain Dealer,* for example, called Lincoln's handling a "brilliant performance" and praised the president's "scrupulous regard for the letter of the law." The *New York World* agreed that Frémont's proclamation was out of harmony with the Confiscation Act, and that the general was wrong to take such an important step without consulting the administration. In any event, they now averred that the proclamation was largely futile, because the government could not enforce any laws in the seceded states. "We can't even let the slaves know, or protect them, and therefore, emancipation would not be an instrument for subjugation." Nevertheless, they still hastened to assert that General Frémont's proclamation "declares no punishment which the rebels do not richly deserve."[17]

Even Republican newspapers, such as *Frank Leslie's Illustrated,* were pulled up short, realizing that Frémont's actions had brought a military commander dangerously in conflict with the executive. *Leslie's,* whose editorial policies had always been strongly antislavery, had been initially much more approving of Frémont. The editors had declared that Frémont had interpreted the sentiment of the nation correctly, even though his actions went beyond the confiscation

16. Thomas Ewing to Colonel Hugh Ewing, Ewing Family Papers, LOC, November 2, 1861; Trefousse, "Lincoln and Race Relations," in Greenberg and Waugh, *The Price of Freedom,* 2:319.

17. *Cleveland Daily Plain Dealer,* quoting the *National Daily Intelligencer,* September 21, 1861; *New York World,* September 17, 1861.

law. They had thought that the Confiscation Act was far too weak, and stated that "it is idle, discouraging to all earnest men, and damaging to our cause" to discriminate between the different kinds of rebel property. "We stultify ourselves, and justly incur the charge of weakness and vacillation, and, what is worse, treachery to the holy cause of human freedom, when we boldly confiscate the ships, and houses, and cattle of the rebel in arms, and yet refuse freedom to his slave, whom he claims as property, except such slave has actually been employed against the nation." Slavery, in the writer's view, was an atrocity, not a "delicate question." When the editor had first heard that Lincoln had revoked Frémont's proclamation, he called the rumor "painful." Nevertheless, Leslie's realized that the "President has to discharge his duty strictly." Again, the writer of the editorial reiterated that the fault was with the recently enacted law, which was only a half-measure. "As it stands, it provokes just as great hostility among the rebels as an unconditional confiscation of their slaves could have done." Leslie's hoped that in the coming December the Congress would amend the Confiscation Act so that it would meet the exigencies of the time.[18]

One point upon which all but the radicals could agree was that military actions must bow to civil authority and to the chief executive. Earlier that year people on the home front had thought Butler's contraband policy a very good joke, and had expected that Union Army officers would take responsibility for the fugitive slaves, as Butler had done at Fortress Monroe. But now, with the Frémont experience behind them, the public began to worry that the military authority might take too much power into its own hands. One pamphleteer thought both Butler's and Frémont's actions dangerously wrong. "War is a mighty, absolute potentate," he warned; such a tyrant recognized no law but "[his] own necessities, and deals summarily" with any code that interferes with that "higher law." Indeed, Frémont's intemperate action had shocked the northern home front into the stark realization that they could not leave such crucial decisions to the military. Lincoln's handling of Frémont's proclamation inspired renewed confidence and trust in his administration and reassured northerners that he was no tyrant. Moderate Republican newspapers insisted that Frémont had to submit to the president and to the congressionally enacted law. Massachusetts's Springfield Daily Republican declared that although Frémont's initial proclamation had been "just the thing," and much nearer to what

18. Frank Leslie's Illustrated Newspaper, September 21, 1861.

the country needed than the confiscation law, it was important that their read-ers remember what they were "prone to forget: that the war was being fought for the Union, the constitution, and the law." The recent act defined the nation's duty, and the president was showing himself faithful to the Constitution. The *Boston Daily Evening Transcript* also insisted that military subordination to the civil power was absolutely indispensable. General Frémont might think the rev-ocation a "most unfortunate error of judgment in the President," but it was un-questionably his obligation to obey.[19]

The solution was to rewrite the confiscation law. A *Cleveland Daily Enquirer* editorial regretted that the administration and Frémont were "Out of Joint." According to the *Enquirer* (like the *Plain Dealer,* also a Douglas-endorsing pa-per), both sides were more or less right, at least in some respects. Frémont was quite correct, the *Enquirer* declared, in thinking that a rebel had no rights, not even to life, but the president was equally correct in his interpretation of the Constitution. Like *Frank Leslie's,* the *Enquirer* saw the problem as originating with the weak Confiscation Act, which should have confiscated the slaves of anyone in arms against the government, not just those used as military weap-ons. Further, the editorial made it clear that the problem was not so much with Frémont's *actions* but with the fact that he did not first consult the administra-tion. The primary cause of discontent was the fear that military power was in danger of usurping the civil authority. Northerners may have wanted to prose-cute a vigorous war, but they feared a powerful standing army led by a hot-headed, radical general. Their response to Frémont's proclamation and Lin-coln's revocation revealed that much of their rhetoric vanished when they were confronted with their radical ideas in application, especially when those ideas threatened to liberate thousands of people in bondage.[20]

Abolitionists considered the president's rebuke to Frémont a tragic missed opportunity. Charles Sumner declared in frustration: "How vain to have the power of a god and not to use it godlike." Radical Republican newspaper edi-torials, like those published in the *Chicago Tribune* and the *New York Tribune,* strongly criticized the president's action. The *Chicago Tribune* thought Fré-

19. Sprague, *Glorifying God,* 53; *Springfield* (Mass.) *Daily Republican,* September 17, 1861; *Bos-ton Daily Evening Transcript,* September 17, 1861.

20. *Cleveland Daily Enquirer,* September 5, 1861; for a similar views, see also the *New York Eve-ning Post,* September 21, 1861, and the *Harrisburg* (Pa.) *Sentinel,* September 21, 1861.

mont's emancipation edict was like "a light set upon a hill," and the government that set out to "undo what he did will be punished." The *Tribune* could not believe that Lincoln and Seward could now take this step backward. In the end, John C. Frémont was removed from his command in the Western Department, for a host of other reasons in addition to his refusal to amend the proclamation. The laws and the executive had reasserted themselves for the moment and had shown that military authority must not supersede civil law. The northern public's previous hotheaded rhetoric on taking rebel slaves and property subsided with guilty relief when confronted by a strong president who would not allow the laws to be overridden. It may be that the border states were, as the *New York Herald* put it, "saved for the Union," but it was also clear that Lincoln had understood the sentiments of the loyal Democratic opposition and its reservations about emancipation by military edict. The public had been agitating for a stronger prosecution of the war. But when Frémont's proclamation forced them to confront these ideas in practice, they retreated to a moral and legal higher ground, behind a chief executive who appeared to be firmly on the side of the Constitution and the laws.[21]

Northerners' reactions to Frémont's proclamation and Abraham Lincoln's revocation depended a great deal upon where they lived and upon their party affiliation. There were significant differences in the public mind on exactly how much authority military commanders ought to wield over rebellious populations. Still, among all but the most radical Union citizens, one can find two broad areas of consensus, at least in the early fall of 1861. First, most northerners would have agreed that military commanders had to obey the chief executive, and second, that the Union Army could take slaves from rebels in arms against their government. According to James M. McPherson, similar attitudes could be found among Union soldiers in the first eighteen months of the war. Although many soldiers thought the rebels deserved to be punished for their treasonous acts, in 1861 and early 1862 the majority were not yet ready to embrace a sweeping emancipation policy. Union Army policy during the first year of the Civil War focused on military victories and deplored interference with civilian property. While it was true that some Union soldiers helped themselves to rebel property early in the war, such actions were considered reprehensible and were harshly punished. A general policy of attacks on enemy property and

21. *Chicago Tribune*, September 9, 1861; *New York Herald*, September 18, 1861.

infrastructure, and a policy of subsisting on enemy territory through forage, did not arise until after 1862. In the meantime, conciliatory generals refused to countenance any efforts at freeing slaves who entered their bivouacs or attempted to join their regiments. General Henry Halleck's General Order No. 3, issued in November 1861, barred fugitive slaves from his marching lines. Halleck justified his decision by asserting that "it does not belong to the military to decide upon the relation of master and man."[22]

Other military officers, of course, permitted and sometimes even encouraged the fugitives to enter their camps. Some soldiers fiercely resented the Democratic generals' orders to return fugitives to their former owners. One Union soldier, for example, called General Don Carlos Buell's conservative policy "that of an amiable idiot." It made no sense to "fritter away the army and the revenue of the government in the insane effort to protect men who have forfeited all right to protection." But what would happen to those slaves after they had fled to Union Army marching lines, or after they had been confiscated, was a much more divisive problem. Perhaps because most northerners had always acquiesced in the notion that slaves were property protected by local law, or perhaps because of deeply rooted racial prejudice, it did not seem to occur to any but the most radical Republicans that the slaves might be left to work out their own future after liberation. Northern rhetoric on the subject of freed slaves was redolent of the most profound bewilderment, but almost everyone seemed to believe that the government or the Army should control the freed people's future. An extremely common phrase that appeared in hundreds of letters, newspaper editorials, pamphlets, and sermons was "what shall be done with the freed slaves?" Few northerners believed that freed slaves should have control over their own futures, nor did many suggest that it might be possible to pay the former bondspeople a fair wage and protect their rights. Although racial prejudice was distressingly evident in newspaper editorials and private correspondence, the northern attitude against emancipation was probably not entirely as callous as it sounds. Many northerners believed that the freed slaves would be incapable of supporting themselves and would starve. One of John Sherman's constituents, for example, was against the "immediate *abolition* of slavery in the seceded states." While he would be eager to hear that this "foul

---

22. Grimsley, *Hard Hand of War*, 19–21; McPherson, *For Cause and Comrades*. See also Grimsley, *Hard Hand of War*, 136–7. Halleck quoted in Freehling, *The South vs. the South*, 96.

blot upon our country was forever and totally erased," he could not see how that could be accomplished "*at present.*" Similarly, a letter to the editor of the *Boston Daily Evening Transcript* by one "Libertas" was entitled "War for Freedom, but not for Abolition." A long war would bring "violent emancipation," which would inevitably result in a war of the races. Surely not even thoughtful black people or abolitionists would want that. Libertas suggested a "humane apprenticeship" as a solution, which he hoped would maintain northern control over black labor for some considerable time.[23]

The problem was that in 1861 no one could predict what would happen. Fugitives had been fleeing their bondage, but they still only numbered in the thousands. No one knew with certainty that after widespread emancipation black southerners would refrain from retaliating against their former oppressors. In fact, the slaves' willingness to take matters into their own hands and escape from bondage proved that they were more enterprising and independent than northerners had believed. Even those who were sympathetic to slaves thought that they would not remain submissive much longer. One anonymous pamphlet issued a dire warning to those who thought they could win the war and leave black persons in bondage. "Think you, the colored population will sit idly by and see the chains riveted upon their necks? No, after all the light that has been scattered among them, they will do no such thing." If Congress refused to give the slaves their freedom, then they would "arise and take their liberty . . . and take it with a vengeance, too." Did northern whites think the slaves would then "show mercy to those from whom they have received none?" That was not to be expected. "So prepare either to give them their freedom or have them rise and take it by force, which they will do as sure as there is a God in Heaven!" Antislavery sentiment was on the rise in the North, both for humanitarian and pragmatic reasons, but Libertas's argument would have struck fear into the hearts of conservative northerners.[24]

It was becoming increasingly clear that the war would have a hand in destroying slavery. The resulting freedom of thousands—perhaps millions—of black people posed serious problems for racially prejudiced white northerners. This was also true of some Republicans; the fact that they desired the end of

23. Beatty, *Memoirs of a Volunteer*, 91–2; S. B. Woodward to John Sherman, Sherman Papers, LOC, August 5, 1861; *Boston Daily Evening Transcript*, August 26, 1861.

24. Anonymous, *On Political Economy*.

slavery did not necessarily mean they wanted to cope with the presence of black people in the North. Even radical jayhawkers such as Jim Lane of Kansas could not quite hide their bigotry. Although he wanted to hit the South hard and destroy the wicked institution of slavery, Lane did not desire to live in a nation of freed slaves. He wanted the two races separated and "an ocean rolling between them." He was certainly not alone in this opinion, which was hardly new. Since the early days of the sectional conflict, many white northerners who had wanted to keep the institution of slavery out of the territories felt this way, not because they felt any compassion for individuals in bondage, not because they were compelled by the guiding principle of freedom, but rather because of their dislike of black people.[25]

For many Americans, including the president, the only reasonable answer to the conundrum of confiscating human property that could neither be re-enslaved nor set completely free was to send the former slaves out of the country. Many newspapers, especially those of a Democratic persuasion, approved enthusiastically of colonization schemes. It seemed an ideal answer to the problem of the impending end of slavery. Indeed, most confiscation bills, including the one Trumbull would propose later in the second session of the 37th Congress, contained a provision for colonization. Even though many northerners believed with Jim Lane that the "slave property of every rebel [should] be confiscated and the rebels [should] be brought to condign punishment," most of them wanted all the confiscated slaves "separated from us by colonization." President Lincoln had toyed with the idea of sending freed slaves to Chiriqui in Panama to mine coal, and when that proved to be fruitless, he encouraged colonization in Ile á Vache in Haiti, which by 1863 proved to be a dismal failure when nearly a hundred freed people died of starvation and smallpox.[26]

In early 1862, Lincoln tried to persuade black leaders to take their people to "tropical countries," telling them that the two races would never live at peace with another. He did not inspire them with much enthusiasm for the scheme. Black people living in the North were outraged by the idea of colonization. Since the 1820s, they had been holding meetings in all of the major cities, vig-

---

25. *Cong. Globe,* 37th Cong., 1st sess., 190.

26. Ibid.; Trefousse, *Lincoln's Decision,* 42. Abraham Lincoln received a delegation of black men on August 14, 1861, headed by Edward M. Thompson. Boritt, *Lincoln and the Economics of the American Dream,* 258.

orously denouncing colonization as anti-Christian, hypocritical, and unenlightened. In fact, white abolitionists and most Republicans also opposed all such ideas vehemently. Eventually Republicans in Congress were forced to vote in favor of appropriations for colonization because they knew that most white northerners would simply refuse to back any emancipation or confiscation legislation that did not provide some method of ridding America of the freed slaves. Radicals, of course, thought colonization cruel and unfair. "Do not drive the negro out of the land on which he stands," an abolitionist named W. G. Snethen implored. "Let him stay there. The land really belongs to him. His race has bought it and paid for it through blood." Snethen scorned all schemes for removing black people from the nation. He thought that once the slaves were liberated, "necessity [would] work out his future relation to the white man." But few white northerners agreed that "necessity" should be allowed to work out their future relationships with the freed slaves. Colonization was also far too expensive a proposition. The Second Confiscation Act did contain a provision for colonization, but with the total lack of support from the black community in the North, the unwillingness of the freed people to leave their homes, and a growing belief among some white northerners that such proposals were both unfair and impracticable, colonization schemes came to an unlamented end. Even a conservative legal theorist like Sidney George Fisher, who believed that black people did not need and should not be granted political rights, stated that the freed slaves could not be "sent away." At the same time, Fisher believed that colonization would extend to freed people "all of the rights and privileges of free men" in their new homes, which was not something they could expect in America.[27]

If colonization were not the answer, how would the nation cope with freed slaves? Fisher commented on the fact that emancipation in the West Indies and British Guinea had been immensely successful, and he hoped that with the establishment of a gradual emancipation plan, and careful supervision by the "superior white race," emancipation would work equally well in the American South. But in the first year of the Civil War, few northerners had relinquished the notion that slave labor was a legitimate form of property. Neither the fed-

---

27. Franklin and Moss, *From Slavery to Freedom;* W. G. Snethen to Lyman Trumbull, Trumbull Papers, LOC, July 12, 1861; Trefousse, *Lincoln's Decision,* 114; Fisher, *Trial of Our Constitution,* 181; Belz, *Emancipation and Equal Rights,* 66.

eral nor the state governments could interfere between the slaveholder and the slave, partly because the slave had always been seen as a legitimate form of property, and partly because, whether one liked the institution of slavery or not, the slave "owed" his or her labor to the master. The wording of the Confiscation Act had acknowledged this relationship, but had deliberately interfered with it in cases in which the slave's labor was used to aid the rebellion. At the same time, hardly anyone could bring himself to deny the basic humanity of slaves. If slaves were confiscated because their owners forced them to participate in the Confederate war effort, did they then deserve to be kept in a state of bondage? This question resulted in painful ambivalence for many northern citizens in 1861–1862. Pamphlets, speeches, sermons, and letters revealed absolute perplexity about what actions the government should take with regard to freed slaves. Secretary of the Interior Caleb B. Smith commented that although he still firmly believed that the war was not "against slavery," southern madness itself would "crush out the institution." When this happened, he would have no tears to shed, but he still did not recommend any legislative effort to bring about this result. Perhaps because they were at such a loss, many northerners thought the problem should be left to Divine Providence. For example, pamphleteer William B. Sprague believed that whatever "ultimate advantage to the cause of freedom . . . shall result from this temporary interference with the workings of the institution, it must be left to Providence to determine." The *Christian Examiner* ran an editorial asserting that the only guarantees the United States could have against the constant recurrence of rebellion and "nullification" would be either the "military subjugation of the Slave States, or emancipation of their slaves." The first would imply keeping a large standing army and a change in "republican institutions," and would therefore be unacceptable. The only solution the *Examiner* could propose was to hope that the government would find a way to end the institution of slavery in the border states (the editorial did not comment on slaves living in the Confederacy) and then eventually colonize the freed slaves. Although Republican voters repeatedly pushed Congress to enact punitive legislation, they did not necessarily want the politicians to take action against the institution of slavery. Therefore, confiscation laws that freed slaves without retaining ownership over them did not conform to the public's desire to retain control over this problematic form of property. Traditionally, Republicans (including President Lincoln) had believed that the Constitution's framers expected slavery to die out; this would be a natural progression of events. Moderates perceived legislative action on slavery as inappropriate because it contradicted stated war aims and struck at fundamental principles of noninterference with local institutions. Moreover, sweeping emancipation would be extremely difficult to control.[28]

Even some radical writers experienced difficulties imagining the future of an America without slaves. They understood that emancipation would confer benefits on the bondspeople, but could not quite envision the practical realities of this transformation. According to the *Chicago Tribune,* what disposition the "Government may make of the confiscated slaves" was still to be determined, although they would not be returned to their former owners. Although the *Tribune* maintained that it was within the government's purview to "dispose" of the former slaves, the paper still conceded that "a loyal slave is entitled to infinitely more respect and consideration at the hands of Government than his rebel master." The editors of the *Springfield* (Illinois) *Daily Republican* were also puzzled by the problem of the future of confiscated slaves. The *Republican,* though not a radical paper, was always staunchly pro-Lincoln and usually supported moderate or gradual emancipation policies. Nevertheless, its editors felt it "beyond them" to solve this question and thought it best to leave it to Providence. "If emancipation is what this war means, we shall know it in good time. It would be cheaply purchased at the price of all the sacrifice we are likely to be called upon to make." Pamphleteer Alfred H. Love agreed. Although he felt that slavery was wicked, he did not want anyone to use "wicked means even to free the slave!" The idea that this was a war for the "rights and liberties of the negro, north and south—is it not illusory?" He did, however, believe that in some unspecified way, black people would eventually get all their rights under the government. The *Christian Examiner* also found itself stymied. Although the editor did not "clearly see how this war is to put an end to slavery," he had faith that Divine Providence had obviously taken the matter into its own hands, and the institution would soon die, though "not perhaps immediately or suddenly." This could be accomplished in several ways, none of which implicated northerners directly in the process. First, the border state slaves would soon begin escaping to the North; second, they would be liberated through Butler's contra-

28. Fisher, *Trial of Our Constitution,* 309; Friedman, 275–7; Bassett, *A Discourse on the Wickedness and Folly of the Present War;* Caleb Smith's speech was reported in the *National Daily Intelligencer,* August 21, 1861; *Christian Examiner,* July 1861, 112; Sprague, *Glorifying God,* 52–3.

band policy, or else the slaves would be freed by "generals in command under the war-power." The evident bewilderment of these commentators could be seen as a refusal to acknowledge the potential rights of freed people, but it might also suggest that radical social changes, once viewed as too drastic to be seriously considered, were now deemed to be a distinct, if frightening, possibility. Even six months earlier, only abolitionists like John Rock, Frederick Douglass, and Wendell Phillips would have contemplated the notion that slaves could be widely emancipated. Now even moderate northerners pondered the possibility, albeit in a perplexed and hesitant way.[29]

Still, for most northerners, radical or not, the problem of slavery was directly linked to the issues of warfare, revenge, and military necessity. No matter how much conservatives and moderates dreaded the necessity of emancipation, militant northerners always pointed to the inevitability as well as the justice of punishing the South. A writer for *Frank Leslie's Illustrated* said that although the northern people had tried to close their eyes to the fact that slavery was at the bottom of all their difficulties, they were now beginning to wake up. *Leslie's* cited Lovejoy's Resolution and the debates over the Confiscation Act as proof. The writer admitted to having worried about the possibility of a servile insurrection against white people. But piratical raids, "cruelties . . . practiced on men and women of Northern birth," rumored southern black regiments, and Indians "seduced" to the Confederate cause, had now made the northern people willing to punish the rebels. Besides, *Leslie's* added somewhat blithely, since southerners claimed the slaves as property, they could not reasonably object to confiscation. "Technically, the owner loses a money value, which is the penalty of treason, but in fact the country enters on a stupendous scheme of Emancipation." Calvin Fletcher, as usual less hopeful, wrote in his diary that this was to be a "bloody war," but he also believed that "the free or union states will be forced by adversity to declare Slavery at an end & put arms into the hands of the sl[a]ves & proclaim liberty to the Captive."[30]

That was precisely what Union-loving border state residents feared most. While full-fledged abolitionists were still in a minority in 1861, they were no

29. Chicago *Tribune*, July 20, 1861; *Springfield* (Mass.) *Daily Republican*, July 10, 13, 1861; Love, *An Appeal*, 12, 15; *Christian Examiner*, July 1861, 111.

30. David Wellman Jr., to John Sherman, Sherman Papers, LOC, August 13, 1861; *Frank Leslie's Illustrated Newspaper*, August 24, 1861; Fletcher, *Diary*, entry for August 17, 1861, 173.

longer quite as despised as they had been before the outbreak of hostilities. By now many more northerners were at least willing to admit that slavery was at the root of their troubles, and even some Democrats contemplated an attack on rebel property—including their slaves. This turn of public opinion was deeply disturbing to border state slaveowners, who still hoped that the guarantees of private property would hold good and that the Union Army would continue to respect slave property. But both of these concepts—considered inviolable before the war—were now severely under attack. Not only was slave property being questioned, but simply owning slaves now called into question one's loyalty to the Union.

On December 5, 1861, Secretary of War Simon Cameron brought the problem of human property more glaringly to the forefront. His annual report to the 37th Congress, which had now reassembled in Washington, was released at the same time as Lincoln's message to Congress. He shocked the nation's conservative newspapers when he leaked his report to the press, without first obtaining the president's approval. The report contained strong language advising the Army to confiscate and arm all the slaves of rebels. Cameron made it clear that as far as he was concerned rebels had no rights under a Constitution they had spurned. Moreover, since the "labor and service of their slaves constitute the chief property of the rebels, such property should share the common fate of war." So far so good. But he struck a raw nerve when he added that it was "as clearly a right of the Government to arm slaves, when it may become necessary, as it [was] to use gunpowder." Judging from the reaction in the northern press, Cameron's hasty action was a significant turning point in the shift in northern public opinion on the capabilities and identities of black southerners. Not only had slaves been fleeing their bondage in increasing numbers for the past ten months, now a senior administration official was blurring the distinction between slaves as property and black men as autonomous, and potentially dangerous, human beings.[31]

Cameron's intemperate action also seriously threatened the border states' continued allegiance to the Union. President Lincoln immediately ordered Cameron to recall the printed copies of his report and to amend the offending paragraph, but his order came too late. Several newspapers had already received the original report and reprinted it verbatim. The *Philadelphia Inquirer* sharply

31. McPherson, *Political History*, 249, 416.

criticized the controversial portion of the report because it took "very ultra ground with reference to slaves in the insurgent States, and distinctly advocate[d] the policy of arming them for military service." The *Inquirer* praised the "moderate and conservative views of the President," who had after all only asked Cameron to delete the references to arming the slaves, but left in the statement that they could be confiscated as a matter of military necessity. The extremely conservative *Louisville Journal,* which would later in the war become nearly a copperhead paper, had also received a copy of the report. The section on arming slaves, said the *Journal,* would alienate the border states and demoralize the Army. But "worse than this, it would introduce into a war that is now humane and holy a savage ferocity and brutality that every Christian man and woman should shudder to contemplate." In all other respects, however, the *Journal* pronounced Cameron's report an "able document." Radicals, of course, were angered over Lincoln's modification of the document. One Republican from New Jersey insisted that Lincoln's cautious action had "absolutely broken down all enthusiasm in his favor," and that the president had now carelessly thrown away any chance he might have had "to make a name for himself in history."[32]

The moderate northern newspapers' reactions to Cameron's report reveal that northerners were growing reconciled to the confiscation of slaves, so long as such actions were unaccompanied by widespread emancipation edicts. The *Philadelphia Inquirer,* a moderate Republican paper that had hitherto always inveighed against general emancipation, explicitly complained about General Charles Stone's returning slaves to their rebel owners. The *Inquirer* found it "difficult to see on what grounds [the general] returns slaves to their owners, when he knows or has abundant evidence before him that their masters are aiding the Rebels." The writer of this editorial said that he felt "impressed that a *very civil* war is being carried on along some portions of the upper Potomac." A more conservative Democratic paper, the *Frankfort* (Kentucky) *Daily Commonwealth,* stated that although the institution of slavery had a right to "protection," it did not deserve this protection "at the expense of all the

---

32. Nicolay and Hay, *Abraham Lincoln,* 5:125–6; see also, McPherson, *Battle Cry,* 357; *Philadelphia Inquirer,* December 5, 1861; *Louisville Journal,* reprinted in the *Frankfort Daily Commonwealth,* December 13, 1861; John H. Bayard to Lyman Trumbull, Lyman Trumbull Papers, LOC, December 8, 1861.

other interests of man or of government itself." A few days later, the *Commonwealth* published a letter advocating the confiscation of "all negroes belonging to secessionists, without regard to what is done with them afterwards." The *Springfield* (Massachusetts) *Daily Republican,* another paper that had always opposed sweeping emancipation schemes, opined that "no loyal American opposed confiscation," and supported this contention by quoting the *New York Journal of Commerce,* an extremely conservative Democratic party organ, which baldly and rather callously stated that "we can confiscate slaves like horses and cotton."[33]

Whether indeed the Union armies or the federal government could confiscate slaves "like horses and cotton" would become one of the more urgent topics for debate among the members of the 37th Congress, who had now reassembled in the capital for their regular session, ready to argue over legislation that would permit a more powerful attack on southern land, crops, and slaves.

33. *Philadelphia Inquirer,* December 17, 1861; *Frankfort* (Ky.) *Daily Commonwealth,* December 13, December 19, 1861; *New York Journal of Commerce,* quoted in the *Springfield* (Mass.) *Daily Republican,* December 9, 1861.

CHAPTER 6

The Second Confiscation Act
Debated in Congress

I N EARLY DECEMBER 1861 the 37th Congress, which had been in recess since August, reconvened in the nation's capital for the regular session. The members found the city considerably altered from the sleepy southern town it had been prior to the outbreak of the war. Visitors noticed that the capital had become a "northern" city, bustling with commerce and industry. The military presence was conspicuous; volunteers from many states were marching, drilling, and brawling in the streets, and scores of entrepreneurs hoping to profit from the war were busily turning the capital into a thriving commercial metropolis. A Presbyterian minister from Virginia now found Washington "as much a center of business as New York," and he thought that most of the money-making was probably connected with the Army. "All classes of tradesmen seem to be flourishing, and thousands of 'Yankees' are taking up their abode there as indeed in every other place near which the Federal forces fix themselves." He was certain that if the war were to continue much longer, and the Union cause prevail, the whole South would soon become "so permeated with Yankee influence as to make resistance against it useless." [1]

The Yankee influence was indeed making itself felt. As the congressmen and senators gathered together in the Capitol chambers for the opening of the regular session, it quickly became obvious that conservatives had lost ground. There were 106 Republicans, 42 Democrats, and 28 Unionists in the second session of the 37th Congress. The most extreme southern sympathizers, like

1. James Ward, unpublished manuscript diary, LOC, entry dated December 19, 1861.

Kentucky's Congressman Henry C. Burnett and Senator John Breckinridge, had now departed—either to the Confederate Congress or to the Confederate Army. Several other border state members of the Senate and the House, including Indiana senator Jesse Bright, had been expelled. Their exodus would make it easier, Republicans hoped, to use their "Yankee influence" in order to pass harsh anti-southern legislation. Republicans at home were making it clear that they wanted their representatives to pass laws that would strike at enemy citizens, both to effect retribution against the rebels and to harm the Confederate military effort. Congressional Republicans, always responsive to their impatient constituencies, hoped to take advantage of their majority in both houses in order to fight and win the war on their own terms. They intended to reconstruct the Union according to the principles of their party: with the might of free labor, and without slavery. Furthermore, they were also determined to make it impossible for the South ever to rebel again. In order to accomplish these goals they had to find a way to gain control over the war effort by prevailing over conservatives and by persuading moderate Republicans (including, of course, President Lincoln) and Unionists to support their legislation. Republicans had to make many concessions to Democratic members of the various committees that deliberated on the confiscation bills in order to pass their punitive program. In their hands Republicans held what one historian has called a weapon that would aim the "mightiest blow" against disloyalty: a law that would confiscate private property from the rebels, punish them for their rebellion, and free their slaves. In their pursuit of these radical goals, however, Republicans were invariably constrained by their moderate colleagues and commitments; the legislation they enacted depended upon enforcement by the federal courts, not the Union armies, and the punishment they inflicted was restricted by narrow legislative limitations, by the president's constitutional scruples, and by the northern home front's unwillingness to support emancipation.[2]

The previous summer, during the brief special session, the lawmakers had struggled against the oppressive heat and the pressure of time to cope with the

---

2. Bogue, *The Congressman's Civil War*, 172. See also Bogue, *The Earnest Men;* Silbey, *A Respectable Minority.* For Republicans' long-term goals in the wartime Congress, see Foner, *Politics and Ideology,* 131; Holt, "Abraham Lincoln and the Politics of Union," in Thomas, ed., *Abraham Lincoln and the American Political Tradition,* 117; Rawley, *Politics of Union,* 61.

national emergency. Now that Congress was meeting in its regular session, many urgent duties occupied the members. They had to finance the war, enlarge the Army and Navy, and manage the domestic affairs of the nation. Republicans and Democrats cooperated on many important financial issues, including bills to raise funds for the war effort, tax laws, bonds, and laws increasing the size of the regular and volunteer armies. But bipartisan cooperation disappeared over emancipation and over punitive measures. Democrats opposed all efforts to free the slaves and confiscate rebel property. Both radical and moderate Republicans wanted to pass punitive legislation, but radicals also wanted to attack the foundations of the constitutional protections of slave property. Both objectives garnered strong opposition from Democrats as well as from some moderate Republicans, who feared that such acts would cripple the Constitution and increase the difficulty of reuniting the nation after the war. Historian Hans Trefousse has pointed out that the enactment of harsh measures helped Republicans win votes among their own constituencies (and possibly among War Democrats as well), but all politicians had to pay attention to the popular ambivalence on slavery. Moderate Republicans and War Democrats, therefore, struggled to gain control over the final form punitive measures would take.[3]

The decision over who was to retain the ultimate control of the war effort remained one of the more crucial dilemmas to be resolved in the 37th Congress. This was especially urgent now that General George B. McClellan, grievously ill with typhoid fever and refusing to communicate his plans, appeared to have been thoroughly stalemated in Virginia. Winter was coming, and very little had been accomplished; no one knew what the general intended to do, or when he would advance his army toward Richmond. The home front, especially after the miserable defeats at Bull Run in July and at Ball's Bluff in late October, which had cost them the life of Senator Edward Baker, had grown impatient beyond endurance. Because of the military delays and defeats, Congress convened a Joint Committee on the Conduct of the War, whose purpose was to investigate the desultory progress of the Union armies, fraudulent military purchases, and the alleged incompetence that had led to Senator Baker's death at Ball's Bluff. This would bring the lawmakers more directly in supervision of the military ef-

3. Rawley, *Politics of Union,* 41; Silbey, *A Respectable Minority,* 34; Trefousse, "Unionism and Abolition," 106–8; see also Trefousse, "Lincoln and Race Relations," in Greenberg and Waugh, *The Price of Freedom,* 2:319.

fort. One of the more important battles for congressional Republicans, then, was to find a way to exert control over military operations and over the treatment of enemy citizens, both of which they considered of paramount importance in prosecuting the war successfully. Republicans and even many War Democrats believed that in order to achieve a victory over the rebels it was necessary to bring the war home to individual enemy citizens and deprive them of their ability to support their army with food, slave labor, and financial assistance.

Northern voters focused more on punishment and on forcing the rebels to pay for the cost of the conflict, but the politicians also saw property confiscation as a way of prosecuting a faltering military effort and gaining control over the overall direction of the war. Of course the more radical Republicans also wanted to use confiscation bills to undergird their emancipation program, but they had more direct ways of striking at slavery. Congressional Republicans launched a two-pronged attack on the institution. First, the legislators passed bills that chipped away at slavery in areas that were arguably under congressional control: in the conquered areas of the South, where slaves were fleeing their owners and joining Union Army camps; in the western territories, where the Constitution granted Congress some control (even though the laws that freed slaves in the territories struck at the *Dred Scott* decision); and in the District of Columbia. The second—and much more serious—attack on slavery occurred under the proposed confiscation legislation. This came under much more debate in Congress because such legislation raised significant questions about who controlled the conduct of the war, and because, according to conservatives such as Congressman John Crittenden, it directly interfered with internal institutions within states. Emancipationist legislation extended congressional control (to its utmost limits) over the South's peculiar institution, but it did so within constitutionally sanctioned parameters. The confiscation bills, on the other hand, cast a wider net because they contemplated an attack on all Confederate property that was being used to support the rebellion, and thus endangered constitutional protections of private property rights. The confiscation laws simply set the slaves free forever, without transferring their ownership to the federal government. Because these laws assailed the property status of slaves, conservatives held that they struck directly at the institution of slavery. Eventually Republicans in the 37th Congress passed twenty-six antislavery laws, including the abolition of slavery in the District of Columbia and in the territories. But no branch of government possessed the power to enact sweeping emancipation. Congressional Republicans (both moderate and radical) understood that they had to begin to assail the constitutional protections of some of the property rights of rebels while they were simultaneously attacking the institution of slavery. They could not have emancipated any slaves at all without strengthening their grip on constitutional war powers or without debating the protection (or extinction of) Confederate property rights. Radical legal theorists such as William Whiting, Timothy Farrar, and Francis Lieber would eventually hold that in wartime, constitutional war powers were superior to all other authorities. The Constitution must be construed as powerful enough to save itself, especially in times of emergency when the welfare of the people required a strong government. That said, radicals primarily understood confiscation as a military measure, with the side benefit, though not the sole purpose, of emancipating the slaves of rebels. Historian Mark Grimsley has pointed out that milder antislavery measures and proposals, such as gradual compensated emancipation in the border states, would not achieve any military benefits, such as depriving rebels of slave labor. In contrast, the confiscation laws specifically attacked "contraband"—private property that was being used to support the rebellion. Democrats argued that such laws, therefore, endangered constitutional protections of private property rights, possibly for all Americans. Conservative legal theorists such as Joel Parker would have agreed; Parker held that emancipation should be limited to military actions, and should be only temporary. Otherwise, he felt, emancipation would interfere with constitutional limitations on the federal government's right to interfere with state institutions.[4]

In their effort to attain their goals of confiscation and emancipation, the more radical Republicans were continually thwarted by the increasingly moderate Republican and Unionist voice in Congress. Although Republicans maintained a numerical majority over Democrats, it was the moderate Republicans (together with Democrats) who were most able to influence the punitive bills as members of the various committees that actually considered and reframed

4. Maltz, *Civil Rights, the Constitution, and Congress*, 13; for Lincoln's interpretation of the war powers granted to him by the Constitution, and of the specific powers granted to Congress, see Benedict, "The Lincoln Presidency and the Republican Era," in Fausold and Shank, eds., *The Constitution and the American Presidency*; Grimsley, *Hard Hand of War*, 137, 69; Paludan, *Covenant with Death*, 136.

the laws. Moderates might have countenanced property confiscation, but they always opposed anything resembling widespread emancipation. The more radical Republicans endorsed a confiscation program again and again in their caucuses, and supported it vehemently and at great length in their speeches, but their punitive bills could not survive the committee deliberations intact. Although some historians, including James G. Randall, have asserted that radicals enjoyed "full sway" in passing this legislation, it was the moderates (including President Lincoln) who ultimately controlled its scope and long-term results.[5]

There were many competing entities struggling for control over the conduct of the war: the Army, the president, the multiple factions in Congress, the press, and the northern public. The Army was led, in part, by Democrats such as George McClellan, Henry Halleck, and Don Carlos Buell, who refused to attack the private property of traitors. President Lincoln had already made it clear that he would not be rushed on his policies toward enemy civilians or toward slavery. Lincoln certainly insisted that wartime legislation conform to the Constitution. The president had to maintain a larger view of the national crisis and of the various groups whose support was required for a victorious conclusion to the war effort. He always managed to keep a firm hand on the reins. Because radical Republicans were primarily responsible to their own constituencies, however, they were less attuned to—or perhaps less concerned with—the competing viewpoints on the home front. A third entity contending for wartime political control were the congressional moderate Republicans, who would do their utmost to soften harsh legislation, and sometimes appeared to side with War Democrats as well as with some conservatives. By contrast, the prowar voters always drove their harsh opinions forward. Republicans' correspondence files are replete with letters pleading for action and for a more vigorous prosecution of the war effort. Democrats were not the most significant opponents of Republican hard-war initiatives. In fact, conservative ("Peace") Democrats had relatively little influence or power in either house. Radical Republicans would now discover, in the more expansive pace of the long session, that their greatest—and ultimately most successful—rivals for political control of the war effort were the moderates of both parties. In both sessions of the 37th Congress, men such as Illinois senator Orville Hickman Browning, Garret

5. Paludan, *Presidency*, 127. Randall and Donald, *Civil War*, 284.

Davis of Kentucky, and Jacob Collamer of Vermont continually softened and weakened punitive legislation.[6]

The Frémont debacle had shown that the First Confiscation Act was too weak to accomplish its object, and that the president would hold the federal armies to the letter of the law. If Congress wanted the armies to move against rebel property, then Congress would have to enact a tougher law. In the meantime Lincoln, no doubt aware of public sentiment but as always politically cautious on any issue touching on slave property, acknowledged the northern public's widespread desire for stronger punitive measures. The president's opening message to Congress on December 5, 1861, alluded to the possibility of enacting a new confiscation law, one that would be more effective and farther-reaching. He commented briefly on some of the consequences of the First Confiscation Act, including the fact that a few slaves had been freed under its provisions. Although the president emphasized that he had been "anxious and careful that the inevitable conflict . . . should not degenerate into a violent and remorseless revolutionary struggle," he nevertheless suggested careful consideration of a "new law upon the same subject." The speech could be read as an invitation to Congress to enact a harsher law, but the president's prudent rhetoric left his intentions open to interpretation. He did not explicitly encourage Congress to pass such a law; as a result, one of Trumbull's constituents fumed that "Mr. Lincoln had his *face Southward* when he wrote this *thing*."[7]

The purpose of the First Confiscation Act, passed at the end of the previous session, was to seize any rebel property that had been used to promote the war effort. The three primary goals of that law were to punish southerners, to take back the munitions, forts, arsenals, revenue cutters, and other federal properties that had been seized, and to deprive rebel armies of the labor of slaves. Although the law did not explicitly emancipate the confiscated slaves, the general understanding on the home front and in Congress was that the slaves would not

6. Mark J. Rozell, "Executive Prerogative: Abraham Lincoln and American Constitutionalism," in Williams and Pederson, eds., *Abraham Lincoln, Contemporary;* Belz, *Abraham Lincoln, Constitutionalism,* chapter 1, and Kammen, *Machine,* chapter 4; Holt, "Abraham Lincoln and the Politics of Union," in Thomas, ed., *Abraham Lincoln and the American Political Tradition,* 113–4; Randall and Donald, *Civil War and Reconstruction,* 284.

7. Basler, *Collected Works,* "Address to Congress," December 5, 1861, 5:48–9; S. York to Lyman Trumbull, Trumbull Papers, LOC, December 5, [1861].

be treated like "ordinary" property. After confiscation they would not be held in possession by the government, but rather, set free. Among the radical element in Congress and more generally on the home front, there had been a great deal of criticism that the First Confiscation Act was too weak to accomplish anything, mainly because it was too limited. The law seized only property specifically used in a military capacity but left all other southern rebels in possession of the mighty tools to prosecute their rebellion: land, crops, and slave labor. What was worse, according to some northerners, was that the First Confiscation Act did not provide for the reimbursement of the losses of individual northern citizens whose property had been stolen by rebels. Early in the session Indiana representative George Julian derided the act as "that wretched legislative blunder," and as the fruit of the administration's reprehensibly "fastidious and gingerly policy." Ohio congressman Albert Gallatin Riddle, who like Julian was an antislavery radical, colorfully denounced the act as "that poor, feeble, emasculated thing," a "eunuch" of a law, indeed one that had been "born without sex." The radicals' dissatisfaction with the limitations of the Confiscation Act led to their desire for a stronger law, and in this they were spurred on by a disgruntled home front. The difference between congressional radicals and Republican voters at home was that abolitionist politicians were deeply interested in confiscation as an emancipation measure, while the public saw it primarily as punitive and as a way of making southerners pay for the costs of the war. That meant that even some moderates—including many War Democrats—at home were able to endorse wholeheartedly the idea of taking private property from rebels, while many of them still strongly resisted emancipation. In the spring of 1862 this difference would lead to a rift between politicians and their constituencies, especially among Republicans.[8]

Once again the first substantive bill introduced in the Senate of the 37th Congress was a confiscation law. On December 3, immediately after the opening prayer, Illinois senator Lyman Trumbull gave notice of his intention to introduce a bill for the "confiscation of the property of rebels and giving freedom to the persons they hold in slavery." And it was to do so whether such property had been used for waging war or not. This law would be substantially harsher

8. These remarks were made on January 14, 1862, *Cong. Globe,* 37th Cong., 2nd sess., 330; remarks of Albert G. Riddle on January 27, 1862, *Cong. Globe,* 37th Cong., 2nd sess., 499.

than the First Confiscation Act, which limited all seizures to contraband. Trumbull had initially proposed this bill in the summer session, where it had disappeared in the committee process and had been replaced by the more moderate bill that became the First Confiscation Act. Trumbull was now reviving it because he believed the time had come for a more sweeping law. Two days later, Trumbull rose in the Senate to introduce his confiscation bill, and delivered one of the most famous speeches of his career.[9]

Perhaps in answer to criticisms of the limitations of the First Confiscation Act, Trumbull wanted to leave no doubt about the sweeping nature of the bill. He opened by saying that his proposed law would provide for the "absolute and complete forfeiture forever to the United States of every species of property, real and personal, and wheresoever situated within the United States." Second, it was his intention to defray the expenses incurred in the suppression of the rebellion; any proceeds would go to the just claims of loyal creditors. This provision was especially important to the public, who had demanded since last winter that the South should be made to pay for the war. The absence of such a provision from the First Confiscation Act had been harshly criticized by northerners. The Second Confiscation Act explicitly contained punitive clauses, including fines, which had been absent in the First Confiscation Act. Therefore, the conflicted question of loyalty would now become more crucial.[10]

Trumbull minced no words about the slaves of rebellious owners. His proposed law "declared and made free" all the slaves of persons in arms against the government. Somewhat disingenuously, Trumbull explained that the right to free slaves was "equally clear" with that to confiscate the rebels' property, because "it is as property that [the rebels] profess to hold" the slaves. He was not treating the slaves the same as "other property," however, because the federal government was not to receive title to the freedmen. This wording had also appeared in the First Confiscation Act. Both bills confiscated the slaves' *labor,* not the slaves themselves. For radical Republicans and abolitionists, emancipating slaves actually meant giving them power over their own labor and over the fruits of that labor. Specifically, it was the right to control one's own labor that

9. Horace White, quoted in Roske, *His Own Counsel,* 81.

10. The provision reimbursing northerners from confiscated rebel property had disappeared from the final version of the First Confiscation Act. It was removed during the select committee deliberations.

was at issue here, and for this reason the confiscation measure was a much more radical attack on the institution of slavery than might be apparent at first glance. In other words, Trumbull's bill not only confiscated the slave's labor from disloyal southerners, but more importantly granted the freed slaves the right to dispose of that labor as they saw fit. The Second Confiscation Act declared that all slaves either captured or fleeing from rebel owners would be forever free, and "not again held as slaves." In response to the northern home front's frequently reiterated fears, however, Trumbull's bill contained a provision for colonizing the freed slaves, or at least "such of them as may be willing to go." Trumbull expressed a hope that some "tropical country" could be found for them where their rights as freed people would be respected. Republicans disliked this portion of Trumbull's confiscation law, but felt forced to include a colonization clause to appease their more moderate colleagues and constituents.[11]

Trumbull stated, somewhat defensively, that to his mind, Congress had an unquestionable right to pass a confiscation law, but he was also careful to assert that the bill was not based on the ground which had been "advanced in some quarters," that in wartime the military was superior to the civil power, or that military necessity could take precedence over the Constitution. Indeed, Trumbull emphasized that "necessity" had always been "the plea of tyrants," and if the Constitution ceased to operate "the moment a person charged with its observance thinks there is a necessity to violate it," then the nation's founding document would become worthless. Trumbull was not a radical; prior to the formation of the Republican Party, he had been a Democrat, albeit with strong antislavery principles. As a congressman and later a senator from Illinois, he had always been a careful defender of the Constitution; indeed, later on radicals such as Benjamin F. Wade and Zachariah Chandler would criticize the final version of his confiscation bill as too lenient. But this bill was much more sweeping than the First Confiscation Act and for now, at least, his more radical colleagues considered Trumbull to be on the "side of the angels."[12]

Trumbull's speech, deceptively straightforward, disarmed his more moderate critics because it appeared unequivocally to establish the Constitution as the

11. *Cong. Globe,* 37th Cong., 2nd sess., 18; Curry, *Blueprint,* 79.

12. *Cong. Globe,* 37th Cong., 2nd sess., 18, 19. The "plea of tyrants" phrase originally came from John Milton's *Paradise Lost,* book 4, chapter 4, and was quoted in a famous speech by William Pitt before Parliament in 1783.

basis for his bill. But his assertions about the Constitution imperfectly masked a nagging uncertainty about the propriety of taking private possessions from American citizens without the due process of law. Indeed, Trumbull argued explicitly that the Constitution could not be set aside in order to enact war measures. He therefore had to resort to an extra-constitutional legal trick in order to justify taking private property of rebellious southerners, and in order to free their slaves he had to cast doubts on their right to own human beings. As in the First Confiscation Act, Trumbull's new bill proposed to confiscate rebel property under *in rem* proceedings, a process usually reserved to customs officers. The property itself (not its owner) was held to be guilty, and could therefore be confiscated without a jury trial. Conservatives considered this process nothing more than "legal sleight of hand," since *in rem* proceedings had only been used to justify confiscations of property captured at sea, not on land. Moreover, the First Confiscation Act confiscated only property used to wage war (which presumably could be termed "guilty" property), while the Second Confiscation Act contemplated taking *all* private property belonging to rebels. In this way Trumbull attempted to negotiate—or, perhaps more accurately, failed to negotiate—the slippery terrain of the confiscation of private property from American citizens. At the same time, there was a significant difference between Trumbull's proposed bill and the First Confiscation Act. The prior confiscation law did not seek to ascertain the guilt or innocence of the owner; Trumbull's new bill was, even in its early stages, an attempt to redefine the crime of treason and to punish rebels. For this reason the bill raised important questions about the meaning of loyalty, and the congressional power to determine the nature and limits of treasonous behavior.[13]

Newspapers around the country reported Trumbull's speech verbatim, and the Illinois senator, who had also made it his business to send printed copies to his own constituents, received hundreds of letters praising it. His careful constitutional stance reassured moderates that the policies in Washington would be carried out within the letter of the law. The *Philadelphia Inquirer* said that "whatever may be thought of the policy of Mr. Trumbull's measure, no one can

---

13. Benedict, "Preserving the Constitution," 65–90. The bill referred to "any person" deemed guilty of treason against the American government, so presumably it also reached aliens' property. However, the debates for and against confiscation rarely considered the rights of alien residents. White, *Life of Lyman Trumbull,* 173.

fail to accord him the high praise of approaching the question with the calm and thoughtful spirit befitting a Senator." The editor thought the plea of tyrants phrase displayed the "proper spirit" to deal with the "troublesome property of the Rebels," by which he meant slaves. Even a conservative Missourian tersely agreed that Trumbull's "Constitution stance is good," even though he believed that "confiscation is wrong." [14]

Many people who read Trumbull's speech in their morning papers, or who had received copies of it in printed form, responded well to the "plea of tyrants" phrase. But they appeared to miss its obvious contradictions. Tyrants rarely take the trouble to plead in defense of their actions, even in justification of their more egregious deeds. If they wished to avoid the charge of tyranny, northern politicians would have to base their actions on a higher ground than military necessity. Yet there was a deep irony in the notion that the North could avoid arguments of necessity in the midst of a civil war, especially since they were fighting to maintain a democratic government founded on individual citizens' rights and liberties. The Bill of Rights protected property ownership; nevertheless, one of the radicals' primary justifications for taking property was that it would be impossible to win the war without an attack on rebel property. Republicans asserted that the Constitution granted extraordinary powers in times of internal rebellion. Furthermore, war powers were only emergency powers; once the emergency was resolved, the national government would return to its normal functions. Perhaps to avoid charges that his bill was based on powers not explicitly granted by the Constitution, Trumbull relied on classical loose constructionist arguments, including the section in the Constitution that gave Congress the power to make "rules concerning captures on land and water" as well as the section that granted the right to make "all necessary and proper" laws to maintain the life of the nation. (Article I, Section 8).

Some of Trumbull's critics, however, found inconsistencies in both the speech and the proposed law. Most Democratic papers (at least, all but the most fervent copperhead organs) wanted to place themselves squarely on the side of vigorous prosecution of the war, but were troubled by elements of the law that appeared to promote wholesale emancipation, such as the provision that liberated the slaves of rebels without retaining ownership of the slaves' labor, which

14. *Philadelphia Inquirer,* December 6, 1861; Charles S. Whittelsey to Lyman Trumbull, Lyman Trumbull Papers, LOC, December 28, 1861.

conservatives considered unconstitutional. For example, while the conservative *New York Herald* thought Trumbull's speech had "some features deserving of commendation," the editor also perceived some great dangers. The Illinois senator's speech was inconsistent, and what was worse, it was "visionary and impracticable," like the ideas of all the other abolitionists. "He proposes to carry on the war strictly within the bounds of the Constitution, and yet his own bill violates it in the most flagrant manner," the editor complained. Even in its present incarnation, before the confiscation law had become subjected to moderation by conservatives in debate and through the committee process, the *Herald* observed that the bill would be difficult to enforce. The editorial stated bluntly that the law "practically amounts to nothing," because it did not provide a clear method for taking rebel property. This problem would never be resolved, and would result in what most historians would argue was the primary cause of the Second Confiscation Act's failure.[15]

Trumbull's bill was referred to the Senate Committee on the Judiciary in mid-December. Meanwhile, his friend and colleague Republican Illinois congressman Isaac N. Arnold proposed a similar bill, which was referred to the House Committee on the Judiciary and would not resurface until late March 1862. On December 19, Republican caucuses from both houses of Congress met and endorsed confiscation as a party policy. The Senate bill was reported back a month later, but would not be taken up for debate until nearly the end of February. In the meantime, while the bills were still in committee, the northern press painstakingly reported the congressional deliberations and reprinted all but the longest speeches verbatim. Over the next eight to ten weeks Congress became deeply involved in debating the conduct of the war, especially during speeches for and against confiscation. Therefore, one unintentional result of the political debates was that many northerners, especially Republicans, began to believe that their government was discussing the war rather than fighting it. From the moment Congress opened on December 4, newspaper editorials from both sides of the partisan press vehemently demanded a more vigorous prosecution of the war. Similarly martial views appeared in many of the letters northern citizens wrote to their representatives in Washington, as well as in pamphlets and in sermons. Since the secession crisis, many citizens, including prowar Democrats, thought that the Union armies should assail the private

15. *New York Herald,* December 8, 1861.

property of traitors, including slave labor, which was clearly a valuable resource for the Confederacy.[16]

The problem was that Republicans at home, and indeed anyone who thought the war should be fought with more vigor, felt that the administration remained deaf to their demands. They simply did not understand the necessity of arguing over legal niceties when the nation was wracked by a gigantic rebellion. They blamed the constitutional restrictions placed on the Army and on Congress. During the summer of 1861, Democratic generals such as George B. McClellan and Don Carlos Buell had explicitly proclaimed their intention to protect southern civilians' private property (including their property in slaves), and President Abraham Lincoln had revoked General John C. Frémont's proclamation of martial law and emancipation in Missouri, much to the chagrin of northern war hawks. Moreover, the administration had always been circumspect in regard to slave property and had refused to take any steps that might drive the volatile border states into the arms of the Confederacy. In spite of Lincoln's suspension of the writ of *habeas corpus* along military lines throughout the North, as well as his institution of a blockade of key southern ports in April 1861, bellicose northerners still believed that the administration was far too cautious in matters of warfare against southern civilians and their private property. Indeed, one man, whose frustration moved him to threats of violence, expressed his disgust with Lincoln's "mildness and Meekness," and declared that he "wished some Brutus would arise who loved the country more than Abraham Lincoln."[17]

Less bloodthirsty northerners also perceived a link between the government's hesitant policies (including the continual concessions to border states) and the Army's marked lack of success. Some, like John Montelius of Freeport, Illinois, even imputed treason to the administration's unwillingness to wage a harsh war and confiscate southern property. In a letter to Illinois congressman Elihu Washburne in late December 1861, Montelius expressed his disgust that the war was "progressing like a *crab, backwards.*" He asserted, rather comprehensively, that the country had been betrayed into the hands of secessionists

---

16. Perkins, ed., *Northern Editorials,* 4.

17. See, for example, speeches contained in Stevens, *Proceedings,* passim. For a discussion of the Lincoln administration's policies toward the border states, see Gienapp, "Abraham Lincoln and the Border States," 13–46.

"from Old Abe downwards to the lowest corporal." Like many of his contemporaries, Montelius was frustrated with the government's chronic hesitation to use all the weapons at its disposal to fight the war. Similarly, another of Elihu Washburne's correspondents fumed that the politicians were still "ignorant of the feleing [*sic*] of uneasines[s] & discontent which pervades the Country." He declared that there was a "screw loose somewhere" and contemptuously called the administration's policy "masterly inactivity . . . pursued with a vengeance." These complaints usually arose from dismay over the chronic military defeats and delays, as well as a desire to exact personal revenge on rebel citizens, and from a growing impatience with the politicians' unwillingness to contravene constitutional protections of the rebels' civil rights. The lawmakers in Washington appeared to be nothing more than pedantic attorneys, nitpicking over legal niceties. A resident of Ohio, for example, confessed himself "*astonished* at the *hairsplitting* opinions of our Lawyer Senate and House." He thought that treason must indeed have a powerful stronghold if the rebels' real estate could not be confiscated, simply because it was protected by the "guarantees of a Constitution they [had] long ago repudiated." [18]

These letters came from Republicans, but similar—if somewhat less radical—views could be found in northern newspapers of various political persuasions. Many Democratic editorials also demanded a vigorous prosecution of the war, which usually included harsh measures toward individual southerners, even if they stopped short of emancipation. Indeed, the only newspapers that argued persistently against the confiscation of southern property were such copperhead organs as the Columbus, Ohio, *Crisis* and extremely conservative Democratic papers, such as the *Albany Atlas and Argus*. Far more representative were journals like the *Louisville Daily Democrat,* a proslavery, pro-Union Democratic paper, which supported the idea of confiscation (including the confiscation of slaves) but thought the legislation pending in Congress was too sweeping, because it appeared to encourage widespread emancipation. [19]

18. John Montelius to Elihu Washburne, Elihu B. Washburne Papers, LOC, December 28, 1861; Potter, *Lincoln and His Party*; A. J. Betts to Elihu Washburne, Elihu B. Washburne Papers, LOC, December 26, 1861; Cephas Brainerd to George Julian, Joshua R. Giddings–George W. Julian Correspondence, LOC, January 28, 1862; P. A. Allaire, M.D., to Lyman Trumbull, Trumbull Papers, LOC, December 10, 1861. Dr. Allaire said he was quoting an unidentified neighbor. Justin Hamilton to John Sherman, Sherman Papers, LOC, May 24, 1862.

19. The *Albany Atlas and Argus* generally opposed all confiscation measures, although the paper did publish a letter from a reader claiming he was less than "tender" about southern prop-

The Senate confiscation bills remained under consideration in the Committee on the Judiciary until February 25, 1862. In the meantime, to obviate arguments about the disputed right to pass legislation that controlled the war effort, the lawmakers in both houses had to work out who was going to be primarily responsible for the conduct of the war. Representative John B. Steele of New York probably put it best when he remarked early in the session, "Well, I think there will be more than two minds at cross purposes if this Congress undertakes to direct this war." Should Congress, in fact, try to direct or legislate on the war? Conservatives and most moderates in Congress were convinced that the legislative branch of government did not have that right, because according to them the Constitution left such powers to the president as commander-in-chief of the Army and Navy (Article II, Section 2). (Undoubtedly, however, they would vigorously have opposed confiscation by presidential edict.) In response to this rather disingenuous argument, which implied that President Lincoln should have full control over the war effort, proconfiscation men argued that the Constitution provided for expanded powers in wartime. Congress had the right of "calling forth the militia to execute the laws of the Union, suppress insurrections, and repel invasions" (Article I, Section 8). But conservatives asserted in return that even if this were so, the war powers as defined by the Constitution were in themselves sufficient and did not require additional legislation. The Constitution did not need to be bolstered with "mischievous" legislation like the Confiscation Act. Senator Garrett Davis of Kentucky asserted that Congress had only the power to make war, not to "do more." According to Davis, Congress could declare war, but had no legislative power over the armed forces (other than, presumably, authorizing appropriations for enlarging the Army.) If Congress enlarged constitutional war powers in order to seize legislative control over the war effort, conservatives reasoned, then it might also gain control over the social institutions of the South, the treatment of rebellious citizens, and the ultimate interpretation of the Constitution itself.[20]

---

erty rights, even property in slaves. Most other Democratic papers in my research sample favored some form of confiscation of rebel property. Curry, in *Blueprint*, 81, also found similar results.

20. Benedict, "A Constitutional Crisis," in McPherson and Cooper, eds., *Writing the Civil War*; 155; Hyman, "Reconstruction and Political-Constitutional Institutions," in *New Frontiers*, 24–5; remarks of John Steele on April 22, 1862, *Cong. Globe*, 37th Cong., 2nd sess., 1761; remarks of Garrett Davis on April 22, 1862, *Cong. Globe*, 37th Cong., 2nd sess., 1759.

The question of constitutional war powers was especially difficult for the members of the 37th Congress because there was so little legal precedent or opinion for them to consult. Legal theorists such as Francis Lieber and William Whiting, solicitor of the War Department, did not address the question until late 1862 and early 1863, when both published important treatises on war powers, the right of confiscation, emancipation, and the suspension of civil liberties. Timothy Farrar published an article proclaiming similar ideas about war powers in January 1862, but none of the proconfiscation legislators mentioned it in their speeches. In any event, both Lieber and Whiting treated the question of constitutional war powers in a manner that would have been much more sympathetic to radical war aims. Both considered that, within certain limitations, advancing armies had a right to confiscate enemy property. The Constitution, according to Lieber and Whiting, adequately provided for such actions in times of civil unrest.[21]

Before the Civil War, the legal aspects of the confiscation of private property had only been considered in relation to wars with Great Britain. In 1796, in *Ware v. Hylton,* Chief Justice John Marshall found that "independent nations" had an "unquestioned right of confiscation." In that case, the state of Virginia had seized and sequestered debts owed to British subjects. After the War of 1812, Marshall again found that "war gives the right to confiscate" enemy property, but held that a special act would have been necessary to authorize the confiscation of private property. Since no such law had been passed, the property in question (the cargo of a British vessel) had to be released. During the confiscation debates in the 37th Congress, both cases were cited in support of a confiscation law. Republicans occasionally cited European legal theorists, such as Emmerich Vattel, J. J. Burlamaqui, and Hugo Grotius, but they did so in a desultory fashion, rarely defending themselves from the conservative contention that the Constitution did not require enlargement by foreign authorities.[22]

21. Francis Lieber, General Order No. 100, *OR,* ser. 2, vol. 5, 671–82; Whiting, *War Powers of the President;* Farrar, "The Adequacy of the Constitution."

22. Quoted in Randall, *Constitutional Problems,* 300–1.Henry Wheaton, author of *Elements of International Law,* was one of the most widely cited authorities during the congressional debates over confiscation. His *Elements* had gone through several editions by the time of the Civil War; the most recent one available to the members of the 37th Congress was the sixth, published in Boston in 1855. See Randall, *Constitutional Problems,* 535, 297–300, and Grimsley, *Hard Hand of War,* 14–6.

But there was also legal precedent for the conservative anticonfiscation position. Although New York chancellor James Kent did appear to favor wartime
confiscation in the abstract, he observed that according to modern authority,
confiscation was "contrary to the right." Further, Henry Wheaton, writing in
1855, had declared that private enemy property and debts should not be
confiscated, though also admitting that this rule was "not inflexible." Secretary
of State John Quincy Adams wrote letters of instruction during the War of 1812
to Henry Middleton, then serving as ambassador at St. Petersburg, which provided support for anticonfiscation arguments. In his letters of instruction,
Adams vehemently denied the belligerent right of emancipation asserted by
Great Britain against American slaveholders. Adams declared the British attempts to entice American slaves to leave their masters to be in contravention
of the 1814 Treaty of Ghent. The British nation, he asserted, considered "slaves
as property," and must therefore recognize them as such by the terms of the
treaty. Thirty years later, however, Adams reversed himself, thus providing the
basis for proconfiscation and emancipationist arguments. In 1842, he declared
that in times of invasion, military authority replaced "municipal institutions,"
and military commanders could therefore legally emancipate slaves belonging to enemy citizens. From the moment a state became a "theater of war," he
stated, "the war powers of Congress extend to interference with slavery in every
way." During the congressional debates over confiscation, both Republicans
and Democrats made use of Adams's opinions to support their arguments.[23]

The conservatives' chief difficulty lay in wresting the power to control the
war from the Republican majority in Congress; therefore, they attacked the
confiscation bill by simply denying that Congress had the authority to control
military action. This power, they argued, belonged only to the president as
commander-in-chief. This is a rather surprising view for men who would—as
elected politicians—presumably have the power to water down any harsh legislation and who, in fact, later successfully limited the effects of the Second

---

23. Randall, *Constitutional Problems,* 301, 343–4; 375–6. Anticonfiscation men did not refer to
the letters of instructions per se, but cited the final outcome of the situation to support their argu-
ments against emancipation as a belligerent right. James G. Randall has observed that because the
U.S. government denied the British right to emancipate American slaves, this remained as the
official State Department position until the Civil War. Unionist Rhode Island congressman William
Sheffield referred to Adams's 1812 policy on January 28, 1862, *Cong. Globe,* 37th Cong., 2nd sess., 501.
Lyman Trumbull referred to Adams's 1842 proconfiscation policy on July 25, 1861, *Cong. Globe,* 37th
Cong., 1st sess., 260.

Confiscation Act. But because Lincoln had made it clear that he intended to leave emancipation to the border state slaveholders' individual consciences, Senator Lazarus Powell of Kentucky said that only the president, not Congress, had the power to declare any form of martial law. He declared that "the only safe, prudent, and constitutional rule" was to allow the great emergencies to "provide for themselves," subject to revision by the president as commander-in-chief. Democratic congressman John B. Steele from New York firmly believed that if Congress were careful to toe the line of its authority, the war would end in six months. It was probably safe for them to make this argument because Lincoln had been demonstrably reluctant to interfere with the rebels' property rights, much to the congressional radicals' dismay.[24]

The proconfiscation men's most cogent (and probably most insincere) rebuttal to this specific argument was simply that leaving the direction of the war to the chief executive would turn the president into a dictator. It is unlikely that the more radical Republicans, who always tried to push President Lincoln on the slavery issue, entertained fears about the chief executive's dictatorship. Lincoln in no way resembled the tyrants who had plagued France, Germany, Russia, and Poland twenty years earlier. When radical Republican senator Benjamin F. Wade debated the more moderate Republican William Pitt Fessenden on this point, he charged that his colleague from Maine seemed to think that once war was declared, "representatives of the people lose all power to control the action of the war." In that case, it would be much simpler "to declare your President a dictator, and make him a tyrant bestriding the Government with unlimited sway, unrestricted by Congress in any particular." Trumbull, debating Edgar Cowan, thought that what so horrified his opponent was not that "rebel property, to a limited extent," was to be confiscated. Instead, Trumbull said, Cowan objected that it would be done by the duly elected representatives of the people, and not "left to the will and caprice of the President without limitation or restraint of any kind or character upon his power." Neatly turning tables on his more conservative adversary, Trumbull then said that such a notion would be "in very defiance of the Constitution." In fact, this strategy of limiting executive power by painting the president as a potential dictator, and thus wresting control over the war effort to the legislative branch, was so successful that Re-

24. Remarks of Lazarus Powell on April 16, 1862, *Cong. Globe,* 37th Cong., 2nd sess., Appendix 109.

publicans employed it effectively throughout Reconstruction, against Andrew Johnson.[25]

Evidently, what most frightened the conservatives in both houses was the notion of a Republican Congress controlling warfare. A Rhode Island Democrat, Congressman William Sheffield, for example, said that because Congress was only responsible for making laws in peacetime, and because "peace and war are incompatible," then the powers of Congress ended when the Army was in the field in battle array. The executive was at the head of the Army as commander-in-chief, and the laws of peace had to "give way, as of necessity, to the laws of war." The position taken by most Democrats was that Congress's powers were civil, not military, and war should therefore be left to the chief executive, but Sheffield's example attributed a great deal of power not only to the president but also to the Army. Clearly, the conservatives of the 37th Congress were less afraid of Abraham Lincoln, even with the Union Army at his command, than they were of the radical Republicans in their midst. John S. Carlile of Virginia stated that the Constitution gave Congress all the power it had, and that Congress could not arrogate to itself additional powers, even in wartime. He dreaded to see U.S. citizens at the mercy of an "unrestrained Congress."[26]

In late February 1862, the Senate bill was ready to come back for debate, although confiscation measures remained under deliberation in the House Committee on the Judiciary for nearly six more weeks. Over the following five months, the main focus of the debates for and against confiscation revolved around the constitutionality of depriving American citizens—even citizens in rebellion—of their private property. Democrats, such as Kentucky congressman John Crittenden and Delaware senator James A. Bayard, and moderate Republicans, such as Edgar Cowan, concentrated their efforts on proving that the Constitution prohibited such legislation. Their position was that since secession was illegal, and the federal government had refused to recognize the

25. Benedict, "A Constitutional Crisis," in McPherson and Cooper, eds., *Writing the Civil War;* 46; this debate took place on January 29, 1862, *Cong. Globe,* 37th Cong., 2nd sess., 514–8. For example, Orville H. Browning had been arguing since the beginning of the session for the "extermination" of treason and slavery, but he also believed that Congress did not have access to these or any other "extraordinary" powers (remarks of Oliver H. Browning on April 29, 1862, *Cong. Globe,* 37th Cong., 2nd sess., 1856).

26. Remarks of William Sheffield on January 24, 1862, *Cong. Globe,* 37th Cong., 2nd sess., 501, 502; remarks of John S. Carlile, *Cong. Globe,* 37th Cong., 2nd sess., 1158.

Confederacy as a legitimate belligerent power, the rebels had never successfully abdicated their citizenship. Therefore, their rights as citizens, including their right to own human property, ought to be respected. Moreover, conservatives feared any interference or broadening of constitutional powers during wartime, disbelieving their more hawkish colleagues' assurances that relations between the government and individual citizens would return to normal the moment the war ended.[27]

Attacking fundamental constitutional guarantees of private property, even of rebellious citizens, conservatives and moderates argued, would backfire after the war was over. Conservative legal theorists, such as Joel Parker, uttered warnings that the Constitution would not withstand severe attacks on its guarantees. Kentucky congressman John J. Crittenden had already pointed this out during the summer session, but no one had taken him seriously at the time. Ohio congressman Samuel Shellabarger now warned his radical colleagues that "bad means *never* have good ends." Once the nation abandoned its Constitution, moderates and conservatives feared, all free institutions would be threatened. They agreed with Trumbull that while fighting to preserve the Constitution, they had to be careful not to violate it. Otherwise, as Kentucky representative John W. Menzies said, they would be "doing the work of the rebels" in destroying the Union and driving loyal border state men out of it. Pennsylvania's Edgar Cowan, one of the most steadfast moderate Republicans in the Senate, worried that it would be impossible to reconstruct the nation according to its founding principles after enacting confiscation legislation. Conservatives were poignantly aware that the very language with which Americans addressed these issues was transformed. "Words and ideas," Cowan fretted, were changing; the notion of reform, which so exhilarated his zealous radical colleagues, held a deep threat for conservatives. Radicals were attempting to use this legislation to reform the South and to wipe out the sin of slavery, but conservatives, reared on less utopian principles, thought that the time-honored ideals of property rights and local rule were the essence of American republican government. The precise definition of property, then, had to be left to the individual conscience. In mid-nineteenth century America, however, this was already a reactionary idea. American courts had established that private property rights had to yield

27. Vorenberg, *Final Freedom*, 15; Benedict, "A Constitutional Crisis," in McPherson and Cooper, eds., *Writing the Civil War*, 156.

to the welfare of the community. But conservatives, especially those in Congress, had to entrench themselves in a more inflexible reading of private property rights in order to safeguard America's social institutions. For conservatives in the 37th Congress, and for many of their constituents, these transformations in the language of property rights and war powers threatened the existence of the Republic. "Pass this bill," Cowan warned, and "we will then have done that which treason could not do; we, ourselves, will then have dissolved the Union; we shall have rent its sacred charter." [28]

In early March, much to the disgust of radicals, moderate Republicans led by New Hampshire senator Daniel Clark met in a caucus in order to get the confiscation bills referred to a select committee. Some thought that Clark's insistence on referral "saved" the confiscation bill, and the committee "improved it" by adding a judicial process. In effect, however, the committee referral would be the end of Trumbull's stringent bill. The judicial provision (Section 7) would be one of the key factors in making it nearly unenforceable later on. The strict judicial process demanded in the legislation meant that no estates could be confiscated, nor slaves permanently liberated, without suit being brought in a court of law, even though the law had previously contained a provision for confiscating the property *in rem,* which would have obviated any need for a court proceeding. According to historian James Rawley, Vermont senator Jacob Collamer had criticized the absence of judicial proceedings from the confiscation bill because, as it stood, it appeared to violate the Constitution, and also made it clear that Republicans were breaking their earlier promise not to emancipate the slaves. The judicial proceedings, which would have to be heard on a case-by-case basis, would have hopelessly snarled the courts for years to come. This would have presented insurmountable obstacles for persons freed by the confiscation laws, if one assumed that slaves were to be treated like all other property under the law. (Eventually the Emancipation Proclamation resolved this problem.) The committees deliberated over several bills over the coming weeks, and all of them were reported back to the Senate considerably softened and weakened. Trumbull opened the second series of debates on confiscation in

28. Huston, *Securing the Fruits of Labor,* especially chapter 9; Paludan, *Covenant with Death,* 109; remarks of Samuel Shellabarger, February 24, 1862, *Cong. Globe,* 37th Cong., 2nd sess., 937; remarks of John W. Menzies on May 22, 1862, *Cong. Globe,* 37th Cong., 2nd sess., Appendix, 147; remarks of Edgar Cowan, March 4, 1862, *Cong. Globe,* 37th Cong., 2nd sess., 1053.

the Senate, which would last from April 6 through May 6. The bill that was finally reported back from the committee was so weak that only four senators supported it; as a result, it was then recommitted to the select committee. When the committee discharged its duties, once again the weakest bill, Jacob Collamer's, came back to the Senate on May 14.[29]

Congressional moderates, especially those who served on the committees deliberating on punitive legislation, wanted to be able to influence and soften its harshest effects, without conceding to radicals the right to emancipate slaves, nor to conservatives the notion that the Congress had no right to legislate on the conduct of the war. Therefore, for example, Ohio senator John Sherman proposed a substitute that severely limited the reach of the confiscation law by carefully enumerating the six categories of persons whose property was liable to seizure. Many other moderate Republicans, such as Maine senator Lot Morrill and Illinois senator Orville H. Browning, proposed amendments and substitutes to confiscation legislation that limited the scope and severity of those laws. Some moderates, such as Ohio congressman John Gurley, even proposed their own confiscation bills. Almost all Democrats voted against all confiscation bills, even though the more martial of them occasionally claimed to approve of the principle of taking land and crops (but not slaves) from rebellious southerners. Still, those congressmen and senators who, like Orville Hickman Browning, favored confiscation but opposed such drastic measures as widespread emancipation or permanent confiscation were torn between conflicting goals.[30]

Ironically, although congressional moderates faced the hardest task—waging war without violating the fundamental principles of the Constitution—ultimately they were more successful than either radicals or conservatives in their efforts to influence punitive legislation. On the other hand, they were also probably most responsible for the worst defects of the confiscation laws. For moderates, the Constitution stood for law, order, and majority rule; they were less interested in its role as a guarantee for abstract virtues. Pragmatic and forward-thinking, they were happy to accommodate both sides when it suited their ends. Moderate Republicans (such as Congressman Albert G. Porter of Indiana) in both houses generally supported confiscation legislation, but worried

29. Rawley, *Politics of Union,* 62.

30. See Appendix 2, Second Confiscation Act, Section 5. There was only one exception: Democratic senator James McDougall of California voted in favor of the First Confiscation Act.

over the emancipation clauses, while moderate Democrats (such as Indiana congressman William S. Holman) verbally supported confiscation but never voted for it. Numerically, however, moderates had the strongest showing, because both Republicans and Democrats numbered moderates in their ranks, and both had strong influence in the Committees on the Judiciary. Moreover, with the 1862 congressional elections looming in the coming fall, radical Republicans could not afford to alienate their more moderate colleagues and constituents.

Congressional moderates took refuge in pragmatic arguments, both as to the unwisdom of extreme measures and the difficulties of future sectional reconciliation after harsh legislation. Although they opposed extreme measures, like the abolition of slavery, moderates rarely admitted explicitly that confiscation was unconstitutional. They did not hesitate to use constitutional arguments to justify confiscation, but they also believed that it was possible to reinterpret the language of the law. Of course, such bet-hedging tactics did not win the approval of congressional conservatives. New York Democratic congressman Samuel Steele had been shocked to hear "men deliberately argue that certain measures are unconstitutional, and in the next breath urge their adoption," merely for the "purpose of advancing a favorite theory." He told his radical colleagues that if they disregarded the Constitution, and "[trampled] upon the rights guarantied by it to States or individuals," they were "no better than the rebels" who were in arms against the government.[31]

But moderates had to negotiate between radicals, who (according to conservatives) threatened the sanctity of private property rights, and conservatives, who opposed all attempts to legislate a harsh war. As a result, they often appeared to be willing to soften the Constitution's restrictions in order to achieve the restoration of the Union. Although Maine senator Lot M. Morrill admitted explicitly that the Confiscation Act was "extreme legislation," he also thought that the Constitution "must not be construed to harm itself." Conservative legal theorists such as Joel Parker agreed with this view, as did the president. Although Lincoln had sworn to uphold the Constitution, he believed that the survival of the Republic and of popular government was more important than adhering to the letter of the law. Later that summer, however, he would insist that the legislators bring the final version of the Second Confiscation Act in line

31. Remarks of Samuel Steele on January 22, 1862, *Cong. Globe,* 37th Cong., 2nd sess., 403.

with the Constitution. Like President Lincoln and all other moderates, Morrill saw the seizure of rebel property as a matter of self-preservation. Illinois senator Orville H. Browning, characteristically, tried to argue both positions at once. "Let us show them that we venerate the Constitution more than we hate and detest their local domestic institution." On the other hand, if it were discovered that the South was fighting for slavery, then he was ready to "wage upon slavery a war of total and utter extermination." He vowed that there was nothing on this earth "that could stand between him and his beloved native land." The moderates, then, tried to employ both principled and pragmatic arguments. These two approaches did not always contradict one another, but they were difficult to reconcile. For example, Ohio representative John A. Gurley's typically pragmatic approach advocated a straightforward interpretation of the Constitution. A moderate Republican, Gurley had proposed his own confiscation bill early in the second session. Pointing out that there had been "enough speeches in the two houses to fill a large volume both for and against the Constitution," he preferred to assume a "common-sense position." The men who originally framed the Constitution never intended, he asserted, "that its provisions should be so construed as to destroy any of its own safeguards; that it should never be erected into a defensive barrier against a Government of which it is itself the solid basis." The Constitution should not become a weapon in the hands of the disloyal to disrupt the government further. If it were truly the basis of a republican government, then surely the governed (and their lawmakers) had a right to interpret the founding laws in their own favor.[32]

Moderate Republicans' pragmatic arguments in favor of confiscation, combined with their cautious attitudes toward black southerners, would win out in the end, and accurately reflected their constituents' attitudes. The moderate influence over punitive legislation made it difficult to effect the punishment of rebellious southerners and the extensive confiscation of their property, which led to dissatisfaction of more militant Republican voters, and may have influenced their widespread abstention from the polls in 1862.

32. Remarks of Lot M. Morrill on March 5, 1862, *Cong. Globe*, 37th Cong., 2nd sess., 1074; remarks of Oliver H. Browning on March 10, 1862, *Cong. Globe*, 37th Cong., 2nd sess., 1139; remarks of John A. Gurley on May 26, 1862, *Cong. Globe*, 37th Cong., 2nd sess., Appendix, 235.

CHAPTER 7

Slavery and the Constitution

B Y EARLY MARCH 1862, Massachusetts congressman
Henry Dawes was tired of hearing the Democrats' endless harping on the sanctity of the Constitution. The House Committee on the Judiciary was still deliberating on the various confiscation bills, but there were rumors that the committee could not come to any consensus and was ready to abandon the project entirely. Dawes now bluntly told his colleagues in the House what he thought was the "plain import" of the impassioned anticonfiscation rhetoric they had been listening to for the past months. Dawes explained that according to the proslavery men in Congress, the existence of slavery was indissolubly bound up with the Constitution, "and so an element of the essential life of the nation." Such men, he maintained, were trying to convince a gullible nation that slavery and the Constitution must "stand or fall, survive or perish, together." Further, and even more reprehensibly, conservatives were claiming that slavery was "not the guilty cause of our troubles, and that to destroy it would be to destroy the Constitution of the country." Dawes contemptuously called such ideas "oft-asserted and as oft-refuted political heresy," but the fact remained that many Americans, especially those elected to public office, were afraid to tinker with slavery precisely because they feared bringing down the structure of the Constitution. Conservatives charged the proconfiscation men with wanting to kill the Constitution rather than allow the country to continue to exist with slavery. They attributed to radicals the motto "Slavery and Constitution shall die together rather than that both shall live." But this was precisely the crux of the debate: could the Constitution live without slavery? Would an attack on the en-

emy's private property rights—even such questionable property as human beings—destroy the foundation of the nation?[1]

According to radicals, President Lincoln—who had reined in Frémont's
attack on slave property last autumn, and who stubbornly insisted that the border states ought to take the lead in emancipating their slaves—valued the Constitution above the Union. Ohio radical Albert G. Riddle was deeply contemptuous of what he perceived as the president's refusal to attack the institution of
slavery and gibed that the president "coldly and timidly seats himself on the
narrowest letter of the Constitution, and hesitatingly applies its feeblest and
shortest instrumentalities to events bearing upon slavery." Because the rebels
had gone "out of and away from the Constitution," the defenders of the Union
would now have to "go out after them." Riddle and the other radicals misunderstood the president's commitment to the Constitution. True, Lincoln was
deeply committed to the preservation of the nation's founding document, but
ultimately he thought of the Constitution as a framework that safeguarded liberty for all American citizens, not as a sacred entity that transcended territorial
integrity and the survival of republican government. Riddle's scornful comment placed Lincoln in the conservative camp with men such as Delaware senator James A. Bayard and Ohio congressman Samuel S. Cox, who believed that
modifying the Constitution even to a slight degree would eventually lead to its
downfall. But many radicals were now beginning to believe that the Constitution required reformation in order to rid it of its shameful compromises with
slavery, and that to do so would not endanger its continued existence. Riddle
ended with a warning that the world as they knew it was about to change. Moreover, he knew that the cautious views in Congress did not match those of
the northern people, whose "intuitions outrun our argumentation," and who
"reached home long ere we reach our tardy and halting conclusions."[2]

Riddle's observations, at least about the Republican voters, were accurate.
They wanted the Union armies, and their representatives in government, to
strike hard at the enemy. They were also growing increasingly critical of the

1. Curry, *Blueprint*, 85; Vorenberg, *Final Freedom*, 15; remarks of Henry L. Dawes on March 4,
1862, *Cong. Globe*, 37th Cong., 2nd sess., 1054; Democratic State Central Committee, Indiana, *Facts
for the People!*, 6.

2. Belz, *Abraham Lincoln, Constitutionalism*, 41. See also Hyman, "Reconstruction and
Political-Constitutional Institutions," in *New Frontiers*, 48, 27; remarks of Albert G. Riddle on
January 28, 1862, *Cong. Globe*, 37th Cong., 2nd sess., 499.

compromises and protections given to the institution of slavery. And when it came to the Constitution, they thought it no longer deserved their unquestioning loyalty or allegiance. Illinois senator Orville Hickman Browning also observed this shift in public opinion. He commented that Union citizens were losing respect for the Constitution. They appeared to think, he said, that "the Constitution so fetters the Government" that it would be impossible to strike "hard, powerful, and efficient blows" against the rebellion without breaking away from its restraints. Although Browning deplored this attitude, he was nevertheless correct in his assessment of public opinion. While antebellum Americans' ideas about the Constitution were often inaccurate, Republican voters' commentary on the congressional actions and debates reveals a significant shift in public opinion on the Constitution. Where they had hitherto revered the Constitution as an inviolable whole, they now turned a critical eye on the document, especially its compromises with slavery. They began to blame its protections and guarantees for the continuing military delays in prosecuting an advance on the Confederate capital, as well as the inability of Republican politicians to enact punitive legislation. Richmond was still in Confederate hands. General McClellan did not set out on his Peninsula Campaign until early April 1862, and would not reach the outskirts of Richmond until the end of May. After further delays and defeats, the campaign ended in failure. In the meantime, the heavy losses accompanying the questionable victory at Shiloh in Tennessee (April 6–7) horrified and disheartened many northerners. The military reverses seemed all of a piece with the administration's chronic hesitation to wage a decisive, vigorous war.[3]

By the spring of 1862, whenever militant northerners looked for the reason for the Army's "wonderful holding back and delay," they blamed the administration's hesitancy in dealing a deathblow to slavery. J. H. Jordan, who frequently sent John Sherman drafts of articles he was writing for local newspapers, thought he had hit upon the correct explanation of the administration and Army's hesitancy. He stated it was due to a "fear of *disturbing* or *interfering with* Slavery." Conservatives fully believed that any attack on private property, especially on slave property, would destroy the Constitution and would make it impossible ever to reconstruct the nation according to the hallowed principles of

---

3. Remarks of Orville Hickman Browning on April 29, 1862, *Cong. Globe,* 37th Cong., 2nd sess., 1858; Hyman, *A More Perfect Union,* 5; Kammen, *Machine,* 83.

the American Revolution. Republican voters, however, experienced few misgivings about the constitutional guarantees of slave property, or indeed of any property belonging to persons currently in arms against their own government. Republicans, and even many War Democrats, had argued since the secession crisis that rebel property should be confiscated as a military measure, to pay for the costs of the war, and to weaken the southern war effort. Confiscation laws were a part of the North's legislative arsenal, much like the laws passed to increase the size of the Union Army and Navy, to raise taxes and pass bond issues to finance the war, and to gain control over railroads and telegraph lines in order to strengthen communication and transportation networks. Judging from newspaper editorials on both sides of the partisan press, most prowar northerners felt that the time had come to strike harder blows at southern property, and were uninterested in fine-grained legal debates over who had control over the war effort, precisely what kind of property slaves were, or which punitive measures the Constitution permitted in times of internal rebellion. If slave labor was supporting the rebellion, then that labor must be confiscated, regardless of legalistic niceties. But that did not mean that northerners favored immediate emancipation. For the most part, the Republicans' radicalism was reserved for punishment of southerners, whose citizenship was at best questionable now in any event. They did not desire a radical overthrow of all southern social arrangements. Their critique of the Constitution revolved around its compromises with the "slave power," and with its protections of rebellious citizens' property rights. While this critique was intimately connected to a rising willingness to strike at the institution of slavery, it did not necessarily envision the widespread or immediate emancipation of black southerners.[4]

Indeed, if northerners had wanted an extreme or radical administration, one New York pamphleteer pointed out, they would undoubtedly have elected more radicals into Congress and possibly also "to the Presidency." The Republican Party had chosen Abraham Lincoln over William H. Seward as its candidate for the 1860 presidential election precisely because Seward was generally perceived as too radical. The pamphlet's author, a moderate Republican named Thomas J. Sizer, explained that slavery was deeply imbedded in America's na-

4. J. H. Jordan to John Sherman, Sherman Papers, LOC, January 25, 1862. For limited northern desire for emancipation in opposition to congressional debates over slavery, see Abbot, *Cobbler in Congress*, 143.

tional system and in the Constitution and that that was why the war was not being fought more vigorously. He pointed out that a bold man might have conducted the war with more determination, which was what public opinion now
appeared to demand. But he reminded his readers that the nation "had carefully
avoided choosing a bold man." He explained that the present generation of
northerners had been "assiduously educated into hatred of abolition." Those
who wanted a more vigorous antislavery policy had to remember "how strong
are the prejudices of a life-time, even among educated and reasoning people."
Here Sizer was referring to the anxious years prior to the outbreak of the war,
when few Americans would have called themselves abolitionists. Although attitudes toward slavery appeared to be changing now, those Americans who were
calling for a direct attack on the institution had to remember that in the past
forty years there had been a long history of compromise with, and conciliation
toward, the slaveowning interests. This was still true in the spring of 1862, when
two more northern states ratified the proposed constitutional amendment
guaranteeing slavery in the South in perpetuity. A desire for a vigorous prosecution of the war, and for punitive measures against rebels, did not necessarily
include a desire for the destruction of slavery.[5]

Further, the northern radicals could not blame an administration that was
merely carrying out the long-term wishes of the American people. For many
years, the free states constantly yielded to the encroachments of slavery because
the American people loved their republican government and did not wish to see
it torn asunder by sectional strife. In fact, Sizer pointed out, most Americans
firmly believed that "Slavery is a part of our system." It had become the standard practice of proslavery factions to "[extort] acquiescence" to their demands
by praising the Union and the Constitution. This occurred with such frequency,
he asserted, that whenever "a speaker or an editor entered upon the subject, all
knew at once that he meant *Slavery*." However, all this was changing. Now that
slavery had begun striking at the republican system of government, instead of
merely relying upon its guarantees, the northern people were becoming "eman-

---

5. Sizer, *The Crisis: Its Rationale. Part II—Restoration of Legitimate Authority the End and Object of the War.* For the federal government's appeasement of the southern slaveholding interests, see Fehrenbacher, *The Slaveholding Republic.* For states that continued to ratify Crittenden's
Thirteenth Amendment in 1862, see Bestor, "The American Civil War as a Constitutional Crisis,"
327–52.

cipated from the mental thraldom" of slavery. This point was not lost on his readers. Many northerners now spoke slightingly of the Constitution precisely because it had become synonymous with the institution of slavery.[6]

Even such a conservative border state newspaper as the *Frankfort* (Kentucky) *Daily Commonwealth* published a bitterly contemptuous editorial in late 1861 about the association between the Constitution and slavery. The editor asserted that traditional constitutional ideas had been perverted, and that "freedom, constitutional liberty, the Union of these States and American nationality" were all now said to "depend upon slavery." In fact, according to border state slaveowners and conservatives in Congress, there was "no interest of men in society that should be so carefully guarded as slavery." One could hardly dare to "say anything that looks like touching that institution," even if the "great principles of free suffrage and equal rights amongst white men are involved and liberty to be lost." While the editor of the *Commonwealth* thought it was true that slavery was protected under the Constitution, it should not have this protection "at the expense of all the other interests of man or of government itself." The moderate Republican *Boston Daily Evening Transcript* also deplored the fact that any suggestion of confiscating southern land and crops was regarded "as an outrageous attack on the sacred rights of property."[7]

In the mid-nineteenth century, the mere intimation that the Constitution could be temporarily set aside, or even revised, would have been seen—by conservatives—as radical or even anarchical. Conservative congressmen and senators made exactly this claim throughout the second session of the 37th Congress. All Americans had been taught to revere the Constitution. Indeed, slaveowners in the South had been asserting for some forty years before the outbreak of sectional violence that the Constitution was a kind of "holy writ" that could not be altered for fear of destroying it altogether. William Lloyd Garrison's famous slur on the Constitution as a "covenant with death and an agreement with hell" had brought him harsh criticism throughout the country—North as well as South. But that had occurred two years before the secession crisis; now northerners were ready to take greater liberties. Like the radical Re-

6. For a similar view, see also E. M. Norton to John Sherman, Sherman Papers, LOC, February 20, 1862.

7. *Frankfort* (Ky.) *Daily Commonwealth*, December 13, 1861; *Boston Daily Evening Transcript*, March 3, 1862.

publican senators and congressmen, proconfiscation northerners flatly refused to regard the Constitution as an inviolable entity. Therefore they were able to divide the document into its component parts, sustaining some and discarding others; but they were much less circumspect than the politicians in Washington about the language with which they expressed their critiques. Pamphleteer George Candee, for example, asked "if the Constitution is on the whole good but has one flawed clause in it," then would it not be better to "violate the law?" Candee believed that politicians were bound by their oath to disregard such a clause. The Constitution, he declared, was not a "Divine Revelation." Others saw in this new interpretation of the Constitution an opportunity for renewal and redemption. Rewriting the Constitution would be like "sloughing off the old skin for a new one." Virginian F. D. Parish thought the country was in a transitional state. America, like a snake, was growing a new skin. If the nation were not permitted to shed its skin, it would die, and the carcass would "fall into and enrich the Earth, perhaps to create a more abundant Harvest in an age of more integrity." Clearly, the old skin was a metaphor for the Constitution, and the natural process of transformation, set in motion by a tragic civil conflict, could serve to renew the nation's original revolutionary purpose.[8]

Some northern commentaries on the Constitution were downright contemptuous, openly avowing sentiments that were heard only among the most radical element in Congress. One author of a war-era pamphlet demanded to know *who* was so "profoundly exercised" for the safety of the Constitution? "The Constitution is nothing but a paper—a mere parchment—good for nothing except in so far as it answers the great end for which it was framed. The moment it fails to do this, we not only may, but should, cast it aside and make another." But the Reverend Levi L. Paine, in a sermon he preached in Connecticut, thought the matter demanded more immediate action. "I am in favor of a new Constitution as soon as we can constitutionally procure it; not a moment sooner; not an instant later." Paine wanted a charter that would be a "palladium of liberty, not a network with which to entangle freedom." Clearly he believed that the country's founding document was not strong enough or moral

8. Paludan, *Covenant with Death,* 4; Candee, *Plan for Conquering Treason,* 6; F. D. Parish to John Sherman, Sherman Papers, LOC, April 18, 1862. For similar vehement critiques of the Constitution, see also Strong, *Diary,* entry for November 6, 1861, 191; *Boston Daily Evening Transcript,* May 6, June 30, 1862; *Chicago Tribune,* May 30, 1862.

enough to save the life of the nation. By the spring of 1862, when the war in the East appeared to have been stalemated, many Republicans at home assumed that the document could not accomplish the task at hand, which was to save the nation and to restore the Union. Some went so far as to declare that the Constitution had now become irrelevant; others criticized the document on the basis of its internal contradictions. Senator Trumbull received a letter that warned, "You cannot carry on a war like this '*according to the Constitution!*'" The Constitution allowed the president and Congress to put down an insurrection, but made no provisions for what the writer called a "regular war." In other words, loyal Americans had to reinterpret the law in order to ensure victory over the rebels. Another of Trumbull's constituents thought the Constitution was contradictory in itself (he called it an "agrigate of ceeded powers" [*sic*]) and therefore questioned its rationality and efficiency. The government must now retake the powers it had so wantonly ceded to the states and to individual citizens. Political theorist Sidney George Fisher, whose ideas about the Constitution and about slavery most closely resembled those of the northern home front, worried about the difficulties inherent in amending the written Constitution. The amending power inherent in the Constitution had originally been intended as a kind of "safety valve." The fact that this safety valve had failed, however, he felt, was amply demonstrated by the southern rebellion.[9]

In early February 1862, General Ulysses S. Grant achieved signal victories in the western theater of the war with the capture of Fort Henry on the Tennessee River and Fort Donelson on the Cumberland. The capture of these two forts and of Nashville on February 23 caused a sensation in northern newspapers. More importantly, these successes virtually assured that the border states, especially Kentucky, were now safe for the Union. Although the northern home front always focused more closely on the eastern theater of the war, these developments did make it easier—for politicians, at least—to contemplate a more direct attack on the institution of slavery. Congressional radicals and emancipationist moderates were, in fact, growing bolder in questioning the right to own human property. Until this point, Republicans had promised to re-

9. Sloane, *The Three Pillars of a Republic;* Paine, *Political Lessons of the Rebellion,* 7; Fisher, *Trial of Our Constitution,* 26–7; J. H. Jordan to Lyman Trumbull, Trumbull Papers, LOC, December 28, 1862; Thomas P. Cowan to Lyman Trumbull, Trumbull Papers, LOC, December 29, 1861.

spect loyal slaveholders' right to their human property. The previous summer even Thaddeus Stevens had grudgingly declared himself willing to do so. But now some Republicans were retreating from their promises. During the debates over the First Confiscation Act, some of the more moderate Republicans had discovered a way to chip away at the legitimacy of human property without necessarily dismantling all of the slaveowners' constitutional rights. Although they had agreed that slaveholders might have some legal rights to their slaves' service or labor, they had assailed the right to own the human being himself. Republicans now expanded this argument, and supported it by reminding their opponents that the Constitution never explicitly referred to slaves, but rather to "persons held to service." In one of his proposed amendments to the new confiscation bill, Ohio senator John Sherman made a clearer distinction between "property in the service or labor of a slave" and what he called "other property." In this phrase, Sherman was careful to differentiate between the slaveholder's right to the slave's *labor* and the right to own the slave himself, body and soul. According to Albert G. Riddle, the nation's fundamental law recognized slaves only as persons, and did not "erase from them the universal quality of subjects." He thought that the phrase "persons owing service" was perhaps a sort of "recognition of an obligation imposed on them by another power," but that this obligation was more akin to that imposed on minors or apprentices, and did not deprive slaves of their innate liberty.[10]

Perhaps because of the northern public's growing willingness to attack constitutional protections of Confederate property rights (especially property rights in human beings), congressional conservatives became extremely reluctant to link the Constitution and slavery. In spite of their chronic harping on the Fifth Amendment during the confiscation debates, few of the Democrats in the Senate or in the House were now willing to commit themselves to a plainly worded statement on the subject of the right to own *human* property. By spring 1862, the subject had become so suspect, so fraught with rancor, that when discussions on slavery became too pointed, some Democrats accused their opponents of bad manners. New York congressman John Steele scolded his col-

---

10. For the role of western victories in the battle against slavery, see Paludan, *Presidency*, 125. See also Gienapp, *Abraham Lincoln and Civil War America*, 104; remarks of John Sherman on April 23, 1862, *Cong. Globe*, 37th Cong., 2nd sess., 1784; remarks of Albert G. Riddle on January 28, 1862, *Cong. Globe*, 37th Cong., 2nd sess., 498.

leagues, telling them that he thought it in execrable taste that they were tearing open "old sores," and introducing in "this, the most responsible body the world ever saw, a political discussion." But he found little sympathy among his opponents in the House. Indeed, Republicans had become so willing to broach the problem of slavery that the mere mention of the subject was now considered "clap trap," meant to impress the public with the politicians' warlike spirit. One of Elihu Washburne's constituents wryly observed that "a great many" men in Congress tried to make themselves a reputation the first day or two of the session by offering bills touching the "'irrepressible' gem'an of color." But there also seemed to be a wild sense of sudden freedom in the way some of the congressmen expressed themselves, as though they were relishing the loosening of antebellum restraints on discussing slavery. In a clever play on words, Kansas congressman Martin Conway now argued that "the abolition of slavery is no longer a 'contraband' position." Conway proclaimed that debates over slavery had become "the overruling necessity of a nation." Necessity, then, was easing the way for congressional interference with southern property rights, specifically their rights in human property, which could no longer be quite so confidently defended with constitutional arguments.[11]

The radical Republicans of the 37th Congress took full advantage of their new freedom to discuss and attack the institution of slavery. Moderates generally urged caution on this issue, but no longer placed serious obstacles in the way of antislavery legislation. During the second session, from December 1861 through July 1862, Congress debated and enacted many important laws assailing the institution of slavery. Among these were the prohibition of Union Army officers and soldiers to return fugitive slaves to their owners (signed into law on April 13, 1862), the emancipation of slaves in the District of Columbia (April 16, 1862), and the abolition of slavery in the territories on June 19, 1862. The positions Republicans and Democrats took on the various emancipationist proposals were predictable enough, following the general party platforms. Democrats thought that Congress had no power to legislate over slavery because it was a state institution. Republicans, of course, proposed various forms and degrees of emancipation, and were able to command enough of a majority among both

11. Remarks of John Steele on December 17, 1861, *Cong. Globe,* 37th Cong., 2nd sess., 81; William Cary to Elihu Washburne, Elihu B. Washburne Papers, LOC, December 14, 1861; remarks of Martin Conway on December 17, 1871, *Cong. Globe,* 37th Cong., 2nd sess., 82; Trefousse, "Unionism and Abolition," 107.

radicals and moderates to pass twenty-six antislavery laws. Despite Republicans' earlier guarantees that there would be no federal interference with the institution, the constitutional protections of slavery were now seriously under attack in both houses of Congress. This is hardly surprising, given the escalation of the war, but it did represent a marked contrast from the first session of the 37th Congress, in which slavery and emancipation had not been the subject of debate, due to the adoption of the Holman Resolution in the House and the administration's concerns about the border states' continued loyalty to the Union.[12]

On the other hand, moderate Republicans, especially in the Senate, were uninterested in using the confiscation bills as a means to guarantee or protect the freed slaves' freedom or civil liberties. These bills were primarily intended as military measures, which was what the northern public had been demanding all along. At the beginning of the session, the confiscation proposals under consideration in the House of Representatives had been split into two separate bills—one for the confiscation of property and the other an emancipation bill—but these bills were eventually subsumed into the more general Senate bills, all of which contained colonization clauses. Moreover, when radical Republicans in the House, such as Albert G. Porter of Indiana, attempted to delineate and safeguard the process of emancipating slaves, moderate Republicans in the Senate quickly moved to scotch such proposals, deeming them unnecessary and dangerous because they radically altered *all* the slaves' status as property, even those slaves owned by loyal slaveholders. In fact, the slaves' status as property had already been subtly altered by the First Confiscation Act, which indicated that it was the slaves' *labor,* not their persons, that was being confiscated. The clauses that guaranteed the slaves' future liberty, however, went too far for congressional moderates. Still, in 1862 Congress struck down several laws that discriminated against free black people in Washington, D.C., and passed the Militia Act on July 17, 1862, which opened service in the federal militia to black men.[13]

Nevertheless, as willing as Republicans now were to bring up the subject of slavery, Democrats were strangely reluctant to engage with them. In fact, dur-

12. The Holman Resolution, adopted during the special summer session of the 37th Congress, stipulated that Congress would discuss only topics of immediate relevance to the war.

13. Belz, *Abraham Lincoln, Constitutionalism,* 5; Belz, *Emancipation and Equal Rights,* 67; Belz, *A New Birth of Freedom,* chapter 1.

ing the confiscation debates in Congress, few Democrats talked about slaves at all unless they were engaging in bitter diatribes against black people. Race played a large role in the Democrats' and border state men's almost desperate arguments against releasing black southerners from bondage. Indeed, even New Englanders were capable of uttering ugly expressions of racial prejudice. In one of his anticonfiscation speeches, Vermont senator Jacob Collamer reminded his colleagues that the nation could not bring the "filthy negro" to the same level as the white man. He ended his speech with the pronouncement that "the white man shall govern and the nigger never shall be his equal," at which the galleries burst into wild applause. The acclaim from the galleries would probably have been echoed in most parts of the North. Radicals viewed slaves as potentially useful citizens who were entitled to political and social equality, while conservatives were deeply prejudiced against black people and dreaded their freedom. Moderates attempted to skate somewhere between these two positions, hoping that the war would free the slaves but believing that they were not ready to participate equally in American society. Legal theorists were of little help in this dilemma; even those who detested slavery rarely committed themselves to a clear statement on the potential social and political rights of the freed people. Francis Lieber, for example, who supported confiscation war measures, nevertheless condemned intermarriage between the races and therefore questioned the possibility of granting equal rights to black people, although he did believe that all human beings deserved access to civil liberties. On the other hand, Sidney George Fisher, who also loathed the institution of slavery, held that black people did not deserve, and would be incapable of appreciating, civil liberties or political equality. Still, many northerners—at least, all but the most conservative Democrats—were beginning to consider southern black people to be a valuable potential resource for the Union armies, although they clearly differed in their views of black people as future citizens and voters. There was, then, for the moment at least, a general agreement—whether expressed sincerely or as a matter of expedient pragmatism—that slaves were property and should therefore be confiscated from their rebellious owners as a military measure.[14]

14. McCrary, "The Party of Revolution," 330–50; remarks of Jacob Collamer on May 6, 1862, *Cong. Globe,* 37th Cong., 2nd sess., 1923; Gossett, *Race,* 94; Fisher, *Trial of Our Constitution,* 178, 290; Richardson, *The Greatest Nation,* chapter 7.

Because Democrats were attempting to minimize the discussion of slavery, they tried—as they had done since the beginning of the sectional crisis—to deflect attacks on the institution by pointing to "abolition fanatics" as the true agents of the rebellion. But such arguments were no longer quite so convincing. On the whole, conservatives found it increasingly difficult to maintain that slavery was *not* the primary cause of the war, and the recent enactments of antislavery legislation had shown that Republicans no longer considered slavery an institution worthy of protection. Indeed, since the passage of the First Confiscation Act and other antislavery legislation, the very concept of slavery as an American social institution, rather than simply as a relationship between a laborer and the individual who laid claim to "ownership" of that labor, was now under question. For that reason, if for no other, the right to own human property had lately seemed less defensible on the lips of border state representatives. Even so, they rarely stated explicitly that slaves were property; they merely said that slaves should be treated *like* other property, or more usually, "like ordinary property." For example, in arguing against the emancipation clauses of the proposed confiscation bill, Senator Garrett Davis of Kentucky pleaded, "all I ask is that our slaves shall have the same fate with all other property." That phrase in itself is revealing because it betrays an uncomfortable awareness that slaves represented a type of extraordinary property.[15]

Kentucky representative John J. Crittenden was one of the few members of Congress who spoke explicitly on human property, but even he—the purest of the old-line conservatives—refused to embroil himself in a debate on the virtues of the peculiar institution. He told his fellow congressmen that he did not propose to discuss "the question of the merits or demerits of slavery." He had no desire to debate what he called the "moral and religious" aspects of the problem, because he believed that the great compromises of the Constitution had settled those arguments long ago. The Constitution considered slaves property, and what was more, Congress had always concurred in this idea. In this, however, Crittenden was mistaken; the framers had not included the word "slave" in the Constitution, and had never specifically referred to slaves as property, but rather as "persons held to service." But Crittenden now came to the heart of his speech, in which he equated the right to own slaves with what he claimed to be the "great object" of every government. According to the Kentucky congress-

<hr>

15. Remarks of Garrett Davis on May 1, 1862, *Cong. Globe*, 37th Cong., 2nd sess., 1903.

man, the purpose of every good government was the security of property. No doubt most Americans would have agreed with him; but the more warlike among them would have argued that the southern rebels had disrespected northerners' right to jointly owned federal property when they had seized the forts and arsenals in the previous year. Moreover, many northerners—both politicians and voters—were beginning to believe, whether explicitly or tacitly, that the definition of property was changing. During the past fifty years, American ideas about property, especially property in real estate, had already undergone a transformation from regarding land as a static possession to treating it as a dynamic source of wealth and independence. Property might indeed be sacred, but Republicans no longer agreed with proslavery Democrats that property in human beings was explicitly protected under the Constitution; nor did they believe that property rights were unassailable and unlimited. American law had permitted interference with private property rights if such intervention was deemed to the benefit of the community as a whole. Civil liberties had to bow to the rule of law. In other words, the exigencies of an internal rebellion might curtail private property rights, and might even place limits on the kinds of property an American citizen had a right to own. Indeed, the southern insistence that the Constitution protected the institution of slavery, and treated slaves purely as chattel property, was already an anachronism in 1862. And because nineteenth-century Americans considered labor to be the source of wealth and capital, the labor that was owed to a rebel—that is, labor that was legally considered to be property—would be an especially important object of confiscation. Republicans like Abraham Lincoln also insisted that every man, including every black man, was entitled to the fruits of his own labor. But this idea was heard less often in congressional speeches than the notion that, for the moment, rebels had no right to the protection of property that was being used in support of the war effort.[16]

According to Crittenden, however, the security of *all* property was necessary for peace, prosperity, and harmony, and no government could expect to prosper without it. Property "elevates the man; it gives him a feeling of dignity." Indeed the sanctity of property was so deeply rooted in the American mind that

---

16. Friedman, *History*, 235–6; Hall, *The Magic Mirror*, 99, 114; Novak, *The People's Welfare*; Peterson, ed., *Democracy, Liberty and Property*, 102; Boritt, *Lincoln and the Economics*, 176; Huston, *Securing the Fruits of Labor*, 131–2.

it had become the "animating spirit of the country." Crittenden thought that with an ample supply of men and arms, there ought to be no need to attack fundamental American ideas of the right to property ownership. But nowhere in this impassioned speech did he actually defend the right to own human property, except to say, somewhat lamely, that Washington himself had held slaves before and after the ratification of the Constitution. But proslavery border state representatives had already lost a great deal of ground. Indeed, Crittenden put forward these arguments on April 23, a week after president Lincoln had signed the law that released slaves from bondage in the District of Columbia.[17]

A further complication in the debate over the confiscation of human property was the conservatives' inability to convince their opponents that not only were slaves legitimate property, but also that slaves did not differ qualitatively from any other kind of property, such as land and crops. This was essentially a contradictory and irrational position, because such an argument would no doubt make it easier to confiscate slaves along with other rebel property. But conservatives hoped that in this way they would be able to bow to public pressure to confiscate Confederate private property without having to free any slaves captured along with livestock or crops. Because slaves did not differ essentially from other forms of property, conservatives claimed, the government would have to retain ownership of them, and would thus be able to avert the threat of widespread emancipation. The idea that human property was identical to all other types of property was actually somewhat revolutionary, because American law had always acknowledged that slaves were a different kind of property, both obliquely in the Constitution and more explicitly in local or state laws, which contained provisions for extra safeguards and protections of human property. Such arguments strike us now as callous in the extreme, but nineteenth-century Americans—even many of those who were now advocating the confiscation of human beings—had not yet been able to rid themselves of the notion that coerced agricultural labor was a vital resource, whether for the Confederacy or for the nation as a whole. This would become more glaringly obvious later in 1862 as the northern public contemplated the widespread emancipation of the South's labor force.[18]

17. Remarks of John J. Crittenden on April 23, 1862, *Cong. Globe,* 37th Cong., 2nd sess., 1803.

18. Fehrenbacher, *The Slaveholding Republic.* For the southern constitutional defense of slavery, see also Tise, *Proslavery.*

When Lyman Trumbull had introduced his original confiscation bill the previous December, he had simply proposed to emancipate slaves, without subjecting the confiscation of human property to the same legal restrictions as "ordinary" property in land and crops, which required condemnation proceedings by the attorney general. That bill had been referred to the Committee on the Judiciary and was reported back on March 10, 1862, with a much more rigorous provision attempting to distinguish more carefully between loyal slaveowners and rebels. In order to obviate further discussion, Trumbull substituted another bill, which, according to Democrats, still did not discriminate adequately between guilty political and military leaders and innocent citizens, who upon proof of their loyalty ought to be able to retain their human property.

Several moderate Republicans proposed other bills or amendments to refine further Trumbull's new bill. For example, on April 10, Ohio senator John Sherman proposed a substitute to the bill reported back from the Committee on the Judiciary, because he thought that bill drew "artificial distinctions" between slaves and what he called the "other property of the same rebels." He thought this showed that the government was now "pursuing the right of confiscation rather against slavery than against the rebels." Confiscation was supposed to be a weapon against traitors, not a tool for emancipation. If moderates like Sherman were troubled by the emancipation clauses in the Confiscation Act, it was not because they approved of slavery—most of them certainly did not. Rather, like conservatives, they believed that freeing the slaves was not the primary aim of the war and therefore should not be the primary aim of confiscation. So long as slaves were treated like other property, congressional moderates could justify their actions as war measures, rather than as radical social reform.[19]

But slaves were not "ordinary" property, and now that they were fleeing from bondage it was becoming increasingly difficult to convince anyone that they were. Indeed, American courts had not sought to maintain the fiction that slave property was legally identical to "ordinary," nonhuman property. Moreover, slavery required much more rigorous safeguards than houses, livestock, crops, or money in the bank. Because of the increase in the slave population, and the chronic southern fear of slave insurrections, slaveowners had always demanded the right to acquire new lands west of the Mississippi, and even eyed

---

19. *Cong. Globe,* 37th Cong., 2nd sess., 1604. Sherman's amendment eventually became the fifth section of the second Confiscation Act (see Appendix 2).

Cuba and Latin America as possible venues for the expansion of slavery. Defenders of slavery continually had to fight and compromise with free-labor advocates for new states and territories. The previous year had seen bitter contention about a new constitutional amendment guaranteeing slavery in perpetuity, which had been proposed (and ratified by several states) as part of the Crittenden Compromise. That amendment, along with all its attendant guarantees and protections, had died without hope of resurrection. The Peace Convention of 1861 had foundered on precisely the issue of the expansion of slavery into the territories, which had also formed an important plank in the Republican Party's platform. There was to be no extension of slavery westward; the new territories and subsequent states were to be kept open for free labor. Although in their first session the members of the 37th Congress had passed the Crittenden-Johnson Resolution, agreeing that it was not their intention to interfere with state institutions, there was now no hope of such bipartisan cooperation on this issue. And by now the most ardent defenders of human bondage had left Congress for the Confederacy.

For these reasons, the increasing awareness of the insecurity of slave property struck harder than insecurity of other, less questionable forms of property. Conservatives and moderates realized that radicals were not only besieging rebellious southerners' right to hold lands and crops: they were attacking the fundamental idea of slaves as legitimate property. For those who opposed slavery, however, the very fact that human property needed greater protection than "ordinary" property was sufficient proof that it did not deserve to be protected by the Fifth Amendment. Such discriminatory practices were clearly unconstitutional. Moreover, slavery had always conferred greater power and higher status—even an "aristocratic" distinction—upon slaveholders, which was contrary to American democratic ideals. Congressman Martin Conway of Kansas stated that "security is the great necessity of slavery; security is what it wants and must have." All Americans understood that the "value of property in slaves, like that of any other, depends on its tenure," but that was precisely the rub. A "secure tenure," he said, was much more difficult to obtain for slaves than for "ordinary property," which, he claimed, would be safe under all but the "wildest anarchy." Since he was an opponent of confiscation legislation, Conway appeared to hint that he considered such laws to be tantamount to "wild anarchy," but even he did not believe that slave property should receive greater consideration than property in land and crops. According to Republican Pennsylvania senator David Wilmot, slaveowners claimed "special guarantees" for the protection of slavery, and demanded exemption for it from the "hazards and necessities of war," but because slaves were an important resource for the Confederate war effort, they should be treated exactly like all other war matériel.[20]

That was precisely the point. If slaves were war matériel, they could be confiscated. But in spite of the fact that conservatives were constantly arguing that slaves should be treated "like other" property, they still demanded, as Wilmot had pointed out, special guarantees for this specific type of property. In their chronic linking of human property to the constitutional protections of all other private property, conservatives had finally pushed the radicals too far. Radicals and antislavery moderates had been willing to accept (for pragmatic reasons) the conservatives' contention that slaves were a legitimate form of property, but the callous refusal to recognize black persons' innate humanity was now offensive. Massachusetts Republican congressman Henry Dawes was appalled that there was "a class of persons . . . who, while they entertain no doubt of our power and the expediency of its exercise, to confiscate the property of rebels, still deprecate all interference with their slaves." He complained that those who argued for property confiscation that excluded slaves "constantly raise[d] imaginary distinctions, putting slave property on grounds high above other rights of property which should exempt it from the casualties common to all municipal rights." According to such arguments, slavery was supposed to possess a "constitutional immunity, wholly unknown to and above all other rights of property." Dawes refused to regard slavery as "possessing a sanctity akin to that which attaches to the Constitution."[21]

The final version of the Second Confiscation Act never explicitly referred to a loyal slaveholders' absolute right to own slaves, but rather always defined the right to own "labor allegedly due" to the owner. Under southern states' Black Codes, slaves had no right to make contracts on their own behalf, but the law

---

20. Huston, *Securing the Fruits of Labor*, 297; remarks of Martin Conway on December 17, 1861, *Cong. Globe*, 37th Cong., 2nd sess., 84; remarks of David Wilmot on April 30, 1862, *Cong. Globe*, 37th Cong., 2nd sess., 1873. David Wilmot had become a "Free Soiler" when he entered Congress in 1849. In 1856 he joined the Republican Party as a protest against the expansion of slavery into the territories.

21. Remarks of Henry L. Dawes on March 4, 1862, *Cong. Globe*, 37th Cong., 2nd sess., 1054.

presumed that because they were in a state of bondage they nevertheless "owed" their labor to their owners. By interfering in this relationship and by refusing to grant the labor the slaves "allegedly owed" to anyone else (such as the U.S. government or an Army officer) the confiscation laws were, in fact, granting the slave control over his or her own labor. This was not merely a shift in semantics; in 1862, this was a radical step toward federal interference with American citizens' right to own human beings, body and soul. The Second Confiscation Act emancipated slaves rather than transferring their ownership to the federal government; it also placed the freed slaves loosely under the control of the president. The law authorized the president to "employ as many persons of African descent as he may deem necessary and proper for the suppression of this rebellion, and for this purpose he may organize and use them in such manner as he may judge best of the public welfare." This attitude was in harmony with northern public opinion on the future emancipated slaves. The northern home front hoped to keep the freed slaves in a quasi-free relationship with the government or the Army, without necessarily returning them to an entirely unfree condition. Within a few months of the outbreak of war, even those northerners who expressed virulently racist sentiments realized that many slaves were deciding their future for themselves. It was doubly difficult to claim ownership of property that was exercising free will. Democratic senator John Henderson of Missouri pointed out the problem of maintaining property in human beings when those human beings spurn that role. He thought that the confiscation law would permit slaves to make a judgment on the loyalty or disloyalty of their masters. This was especially troubling because, according to Henderson, there was "no practical appeal from the decision of the slave." Although as a border state senator, Henderson always vehemently opposed confiscation, he was also aware of the myriad difficulties and contradictions inherent in attempting to maintain possession of human beings with free will.[22]

Since the secession crisis, the majority of northerners—of whatever political conviction—had been firmly convinced that property confiscation was equivalent to a vigorous prosecution of the war. While conservatives generally deplored extreme measures, few loyal Democrats wanted to be thought "soft"

22. See Appendix 2. Remarks of John Henderson on April 8, 1862, *Cong. Globe*, 37th Cong., 2nd sess., 1575.

on the war effort, in spite of their misgivings about emancipation. Confiscation struck at southern land, crops, money, arms, and livestock. On the other hand, emancipation would undermine not only a social institution that was helping to maintain the superiority of the white race, but also, according to Democrats, the constitutional protections of all property rights. Unlike wartime confiscation, emancipation was the permanent destruction of an entire class of property rights—the property rights in human beings. Confiscation and emancipation were not synonymous in conservatives' minds, but what conservatives (and many moderates) failed to realize was that all confiscation legislation would soon play a significant role in the escalation of "hard war" sentiment in the North. Northern citizens had been pushing for punitive legislation, but the congressional debates and the passage of antislavery laws also served to further exacerbate public opinion on the treatment of rebel citizens. As northerners reacted to congressional debates, their views frequently became highly charged with expressions of anger and vengeance. The growing punitive sentiment was not lost on congressional moderates. Therefore, even such conservative senators as Kentucky's Unionist Garrett Davis and Pennsylvania's Republican Edgar Cowan were able to argue good-humoredly over which of them was the more ardent "confiscation man."[23]

Unfortunately for conservatives, however, it was impossible to marshal logical arguments in favor of confiscating slaves without setting them free. While it was true that many northern voters were rather in favor of such a plan, politicians in Washington were much more reluctant to argue that slaves could be confiscated without being liberated. Similarly, conservatives who opposed emancipation, while pretending to approve of a vigorous conduct of the war, confronted an impossible logical hurdle. It was absurd to consent to property confiscation, all the while maintaining that slaves were a legitimate form of property, and then deny the right to take them along with other possessions. Some members of Congress still hoped that it would be possible to confiscate slaves without necessarily interfering with their status as property. But because this idea placed slaves squarely in the position of cattle, such an argument required an implicit assertion that they were not fully human or that it might be

---

23. The discussion between Edgar Cowan and Garrett Davis took place on May 6, 1862 (*Cong. Globe*, 37th Cong., 2nd sess., 1965). Cowan was a Republican, but he was extremely moderate. He voted against the Second Confiscation Act.

possible to re-sell or re-enslave them after the war. Considering the shift in attitudes even among conservatives in Congress, none of them felt able to make this kind of statement.[24]

In the end, congressional moderates who wanted to confiscate property without liberating slaves had to bow to *force majeure*. No Democrat voted for the final version of the Second Confiscation Act. Naturally, the conservatives' desire to separate slave property from other "kinds" of property fell on deaf ears. They were simply outnumbered. Nevertheless, the confiscation bills had come back from the moderate Committees on the Judiciary considerably softened and with many careful restrictions, and without any guarantees for the freed people's future liberty or civil rights. Even so, none of the committee's moderates were able to keep Congress from including slaves among the property to be confiscated, nor were their voluminous speeches influential in keeping those slaves safely in bondage or under permanent federal (or Union Army) control.

But perhaps moderate congressmen who wished to safeguard white southerners' civil rights, while still fighting the enemy with all the weapons at their command, were willing to relinquish some hold over the "sanctity" of slavery, while at the same time carefully restricting the government's, and the Army's, ability to capture rebel property. The Second Confiscation Act did not indicate who was to be responsible for adjudicating the guilt or innocence of persons accused of treason, for seizing the property of the guilty, or indeed how this capture would be carried out. Over vehement conservative objections, however, the law did set slaves free without further ado, especially if one did not treat them as "ordinary" property in the condemnation proceedings. As a result, the final version of the Second Confiscation Act made it relatively easy to emancipate slaves, and difficult (at least, legally) to confiscate any other kind of property. The relative ease or difficulty of legal confiscation may be a nice point in light of the routine and widespread confiscation and destruction of southern

---

24. I found evidence for the view that confiscated slaves should be re-enslaved or re-sold in northern manuscript letters (see chapter 9), newspaper editorials, and pamphlets, but I found no evidence that anyone in Congress thought so. On July 14, 1862, Abraham Lincoln did, however, send a message to Congress asking them to consider the inclusion of an addendum to a compensated emancipation bill which made it possible for states to re-enslave their freed slaves if they returned the government's compensatory payments. See Freehling, *The South vs. the South*, 107.

property by the Union armies, but the constitutional guarantees of private property rights forced Republicans to engage in prolonged debates over this controversial legislation. Still, they managed to obtain enough votes from both radicals and moderates to launch a grave attack on property in slave labor. When the final version of the law came up for a vote later that summer, the Democrats in the 37th Congress would have to acknowledge themselves beaten.

CHAPTER 8

The Northern Public, Slavery,
and Hard War

O N APRIL 23, 1862, after reading one of Senator John Sherman's moderate speeches on confiscation in his newspaper, the father of two Union soldiers fired off an angry letter protesting that Sherman was still being far too careful of rebel property rights. He now demanded that the Ohio senator immediately furlough both of his boys. "If you cant confisticate the property of the Rebbles," he declared, "you cant ceepe my sons." He was not prepared to sacrifice the lives of his beloved sons for a government that was unwilling to fight the war with all the weapons at its disposal. The only way to win, he told Sherman, was to "ask no quarter and give none, destroy the [w]hole country, and slay everything you come toward." Belligerent northern citizens, in contrast to their more cautious representatives in Washington, had no trouble linking the confiscation of rebel land, crops, and slaves with national war aims. They were tired of the politicians' endless harping on rebels' private property rights, they were tired of continual efforts to conciliate slaveowners in the South and in the border states, and above all, they were tired of all forms of negotiation, compromise, and discussions about principles. Militant northerners had no interest in reconstructing the Union "as it was"; indeed, what many of them wanted now was an *"overwhelming, crushing, exterminating* blow." Judging from this correspondence, northerners also believed that Congress was able to exercise a great deal of control over the Union military effort.[1]

1. R. Buckley to John Sherman, Sherman Papers, LOC, June 8, 1862; Sherman Blocker to John Sherman, Sherman Papers, LOC, April 23, 1862; A. B. Allen to Zachariah Chandler, Zachariah Chandler Papers, LOC, April 23, 1862.

Winning the war would involve personal attacks against individual southerners, not conciliation or negotiation with rebellious states or with the Confederate government. Republicans in Congress and at home believed that the
confiscation of southern property was a military necessity, but the voters also
saw it as a way of achieving retribution against the rebels and reimbursement
for losses incurred as a result of the war. This view was not entirely as shortsighted about the future of the reunion of the states as it may sound. While conservatives and moderates in Congress lamented the harshness of confiscation
legislation, claiming that it would make a peaceful reconstruction of the Union
nearly impossible, Republican voters at home thought that there was simply no
point in fighting the war if the South were left intact to rise again or if, at the
very least, the South were not thoroughly brought in line with northern values
of free labor, industry, enterprise, and democracy.

Deliberations about principles (or, indeed, reliance on all forms of rhetoric)
were now thoroughly discredited; bellicose northerners equated oratory with
compromise, weakness, and even with the old wicked institution of slavery.
Moderate Republicans in Congress might have hesitated to use military necessity as a justification for harsh wartime legislation, but their constituents contemptuously dismissed such quibbling. They were far less hesitant to equate
confiscation legislation with a military victory and with personal retribution
against individual southerners. For example, an Indianan begged Elihu Washburne not to allow Congress to adjourn "until you pass a strong and stringent
confiscation act and provide that the leaders of this rebel[l]ion shall be hung—
confound this sympathy for them." An Ohio resident responded to a speech
Senator John Sherman gave in mid-March on the probable extinction of slavery as a result of the war. He told Sherman that popular feeling ran high for the
passage of a stringent Confiscation Act that would "reach all rebels in *every possible way.*" Moreover, the administration had been far too tender of the "supposed rights of the rebels under the Constitution." He ended his letter with a
strongly worded warning. He told Sherman that "the masses are ripe and ripe
for the most thorough kind of dealing with the southern hell hounds (pardon
the expression)."[2]

But progress on any "thorough kind of dealing" was painfully slow.
Throughout the month of May the confiscation bills remained under delibera-

---

2. A. Bleck? [signature illegible] to Elihu Washburne, Elihu B. Washburne Papers, LOC,
March 12, 1862.

tion in the Senate Committee on the Judiciary. Around this time the House committee reported back two separate bills: H.R. 471, a property confiscation measure, and H.R. 472, an emancipation bill. The congressmen agreed that the measures would be debated jointly beginning on May 20 and that a final vote would be taken on both bills on May 26. During that week the congressmen presented enough speeches to fill a separate appendix volume of the *Congressional Globe*. In fact, the House had to hold evening sessions on May 22 and 23 to accommodate all the members who wished to speak on confiscation. The militant northern home front reacted to this outpouring of oratory with predictable irritation, especially because only the most radical congressmen, such as Thaddeus Stevens, were willing to commit themselves to the seizure of "every foot of land, and every dollar of [rebel] property." Most Republicans in Congress were much more circumspect in their discussions of confiscation; they had no desire to figure as tyrants in the eyes of their more moderate colleagues, whose votes they needed to pass punitive legislation.[3]

Much of the Republican home front's impatience with rhetoric was tied to the political debates over the constitutional guarantees for rebel civilians' property rights, but war-minded northerners were equally tired of pronouncements by military officers. The officers' more pugnacious proclamations were inevitably revoked by the president, while their more peaceful edicts simply aroused the ire of militant citizens. Until 1862, most Union generals followed a conciliatory policy toward white southerners, which included respecting their property and returning runaway slaves to their owners. In a December 1861 editorial entitled "Slavery, the War, and Proclamations," the *Boston Daily Evening Transcript* declared that the Union now consisted of "a people and an army led by a debating club." An anonymous pamphlet published the following summer similarly decried the propensity of politicians and Army officers to content themselves with beautiful rhetoric as a substitute for aggression toward the enemy. According to the author, an army led by words alone could not achieve significant military victories, "unless our armies advance and read them to the enemy." The *North American Review* observed sarcastically that "siege guns, shells, solid shot, telescopic rifles, and Minié bullets are as nothing when compared with a proclamation." Nineteenth-century Americans loved a good speech, but by mid-1862, Republican voters had reached the end of their patience with oratory. Northern newspapers reported endless proclamations and

3. Quoted in Brodie, *Thaddeus Stevens*, 166.

"general orders" issued by Union Army officers, especially those addressing the southern civilian population. Therefore it appeared that while the home front seethed as Congress pondered the constitutional rights of rebels, the northern armies had to content themselves with proclamations that sounded grandiose and accomplished nothing. By late May, General George B. McClellan's Virginia campaign was grinding to a halt. Robert E. Lee was driving McClellan off the Peninsula, and General Thomas J. "Stonewall" Jackson was pushing General John Pope back toward Washington. In the early days of the war northern newspapers had rhapsodized over General McClellan's blue eyes and self-possessed demeanor, and young women had idolized the handsome general. But now many citizens were beginning to grow impatient with his endless delays. One young Ohio lady looking at a portrait of McClellan, when told it was a good one, commented that any artist could get a good likeness of the general because he was always "setting still." And one of Elihu Washburne's correspondents, who was thoroughly disgusted, thought that while "our western Soldiers [were] doing Bravely," General McClellan was an "old foggey." Abolitionist Frederick Douglass also commented with biting sarcasm that "it is enough to exhaust the patience of Job, to read every morning, for six months, that 'all is quiet on the Potomac,' [and] that the rebels are evidently expecting an attack, which expectation our Generals are determined to disappoint."[4]

Many Union citizens believed that the idea of fighting a war along stated principles, and engaging in rhetoric about these principles (such as discussions concerning the constitutionality of certain military actions, or adherence to international codes of civilized warfare) epitomized modern weakness. Around this time the term "modern warfare," inevitably used in a pejorative, contemptuous sense, began to appear frequently in northern pamphlets, newspapers, and private correspondence. Northerners thought that the real definition of warfare lay somewhere in the heroic past, when warriors had not hesitated to

4. *Boston Daily Evening Transcript,* December 20, 1861; Democratic State Central Committee, Indiana, *Facts for the People!,* 6; [Joel Parker], "The Character of the Rebellion, and the Conduct of the War," *North American Review,* October 1862; Basler, *Collected Works,* 4:531–2. For a similar view, see the *Philadelphia Inquirer,* December 21, 1861; Grimsley, *Hard Hand of War,* 3; Doughty and Gruber, *The American Civil War,* chapters 2 and 3; Sutherland, *The Emergence of Total War,* chapter 1. This anecdote was recounted in a letter by Edwin B. Nugent to Israel Washburn, Israel Washburn Papers, LOC, September 11, 1862; Tilson Aldritch to Elihu Washburne, Elihu B. Washburne Papers, LOC, March 7, 1862; from "The State of the War," quoted in Foner, *Life and Writings,* 209.

strike a mortal blow against an enemy. Many northerners, especially Republicans, now concluded that modern warfare was synonymous with abstract principles, flowery speeches, extreme courtesy toward enemy soldiers, and a too-careful regard for the foe's rights and goods. Modern warfare was characterized by explanations, excuses, and persuasion. But common sense dictated that war should cause destruction and suffering for the enemy. According to historian Charles Royster, no Civil War general had read Prussian military theorist Karl von Clausewitz's *On War*, which had not yet been translated into English. A standard nineteenth-century definition of war appeared in a publication by the famous pamphleteer Charles Janeway Stillé, who may have been influenced by Clausewitz: "For what is all war but an appeal to force to settle questions of national interest which peaceful discussion has failed to settle; and what is an army, but only another argument, the *ultima ratio,* which, if successful in decisive battles, must give the law to the conquered?" [5] That is, since political arguments had failed, the Union Army would now have to use force to reestablish the laws of the land. Force would triumph where reason had foundered. Even the Reverend James Ward, a conservative pro-Union minister living in Alexandria, Virginia, demanded a hard war policy. He espoused Christian principles of forgiveness, forbearance, and charity—even toward the enemy—and had little sympathy with the harsh rhetoric of his more warlike contemporaries, but there were limits to Reverend Ward's patience. Early in December 1861, after commenting on the opening day of the regular congressional session, he confided to his diary that "[a]ll our loyal people ask that the houses and lands and gold and silver, and stocks and securities, and cotton and powder and cannon and ships of Jefferson Davis and his robber associates, should be confiscated, and, rather than it should be used to damage and destroy the Union, should be annihilated." [6]

A similar denunciation of "modern" warfare appeared in a pamphlet published in 1862 by New York businessman Sinclair Tousey, who was deeply contemptuous of what he called "this new soft war policy." Harsh war was a military necessity, and soldiers who were fighting at the front should be supported

5. Charles Janeway Stillé, *How a Free People Conduct a Long War: A Chapter from English History* (Philadelphia: Collins, 1862) reprinted in Freidel, *Union Pamphlets of the Civil War;* Royster, *Destructive War,* 353; Stillé traveled extensively in Europe, and may have read *On War.* James T. Ward, manuscript diary, LOC, entry dated December 5, 1861.

6. Grimsley, *Hard Hand of War,* 31.

by decisive measures at home. "It is a new idea," Tousey claimed, "that in war a measure tending to weaken your enemy is vindictive. War means destruction. To destroy your enemy is not vindictive." In fact, it was the nation's duty, "in justice to those who fight [our] battles," to assail the enemy in all his weak points, specifically his property and his slaves. Such a policy would destroy the southern armies because the Confederacy's white men would now be forced to produce or starve. Further, he had nothing but contempt for those weak-minded northerners who sought to enjoin against the confiscation of slaves. "The skulls of our brave boys are made into drinking cups by the very rebels whose slaves we propose to confiscate, and when we say deprive them of the power to polish more skulls, we are accused of being 'vindictive.'" Tousey's view was representative of not only the warlike element on the home front, but also of many Democrats who otherwise deplored interference with the institution of slavery. The moderate press, while not explicitly endorsing sweeping confis-cation legislation, nevertheless supported the idea that warfare should be de-structive to the enemy and calmly accepted the fact that it would ultimately cause the civilian population to suffer.[7]

However much the northern public may have wished for decisive action on the part of the government and the Army, their hopes were continually frus-trated by conservative political opposition to harsh legislation and punitive ac-tion. In early March, Indiana banker Calvin Fletcher pointed out the difference between home front opinion and that of the government, which had "tried to plaster up secession to make it as easy as possible to win the disap[p]ointed back to obedience. I think it needs a retribution of greater severity than our public authorities are disposed to give it." Radical newspapers like the *Chicago Tribune* denounced conservative members of Congress who voiced their op-position to the Second Confiscation Act. "The reactionary party in Congress have mustered all their forces to defeat the confiscation act," the *Tribune* pro-nounced. Their conservative ideas were born of a "mawkish kindness" that flinched at proposals to seize enemy property. It appeared that the administra-tion had decided that their harshest weapons should be "sugar plums." Such policies, most Republicans believed, only served to strengthen the rebellion. The only way to achieve victory was to punish the traitors, "impoverishing and

7. Tousey, *A Business Man's Views of Public Matters*, 35; see also *Daily National Intelligencer*, March 8, 1862; *Philadelphia Inquirer*, April 5, 1862.

subjugating them." In fact, many northerners now became quite blunt in their avowal that the only way to win the war was to crush the rebels. There was no time now for "silly sentimentality" (no doubt referring to the conservatives' frequent asseverations that southern rebels were fellow citizens). Whoever struck the "freest, fullest, *foulest* blow" would win the war.[8]

There was little evidence of "mawkishness" among Republican citizens. Vehement sentiments toward individual rebels were especially evident in speeches whose purpose was to inspire public support for the Union cause. Throughout the first two years of the war, all the major cities in the North held mass rallies and invited prominent men of affairs to give speeches in support of the war effort. Somewhat paradoxically, rhetoric about the sanctity of the Constitution could coexist comfortably with bloodthirsty language about personal attacks on rebellious citizens. Militant northerners never hesitated to brandish the Constitution or the Union when it suited them to do so, even though they also frequently criticized the document. The point of such speeches was to rouse fervor, not necessarily to put well-reasoned arguments before the people. In articulating ideas about the conduct of the war, Union rally speeches made use of ferocious, if somewhat vague rhetoric, usually to wild applause. At one such rally held in Union Square, a New York attorney named Charles King exhorted his audience to "go forth and make the war as fierce and bloody as it is possible for a civilized nation to make it. No moderation is shown to us; let us show none to them." He thought the U.S. government had heretofore "acted too much on the defensive; let us now act on the offensive. [Cheers.]" Further, the North should be more aggressive and stop guarding rebel property: "This may be magnanimous, but it is not war." Republican voters' frustrations with the administration's hesitant policies, and with the dilatory nature of the Army's progress, would soon prove costly to their party leaders. In the fall 1862 congressional elections, Democrats gained a great deal of ground, adding thirty-five seats. Democrats also elected governors in New York and New Jersey. Most Republicans blamed their severe losses on Lincoln's cautious policies and the anger of

8. Fletcher, *Diary,* entry for March 6, 1862, 7:367; *Chicago Tribune,* March 5, 1862; unidentified newspaper clipping, enclosed in a letter written by F. B. Hubbell, editor of the *Daily Whig,* (Kentucky) to Robert J. Breckinridge, Breckinridge Family Papers, LOC, May 28, 1862; John C. Breckinridge to Robert J. Breckinridge, Breckinridge Family Papers, LOC, September 14, 1862. This is not the disloyal former senator John C. Breckinridge, but rather a Unionist relative bearing the same name.

northern Republicans who had demanded harsh measures against the rebels, and who subsequently abstained from voting in local and state elections. Union soldiers, many of whom were shifting their allegiance toward the Republican Party, would likely have lessened the Democratic victory. Lincoln commented on the fact that because they were away at the front, they had been unable to cast their votes in the 1862 elections; he would resolve this difficulty in 1864 by instituting absentee ballots.[9]

Although northerners had been besieging Congress for punitive legislation against the rebels, complaining that neither the government nor the Army nor the president seemed willing to take decisive action against the traitors, they had not favored a radical emancipation policy. Many historians of the Civil War era have observed that northern public attitudes toward slavery were changing rapidly in 1862, but northerners primarily viewed the confiscation of slave labor as a military measure, not as a way of overthrowing southern social institutions or as a means of elevating black people to full participation in American political life. Indeed, many northerners would have deplored a confiscation policy that emancipated slaves without retaining any control over their future. Even many of those who spoke out sharply against the institution of slavery retained deeply rooted ideas about the inherent intellectual and moral inferiority of black people, their unwillingness to work without coercion, and especially their inability to participate in self-government. While it was obvious to nearly everyone that slave labor was enormously important to the southern war effort, only the most radical Republicans wanted the government or the Army to move beyond confiscation. Many considered manual labor to be the appropriate sphere for black southerners, but they firmly believed that once freed the slaves had to remain under the control of the government or the Army. In an editorial entitled "The War Policy as to Slavery," a moderate Massachusetts newspaper probably best summed up majority opinion about what action the government and the military should take toward slaves. The *Springfield Daily Republican* had long been publishing editorials against slavery, but like most northern newspapers maintained that the end of the institution should not come suddenly. The editor thought it perfectly legal for commanders to "use"

9. Stevens, *Proceedings*, 28; for a similar view, see Strong, *Diary*, entry dated November 28, 1861, 193; Holt, "Abraham Lincoln and the Politics of Union," in Thomas, ed., *Abraham Lincoln and the American Political Tradition*, 130; McPherson, *Battle Cry*, 562.

the contraband when they came to fixed locations like forts, but that even though general emancipation might be "legal as a military necessity, it would certainly not be universally popular among the Northern home front." Like many of his contemporaries, the editor of the *Republican* believed the best thing the government could do now was to "prosecute the war to the utter suppression of the rebellion," but to let slavery strictly alone, "except so far as it . . . suffers the consequences of the war." Indeed, even some ardent antislavery activists thought the government should allow the fortunes of war to enact abolition. The firebrand J. H. Jordan proclaimed, in one of the many articles he sent to Ohio senator John Sherman, that it would be better if the government would "let the *armies* do the 'confiscating'—so far as the negro is concerned!" By 1862, Union soldiers were growing increasingly willing to receive fugitive slaves into their marching lines (if not actively sheltering them) because the fugitives proved themselves useful as laborers and informants. As one Union private put it, "If a *culled man* will dig trenches and chop timber and even fight the enemy, he is just the fellow we want." Such attitudes would make General Henry W. Halleck's 1861 General Order No. 3 forbidding fugitives' entry into Union camps nearly unenforceable.[10]

On the home front, the more thoughtful proponents of confiscation recognized that considering slaves to be property for purposes of confiscation might unleash a host of complicated theoretical and legal difficulties. For example, Lyman Trumbull's original confiscation bill had not included any specific process for emancipating slaves, beyond merely releasing them from their bondage to rebellious southerners. Moreover, the bill did not strike directly at the institution of slavery; it merely attacked the human property of rebels. That would mean that after the war, some black people would remain in bondage (presumably to loyal white southerners), while others would be nominally free. In early January, an editorial in the *New York Times* had pointed out that this law "would make the United States the greatest slave owner in the world." Since the Constitution still protected the property rights of loyal slaveowners, the government would be unable to free the slaves. Thus, the government would

10. Wiecek, *Sources of Anti-Slavery Constitutionalism in America; Springfield* (Mass.) *Daily Republican*, November 28, 1861; J. H. Jordan to John Sherman, Sherman Papers, LOC, January 25, 1862. In her *Political Opinion in Massachusetts during the Civil War and Reconstruction*, Edith Ware has found similar attitudes (94). Union private quoted in Freehling, *The South vs. the South*, 102.

then become "not only slave holder but slave dealer." The *Times* expounded on the tragic consequences of such a situation. "To wind up this drama, after the tragedy of the rebellion is closed, by a general seizure and sale of all the slaves . . . would turn the whole thing into a most melancholy farce, at which devils might laugh, but mankind would stand aghast." New York businessman Sinclair Tousey, on the other hand, casually dismissed the principle of protecting the property rights of loyal slaveholders, especially the notion that the Army should take only slaves from the disloyal. "We will confiscate every slave in the rebellious States," he declared baldly, regardless of who owned them. Still, although Republican politicians certainly expected to free the slaves of rebels, the Confiscation Acts were never intended to be primarily emancipation measures. So long as loyal slaveowners still supported the Union cause, Congress could not pass a sweeping emancipation law. They were chipping away at the institution of slavery in the legislation they passed during the spring of 1862, but the confiscation bills principally attacked private Confederate property, not slavery.[11]

In the first year of the Civil War most northerners—Republicans and Democrats—had agreed, either reluctantly or eagerly, that slaves were both property and persons. In the months after General Butler's famous "contraband" order, northerners had gleefully pointed to slaves as a legitimate form of property and therefore a fit object for military confiscation. At the same time, however, few Union citizens concerned themselves with the implied constitutional obligations toward the southern slaveowners' rights to their private property, which was being used to prosecute the rebellion. In 1862, partly as a response to the growing numbers of people fleeing their bondage, and also as a response to the disappointing Frémont situation, a subtle shift appeared in northern public opinion. The earlier bewilderment and willingness to leave the problem of emancipation in "Divine Providence" or in the military's hands was now giving way to more deliberate, and often more callous, views on slaves. In 1862 northerners were wrestling with the painful shift between slaves as property—useful to both friend and foe—and slaves as individual human beings who could act and make decisions. Union soldiers increasingly recognized both the usefulness

11. *New York Times*, January 8, 1862; Tousey, *A Business Man's Views of Public Matters* 36; for a similar view, see Grant Goodrich to Elihu Washburne, Elihu B. Washburne Papers, LOC, March 7, 1862.

and the humanity of black southerners. For the civilians on the northern home front, this change came slowly and painfully, and not always compassionately, not even for all antislavery Republicans. In the early nineteenth century, many Americans still adhered to the belief that black people were inherently inferior to white people and would never be able to participate in democratic self-government. Indeed, some American social scientists held to the theory that the black race originated from a different species, and was therefore innately incapable of improvement or advancement, far longer than did their European counterparts, such as Sir William Lawrence and Charles White. Political theorist Sidney George Fisher, who frequently alluded to such theories in his treatise on the Constitution, did not believe that the freed slaves should ever achieve social or political equality with white Americans.[12]

Radicals might have been willing to grant slaves the status of individuals, but moderate northerners experienced greater difficulty sorting out the difference between human beings who belonged to someone else and human beings who belonged only to themselves. An article that appeared in the *North American Review* later in the year explicitly stated that slaves were property and that the rebels themselves had not hesitated to use "any of our property, when it falls in their way, against us." However, the author understood that confiscating this type of property had profound and unpredictable implications. Confiscating slaves might deprive rebels of a valuable resource, but it also altered the slaves' identity. The author commented that whenever anyone suggested confiscating slaves, then "slaves immediately become persons, and very dangerous persons." Confiscation changed the identity of slaves from property to individuals; as property, a slave was subsumed by the institution of slavery and by constitutional protections of private property, but as a free human being a slave had a future, a purpose, and a mind of his own.[13]

Still, the issue at hand was winning the war, not overturning the social institutions of the South. Even though Democrats opposed all interference with slave property, many recognized that one could not leave the enemy in possession of valuable war matériel if one wanted to achieve a military victory. Radicals believed that even conservative Democrats would long ago have passed a

12. Gossett, *Race,* 54; Fisher, *Trial of Our Constitution,* 178.
13. [Joel Parker], "The Character of the Rebellion, and the Conduct of the War," *North American Review,* October 1862, 500–32.

harsh confiscation act if it had excluded slaves. The *Chicago Tribune* ran an editorial in March that declared, "Take niggers out of the list of chattels liable to confiscation, and there would be no trouble now to pass a Confiscation Act." The fact that Congress was still debating the constitutionality of confiscation (because of the Democrats' unwillingness to meddle with slavery) was proof that the administration still hesitated to wage a "real war" and was hoping to "inflict nothing worse than a gentle reproof upon the bad men." [14]

The *Tribune* had it exactly right. Democrats at home would have been satisfied with the passage of a confiscation law if it had excluded slave property, or if it had left slaves securely in the Union Army's possession. In spite of the old guard's reluctant approval of the confiscation of human property, many conservatives still thought that the seized slaves had to remain in some form of bondage. The *Louisville Daily Democrat* expressed precisely this view in a series of editorials it published in 1862. "Whatever may be the policy of the Administration in regard to slave property," the *Democrat* proclaimed, "we have no objection to the confiscation of the negroes of disloyal men in Missouri—men who are in arms against the Government." However, the *Democrat* was swift to assert, "We protest against the slaves being set free." The slaves should be confiscated and remanded to the use of the federal government or the Union Army. Setting confiscated slaves free would inflict a severe injury on loyal Missourians because liberated black people would lower the property value of slaves in the vicinity. The people remaining in bondage would become discontented with their lot and therefore less productive. An anonymous Indiana pamphleteer agreed with this view. According to him, the government ought to sell the confiscated slaves and then use the proceeds to reimburse loyal northerners for any expenses incurred as a result of the war. He complained that instead, the proposed confiscation legislation merely set the slaves at liberty, which he claimed "all the border State members join in denouncing, as an act tending to strengthen the revolt." [15]

Even philanthropic northerners felt that confiscated slaves should remain under the control of white people. Almost no one in the North thought it would be worthwhile consulting the wishes of the freed slaves themselves. Indeed, Sid-

---

14. *Chicago Tribune*, March 5, 27, 1862.

15. *Louisville Daily Democrat*, September 14, December 4, 1861; Democratic State Central Committee, Indiana, *Facts for the People!* For a similar view, see S. G. Lane to Edward McPherson, McPherson Papers, LOC, December 13, 1861.

ney George Fisher, who despised slavery, explicitly spoke out against the notion of asking black southerners what they wanted. He was convinced that they did not even desire to be free, and would in any case be incapable of coping with liberty. Fisher, like many other northerners, believed that if emancipation came too quickly and too completely, the South would be wracked by a "servile revolt."[16]

Abolitionist Lydia Maria Child recognized and deplored northerners' unsympathetic attitude toward the slaves. In an acerbic letter she wrote to former Ohio congressman Joshua Giddings praising a proconfiscation speech he had recently given, she told him that she understood that few had any genuine interest in the welfare of the confiscated slaves. In fact, "the only question [seems] to be whether it will most serve *our* interest to abuse them, or to use them." Frederick Douglass was also fully aware of the white northerners' pragmatism, but he was resigned to it. Speaking of the North's increasing willingness to consider emancipation as a war measure, he said he "gladly welcomed this great change in the public sentiment of the country," but felt he could not "rely very confidently upon it . . . either in regard to its origin or its quality." He understood perfectly that "national self-preservation, national safety, rather than any regard to the bondsman as a man and a brother, [was] at the bottom of much that now meets us in the shape of opposition to slavery."[17]

Douglass was undoubtedly justified in his suspicions. White northerners were more concerned about the outcome of the war than the welfare of the slaves. Throughout the North there was a growing recognition that the war might bring about the end of the institution, but—as much as some northerners might have desired or feared that outcome—the main point was still winning the war and beating the enemy. Some northerners, indeed, considered that emancipation might be useful as a method of "weakening and punishing" the rebels, but were less than enthusiastic about the long-term consequences. In late May one of Elihu Washburne's constituents wrote that it was time to "suppress the rebellion with a *might*, leaving slavery to take care of itself." Similarly, the *Boston Daily Evening Transcript* published an editorial in early July on a confiscation speech by Maine senator William Pitt Fessenden, praising his stance on the vigorous prosecution of the war, which would include the con-

16. Fisher, *Trial of Our Constitution*, 284–90.

17. Lydia Maria Child to Joshua R. Giddings, Giddings–Julian Correspondence, LOC, June 16, 1862; "Future of the Negro People," quoted in Foner, *Life and Writings*, 216, 218.

fiscation of slaves. The *Transcript* assured its readers that although many of them might think that emancipation would "harm the slaves, this [did] not matter because it [was] not a moral but a military measure." Indeed, even anti-slavery Republicans sometimes expressed a cavalier attitude toward freed slaves. For example, in his famous diary, New Yorker George Templeton Strong commented that it was time to enact a fair treatment of "Southern niggerdom," including a "proffer of freedom to every able-bodied slave owned by a rebel." The reason he gave for this, however, was not that it would be the just or the humane thing to do, but that emancipation would "kill rebellion slowly but surely." [18]

At the same time, regardless of their opinions on emancipation, northerners fully appreciated the importance of black people's labor. By 1862 they were still convinced that coerced labor was necessary to the success of the southern plantation economy. Emancipation created a double-pronged problem for white northerners. First, northerners feared that upon liberation all black people would want to come northward, and take work from white laborers. Second (and perhaps just as distressing to white northerners), once they were freed, the slaves' labor would be unavailable to southern agriculture. The *Cincinnati Gazette* pointed out that although slavery might end as a result of the war, the government could not turn 4 million people loose because their labor was essential to the economic well being of the nation as a whole. Whether enslaved or free, black people had to stay where they were because they were "almost the entire reliable agricultural laborers of the South." A writer for the *New York Herald* agreed, stating that it would be "extreme folly" to deprive the country of "such an immense laboring population." The *Herald* editorial stated that vagrancy laws compelling labor would keep the former slaves in line. In spite of the fact that the writer thought the freed slaves deserved "fair wages" for this coerced labor, he admitted that such a system would probably not be "better for the negroes." In the long run, however, it would be "infinitely better for the planters." But any idea of giving the freed slaves social or political equality was "an absurdity of which nobody dreams but Utopian abolitionists like [Horace] Greeley and [Charles] Sumner." [19]

18. Franklin Fairchild to John Sherman, Sherman Papers, LOC, May 27, 1862; William A. Gregory to Elihu Washburne, Elihu B. Washburne Papers, LOC, January 20, 1862; *Boston Daily Evening Transcript,* July 11, 1862; Strong, *Diary,* entry dated November 28, 1861, 3:193.

19. *Cincinnati Gazette,* quoted in the *Louisville Daily Democrat,* May 20, 1862; *New York Herald,* April 17, 1862.

Indeed, few proposals for the future of the freed slaves made sense to mid-nineteenth-century Americans, who believed that the federal government had no business interfering in social problems. A pamphlet published shortly after the passage of the Second Confiscation Act attempted to formulate a solution to the problem of confiscated slaves, but the author, Joseph Alfred Scoville, worried that there was "no reasonable answer." Scoville was convinced that while it would be dishonorable to restore slaves to their traitorous masters, the nation would be obliged to recognize the property rights of loyal slaveowners, as well as to minimize the freed slaves' potentially destructive effect on the national economy, especially if they flooded northern labor markets. This meant finding some way to keep the freed people in the South and to ensure that they would not become a financial burden on the victorious North. The nation was presented with three choices: "1. We may re-enslave him; 2. We may apprentice him; 3. We may make him wholly free at once." Because the first and third choices were unacceptable, according to the author, the only sane alternative was a system of "humane apprenticeship." Further, Scoville thought, it would be good for the freed slaves to be compelled to labor. Hard work would have long-term beneficial effects on the freed peoples' character, although in what way this would represent a change from their previous condition, the author did not explain. Still, he also believed that the black race could "improve over time," but that the government would have to become guardian of the freed slaves for generations to come.[20]

Many northerners considered black people fit only for agricultural labor and undeserving of a choice in the matter of their future; Sidney George Fisher declared that black people did not deserve, and would be incapable of understanding, political rights. They should remain forever subservient to white people, both for their own good and for the good of the nation. But some took their callous ideas a few steps further. A few even proposed innovative uses for black people's labor. One pamphleteer, for example, declared that the confiscated slaves' labor could be turned to good advantage for the North. The Civil War could become a golden opportunity to "open at once the Pacific railroad," since the confiscated slaves could immediately be put to work on laying rails. "They are not fit to be emancipated and thrown upon their own resources; it

---

20. Scoville, *What Shall be Done with the Confiscated Negroes?* Scoville thought that the freed slaves should work for free for five days a week, and be paid for the sixth.

would be but cruel kindness to take them from the plantations, where they are fed and cared for without the trouble of using their brains, and leave them to take care of themselves." However, in spite of his rather unflattering assessment, the author believed that the freed slaves would gradually acquire "manliness and intelligence" under supervision of white men. At the same time, he thought that the profits the North would earn from the roads, cities, and railroad building projects would enable the country to buy the slaves of faithful Unionists at a fair price "and thus guarantee to every citizen the value of his property." In this way slavery would lose its grip on national politics, property rights would be safeguarded, and black people would remain safely under the control of northern whites.[21]

In the meantime, however, many white northerners feared that emancipation would wreak national economic devastation. The problem, as they saw it, was that the freed slaves would refuse to work without some form of coercion, or would move to northern cities. Therefore their liberation would bring great social disruption to both sections of the country. Clearly, the northern government would have to take some responsibility for slaves liberated through confiscation, but the sheer number of freed people would make an easy resolution impossible. Conservative Delaware senator James A. Bayard, writing to his son in the midst of deliberations on the Second Confiscation Act, was convinced that "free negroes will not labor," and that even if peace finally came, "after years of devastation, [they] will again be reduced to slavery." The *Philadelphia Inquirer* agreed, but wished for a better resolution of the crisis for both black and white residents of the South. "We see it stated ... that the slaves do not work as they were wont to do when their masters were at home. They need coercion in order to make them work up to the full measure of their ability."[22]

In pressing for military confiscation of rebel property, some northerners hoped that confiscated slaves would remain under the control of the Army or the local military governors. However, when the commander of the Union forces, General David Hunter, proclaimed martial law in South Carolina, Georgia, and Florida on May 9, 1862, they were not quite ready to accept such a bold interpretation of their wishes. His proclamation declared all slaves belonging to

21. Fisher, *Trial of Our Constitution*, 178, 305; Citizen, *A View of the War*.
22. James A. Bayard to Thomas F. Bayard, James A. Bayard Papers, LOC, June 9, 1862; *Philadelphia Inquirer*, April 5, 1862.

rebels in the "Department of the South" forever free, but he did so without first obtaining the president's approval. Once again, Lincoln learned of a sweeping emancipation edict by reading of it in the newspapers. He swiftly revoked Hunter's proclamation, but did so on the grounds that the general had overstepped his authority, not on the general principle of safeguarding the institution of slavery. He further stated that as commander-in-chief, the power and discretion to free the slaves was reserved exclusively to himself, and hinted strongly that at some future date such an action might "become a necessity indispensable to the maintenance of the government." This point was not lost on the conservative element on the home front. Although the *Louisville Daily Democrat* thought it was proper that Lincoln "decline[d] to allow a subordinate to exercise such a power," the editorial's author nevertheless realized that the president had not made a clear statement protecting the property rights of Unionist slaveowners. "Well, he disapproves Hunter's proclamation, but leaves the future in the dark; still, however, urging emancipation by other means."[23]

Indeed, the president included in his proclamation a reminder to border state slaveholders that the "signs of the times" were becoming increasingly difficult to ignore, and implored them to take some steps toward gradual emancipation while they still had the chance to be compensated for their human property. President Lincoln always insisted that the impulse for emancipation in the border states should come from the citizens themselves. He had no desire to force emancipation on an unwilling and volatile population, especially one that had remained loyal to the Union, and was therefore still protected by constitutional guarantees. Moreover, Lincoln fully intended to control the process himself. While he would not permit himself to be pushed into action against slavery before he was ready—perhaps before he was convinced that the northern public would countenance an emancipation policy—by early June he was nevertheless already contemplating freeing the slaves by presidential edict. In the meantime, he kept his plans to himself, and continued to urge the border state slaveowners to liberate their slaves themselves.[24]

23. Bensel, *Yankee Leviathan,* 179; Holt, "Abraham Lincoln and the Politics of Union," in Thomas, ed., *Abraham Lincoln and the American Political Tradition,* 129; Trefousse, "Unionism and Abolition," 107–8; Basler, *Collected Works,* 5:222–3; *Louisville Daily Democrat,* May 21, 1862.

24. Paludan, *Presidency,* 127; Trefousse, "Lincoln and Race Relations," in Greenberg and Waugh, *The Price of Freedom,* 2:320; Cox, *Lincoln and Black Freedom;* Guelzo, *Lincoln's Emancipation Proclamation,* 126.

Once again many Americans applauded the president's determination to exercise his authority. The *New York Herald,* often critical of Lincoln's policies, praised his proclamation and called it one of the most significant state papers of the war, and a "Great Victory for the Union." The editors of conservative papers such as the *Herald* were clearly uncomfortable with the notion that Army officers arrogated to themselves the power to interfere with social institutions, and lauded President Lincoln's refusal to relinquish the prerogatives of his office. "Hereafter," the *Herald* hoped, "we may expect to escape the unwarrantable and ridiculous efforts of military generals to interfere with the prerogatives of the civil power in attempting to make political capital out of the poor contrabands," thus tacitly acknowledging growing sympathy toward the "poor contrabands" among northern public.[25]

Another, more volatile factor in considering the future of the confiscated slaves was the prevalent northern prejudice against black people. Racial hatred had always been a decisive element in the defense of slavery, and in the restriction of the rights of free black people in the North. By 1860 only six northern states had granted limited suffrage to free black men, and several states had already passed ordinances forbidding the entry of free black people across their borders. Northern Democrats were outspoken in their fear of the sheer multitude of black people, especially since they realized that the South was, as one man put it, a "Black Empire." In May 1862, a Delawarean wrote to Senator John Sherman in response to one of his speeches on slavery. He agreed that the institution was wicked, but confessed himself impatient with the "eternal harping upon it in Congress." He told Sherman that he greatly feared the emancipation of 4 million slaves; indeed, he considered slavery a blessing since he thought the black race a "great peril" to the peace and security of the nation. His solution to the problem of the war and emancipation was to colonize *both* the fire-eaters and the freed slaves, preferably in Texas. Even Senator Sherman himself was not immune to such ideas; on May 19, he wrote to his brother General William T. Sherman that he feared if the rebels did not soon abandon their cause, events would "force a war in the cotton States between the whites and blacks."[26]

25. Israel Washburn to Hannibal Hamlin, Israel Washburn Papers, LOC, May 23, 1862; *New York Herald,* May 20, 21, 1862.

26. Donald, Baker, and Holt, *Civil War and Reconstruction,* 326; for the rights of black people during and after the Civil War, see C. Vann Woodward, "Seeds of Failure in Radical Race Policy,"

Similarly, a few weeks after Senator Lyman Trumbull proposed his confiscation bill in the Senate, he received a letter from a Virginian warning him that it would be difficult to get support for the bill in the border states. The writer was in favor of confiscating the slaves but opposed to the idea of emancipating them, because, as he explained to Trumbull, the "great mass of the loyal citizens in this state & also the states of Maryland Kentucky & Missouri have a great *dred of free Niggers.*" The rebels, well aware of this prejudice, had been playing on these fears, telling white women they would have to "amalgamate" with the freed slaves. "Now how will you like your daughter or sister to marry a great big nigger. I assure you sir this is the kind of slang whang they will use." Although the writer thought it would be perfectly legal to confiscate the slaves, he had no idea what should be done with them, because they were not welcome in the free states. He was also sure that because "not one-fourth of them" would agree to be colonized, the freed slaves would undoubtedly become "vagabonds & nuisance . . . since they can't think for themselves or make a living." [27]

While it would hardly be fair to generalize the most egregiously callous of these sentiments to the entire northern population, it is true that in the first two years of the war most northerners did not consider black people capable of deciding their own future—nor, perhaps, of surviving emancipation *en masse.* How, then, does one make sense of these rather unsympathetic ideas in light of the Republican voters' critique of the Constitution, especially since that critique was, at least in part, based upon a refutation of the constitutional compromises with slavery in the first place? The critique, after all, implied a willingness to "shed the skin" of the snake—that is, to reform American institutions and society. The critique also implied a willingness to subvert some of the founding principles of the Constitution in order to achieve a military victory over rebellious citizens. Indeed, some Americans were growing increasingly impatient with Congress's habit of basing its actions upon "*refined,* highfalutin' principles so as to *hurt* nobody!" [28]

Although they were criticizing the Constitution's compromises with southern slaveholders and were hoping to use the document's war powers provisions

---

in Hyman, ed., *New Frontiers,* 126–7; J. W. Powell to John Sherman, Sherman Papers, May 18, 1862; letter dated May 19, 1862, in Thorndike, *The Sherman Letters,* 151.

27. Amherst Miller to Lyman Trumbull, Trumbull Papers, LOC, January 24, [1862].

28. S. York to Lyman Trumbull, Trumbull Papers, LOC, December 5, 1862.

to deprive the rebels of their property, most northerners were not yet ready to extend its protections to the freed slaves. Clearly, in their demands to attack slavery in order to hurt slaveholders, very few white northerners thought about giving any help to freed people. The rights of black people as autonomous individuals (even without equal social and political rights) would not be established until northern citizens had first shed the notion that human beings could be held as property, or, perhaps more fundamentally, until northerners had found a way to attack the property rights of rebellious white Americans. Moreover, northerners were as yet unwilling to abandon the idea that coerced agricultural labor was necessary to the economic survival not only of the plantation South, but also of the nation as a whole. Few northerners credited black people with much enterprise or intelligence; they also insisted that the confiscated slaves had to remain in the South, under some form of military or governmental control in order to carry on the region's agriculture. In spite of the fact that northerners resented the constitutional compromises with—and protections of—slavery, they were not yet ready to extend their radicalism to a critique of the "peculiar institution," nor, indeed, to their own perceptions of the initiative and capabilities of southern black people.

Given the increasing antislavery sentiment among militant northerners by mid-1862, border state slaveowners were caught in a terrible bind. After the invasion of Kentucky by Confederate forces in 1861 and especially after the western victories in Tennessee in February 1862, there was little likelihood that Kentucky would join the Confederacy. The state legislature had abandoned its neutrality stance the previous autumn, and Kentucky slaveowners now had to confront the fact that they were governed by a Republican president and Congress. Unionist political leaders such as Kentuckian Joseph Holt, who had been secretary of war in the Buchanan administration, and radical congressman Henry Winter Davis of Maryland pleaded with slaveowners to remain loyal to the Union, claiming that only the federal government could (and would in the future) protect their slave property. But border state slaveowners no longer fully trusted such assurances. If they remained loyal, they were subject to threats from the Confederacy, while at the same time their more radical fellow-citizens to the North now questioned their loyalty and, increasingly, their right to own human property. Robert F. Breckinridge's son described the situation in a worried letter. "It is thus we of the Border States, where treason & loyalty overlap, have to suffer, offer our lives to our cause, and yet mo[u]rn when it is victorious." He thought that no matter how nobly the citizens of the border states acted, "'whether in the true or false cause,' they would always be suspected, and suffer from misinterpitation [*sic*]." He thought it would be difficult to get their "northern brethren" to stop suspecting border state citizens and uttering such condescending phrases as, "such a man, though from the border, is true."[29]

Some nonslaveholding border state residents, indeed, were beginning to perceive the "signs of the times," as Abraham Lincoln had phrased it, but had strong doubts about their slaveowning neighbors' willingness to let go of their human property. For example, a Kentucky slaveholder asked Senator Sherman for a copy of one of his confiscation speeches so he could "see both sides." However, he told Sherman that it would probably be difficult to get the border state slaveowners to "give up their slaves to save the Union that they profess to be so mutch devoted too," because the institution was "rather a Sweett Morsell under their tongs." A Missouri citizen agreed with this view. Praising one of Robert J. Breckinridge's Unionist editorials, he observed that the part which "touches on the *evils* of slavery may be a little too strong for your latitude. But if it hurt, it will be because the *truth* strikes hardest." A staunch Republican from Delaware was more strongly in favor of abolition and confiscation. He warned Representative Henry L. Dawes that the "people do complain that the *Deity of Slavery* is so sacred that it cannot be touched except for its protection." He demanded to know why Dawes and other Republicans voted against emancipation, when it was clear that the slaves themselves were "the only *true* Union men in the Slave States?" At the same time, he still believed that loyal slaveholders should be compensated for the loss of their human property.[30]

29. There are numerous examples of speeches by border state political leaders exhorting loyal slaveowners to place their trust in the constitutional protections for human property. See, for example, Holt, *Letter from the Hon. Joseph Holt, upon the Policy of the Federal Government, the Impending Revolution, Its Objects, Its Probable Results if Successful, and the Duty of Kentucky in the Crisis;* Kennedy, *The Border States* (John Kennedy was a Baltimorean). See also Collins, *Second Address to the People of Maryland;* Davis, *Address of Hon. Henry Winter Davis Delivered at Baltimore;* Drake, *The Rebellion: Its Origin and Life in Slavery. Position and Policy of Missouri;* John C. Breckinridge to Robert F. Breckinridge, Breckinridge Family Papers, LOC, February 23, 1862 (the writer was not the former senator John C. Breckinridge, but a loyal relative bearing the same name).

30. J. H. Spelman to John Sherman, Sherman Papers, LOC, May 27, 1862; D. A. Wilson to Robert F. Breckinridge, Breckinridge Family Papers, LOC, March 25, 1862; W. M. Caulley to Henry L. Dawes, Dawes Papers, LOC, May 27, 1862. See also, Ware, *Political Opinion,* 100.

Border state slaveholders were right to be fearful. Republicans mistrusted the loyalty of white Unionists in the border states, especially those who owned slaves. Hard war sentiment among the northern public—even among War Democrats—had grown exponentially, especially in response to the victories in the west and the chronic defeats and delays in the eastern theater of the war. At the same time, border state slaveholders were still citizens whose rights were unquestionably protected by the Fifth Amendment. Although most politicians in Congress, even many radicals, still agreed that the property of loyal border state residents should be protected, the northern home front's attitude was much more intolerant. For example, a Buffalo man writing to Trumbull in favor of confiscation questioned whether the property of "loyal (?) slaveholders" should be protected. The mistrustful phrase "loyal (?)" was attached to many northerners' references to slaveholders who professed unionist sympathies, implying that their loyalty was so doubtful as to be of small account in considering the propriety of confiscating their property and freeing their slaves. An unusually radical view of this kind appeared in the conservative *Cleveland Plain Dealer*. According to the editor, the government and Congress had now listened long enough to the "half way secessionists" of the border states. The paper thought it was time to "let justice be meted out," and recommended that all of them should simply be hanged. Likewise, a Massachusetts man fumed that it was time to stop waging "this accursed slave holders war for the especial benefit of slavery & still be ruled by a few Pseudo Loyalists in Congress."[31]

Indeed, many northerners commented on the insincerity and duplicity of border state residents. One Union Army chaplain contemptuously observed that "all these people would be loyalists . . . if they could get rich by it & save their right of property in Negroes." Their apparent inability to prove true loyalty, because they lived so close to the Confederacy and because they owned slaves, justified depriving them of their constitutionally guaranteed property rights. For example, one Ohio voter wrote to Sherman that he was well pleased with Trumbull's bill, but thought the law should "throw the onus more clearly on the slaveholders." Unless a slaveowner had "*done* or *suffered* worthily for the cause of the United States," his slaves should all be confiscated. The writer thought that the scoundrels who were merely "watching the wind to save their

---

31. A. G. Stevens to Lyman Trumbull, Trumbull Papers, February 9, 1862; *Cleveland Plain Dealer*, May 15, 1862; Carver Hotchkiss to Henry L. Dawes, Dawes Papers, LOC, April 7, 1862.

slaves ready to cry good God, good Devil as the case may be," were "meaner" than the rebels in arms. Abolitionist Lydia Maria Child agreed. "Oh, those Border States!" she exclaimed, in an exasperated letter to Joshua Giddings. She remarked that the "borderers" were as demented as ever on the subject of slavery, but they obviously thought that it was "in their interest to profess loyalty," calling them "*disguised* lunatics."[32]

In contrast to Republicans in Congress, who stipulated that border state slaveowners' rights had to be protected, Republican voters (including many soldiers at the front) entertained much more severe views. They blamed border state representatives and their sympathizers for the weak and dilatory policies of the administration. For example, a Wilmington resident writing to his representative in the House vilified the other Delaware congressmen as "miserable Sympathizers & cooperators with rebels & vile traitors." And one of Trumbull's constituents thought that the "equivocal position of Kentucky has had too much influence in shaping the course of the Administration," while yet another cryptically described the state of Kentucky as a "strange analogy." Kentucky, he claimed, had asked the federal government to raise troops to "kill all rebel slaveholders," but at the same time demanded that Union soldiers carefully guard slave property.[33]

The growing suspicion toward the border state slaveowners, and indeed the fierce tone of northern home front rhetoric, might indicate a desire for wholesale destruction of the southern states or harsh, even cruel measures against all rebel citizens. But despite the rather sweeping nature of some of their expressions, such as a Union Army doctor's demand for the "entire extermination of the villains," northerners believed that in the long run a "feather bed war" would be more cruel than a harsh one because it would last longer and cause more bloodshed and destruction. Such a policy, which northerners called "maudlin" or "namby pamby," would permit southerners to return to power after the war was over. A German immigrant living in Illinois wrote to Elihu Washburne: "If there be any truth established by the universal experience of na-

32. Quoted in Furry, ed., *The Preacher's Tale,* 20; Eli Nichols to John Sherman, Sherman Papers, LOC, January 20, 1862; Lydia Maria Child to Joshua Giddings, Giddings–Julian Correspondence, LOC, June 16, 1862.

33. George F. Wiswell to George Fisher, George P. Fisher Papers, LOC, June 16, 1862; Joseph Barber to Lyman Trumbull, Trumbull Papers, LOC, December 8, 1861; C. K. Williams to Elihu Washburne, Elihu B. Washburne Papers, LOC, December 24, 1861.

tions it is this: that to carry the *spirit of peace* into *war . . .* is a *weak and cruel policy. . . . Languid war* can do nothing which negotiation or submission can not do better, and to act on any other principle is not to save money but to squander it." Another of Washburne's correspondents shared this view. If the country refused to fight the war in earnest, that meant that the "immense public Debt [was] only spent to prepare the way for the Slaveholders to come in & return to their old domineering position." Finally, he asked an unanswerable question: "If it was the intention to subdue the Rebellion why this wonderful Feather bed policy for Secessiondom[?]" Soft war was not only ineffective, but it actually aided the enemy in prosecuting their treasonous designs. The *Boston Daily Evening Transcript* thought that by opposing even "moderate schemes of emancipation and confiscation, [conservatives] practically tell the rebels that they may fight until they are utterly exhausted, and then be received back into the Union without punishment." While this might be called a conciliatory and constitutional policy, it "certainly ignores every principle of common sense." In fact, the confiscation law currently being debated in the halls of Congress was, if anything, milder than the 1790 treason law, which mandated a death sentence and allowed no judicial discretion on the punishment of traitors. Northern voters would no doubt have deemed any sentence short of hanging to be far too lenient.[34]

Although not surprising in the midst of a civil war, this ferocious talk probably reflected impatience with the government as much as rage with the rebels. A man from Ohio demanded to know how long it would take "this people to learn that the only way to treat this ganggrene [*sic*] of rebellion is to strike home." He prescribed a severe policy in strong language: "Give it no quarter, down with it, death to traitors & all who sympathise with traitors is my doctrine. None of this half way namby pamby dealing with traitors." Similarly, the *New York Evening Post* stated baldly that the rebels had forfeited their civil rights by the act of treason and that the only way they would be "purged of their crime" was for Congress to administer the appropriate punishment, without stopping to question the constitutionality of their actions. An Indianan named

---

34. P. A. Allaire, M.D., to Lyman Trumbull, Trumbull Papers, LOC, December 10, 1861; Frederick Hecker, to Elihu Washburne, Elihu B. Washburne Papers, LOC, December 9, 1861; Wait Talcott to Elihu Washburne, Elihu B. Washburne Papers, LOC, January 18, 1862; *Boston Daily Evening Transcript*, July 19, 1862.

Jesse F. Miller informed Elihu Washburne that his blood boiled when he heard "men commiserating with . . . traitors," who were nothing but "vipers who would fain cover our Constitution with Slime and swallow it."[35]

Nineteenth-century women might have been expected to express less war-like sentiments; indeed, women rarely wrote to men they did not know personally, always prefacing their letters with apologies for presuming to do so. A few northern ladies felt so strongly about the conduct of the war, however, that they were moved to communicate their opinions to their representatives in Washington. A woman named A. A. Cochran, who had several brothers serving in the Union Army, wrote a strongly worded letter to Elihu Washburne. She begged pardon for writing, but declared that whenever she thought of the rebels she found it difficult to keep her temper "within bounds." Although she claimed she did not wish to harm the souls of the traitors, she thought "it would be a good thing if they would all repent of their sins, and then—all get killed before they have a chance to backslide." Perhaps Miss Cochran had not thought through her ideas while she was penning her letter to Washburne; before she reached the end, she apparently thought better of her bloodthirstiness, and added a hasty postscript: "Please excuse what I have written, that was uncalled for." Another lady, named Sarah P. Edson, questioned whether the present administration's policy was not "please don't hurt, but protect the enemy." This struck her as nonsensical. She asked radical Indiana congressman George W. Julian, "Must we not *punish to conquer?*" Julian would have agreed with her, but however much the home front demanded punitive measures, and however much the radical politicians desired to gratify their constituents, the moderates in Congress remained determined to ameliorate all legislative proposals to confiscate southern land or slaves.[36]

35. N. B. Yates or Gates (signature illegible) to John Sherman, Sherman Papers, LOC, March 1, 1862; *New York Evening Post*, March 5, 1862; Jesse F. Miller to Elihu Washburne, Elihu B. Washburne Papers, LOC, April 22, 1862.

36. A. A. Cochran to Elihu Washburne, Elihu B. Washburne Papers, LOC; the date is missing, but the letter appears at the end of the March 1862 letter file; Sarah P. Edson to George Julian, Giddings–Julian Correspondence, May 5, 1862.

CHAPTER 9

Southern Land and Slaves

B Y MID-MAY 1862 the confiscation bills were again under discussion in both houses of Congress. In the Senate, during one of his many anticonfiscation speeches, moderate Republican Edgar Cowan claimed, somewhat apocryphally, to be an "especial Apostle of confiscation." But he also feared that the bills presently under consideration were hardly a "fit and proper remedy for reconciling a rebellion." Militant northerners would have disagreed with him, believing that the only way to reconstruct the nation successfully was to begin by thoroughly crushing the rebellion. But that did not mean they were blind to the consequences of punitive measures. In spite of the bellicose tone against rebels and even against loyal border state slaveowners, most belligerent northerners understood that the nation would someday have to be reunited. A Union victory, Republicans felt, ought to entail bringing the southern states to heel and permanently back into the Union. Some northerners may have loudly demanded the "entire extermination" of the traitors, but they had to accept that the government could not order the wholesale hanging of rebels. Indeed, many thought confiscation was a more civilized punishment for the rebels than execution for treason. The *Chicago Tribune* put it this way. "If the Government cannot take [a rebel's] slaves, can it take his life?" The *Tribune* pointed out that a criminal forfeited "every right which would interfere with the arrest of his act." Therefore, would it not be more humane for the government to "take slaves than to kill rebels[?]" Similarly, the *New York Times* argued that confiscation was more peaceful than warfare. "To insist upon bloodshed, when a less fatal alternative is presented, is certainly not the dictate of humanity or prudence."[1]

The Republican voters' ideas about property confiscation, then, hinted at a future policy for dealing with the southern states. There was to be a policy of severity toward the rebels, which ought to include a diminution of their civil rights and the application of an appropriate punishment. Furthermore, northern citizens would be fairly reimbursed for losses incurred during the war. This would naturally involve taking and using southern property (including, according to some especially callous northerners, the labor of slaves) to rebuild the Union and to force the South to become more thoroughly "American." In this way the South would be punished, reformed, and cleansed. Republicans at home and in Congress assumed that this project would be carried out in tandem with the might of congressional legislation and the Union armies, although the precise course of action remained somewhat unclear to most of them. What role would Federal soldiers play in the appropriation of southern land, crops, and slaves? Ought they to be permitted to forage, or even plunder, civilian property? What would happen to the property, once confiscated? And which southerners, in particular, deserved to be the target of harsh legislation? Finally, what were the long-term objects of such laws—were they to be primarily punitive, or ought they to play a role in the reformation of the South?

Some northern newspapers began voicing the curious idea that harsh war would in the long run be beneficial for the South. The *Philadelphia Inquirer* claimed that while warfare had a "grim visage" and a "horrid front," it still had its "humanities and courtesies." Other newspapers echoed this sentiment; some seemed to imply that the Union Army would almost kill the enemy with kindness. The *Boston Daily Evening Transcript* claimed that, indeed, the "sincerest regard to the whole South—setting aside all other considerations—demands now the unflinching prosecution of the war." Since the rebel leaders had "made dupes of many—possibly the majority of its adherents," the rightful authority had to win back its power by force "in order to prove that it seeks to maintain itself only that it may be a blessing to the whole land." The *Springfield* (Massachusetts) *Daily Republican* wrote lyrically about what it called the "fruits

---

1. Remarks of Edgar Cowan, May 6, 1862, *Cong. Globe,* 37th Cong., 2nd sess., 1965; *Chicago Tribune,* May 12, 1862; *New York Times,* May 15, 1862.

of invasion." In this editorial, the paper extolled the many benefits the Union Army would extend to the southern people. They would feed, clothe, and educate poor southerners. Indeed, the *Republican* was entirely convinced that an "invasion like this cannot make enemies."[2]

In spite of their blustering about the private property of rebels, most Union citizens drew the line at plunder. Because they were rarely able to render a clear definition of the difference between the confiscation of property and plunder, however, their arguments betrayed a great deal of ambivalence and confusion. Many newspaper editorials asserted, rather lamely, that such actions would not be "Christian," in spite of the fact that they had been saying all along that the time for gentlemanly warfare was now over. At the same time, however, newspapers like the *Boston Daily Evening Transcript* thought that the Union armies should "find their subsistence in the States they occupy," because this would "obviate the necessity of long supply trains." In this editorial, the *Transcript* appeared to sanction forage, which was in essence the military practice of subsisting on the enemy's land and crops. But neither the *Transcript* nor most other newspapers of the period explained the differences among forage, confiscation, and plunder. Presumably, confiscation could only follow the enactment of specific legislation and would transfer ownership of private property to the federal government. Eventually Francis Lieber wrote General Orders No. 100 for the U.S. Army, which strictly forbade plundering, defined as the lawless looting of private enemy property. In the meantime, there were few clear guidelines or precedents in place for Federal Army commanders to follow. Plunder, as opposed to forage, was defined as wanton looting and implied inflicting personal bodily harm on enemy civilians. Plunder would result in transfer of private property to unruly soldiers—not to the Union government or citizens. In May 1861, General Henry Halleck's treatise on the international rules of warfare appeared in print, which deplored such practices as extensive foraging and plunder. According to historian Mark Grimsley, Halleck's *International Law* supported the government's policy of conciliation. Many northerners, however, wanted southern private property transferred to their own pockets. In 1861, when many Union Army officers still adhered to conciliatory policies, the

2. *Philadelphia Inquirer*, January 2, 1862; *Boston Daily Evening Transcript*, August 20, 1862; *Springfield* (Mass.) *Daily Republican*, May 21, 1862; see also, the *Louisville Daily Democrat*, September 4, 1861.

enlisted men nevertheless occasionally helped themselves illegally to private rebel property through foraging. By late 1861, Confederate civilians had begun fleeing farther southward or westward with their possessions and their slaves, sometimes abandoning their plantations to the advancing Federals. Some officers seized public property, but on the whole they pursued a lenient course against rebel civilians, and severely punished vandalism or theft. Many Union soldiers, however, rejected conciliatory policies by early 1862, both toward rebel civilians' property and toward their slaves. A Major Connolly told his wife that he had degenerated from a "conservative young Democrat to a horse stealer and 'nigger thief'" and that while he was in the field, he was an "abolitionist." By July, Major General John Pope had already declared a policy, which was sanctioned by Lincoln, of subsisting "upon the country" in Virginia. In fact, Pope forced all residents in the area under his command to sign loyalty oaths in order to avoid the confiscation of their property, which in 1862 was still an innovation among Union Army commanders.[3]

However senior military officers might have reacted to plunder, the home front viewed these actions pragmatically. When newspapers inveighed against the practice of plundering, they rarely cited ideological reasons for their opposition to this practice. The New York Times stated that there was "no occasion for our soldiers to plunder in order to obtain supplies of goods or clothing, for the Government adequately provides for all such wants." Further, if soldiers were plundering for private gain, then that would be "doubly dangerous,"— not because it contravened the conventions of civilized warfare or violated the Constitution, but because such a practice "not only breaks down discipline while the plundering is going on, but . . . encumbers the soldier with goods that he will divide his attention with, giving so much less to his main business in the field—that of fighting." An editorial later that summer further reinforced the paper's realistic attitude toward the victims of foraging raids. The New York Times sought to reassure its readers that even though the editor thought plundering ought to be "strictly punished," northern citizens need not fear that the Union Army "will not sufficiently desolate the rebel territory." An army, he claimed was like a flock of locusts "even to its friends."[4]

3. Ash, When the Yankees Came, 28–32, 57; Boston Daily Evening Transcript, July 23, 1862, quoted in Ash, When the Yankees Came, 150, 54; Hyman, Era of the Oath, 35.

4. New York Times, May 31, July 25, 1862.

While it is true that most northerners—when pressed—said that plunder was an unchivalrous act, not befitting a moral Army, they were less troubled by the lack of legality or morality than by its potentially subversive effect on the soldiers themselves. Conservatives thought the war should be fought along internationally accepted standards of military conduct, but even the opinion leaders who were most sympathetic to the South had difficulty sorting out the difference between justly stern measures and unconstitutional ones. Charles F. Blake, the conservative author of a pamphlet on the conduct of the war, opposed both confiscation and emancipation. Nevertheless, he thought that the Army had a right to appropriate food and livestock belonging to the enemy because it might be used to aid the war effort. According to Blake, the confusion surrounding the question arose from a "neglect to distinguish accurately" between the Army's right to forage and the government's power to legislate the conduct of the war. Although he was doubtful about what he called the "civil penalty of confiscation," he nevertheless recognized the "military right to plunder." A confiscation law enacted by Congress was wrong, he believed, because it enlarged the power of the executive far beyond the limits set by the Constitution; but the military had a right to plunder private property, presumably as an act of war against an enemy. In this case, the word "plunder" was being used as a synonym for "forage." But Blake obviously believed that plunder, however he defined it—with all its attendant dangers to the southern civilian population—was less dangerous than confiscation, which appeared to subvert the Constitution.[5]

Regardless of their squeamishness about the plunder of private citizens, militant northerners nearly always targeted individual southerners rather than the rebel states (let alone the Confederate government) in their angry rhetoric. Legal theorist George Ticknor Curtis pointed out that because states could not legally secede, the war would have to be waged against individual rebels. This was certainly in keeping with the majority of northern public opinion on the treatment of enemy citizens. Union citizens had felt personally attacked when secessionists seized their property in early 1861, and they continued to inveigh against individual rebels who remained in arms against their government. Therefore, northerners recognized that they had to distinguish between the guilt of the leaders and the guilt of the southern people, whom they considered

5. Blake, *Rightful Power of Congress*, 19–20.

"dupes." The *Springfield* (Massachusetts) *Daily Republican* said that while the rebels should be forced to pay for the cost of the war, it was of the first importance to make a "wise discrimination" between rebel leaders and the duped masses. Indeed, the word "dupe" was one of the most common epithets applied to nonslaveholding southerners. In February 1862, the *New York Times* published an editorial entitled "The Southern People—Guilty or Not Guilty." The *Times* declared that it was important to be careful not to confound the southern people, who were the "body of the rebellion," with the "rebel *chiefs*, civil and military, who have been its brain and hand." Not that the former had not been "weak, and wicked, and guilty," but they were bound in any case to be punished by the fortunes of war. At the same time, the *Times* predicted "magnanimity upon reconstruction," because the majority of southerners had been victims rather than authors of rebellion and would no doubt repent of their actions. An Ohio man was far less forgiving to southern "doops." He submitted a petition to Senator John Sherman proposing a plan of action for the disposal of "the Trators property." The petition suggested that "every prominent Trator shall be Hung, & thier doops be deprived of all thier *property*, of what ever Sort." Meanwhile, he hoped that some of the "Antiquarian *Fossels*" in the Senate could be "galvanised" to life, but doubted that this would ever occur.[6]

While the 37th Congress was debating the constitutionality of the Confiscation Acts, the Republican voters' attitude toward southerners was far more businesslike. Northern citizens were enraged about the attack on the Union and the Constitution, and the deaths of their loved ones; but they were also aware that the war had to be paid for, and that the lion's share of the responsibility would fall on the shoulders of loyal citizens. Many had been irate since early 1861 about their increasing tax burden as a result of the war and about southern depredations on their business profits. One of Sherman's correspondents stated flatly that the rebels "must be compelled to pay the cost of the rebellion and the arch traitors must pay the forfeit of their lives on the gallows." When he looked about him, he saw "so much disarrangement in business. So much loss of treasure & property so much loss of valuable lives. [S]o much suffering can not be

6. Benedict, "A Constitutional Crisis," in McPherson and Cooper, eds., *Writing the Civil War*, 157; *New York Times*, February 19, 1862; A. Denny to John Sherman, Sherman Papers, LOC, February 21, 1862.

permitted again nay nor allowed to pass without suitable punishment, now, the first two must be repaid [and] the blood of the third must be avenged." He demanded, "What does the Govt mean in not holding [the rebels] to a strict accountability?" Frustrated, he wished the pulse of government could be made to "beat in accordance with the will of the people." Another of Sherman's constituents put it even more strongly. He believed that the time had come when "we must apply fire & sword and confiscate all propperty in the rebel states and apply to the expence of the war."[7]

Indeed, since the secession crisis, northern businessmen had carefully calculated the amount the war would cost them in expenses, taxes, and loss of profits. An anonymous "Citizen" published a pamphlet in 1861 deploring the war's accumulating costs. "Southern traitors have by their acts depreciated the property of the free States a full 25 per cent, . . . wasted [the North's] treasures and blighted its prospects." Surely, all this called for the severest punishment, and, according to this Citizen, the only fair penalty was the confiscation of their property. Like many others, he was horrified at the injustice of imposing "heavy losses on the innocent" without making traitors pay. A *Boston Daily Evening Transcript* editorial stated that "the whole property of the country has, by a causeless rebellion, been woefully depreciated, and a portion of it, equal to the whole assumed value of the Southern slaves, has been practically annihilated." According to the *Transcript,* Congress hardly seemed to care that "eight-tenths of the property of the country, founded on the basis of free labor, is placed in peril, provided the two-tenths, resting on the sacred basis of slave labor, is preserved intact." If a nation of free citizens was ready to swallow this kind of "drivel," the editorial declared indignantly, then they "might as well go back to Buchanan."[8]

Northerners had long believed that southerners ought to be forced to pay for the costs of the war, and hoped that Congress would soon pass a law "confiscating the property of *Rebels* to aid in defraying the war expenses." The writer of this letter told Washburne that this sentiment was so universal that even "Secesh sympathizers" united with the Union men in this hope. An Ohioan thought that the "free states will be taxed enough in blood and treasure to jus-

7. L. S. Abbott to John Sherman, Sherman Papers, LOC, June 9, 1862.

8. John McLaughlin to John Sherman, Sherman Papers, LOC, January 28, 1862; Citizen, *A View of the War; Boston Daily Evening Transcript,* March 5, 1862.

tify as [nearly] as possible the overthrow of the cause of our calamities," by which he meant, of course, slavery. Similarly, the *North American Review* published an editorial on the customary ways of financing war, which should include taxation and a greater reliance on public credit. A third way in which "conquering nations are accustomed to relieve themselves" was to make the conquered party pay, and to confiscate the property of enemies. This was unquestionably just, the *Review* claimed, but it defended its standpoint rather vaguely: the government had "this high justification, that they discountenance all rash, needless, and criminal wars." Besides, the *Review* pointed out, the Confederacy had done it first.[9]

William Howard Russell, a correspondent from the *London Times*, had observed as early as 1861 that southerners hoped for an internal division in the North over financing the war. Russell was convinced that the pressure of finances would "force on a solution, for the State taxes already amount to 2 or 3 per cent., and the people will not bear the addition." It seemed obvious to him that "the North has set out with the principle of paying for everything, the South with the principle of paying for nothing"; but he predicted that this would be "reversed in time." Most northerners would have agreed with him wholeheartedly. When they contemplated the burden of funding the war effort, many northerners became unabashedly practical in their demand for southern property. For example, one of Elihu Washburne's correspondents asked whether Congress would "pass the Bill to make Seceshdom all new teritory & sell it to pay the expences of this Rebelion[?] I hope they will, and I think the majority of your constituents do the same." Daniel Gardner from Massachusetts sent a proposed confiscation bill to Charles Sumner. He wanted to collect from the public as well as private property of "all rebel citizens and corporations . . . all property injuries arising from the rebellion & all debts due from rebels or Traitors to *loyal American citizens* & loyal corporations." Sumner referred Gardner's bill to the chairman of the Judiciary Committee of the House, where it disappeared.[10]

9. Cornelius Mikesell to Elihu Washburne, Elihu B. Washburne Papers, LOC, March 6, 1862; Eli Nichols to John Sherman, Sherman Papers, LOC, January 20, 1862; *North American Review*, December 1861, 668.

10. Russell, *My Diary North and South*, 323; Tilson Aldrich to Elihu Washburne, Elihu B. Washburne Papers, LOC, March 7, 1862; Daniel Gardner to Charles Sumner, Sumner Papers, HL, February 17, 1862.

The demand for punishment of rebellious wealthy slaveowners, combined with the desire for reimbursement for the costs of the war, produced a coolly pragmatic view of the economic value of the southern land, crops, and slave labor. Some northern pamphlets tried to assess the likelihood that southern slaveholders' property could be "harvested" to pay northern war costs, and they usually emphasized the immense national debt the country would someday have to pay. One pamphleteer calculated the future debt to "more than a thousand millions" of dollars. He thought that the actual value of property in the rebel states was about $4.7 billion, "say three billion if exclusive of slavery." He thought that if southern land and crops could be sold to pay off northern war debts, it would go "a good way" toward meeting their obligations. The author recommended that all constitutional limitations on confiscation be set aside because the Constitution did not allow the seizure of a traitor's property beyond his lifetime. The author pointed out that if Congress could confiscate real estate only for the life of the owners, "very little can ever be realized out of it, and this enormous debt must fall with crushing weight upon the wealth and the industry of our country."[11]

Indeed, the politicians' careful regard for the rights of rebels was especially irksome for northerners now that Congress was enacting heavy taxes to pay for the war. The 36th Congress had passed the Morrill Tariff in March 1861, and the 37th Congress had passed another more comprehensive tariff and the Direct Tax Act at the end of the summer session. And as chairman of the Committee of Ways and Means, Thaddeus Stevens introduced a sweeping new tax law that would raise the prices of consumer goods. Radical Illinois congressman Elihu Washburne, who as a member of the Committee on Commerce frequently spoke on both confiscation and taxation, received dozens of anxious letters on this topic. Many of the writers claimed they would pay taxes "cheerfully" if only the war were being prosecuted with more vigor. William B. Dodge sent Washburne a petition that demanded to know, "Are we to make immense sacrifices of blood and treasure to put down this horrid rebellion, and yet spare the embodiment of evil which caused it?" Another of Washburne's constituents asserted that western farmers wanted action: "The people do not desire to be taxed, or sacrafice [sic] their sons, brothers, and neighbors, and then stop short of a final settlement." The subscribers to the petition told Washburne that they wanted the work done "so that it will not need to be done over." The *Boston*

11. Wilson, *Attainder of Treason*, 3–4.

Daily Evening Transcript claimed, rather optimistically, that the people "pined for taxation" and argued that this would "reclaim the nation to common sense." According to the editor, all opposition to confiscation bills proceeded from the idea that the property of rebels was more sacred than the property of Unionists. Everybody knew that the property of the free states was to be seized, by "due course of law," by which he meant taxation, to pay the expenses of the war. According to the *Transcript,* it was unfair that the sufferers should bear all the cost while the criminals escaped "without loss of property or honor." The North's willingness to bear the expenses of the war depended upon the government's willingness to deal harshly with the enemy. Dexter A. Hawkins was sure that twenty thousand dead rebels, even if it meant as many Union dead, "would make money pour like water into the now Empty Treasury." [12]

In their demands for property confiscation, whether out of military necessity, for revenge, for reimbursement, or to help ease the burden of mounting taxes, northerners usually pointed directly to wealthy slaveowning southerners as the guilty authors of the rebellion. The slaveholders represented a hated aristocracy, or "Slave Power," which had long been conspiring to destroy the country's free institutions. Many northern letters, pamphlets, and newspaper editorials now began to cite the South's "un-American" class differences as justification for taking southern land. Further, they argued that depriving this despised aristocracy of their land would be the only workable solution to the conflict. The *New York Evening Post* stated explicitly that "very little injustice can be done [to the] more opulent of the slave-holders of the South . . . by using their property as the means of a complete and harmonious restoration of the Union." Maine senator Lot M. Morrill told his colleagues that they were witnessing the "old struggle of a class for power and privilege which has so often convulsed the world, repeating itself in our history." Not only would a strong confiscation law help win the war for the Union, but it would also bring the defeated South in line with true republican principles. [13]

Many Republicans reasoned, therefore, that the confiscation of rebel prop-

12. For Republican tariff and tax legislation, see Richardson, *The Greatest Nation,* chapter 4. William B. Dodge to Elihu Washburne, Elihu B. Washburne Papers, LOC, December 12, 1861; H. P. Sloan, to Elihu Washburne, Elihu B. Washburne Papers, LOC, December 12, 1861; *Boston Daily Evening Transcript,* April 30, 1862; Dexter A. Hawkins to Elihu Washburne, Elihu B. Washburne Papers, LOC, January 6, 1862.

13. Richards, *The Slave Power; New York Evening Post,* March 5, 1862; *Cong. Globe,* 37th Cong., 2nd sess., 1077.

erty would not only help win the war, it would realign un-American class divisions in the South. Republicans—and Whigs before them—had long critiqued slavery's corrupting influences on American society and politics, as well as the institution's threat to free labor. The *New York Times* baldly declared that the country was involved in a class war. "It is a war of the aristocracy of the South, nominally against the people—the working people of the North, but really against the whole people, and against Democracy itself." It was now time to "strike at the higher classes." Obviously, the best way to do that would be to free the slaves, "not merely from military necessity," but because emancipation would "depress the traitorous aristocracy, who hate the Union and Democracy, and always will hate them." Therefore, the government should confiscate the rebels' estates, and "divide them, not merely among our soldiers, but sell them cheaply to, or bestow them on the poor white men of the South." This would help destroy the power of the ruling classes in the South. At the same time, however, the *Times* adjured their government not to "hurt the poor." When the northern press referred to the plight of the poorer southern whites, however, they rarely discussed them in the same breath with slaves. Indeed, they appeared to hate the institution of slavery more because it threatened the well-being of white people than because it was oppressive to the slaves themselves.[14]

Convinced that poor southern whites secretly hated the slaveowning aristocracy, many northerners believed that, given the right incentives, such people would be happy to return to the Union. Pamphleteer George Candee carefully laid out a strategy that he hoped would not only win the war, but also bring poor white southerners to the side of the Union. He advised the nation to confiscate all the property of "active rebels," to proclaim liberty to all their slaves, "*and to offer liberal bounties in confiscated lands to all Southern men who will volunteer their services to put down the rebellion and maintain the Government.*" This way the Union would lure nonslaveholding whites away from the Confederacy, most of whom, according to Candee, did not own any land, but were dependent upon the upper-class landholders for "support—for existence even." It was only this dependence, as well as the poor whites' "ignorance and prejudice" that attached them to the rebel cause. But if the government would only confiscate the lands of "aristocratic traitors" and offer "liberal portions of

---

14. Huston, *Securing the Fruits of Labor*, 297; *New York Times*, July 25, 1862. For republican ideology and the slave power, see Foner, *Politics and Ideology*, chapters 2 and 3.

them to these poor men who have been deluded and forced into an inhuman war against their own interests and life," the invading armies would find the poor southern whites converted to loyalty to the Union. Section six of the Second Confiscation Act gave southerners a grace period of sixty days during which they could reconsider the wisdom of their rebellion and return to the Union. If they laid down their arms and repented their treason, their property would be secure. Perhaps the legislators hoped that many of the "dupes" of the southern rebellion would avail of themselves of this opportunity to reaffirm their allegiance to the United States.[15]

Candee was confident that nonslaveholding southern whites would hail Yankee immigrants with joy. Northern farmers could then "occupy a share of confiscated lands, taking with them all the institutions of Christianity and civilization, and be received with a hearty good will." Although clearly erroneous, this view of southern society enjoyed widespread popularity in the North. Many northerners believed that only plantation owners held slaves, and that there existed strong class divisions in the South that would be easy to exploit once the "duped" masses could be won back to the Union. A *North American Review* article put it even more strongly. The *Review* declared that the South's inevitable failure would "draw after it a revolution in property." The disloyal race of cotton, sugar, and rice planters of the South would, "as a class, disappear, beggared, perhaps in large proportion extinct." This might be a fearful retribution, but the *Review* did not see how they could escape it. In this way, confiscation legislation became an instrument or expression of Divine wrath.[16]

In contrast to their pugnacious constituents, Republicans in the 37th Congress were careful to refrain from discussing the material value of the land or the possible uses to which it might be put. At most, there might be oblique references to abandoned plantations or lands not used to their fullest potential, a view that had long governed federal policy toward Native American land rights. Some politicians also hinted delicately at the dangers of freeing slaves without making adequate provision for their employment and survival. At one point, Trumbull did briefly discuss the abandoned Port Royal plantations and asked

15. Candee, *Plan for Conquering Treason*, 2.

16. Ibid.; "The Civil War: Its Nature and End," *North American Review*, December 1861, 639–72. For northern attitudes and perceptions of the South, see Stampp, *And the War Came*, chapter 1, and Floan, *The South in Northern Eyes*.

his colleagues in the Senate, "Is [this land] to remain unoccupied? Is it to become a wilderness?" He thought they should treat it the way "all the nations of
Europe treated this American continent when they settled upon it and the savages fled." In fact, according to Trumbull, southerners who abandoned their
own country did not differ materially from "Indian savages." After the Union
Army had conquered the South, they would have a right to "take possession of
that country and apportion it out among the loyal citizens of the Union." Albert G. Riddle, who was more radical than Trumbull, was also more direct. He
was infuriated by the suggestion, which had first surfaced in the original version
of Trumbull's bill, of purchasing land to settle the newly freed slaves. "Buy land!
Of whom and where? Buy land! Why one half of our own is wrested from us."
He thought the North could settle the freed slaves in the "territory once called
South Carolina, if you will; and if we have not then land enough, buy another
half continent, or take the whole of it." [17]

When radical Republicans in Congress and on the home front demanded
the confiscation of southern land, they did so with an eye to keeping the captured real estate permanently under Union control. It was not merely to be
considered war matériel for the duration of the conflict; it was to be used
to safeguard the future of the Republic from future southern aggressions.
One Massachusetts resident wrote to his congressman that there would be
no peace until the Union had reconquered the land, and slavery was dead. He
proclaimed, "the territory of the South must be ours if we make it desolate
as the cities of the plain and all its inhabitants must submit quit or swing." An
editorial in the *Chicago Tribune* also declared that the government would have
to take southern real estate in order to establish a permanent peace. Otherwise, the *Tribune* predicted that the government would need a standing army to
subdue the rebels "if we let them keep their lands and slaves. They will feel no
gratitude." [18]

But many northern voters, especially Republicans, also wanted the South
for themselves. The monetary value of southern land and the benefits of the
southern climate were not lost on them. Even moderate Democratic newspapers—papers that had previously argued against emancipation, and even

17. Remarks of Lyman Trumbull on February 25, 1862, *Cong. Globe*, 37th Cong., 2nd sess., 943;
remarks of Albert Riddle on January 14, 1862, *Cong. Globe*, 37th Cong., 2nd sess., 332.
18. Bensel, *Yankee Leviathan*, 27; Samuel Wiles to Henry L. Dawes, Dawes Papers, LOC, November 25, 1862; *Chicago Tribune*, March 14, 1862.

against sweeping confiscation laws earlier in the war—eagerly envisioned the uses to which fertile cotton-, sugar-, and rice-growing areas could be put, as well as the profits to be earned from these crops. In scrutinizing this potential agricultural windfall, northerners also eyed the black labor force as the only way to realize the value of the southern land. For example, the *Boston Daily Evening Transcript* said that "not only will three out of four millions of enslaved blacks be emancipated, but thousands of square miles of cultivated or cultivatable plantations will be confiscated." Although the *Transcript*'s editor regretted the "hateful necessity of total warfare," he nevertheless declared himself willing to let it have its "full sway when the time for its natural operation shall occur." Similarly, the *Philadelphia Inquirer* discussed various congressional solutions to the problem of what to do with freed slaves. The purpose of such legislation ought to be to "avoid the expense of supporting crowds of slaves in idleness, and furnishing the American mills with cotton." The *Inquirer* explained that there were more than 20 million acres of southern land, "of unsurpassed fertility, capable of producing about fifteen millions of bales of cotton per annum," subject to military confiscation. Some of this land could come from Indian territory west of Louisiana and Arkansas, provided some of the original treaties were rendered "null and void." The *Inquirer*'s editor also looked toward Florida, where, he said, the contraband could be apprenticed to cotton planters. An editorial in the *Cincinnati Daily Enquirer* on John Gurley's confiscation bill also suggested that land could be found in Florida for the freed slaves, "all of whom can find congenial homes in its hot climate and fertile lands, the extent of which is amply sufficient." In no way did this paper suggest giving the land to the slaves; the point was to confiscate the land and "apprentice" the freed slaves to cultivate it (which would not include paying them a wage for their labor). This was a rather surprising attitude for a Democratic paper that had supported Stephen A. Douglas's candidacy for the presidency in 1860; the editorial did, however, recommend obtaining Florida's permission first. Such ideas would not become prominent in Congress, not even among radicals like Thaddeus Stevens and Benjamin Wade, until late 1863 during the first session of the 38th Congress, after the Union Army had achieved significant victories at Vicksburg and Gettysburg.[19]

The confiscation of southern land could also serve as an avenue for social

19. *Boston Daily Evening Transcript*, April 1, 1862; *Philadelphia Inquirer*, December 26, 1861; *Cincinnati Daily Enquirer*, December 12, 1861.

and especially educational reform in the benighted South. As early as 1861, as Union regiments began to occupy areas of Virginia, some New England missionaries and schoolteachers followed. These men and women worked among the contraband and soon developed both liking and respect for them, in marked contrast to northerners who had remained at home. Those who were less personally interested in profiting from southern land and crops still thought the land should be put to good use. A Vermonter suggested to Thaddeus Stevens that abandoned lands in Virginia could be cultivated at once to "feed the army and employ the contraband." The superintendent of public schools in Griffin, Ohio, wrote to Senator Sherman that all Ohio patriots demanded the passage of a confiscation bill. He reminded Sherman that "a large amount of land and other property must come into the possession of the Government," and this would occur in those states "where they need *common schools.*" He suggested that Sherman include "in whatever Bill that may be passed, an article such that one-sixteenth or more of the proceeds realized shall be a *permanent* Common School Fund," thus extending the principles of the Northwest Ordinance southward. This would be crucial to ensure that there would be "loyally educated citizens in those States," and would also do a great deal toward bringing northern values and ideals to the South. Andrew Johnson received a similar letter from his friend Fearless A. Armstrong, who thought that one-third of all property confiscated should be "*devoted to common schools in the respective states, from which the Word of God shall not be excluded.*" [20]

Above all, the confiscation of rebel lands would bring about the Americanization of the South. Confiscated southern lands could be used to promote the northern principles of free white labor and enterprise. The *New York Times* had been publishing opinions since the outbreak of the war recommending "universal confiscation" of real estate so that loyal settlers could occupy southern lands. Northern newspapers had speculated on the wealth and beauty of some of the southern states since the secession crisis. As early as April 1861, before Vir-

20. McCrary, "The Party of Revolution," 330–50. See also Paludan, *Presidency*, 145; James Marten, "A Feeling of Restless Anxiety: Loyalty and Race in the Peninsula Campaign and Beyond," in Gallagher, ed., *The Richmond Campaign of 1862*, 140–2, 146; Elias Lee to Thaddeus Stevens, Thaddeus Stevens Papers, LOC, March 19, 1862; H. C. Robinson to Edward McPherson, McPherson Papers, LOC, March 4, 1862; L. E. Holden to John Sherman, May 5, 1862, Sherman Papers, LOC; Fearless A. Armstrong to Andrew Johnson, January 21, 1862, quoted in Graf and Haskins, eds., *The Papers of Andrew Johnson*, 5:110.

ginia had even joined the Confederacy, the *New York Tribune* had carried editorials extolling Virginia's lovely climate and fertile lands. The *Tribune* had likened the state to a garden but predicted that it was "doomed to be a good deal trampled, and its paths, its beds, and its boundaries are likely to be pretty completely obliterated before we have done with it." The editorial cast a greedy eye on Virginia's property "in houses, in lands, in mines, in forests, in country, and in town," which doubtless would have to "be taken possession of." All this was perfectly fair because, according to the *Tribune,* the "worn-out and emasculated First Families must give place to a sturdier people, whose pioneers are now on their way to Washington at this moment in regiments." Certainly, an allotment of Virginia farmland would be a "fitting reward to the brave fellows who have gone to fight their country's battles." [21]

Similarly, the *New York Times* proposed "sending all rebel inhabitants further South, and occupying their houses with our soldiers." A pamphlet in favor of confiscation also recommended "opening the lands of the South to free white labor [and] arming friendly troops, of every color, creed and clime." In the same vein, the *Springfield* (Massachusetts) *Daily Republican* published a revealing editorial entitled "The Americanization of the South." This editorial quoted from an article that had appeared in *DeBow's Review* on the perils of peace, the danger of "an immense Yankee immigration" into the border states, and the necessity of protecting the South from such an invasion. But the *Republican's* editor believed that should the rebels succeed in dividing the Union, no "Chinese wall . . . would wholly protect the South from [a] peaceful Yankee invasion." In fact, after the restoration of peace, "tens of thousands of industrious and enterprising men from the North and West" would soon discover the "advantages of the soil, climate and position, and the rich but undeveloped resources of these great border states." These vigorous northern men would soon "make their desolate places bud and blossom, and supplant their present sluggishness and poverty by industry and thrift." Further, a large portion of the land in Texas ought to be confiscated, because the nation had a "double and triple claim upon the soil of this most ungrateful of states." The Texan lands should be distributed to Union Army volunteers. In this way the South would "get that infusion of new blood which it needs to secure its renovation." Like

21. *New York Tribune,* quoted in the *Baltimore Sun* on April 26, 1861. For antebellum northern conceptions of the South as degenerate, see Grant, *North Over South.*

many other northerners, the editor of the *Republican* believed that the war would eventually give the nation a unity, character, and destiny "more lasting than that which comes from Constitutions and laws." At the same time, however, the southern press carried similar warnings about the northern invaders; the rebels were equally convinced that a Yankee invasion would corrupt and defile southern civilization.[22]

During the secession crisis, the rebellious states had been called "erring sisters"; now that the bitterness of war tainted the feeling of kinship between the sections, northerners still viewed the southern states as feminine, but began to cast them in a less familiar role. In their eagerness to conquer and reform southern lands, some editorials portrayed the South as a beautiful, desirable, but corrupt woman, one who could only be reformed by the application of the stern masculine authority of northern values. For example, the *New York Times* published a favorable opinion on Francis Blair's confiscation bill, which provided for the sale of confiscated lands and encouraged Union soldiers in the Army to purchase the land. In this way, according to the *Times,* "a new element" was likely to be introduced into the war, which would "regenerate the South." Northern soldiers, more used to the "rugged soil" and "inhospitable climate" of their native states, would be "captivated by the beautiful regions" of the South and eager to become their "owners and occupiers." Such a development was inevitable, the editorial claimed, and would have occurred even if there had never been a war. According to the *Times,* the South would soon be "overrun and overpowered by the more prolific loins and stronger muscles and wills of the North." This was nothing more than the law of "superior forces when brought in contact with inferior." Echoing Senator Charles Sumner's famous 1856 "The Crime Against Kansas" speech, northern editorials focused on the metaphoric and literal sexual impurity of slaveowning southerners (and by implication, of the southern states) as a justification for a manly Yankee invasion. The "sister" metaphor was no longer appropriate after the emergence of the language of conquest, surrender, and redemption through a "peaceful invasion."[23]

Like many others of his time, Sidney George Fisher thought that the south-

---

22. *New York Times,* July 25, 1862; Edward Delafield Smith, *Brief Appeals for the Loyal Cause* (New York: John W. Amerman, 1863); *Springfield* (Mass.) *Daily Republican,* November 29, 1861; Ash, *When the Yankees Came,* 40.

23. Silber, *Romance of Reunion.*

ern people had been sexually and morally corrupted not only by the institution of slavery, but also by the mere presence of black people. The descendants of "Africa," he said, would eventually destroy not only the South but also the rest of the nation, if they were permitted to migrate northward. In the meantime, however, only the purer strains of the "Norsemen" could redeem the degraded South. Fisher was convinced by popular European race theories that held the "Teutonic" to be the "highest type of man," but he feared that "prolonged intercourse" with the "dark races of the South" would bring harm to even the hardiest members of this race. Nevertheless, he believed that the only way to redeem the South from these deleterious influences was by injecting "fresh supplies of Northern force and ability."[24]

Sometimes such sentiments verged on the vindictive, evoking images of violation and rape. In August, shortly after the passage of the Second Confiscation Act, Michigan senator Zachariah Chandler received a letter from an officer who commented with some satisfaction that it was "dreadful to behold the state of prostration" under which the state of Virginia, which he called "the Eden of America," was now laboring. According to this officer, who told Chandler that a confiscation act would serve to bring the southern rebels to heel, the "hard hand of war" was strikingly visible in all "her fertile valleys," and Virginia's crops, which had hitherto promised "an abundant harvest for the support of treason" were now "trampled under foot by those whose lives are pledged to support our free & glorious Constitution." The beautiful, warm climate of the South, which had corrupted the idle slaveowners, would have only a beneficial effect on the hard-working sons of the North. A Yankee invasion, therefore, would effectively redeem not only the South, but also reinvigorate the entire nation. Fisher believed that because the South had allowed herself to become "a degenerate race," she could no longer be trusted to participate equally in American democracy. An association with the South would "corrupt and destroy" the Republic; therefore, the southern states would have to be governed as "subject provinces," or excluded wholly from the Union. A *New York Times* editorial declared that the war would accomplish in a single generation what might otherwise have required centuries in peacetime. In fact, America's Civil War would become the "grand agency in the cause of civilization, which only proceeds by the better supplanting the worse, and often by destroying it." In this way, the

24. Fisher, *Trial of Our Constitution,* 176.

Union Army would bring superior northern culture, values, and racial characteristics to the corrupt, benighted South.[25]

By 1862, several proposals appeared for turning over southern slaveowners'
property to Union soldiers. There was a fairly widespread belief that since these
brave men had risked their lives for the Union, they deserved bounties from
southern land and crops. The practice of awarding land to soldiers had a long
history in the United States. Most states had awarded bounty lands to veterans
of the Revolutionary War, and the federal government set aside vast tracts of
land—more than 3.5 million acres—in the Old Northwest Territory as payment to veterans of the War of 1812. Charles A. Dana wrote to Charles Sumner
that "*bon gré, mal gré* it is what we must come to. It seems that with large bounties of confiscated lands to the soldiers to settle in the recovered territories the
business may be managed." For Dana, there was no difficulty in justifying such
an action. In fact, he hoped that the rebels would refrain from submitting too
easily because the "very madness and malignity of the slaveholder promises to
help us where sense and submission on their part might lead to a temporary
settlement which would be no settlement at all." A Union general published a
pamphlet which also proposed confiscating all the rebel land conquered by the
Union Army, and turning it over to the soldiers and officers "as compensation."
Although General Josiah Perham, who had prior to the war been the president
of the People's Pacific Railroad Company, thought that slaves living on rebel
lands ought to be freed, he still believed that Unionists in the disloyal territory
ought to be protected in their property, and reimbursed for the loss of their
slaves. He also suggested that any Confederate soldier or citizen who chose to
fight on the Union side ought to share in the "rebel territory." According to Perham, all of this was perfectly justified because the rebels themselves had forfeited their constitutional rights and were entitled to nothing more than "one
end of a rope."[26]

Although there were numerous schemes for the future of southern land and
property, and although some of these included using the black labor force to

25. Lt. Henry B. Clare to Zachariah Chandler, Chandler Papers, LOC, August 14, 1862; Fisher,
Trial of Our Constitution, 182; *New York Times,* January 14, 1862.

26. Charles A. Dana to Charles Sumner, Sumner Papers, HL, April 7, 1862; the phrase *bon gré,
mal gré* means "for good or ill." Josiah Perham, *General Perham's Platform: The Most Feasible Plan
Yet Offered for Suppressing the Rebellion* (Boston: Alfred Mudge and Son, 1862). I am indebted to
Andy Coopersmith for calling my attention to this pamphlet.

cultivate these lands, few northerners suggested giving any of it to the freed slaves outright. Only the most radical newspapers and abolitionists expressed such ideas. One rare suggestion came from the militant *Chicago Tribune,* which published a set of resolutions by Maine state senator Ephraim K. Smart "urging Congress to confiscate the rebels' property and liberate their slaves, and arm the slaves as soldiers." Smart proposed giving the slaves their freedom after three years, paying them eight dollars a month, and offering them forty acres of land in Texas or some other "suitable climate." The *Tribune* thought that "all vacant and unoccupied lands in States which have entered into an unconstitutional confederation for the purpose of making war upon the Union, *should by the act of Congress be immediately confiscated to the United States,* . . . for the benefit of slave soldiers and others of African descent." Ohioan W. M. Wilson wrote to Senator Sherman that because the wealth and power that had sustained the institution of slavery was now about to be destroyed, and because the slave-holders would not have the industry and enterprise to recuperate from the de-struction of the war, he suggested that Congress give the lands of rebels to their slaves. At the same time, however, he also thought that the slaves should be "made a fixture to the realty" of the rebel as long as the rebel lived, unless the loyal occupant voluntarily gave up the slaves for colonization as freemen. Per-haps suddenly realizing his own contradictions, he decided that human wisdom could not master the problem; it would have to be left to God's Providence.[27]

After the first year of the Civil War, the nation's capital had come to sym-bolize the conquest of the South by the Union government as well as by north-ern values and ideals. As Reverend James Ward had pointed out in his diary en-try describing his visit to the capital in July 1861, Washington, D.C., was turning into a "Yankee commercial metropolis." As part of the nation's original com-promise with the South, the capital had been situated between two slave states, but it was now ruled by a Republican Congress and president. The District of Columbia should represent the new America that was going to supplant the older one, born of vicious compromises and now fighting for its existence. The founding fathers' compromises with the South, evident both in the Constitu-tion and in the location of the capital so close to the Mason-Dixon line, would soon be rectified by the North's superior strength and will. Former Ohio con-

27. *Chicago Tribune,* January 24, 1862; W. M. Wilson to John Sherman, Sherman Papers, LOC, January 18, 1862.

gressman Jacob Brinkerhoff observed to John Sherman, "you and I know that *social* influences at Washington have always been intensely proslavery—southern, anti-northern, opposed to northern ideas, northern policy, northern sentiments, tendencies, modes of life, and modes of thought." In short, according to Brinkerhoff, the nation's capital had always been a southern town. But once slavery was abolished in the District, the northern horde, about which the southern slaveowners "unceasingly prated," would overrun the South and "cleanse their filthy places." Brinkerhoff was confident that Washington would soon become a northern city, and a "radiating center for the dissemination of northern ideas." The *Springfield Daily Republican* had also observed as early as November 1861 that Washington, in becoming more and more northern, was finally "sloughing off with its effete southern aristocracy the thriftlessness and stupidity" of that class.[28]

For many northerners, then, winning the war for the Union meant more than reuniting the states, rewriting the Constitution, and reforming their relationship with the government. Winning the war would also mean bringing the North physically and morally into the South, thus creating a more truly unified and virtuous nation. By the spring and summer of 1862, however, many northerners—both those in Washington and those left at home—were beginning to realize that winning the war and purifying the nation would be a long and painful process. As a result, some of them began searching for more convincing arguments to justify the harsh measures that would be necessary to achieve a final victory over the South.

28. James T. Ward, manuscript diary, LOC, entry dated December 19, 1861; *Cleveland Daily Plain Dealer*, January 9, 1861; Jacob Brinkerhoff to John Sherman, Sherman Papers, LOC, February 23, 1862; *Springfield Daily Republican*, November 29, 1861.

CHAPTER 10

War Powers and Confiscation

ON MAY 26, 1862, President Lincoln sent a message to the House of Representatives defending former Secretary of War Simon Cameron, who was now serving as minister to Russia in St. Petersburg. The House had passed a resolution on April 30 censuring Cameron for distributing money for military supplies, as well as granting the authority to purchase them, through unofficial channels, which smacked suspiciously of kickbacks and corruption. Lincoln stated that he had known about and agreed to this unorthodox distribution of money because he felt he could not trust the regular government officials. Cameron's action was unconstitutional because it subverted congressional appropriations power. Lincoln used his message as a way of justifying his course of action and incidentally presenting to Congress his view of war powers. "There was no adequate and effective organization for the public defense," he excused himself. Communications had broken down, and Congress had "indefinitely adjourned." In this last statement Lincoln was being somewhat disingenuous, since shortly after the Fort Sumter crisis in April he had given himself a breathing space of ten weeks by setting the opening date for the special Congressional session as July 4, 1861. President Lincoln told Congress that in approving these irregular financial methods, he had found it necessary to "choose whether, using only the existing means, agencies, and processes which Congress has provided, I should let the government fall at once into ruin, or whether, availing myself of the broader powers conferred by the Constitution in cases of insurrection, I would make an effort to save it with all its blessings for the present age and for posterity." Because under normal circumstances the Constitution forbade the confiscation of private property without benefit of a jury trial, war powers became an extremely important issue in the confiscation debates. Proponents of the Confiscation Act had to rely on emergency powers to justify the seizure of private property, while opponents argued that the Constitution did not grant extraordinary powers to Congress to subvert the Bill of Rights, even in wartime. Whichever interpretation of constitutional war powers would prevail would determine the federal government's, and the Union Army's, course of action on property confiscation, the treatment of enemy civilians, the conduct of the war, and the emancipation of slaves.[1]

Lincoln believed that in times of emergency the executive's powers were greatly enlarged and permitted him to go beyond what he called "the existing means" in order to save the life of the nation; indeed, his view of war powers remained consistent throughout his tenure as president. Two years later, in his 1863 message to the 37th Congress, Lincoln would declare that war powers had been the nation's "main reliance" in the crisis of civil conflict. He had regretted the necessity of employing extraordinary powers, but he felt that the country's survival demanded a flexible interpretation of executive authority. The phrase "war powers" has traditionally referred to temporarily expanded powers for the executive and legislative branches of government, and, since the Whiskey Rebellion in 1794, was usually interpreted as emergency or crisis powers. War powers act upon citizens, not on the military, because the Army obviously already has the power to act on enemy soldiers. During the Civil War, President Lincoln considerably expanded the powers of the executive with a series of acts that he said would have been "otherwise unconstitutional" had they not been necessary for the preservation of the Constitution "through the preservation of the nation." In other words, Lincoln appeared to believe that in extraordinary circumstances it was sometimes necessary to subvert the Constitution in order to save it. For the moment, the Constitution still forbade interference with the private property rights (even of rebels) without due process of law, and implied the protection of human property as well.[2]

The Constitution, however, gives war-making powers to Congress, not expressly to the president. Article I, Section 8, of the Constitution grants to Con-

1. Basler, *Collected Works,* 7:52–3; Randall, *Constitutional Problems,* 36–7.
2. Lincoln's First Message to Congress, July 4, 1861, in Basler, *Collected Works,* 4:421; Hyman, *Quiet Past and Stormy Present?,* 17.

gress the power to "declare war, grant letters of marque and reprisal, and make rules concerning captures on land and water." The Constitution also empowers Congress to "raise and support armies, . . . provide and maintain a navy," and to "provide for organizing, arming, and disciplining the militia." Further, Congress had the right to make all "necessary and proper" laws to carry out its functions. The Constitution established the president as commander-in-chief of the Army and Navy, "and of the militia of the several states, when called into the actual service of the United States." Most historians writing about war powers during the Civil War admit that the division of powers in the Constitution is not entirely clear. Indeed, the most important opinions and documents clarifying the use of war powers emerged only after the passage of the Second Confiscation Act. Francis Lieber's General Order No. 100, which clarified the treatment of private citizens and the confiscation of property, was published on April 24, 1863. The Supreme Court's decisions in the *Prize Cases,* which were a series of cases dealing with the capture and confiscation of rebel ships, retroactively approved the president's use of war powers. However, the *Prize Cases* were not decided until late 1863.[3]

Roughly speaking, there were three somewhat overlapping positions on war powers in Congress. Following Harvard University law professor Joel Parker, conservatives did not concede that the president or Congress had any extraordinary authority even in times of crisis, and declared that the Constitution was sacrosanct and adequate in all emergencies. They believed that although Congress declared war, the actual war-making powers belonged under the chief executive as commander-in-chief of the Army and Navy. This represented a dramatic shift from their opinions expressed less than a year before, when they had severely criticized President Lincoln's suspension of the privilege of the writ of *habeas corpus,* his order to call up the militia in April 1861, and the blockade of southern ports as unconstitutional. Although conservatives in Congress had sharply censured these actions, they were outvoted at the end of the special session, when Congress retroactively authorized all these acts as properly belonging to the president's emergency powers. But now the pressure of radical legislation in Congress forced them to reconsider their earlier position on executive authority, and forced them to rely on a moderate president rather than on a

---

3. For Lincoln's view of war powers, see Hyman, *Quiet Past and Stormy Present?,* chapter 2. Lieber, *OR,* ser. 2, vol. 5, 671–82; Randall, *Constitutional Problems,* 25–47.

Republican-dominated Congress in their effort to ameliorate the worst excesses of congressional radicals.

Congressional moderates' views were best represented by political theorist Sidney George Fisher. While still holding to the Constitution as the supreme law of the land, they nevertheless believed that a state of emergency broadened presidential power. Radical Republicans, of course, wanted the Union Army to carry out a harsh, punitive war program and to free the slaves as they entered southern territory. They believed that the Constitution granted Congress unlimited powers in time of crisis, and that the war powers placed the military firmly under congressional control, in dealing with both civilians and enemy armies. Both Francis Lieber and William Whiting supported this view in works published after 1862, and this interpretation of constitutional war powers would remain dominant throughout the war.[4]

The radicals in Congress insisted, throughout the Civil War, on hammering out each war measure on the floor of the Senate or the House. They were unwilling to leave decisions about fugitive slaves, property confiscation, and the seizure of telegraph and railroad lines to the discretion of military commanders but insisted on prescribing the methods by which such actions were to be carried out. In less turbulent times, such caution would have appeared conservative, and would have argued a careful regard for the separation of powers, and for constitutionally guaranteed rights. The war hawks risked watering down their punitive measures by submitting their proposals to partisan debate. But it was nearly always the Democrats and the border state politicians who insisted that such decisions be left to the president and to the military commanders.

In the first two years of the war, the administration and the U.S. military had shown themselves to be driven by considerations of conciliation and political expediency. For example, on May 30, 1861, General George B. McClellan had issued a proclamation in western Virginia assuring the residents there that he had no intention of harming their property or their rights. In the following July, McClellan wrote his famous "Harrison's Landing" letter, which declared that "neither confiscation of property, political executions of persons, territorial organization of States, or forcible abolition of slavery should be contemplated for

4. Paludan, *Covenant with Death*, 140–2; Fisher, *Trial of Our Constitution*, 199; for congressional positions on war powers, see Curry, *Blueprint*, 15–7; Lieber, *OR*, ser. 2, vol. 5, 671–82; Whiting, *War Powers*.

a moment." Although it was true that General John C. Frémont had attempted to free all the slaves of rebels in Missouri in September, President Lincoln had swiftly countermanded Frémont's proclamation. Lincoln was more pleased when, less than a week later, General Ulysses S. Grant in Paducah, Kentucky, issued his own proclamation in which he declared that it was not his intention to "injure or annoy" citizens, but rather to "respect the rights, and to defend and enforce the rights of all citizens." Generals William Tecumseh Sherman and Don Carlos Buell and Major General Henry W. Halleck also issued orders expelling fugitive slaves or ordering their return to bondage. The northern military leaders faced grave difficulties as they attempted to interpret federal policy toward fugitive slaves. There were simply no clear guidelines. When Generals Benjamin F. Butler and Grant attempted to get advice or guidance from the War Department as to fugitive slaves, they had to wait for months for any clear reply. The First Confiscation Act had certainly mandated the confiscation of slave labor actively involved in the war effort, but Army commanders did not feel themselves competent to judge the loyalty of rebel owners. Many of them also did not have the manpower or the supplies to cope with the hundreds of fugitive slaves entering their bivouacs.[5]

On the whole, military commanders followed no specific line of action and instead acted upon their political views rather than orders from on high in deciding on the difficult question of the confiscation of fugitive slaves. They reasoned that if fugitive slaves were not returned to their former putative owners, then the Army was, in a sense, confiscating them as contraband. Since December both the House and the Senate had been considering diverse bills and resolutions clarifying the military's policy toward fugitive slaves. However, even when Congress did enact measures dealing with the fugitive slave problem, such as Lovejoy's controversial resolution of the previous summer, military commanders simply ignored the legislation when it did not suit their political views. Although Congress had passed an Article of War on March 10, 1862, declaring that no Union officer would henceforth return fugitive slaves, officers with strong Democratic convictions ignored this order whenever they could. The frequent personnel shifts at the highest level of the Army made it diffi-

---

5. George B. McClellan to Abraham Lincoln, July 7, 1862, Lincoln Manuscripts, LOC; see Berlin, Fields, Miller, Reidy, and Rowland, *Slaves No More*, chapter 1; Simpson, *Let Us Have Peace*, chapter 2.

cult to enforce policy toward civilians. This situation was rendered even more troublesome by the fact that the administration, at least until the Emancipation Proclamation, did not appear to have a unified policy in the first place.[6]

Within the halls of Congress there was also little consensus as to the exact degree of control the various branches of government exercised over the Army. Although Republicans wanted to keep the power to legislate the war firmly within their own control (as revealed by their tight grasp on the Committee on the Conduct of the War), they could not agree with one another as to the extent or limits of the war powers conferred on Congress. For example, constitutional moderate Lyman Trumbull asserted that there was "not a syllable in the Constitution conferring on the President war powers." According to Republicans like Trumbull and Charles Sumner, the Constitution simply appointed the president commander-in-chief of the Army and Navy, but did not grant him the power to "raise the one nor provide the other." Statements like this obliquely referred to the fact that Congress held the purse strings, and therefore possessed the power to raise the Army and decide its strength. But radical Republicans, such as Albert G. Riddle, took their interpretation of war powers much farther. Riddle thought that in times of crisis, war powers conferred upon the government a "vast and limitless source of law." Meanwhile, despite continued radical pressure, the president refused to take an overtly active role on emancipation. Although his remonstrance to General David Hunter in May had clearly shown a greater disposition to recognize the military value of emancipation, Lincoln still refrained from issuing his own proclamation. Perhaps for this reason, radical senators argued that it was Congress, not the chief executive, who exercised full control of the war powers. Sumner claimed "for Congress all that belongs to any Government in the exercise of the Rights of War," while the president was "only the instrument of Congress, under the Constitution." The controversy over war powers, when directly related to confiscation of property, led the politicians in Washington into some oddly contradictory positions. Antislavery Republicans, such as Riddle, Trumbull, and Sumner, were forced into a position of having to argue a legislative approach to policy decisions, in order to maintain their control over the war effort. A moderate Republican, such as Alexander Diven of New York, on the other hand, had severe

6. White, *Life of Lyman Trumbull,* 176–7.

misgivings about what he sarcastically called the "general warfare" words in the Constitution. He demanded, "does that give Congress unlimited power?" He did not believe that the constitutional clause giving Congress the authority to provide for the general welfare of the United States (Article I, Section 8) permitted the legislators to do whatever they—in their judgment—deemed to be proper, "though it might be in the very teeth of the Constitution." Paradoxically, moderates and conservatives had to argue for a more federalist governmental theory, leaving the authority to conduct the war in the hands of a centralized power. This struggle foreshadowed continuing conflicts in the coming years when radical Republicans found themselves at even greater odds with Lincoln's successor, and had to overcome the objections of conservatives and moderates to their Reconstruction program as well as to their efforts to guarantee and protect the rights of black southerners.[7]

For the moment, however, those politicians who opposed confiscation were fighting an uphill battle. Democrats were more internally united on their refusal to grant extraordinary wartime powers to Congress. But they had also committed themselves to a vigorous prosecution of the war effort, and they were now in the awkward position of being forced to deny themselves the right to control the armed forces. Pennsylvania congressman Hendrick Wright claimed that he would "go for that line of policy which would leave the confiscation of property to the great emergencies as they arise." Congress could not presume to "lay down a rule for the conduct of [the] Army in regard to this particular." Indeed, many conservatives believed that the president and the Army were the sole judges of what actions should be taken against the enemy. For example, Rhode Island representative William Sheffield thought it would be absurd to "pass a law telling the President to fight at Manassas." In his reference to Manassas, he may have been referring indirectly to Congress's continual interference with military matters, which had heretofore only led to disastrous results. Many Americans certainly blamed the radicals' ceaseless shout "On to Richmond!" for the humiliating defeat at Bull Run. Sheffield believed that the president's duty was to "execute the law according to the rules of war and according to his conviction of duty." On the contrary, said Trumbull, the military had to remain subject to the civil power, and "should act and be made to act in

7. *Cong. Globe*, 37th Cong., 2nd sess., 1559, 498.

obedience to the civil power." Further, the Army was certainly acting in obedience to the nation's will "when it goes forth on this errand to put down the rebellion by war and by the slaughter of our enemies."[8]

The conservatives were frightened of the expanded powers of Congress, especially a Congress with numerically superior Republicans who were beginning to flex their muscles on the subject of slavery and on many other economic and social reform issues. Edgar Cowan, the only Republican who would eventually vote against the Second Confiscation Act, declared that "our Government is not one of absolute powers—it is in no respect omnipotent or restrained only by its own sense of propriety or policy." But Trumbull dismissed the notion that Congress could "confer a dangerous power" on the Army simply by legislating that it carry out its military duties. "Sir, is it not a power that is exercised every day by your armies?"[9]

One of the most nagging problems radicals faced in their fight for a more sweeping confiscation law was that they were attempting to broaden the scope of the First Confiscation Act considerably, while relying on the same arguments. They had argued, during the previous summer, that since the Constitution granted to Congress the right to "make rules concerning captures on land and water," Congress had the right to confiscate property and slaves when they were used as war matériel. However, even though Republicans were still arguing that confiscation was a military necessity, they had now turned their attention away from property used in battle and were focusing on private property held by civilians. Therefore, confiscation was clearly intended as a wartime punitive measure of military expediency, or (as many of them put it) a way of frightening rebels back into allegiance with the government. However, the Fifth Amendment expressly forbade the seizure of private property without due process of law, and the Sixth Amendment guaranteed the right to a criminal trial in the district where the crime was committed. The Second Confiscation Act violated both of these civil rights by authorizing the seizure of property and the emancipation of slaves, without affording the accused traitor the opportunity to defend himself in a court of law. (Of course, the Republicans' best defense was that the rebels themselves had closed the courts and therefore could not

8. Ibid., 406, 502, 508.
9. Ibid., 517; *Cong. Globe*, 37th Cong., 2nd sess., 509.

reasonably expect a jury trial.) The Constitution appeared inadequate to the crisis—or, at least, inadequate to the demands of radical Republicans.

Because radicals thought that the Constitution was insufficient to the emergency, they sometimes looked to the rules of international warfare for guidance, or at least for an expansion of their powers. Ohio representative Samuel Shellabarger believed that "in a war against rebellion this Government is endowed with all the powers over persons and property which are the incidents of civilized war, and with the additional power of all Governments over treason." Radicals, such as William Whiting, who was at this point in his career writing opinions for the War Department, and Columbia law professor Francis Lieber, thought that in times of emergency international rules of warfare could supplement or even supersede the Constitution. Conservatives were horrified by this implication, especially since the nation was now presumably at war to prove its superiority to European legal and governmental systems. Rhode Islander William Sheffield said he had always supposed that the "laws of nations and of war existed independent of Congress," and that they were made up of treaties and of the usages and customs of civilized nations. Congress, he said, had no power to "take from and no power to add to the law of nations." [10]

Those who thought that the Constitution was already adequate in any emergency, following conservative constitutionalist Professor Joel Parker of Harvard University, said that confiscation legislation was unnecessary because the Constitution already provided war powers to the executive. This view also was espoused by such moderate Republicans as Maine senator William Pitt Fessenden, who believed that the power to remedy all evils and reach all difficulties "exists, exists better, with greater effect, and to a greater extent in what is called the war power, than we can make it exist by meddling with it." Like his moderate Republican colleagues, Fessenden had voted for the First Confiscation Act but entertained strong doubts about the Second. He thought that the First Confiscation Act was already sufficient to the emergency, and should not be expanded to include the property of southern civilians not actually in arms against the Union Army. If the right to do so existed at all, it should be exercised by the Army, and not legislated by Congress. To this objection radical Benjamin F. Wade replied that although the Constitution certainly granted the pres-

10. *Cong. Globe*, 37th Cong., 2nd sess., 934, 501.

ident the power to confiscate all enemy property, he still thought it "ought to be declared by Congress before it is exercised." Therefore, Wade believed that "Warmaking powers" were among "those dormant powers that require the actions of Congress to call them forth." In fact, prior experience had shown that such laws were in fact necessary. After the War of 1812, Chief Justice John Marshall had returned confiscated property to British sympathizers on the grounds that Congress had not enacted any laws depriving such persons of their property.[11]

Ohio senator John Sherman was more pragmatic and once again returned to the problem of military necessity. In a state of emergency, Congress ought to place itself on a "more intimate and close connection with the Executive." In a comparison of executive and congressional war powers as enumerated in the Constitution, he found simply that Congress had the longer list. "The President has no other duty to perform except simply to carry out the powers conferred on him by Congress." If Congress failed to do its duty, and, for example, refused to give the president the power to seize railroad and telegraph lines, then the chief executive ought to take matters into his own hands. Here Sherman appeared almost to grant tyrannical powers to the president, but he added, somewhat hastily, that it was the duty of Congress "to prescribe the limitations of that power." Jacob Howard put it more bluntly. If one needed only laws as precisely stated in the Constitution, "Why, then, make a law against murder [and] piracy? . . . Why make a law to raise an army to go out and meet the enemy, vindicate the cause of the country and an outraged Constitution, and rescue the land from the curse of rebellion?" Clearly, the crisis had come to a point where harsh laws were not only desirable but necessary. Indeed, the Republicans felt themselves pressed by necessity on all sides. Trumbull would at one point reverse himself on his earlier stated principle of necessity; where he had once stated that necessity was the plea of tyrants, he would eventually cite military necessity as a justification for far-reaching war measures.[12]

Radicals such as Charles Sumner argued that the U.S. government had a dual relationship toward the Confederates; it could act against them as criminals and imprison or fine them, but it could also seize their property because

11. Ibid., 512. For confiscations after the War of 1812, see Randall, *Constitutional Problems*, chapter 2.
12. *Cong. Globe*, 37th Cong., 2nd sess., 515, 1881.

they were simultaneously "enemies outside the Constitution." In other words, rebellious southerners were at once criminals (because they stole federal property) *and* traitors (because they were in arms against the nation.) This notion of a dual relationship was seriously under contention during the confiscation debates. Once again the discussion revolved around the relationship of the Union government to *individual* southerners, who had now become too vast a force to be convicted under the Constitution's treason clause, which defined treason as "levying war against" the United States, or "adhering to their enemies, giving them aid and comfort." The northern home front used a more rough-and-ready measure to establish the rebels' possible guilt or innocence: they simply gauged southerners' loyalty by whether or not they owned plantations and slaves. For many northerners this now included border state slaveowners. Indeed, one of the more difficult problems for Congress to resolve concerned the fate of individual southerners, since the seizure of private property would obviously affect the lives of rebel citizens in an immediate way. Although the federal government was making war against an enemy power, confiscation legislation clearly brought the war home to the families and dependents of the rebels in arms.[13]

The ultimate success or failure of confiscation legislation depended almost entirely on Congress's willingness—or ability—to make a policy that would treat rebellious citizens fairly, while still facilitating a military victory. While the identity of black southerners was changing from property to person, the identity of rebellious white southerners (or more accurately, of white southerners who owned slave labor) was also changing, from citizen to rebel and back again, depending upon the tides of war and of northern public opinion. The northern home front wanted to hurt rebellious southerners personally, but Congress had to take the longer view toward the reunion of the two warring sections. Certainly, it was impossible for anyone to decide how to fight the war until they understood their relationship to rebellious southerners as citizens *and* as enemies. Because the North was fighting the South over the question of the legality of secession, it was impossible to declare that southerners were not still American citizens. Therefore, if southerners were still legally citizens, then they could not be deprived of their private property without a trial that proved them guilty of treason. If the U.S. Congress wished to proceed against them as enemies, then

13. Donald, *Charles Sumner*, 63.

they would in fact be recognizing the rebels' right to secede. But if one did not recognize the right of secession, then all persons in rebellion against the government would have to be treated as traitors, and subsequently face the penalty of execution. It would take another year before the Supreme Court, and legal theorists such as William Whiting, would hammer out the relationship between the government and the rebels. In late 1863, the Supreme Court found, in the *Prize Cases,* that because the war had been forced on the chief executive, he could exercise belligerent rights on the rebels without necessarily recognizing the right of secession. In his opinion on the famous *Amy Warwick* case, Justice Royal Tyler Sprague stated explicitly that the U.S. government had "full and complete belligerent rights, which are in no degree impaired by the fact that their enemies owe allegiance and have superadded the guilt of treason to that of unjust war." [14]

But how much power did Congress have over rebellious citizens? How would Congress protect a government that was, according to the most radical among them, incapable of protecting itself? Such questions were made even more problematic by the fact that the goal of the war was, eventually, to bring rebels back into an obedience of the laws that the government was now attempting to circumvent or expand. In order to accomplish this end, Congress would have to discover the extent and limit of the rights of rebels. The question of the disputed rights of rebellious white southerners was, for the moment, far more important to most northerners than the rights of black southerners— partly because of an intransigent race prejudice and partly because no slaves could constitutionally be set free until the rights of white southerners had been thoroughly defined. Further, the lessons they might have learned from European conflicts, like the sixteenth-century Dutch rebellion against Spain, or the more recent Greek rebellion against Turkey in 1829, could not be applied to the American troubles. The rebels were not attempting to overthrow the government, simply to separate from it. Moreover, the phrase "war powers" was always used to mean temporary, emergency powers. Once the crisis was under control again the government would once again assume a normal relationship toward citizens.

The problem was that it was difficult to know how to treat citizens who were busy committing treason; the many contemporary references to "this giant re-

14. Sprague is quoted in Randall, *Confiscation of Property during the Civil War,* 21.

bellion" made this problem poignantly clear. There were simply too many traitors; one could not execute them all. The Constitution had not envisioned a
rebellion of such magnitude. Senator Edgar Cowan thought that Congress's attempt to legislate the relationship between the government and rebellious citizens was an "absurdity," since "the moment the Congress declares war, the war
power operates upon the enemy, not upon citizens." Still, this was a dangerous
tack for him to take, since Congress would certainly have the right to take extreme measures against a declared enemy whom it had recognized as a belligerent power.

The Second Confiscation Act, in the end, did not attempt to resolve this
problem, which was one of the most important reasons for its ultimate failure.
The framers of the Constitution had certainly envisioned acts of rebellion, as
the wording on *habeas corpus* makes clear, but Congress—like the rest of the
nation—was overwhelmed by what they always called the "gigantic" nature of
the rebellion. The Second Confiscation Act simply empowered the president to
seize and "use" the rebels' property, and to free their slaves. The law did not lay
out a system or a procedure for such seizures, and in fact expressly forbade
Army officers to decide the guilt or innocence of persons claiming to be loyal
and demanding the return of their fugitive slaves. At this time there was no
simple way of determining the loyalty of persons living behind enemy lines. The
only loyalty oaths commonly in use in 1861 and 1862 were aimed at civil servants
and government officials, such as shipmasters, telegraphers, postal contractors,
and pensioners. Presumably leaving the decision to the president was a way of
throwing a sop to conservatives, but the failure to assign clear responsibility
for adjudicating guilt and carrying out the law hobbled the president's purported power in enforcing it. In this way Congress justified the enactment of
the confiscation law by citing the Constitution's grant of war powers, but did
not establish a way to use those war powers to carry the law out to its logical
conclusion.[15]

The Senate took up the House confiscation bill on June 23, 1862. Senator
Clark of New Hampshire now quickly reintroduced the weaker Senate select
committee bill (S. 131), which he had sponsored, as a substitute for the House
bill. Four days of acrimonious debate ensued, during which Republicans focused their speeches on the rival merits of the two bills. The Senate select com-

15. Hyman, *Era of the Oath*, 20.

mittee bill had limited *in rem* proceedings to narrowly defined cases, had introduced stringent judiciary procedures, and had enumerated specific classes of rebels whose property could be confiscated. The House confiscation bill was much more sweeping in the matter of applying *in rem* proceedings, although, unlike the Senate bill, it did not contain any emancipation measures. On June 28, 1862, the Senate adopted Clark's substitute, 28–13. At this time the amended bill went back to the House, where it was defeated and returned to the Senate on July 3, 1862. Senator Clark, however, moved that the Senate insist on its substitute, and called for a conference committee, to which the House agreed. All that remained now was to refine the details of a bill that would render it at once capable of confiscating southern real estate and slaves, without overturning all southern social institutions and without endangering constitutional protections of private property rights. The final round of debates would reveal the nearly insurmountable obstacles to this goal.

The Passage and the Failure of the
Second Confiscation Act

Missouri congressman John B. Henderson took
the place of former senator Trusten Polk, after Polk departed the Senate in August 1861 to join the Confederate Congress. Henderson, also a Democrat but
more moderate than Polk, took his seat the following January, but easily held
his own among his more experienced colleagues with his shrewd, witty, and
fair-minded rhetoric. In a clever speech he sketched out the hypocrisies and inconsistencies of both sides of the conflict. First, he ridiculed abolitionist northerners, who had long been teaching the equalities of the races, demanding universal emancipation "without attempting to elevate the negro in his own State,
and even rejecting all association with him." Further, radicals had been condemning the Constitution as a covenant with hell while at the same time blessing the "sacred instrument because it gives 'liberty' to every human being." But
Henderson was equally hard on southerners. The proslavery enthusiast, he said,
had been claiming the "divinity of slavery," but closed the door against its discussion "lest human reason should subvert the decrees of Omnipotence." The
slaveowning planter demanded new territories as an outlet for slavery, "while
he complains of the waste of labor in the South; he teaches the universality
of slavery and denies the power of the nation to interfere with it, because its
existence depends upon local law." Asserting that Congress had no power over
the subject in the territories, the defender of slavery threatened to disrupt the
Union unless slave codes were enacted for its protection. What was even more
outrageous, such men demanded "non-intervention by those not interested in
the institution," while demanding "the power of Federal law to force it upon an

unwilling people." Henderson was making an anticonfiscation speech, but he was also explaining in part why it was so difficult for his colleagues to come to any consensus. His speech exposed the deeply rooted inconsistencies and self-serving hypocrisies of both sides of the conflict. Indeed, the equivocations of the years of sectional crisis preceding the attack of Fort Sumter would lay the groundwork for an impractical confiscation law. The long-standing northern critique of the constitutional compromises with the institution of slavery (and, of course, with the slave power) contained an element of truth: such political compromises would make it extremely difficult to enact revolutionary changes in American civic society.[1]

Congress had a long history of leaving the practical details of legislation to the discretion of the courts, but in the final version of the Second Confiscation Act the members of Congress simply abdicated responsibility for seeing to it that the law could be enforced at all. The act mixed together both a watered-down version of a criminal treason law and a highly impractical "threat" to the property of rebels who were still in arms against the government. In this way, the Second Confiscation Act tried to serve two opposing functions. First, because it was aimed at the private property of southern planters, it was a symbol of long-term festering resentments against them and their aristocratic social system. Second, the act attempted to ameliorate the punishment dictated by the 1790 treason law, which was death. That law had allowed no judicial discretion on this point. Thus the confiscation law was attempting on the one hand to take revenge on slaveowners and remove them from their high position in American society and government, and at the same time—with an eye toward future reunion—attempting to be somewhat more merciful on them than the 1790 treason law mandated. The Second Confiscation Act established lesser crimes and punishments than the strict definition of treason as stated in the Constitution. Since the 1790 treason law mandated the death penalty, the confiscation law's $10,000 fine was perceived as more lenient.[2]

A further practical problem was the difference between the war aims of the Republican home front and those of Congress. Militant northerners had been agitating since the beginning of the war for a thorough, far-reaching law that

1. *Cong. Globe*, 37th Cong., 2nd sess., April 8, 1862, 1574.
2. Lucie, *Freedom and Federalism*, 15–8, 37–8.

would confiscate rebel property and then use it to pay for the cost of the war. Many had also insisted that Congress include slaves among the property to be confiscated. Although there was little consensus among northerners about the degree and kind of confiscation, and certainly none about the future of the confiscated slaves, one point was uncontested: that the aim of punitive legislation should be the confiscation of southern land, crops, and slave labor. Unlike their belligerent constituents, however, proconfiscation politicians in Congress were less interested in the future remunerative aspects of confiscation and spent little time speculating about potential revenue. Benjamin Wade protested that the Second Confiscation Act was not a "bill for the purpose of making money out of cultivating cotton lands for the government." He hardly supposed that the government would make "any very great sum by this operation," although he admitted that he hoped the government would come out even, and perhaps, that it would "make a little." Once again, when it came to such pragmatic matters, however, northerners were far more interested in the main chance. As important as legal niceties over the various "types" of property were in the halls of Congress (human property versus land and crops, for example) such distinctions were of little interest to those northerners who insisted in having a say in the disposition of all Confederates' assets.[3]

The northern public also wanted to bring the rebels to heel; revenge was always an important factor in their demand for punitive legislation. But punishment was simply not a feasible goal in Congress because moderate Republicans, Democrats, and border state representatives were unwilling to enact harsh measures, and the more conservative members of those groups were still averse to freeing slaves. Therefore, Congress set itself a task that was by definition almost impossible to accomplish. They tried to enact legislation that was to a great extent motivated by northern home front pressure but that in almost no way met any of the wishes articulated by the public. As formulated by Congress, the Second Confiscation Act was supposed to be "prospective," which meant that its primary function was to act as a threat of future punishments, rather than a way of carrying out immediate retribution. Indeed, although President Lincoln expressed many reservations about the law, the fact that it was prospective was the one point he praised. However, many northerners merely saw the sixty-day

3. *Cong. Globe,* 37th Cong., 2nd sess., 960.

warning period as an irritating loophole. Even the Democratic *New York Herald* mocked that a "good jurist" would "probably be able to drive through [the law] with a two horse team."[4]

A further reason for the weakness of the confiscation bill was that radical Republicans tried to enact this legislation in the face of powerful opposition among Democrats and also moderates within their own party, whose constituencies still remained crucial to the outcome of the war. Although Republicans outnumbered Democrats two to one in the Senate and nearly three to one in the House, there were many moderates in Congress and at home who shrank from extreme legislation and insisted on placing all wartime measures on a sound constitutional footing. This demand accounted for the inclusion of the clauses that most limited the effects of the confiscation law: first, the provision that there were lesser penalties for treason and that such penalties should include specific fines ($10,000); second, that the guilt or innocence of the property owner should be adjudicated in a court of law; and finally, John Sherman's amendment severely limiting the number of persons whose property was liable to confiscation without benefit of jury trial.[5]

Moderate Republicans tried to enact a law that would adhere to the letter of the Constitution; but the Constitution was a law in which their radical colleagues and their constituents no longer had unswerving faith, and which was at best ambiguous about the extent or scope of their powers. The fact remained that it was simply impossible to reconcile the myriad contradictory goals that confiscation legislation sought to join together. One could not reasonably expect, for example, to enact a law that would be enforced by Army officers in the field, but that would ensure that no property belonging to loyal Unionists would ever be touched. Although the Second Confiscation Act (as amended by Senator Sherman) did specify the five classes of persons whose property was liable to seizure, the problem still lay in determining the guilt or innocence of the persons involved.

But many of the proponents of confiscation still thought it might be possible to limit the law in such a way that it would not touch the lives of ordinary

4. Veto message to the House of Representatives, July 17, 1862, in Basler, *Collected Works*, 5:328–31; *New York Herald*, July 18, 1862.

5. Paludan, *Covenant with Death*, 27–60.

southerners. For example, New York senator Preston King somehow believed that the "confiscation law will only affect people who have property." Presumably by property he meant significant landholdings or slave ownership; he clearly subscribed to the myth that it would be possible to attack private property rights of leading rebels without endangering the rights of the "plain folk," and that white southerners who did not own slaves also did not own land. The Second Confiscation Act manifested this kind of shortsighted (and erroneous) thinking by enumerating specific persons whose property was to be seized, while allowing others the opportunity of resuming their allegiance to the U.S. government without further harm. That it would be impossible to seize the property of the one before the war was ended, and protect the property of the other in the midst of an invading army, escaped the lawmakers.[6]

Some Democrats who claimed to support a vigorous prosecution of the war effort (although almost none of them voted in favor of any confiscation bill) tried to argue that it was possible to fight a war without breaking any laws of humanity or reason. The doomed Crittenden Resolution, rejected by Congress early in the session, was the best example of this kind of thinking. Maine senator William Pitt Fessenden exposed the internal inconsistency of the Crittenden Resolution as an attempt to wage a war without making that war punitive. According to Fessenden, it was manifestly impossible to engage in civil warfare while refraining from "conquering or subjugating, or overthrowing internal institutions," especially if the nation were forbidden to use "constitutional means to do so." Here Fessenden was hedging his bets, since he was claiming that the confiscation was constitutional, while also saying that it was impossible to "defend and maintain the supremacy of the Constitution and to preserve the Union with all the dignity, equality, and rights of the several States unimpaired." New York congressman John Steele, a Democrat, tried making sense of these two goals. Like many other moderate Democrats, he claimed he was in favor of a vigorous, thorough prosecution of the war "to the utter discomfiture and annihilation of treason and treasonable sentiments, North and South." But he was not "anxious to see the land drenched in the best blood of our nation, and emancipation, conflagration, and death moving hand in hand with slaughtering armies." He obviously equated emancipation with "conflagration

6. *Cong. Globe,* 37th Cong., 2nd sess., 1813.

and death," but neglected to explain how he thought it would be possible to prevent death from moving hand in hand with what he called "slaughtering armies."[7]

The problem was to try to honor the "extreme limits" of the Constitution without stepping so far over the bounds that it would be impossible to return to the law once the conflict was over. Furthermore, not even the most sanguine war hawks could be absolutely certain of the outcome of the war or its effects on the constitutionally guaranteed rights of American citizens. These fears may have been behind the radicals' careful acceptance of such niceties as the constitutional prohibition of *ex post facto* laws and bills of attainder. Indeed, they almost seemed to fall over one another in their eagerness to prove that their proposed bills were neither the one nor the other. Vermont senator Jacob Collamer remarked sarcastically that he wondered why the senators were so "tender" with regard to *ex post facto* laws when they were willing to dispense with all other constitutional guarantees. He asked one other, ultimately unanswerable question: why did his radical colleagues think they could not "make an effective law" if they had to remain within the Constitution? If that was indeed so, he scoffed prophetically, they had "better do without an effective law." Indeed, in their dependence on such legal sleight-of-hand as *in rem* proceedings and their refusal to work out the practical problems of seizing millions of acres of southern land, his opponents could be said to have obeyed his injunction to "do without an effective law." The Constitution expressly forbids both such laws. *Ex post facto* laws retroactively punish persons for crimes committed *prior* to the passage of the law. "Bills of attainder" are legislative assumptions of guilt; that is, a governmental body passes a law convicting a specific person of a crime and then punishing him. Since this violates the Sixth Amendment, such a law is unconstitutional. The Second Confiscation Act is not an *ex post facto* law because it proposes to seize the property of persons "hereinafter" convicted of treason. No doubt this is why Lincoln praised the law as being "prospective."[8]

In addition to — or, perhaps because of — these legal and moral confusions, the Second Confiscation Act was written in such a way that it would prove difficult to enforce. The first two sections of the act stated that rebels found guilty of aiding the rebellion and convicted in a court of law after the passage of

7. Ibid., 402, 404.
8. Ibid., 1962.

the law would be subject to confiscation. The fifth section, however, which had originally been authored by Senator John Sherman, enumerated specific persons, like the Confederate president, vice president, and Congress, as well as officers in the Confederate Army and Navy, and provided for the immediate seizure of their property. Under normal circumstances such seizures would be prohibited by the Fifth Amendment, but the law provided that this property could be seized under *in rem* proceedings. When private homes and plantations were confiscated (like Robert E. Lee's Arlington, Virginia, home or Jefferson Davis's plantation in Mississippi), the title to their property was granted to the Treasury Department, not to private citizens. At this time, most slaveowning planters were still out of reach of most federal courts. Eventually this would change as the Union armies advanced farther into Confederate territory, but in 1862 this had not yet become an inevitable conclusion. By the time of the passage of the Second Confiscation Act, federal courts had reopened in Virginia, Louisiana, parts of Tennessee, and Maryland.

Trumbull tried to defend his bill by explaining that it was "manifestly impossible to try a man for treason in South Carolina." He knew perfectly well that "some have objected that this bill amounts to nothing; that we have not possession of this property." But he thought that if Congress could pass a confiscation law, the federal government could take possession of the property "next year or any time hereafter," by which he presumably meant, after the war was over. What Trumbull did not fully explain was whether he thought the traitors would then have to be tried. The confiscation law simply provided for the seizure of their property without a jury trial, but Trumbull seemed to be hinting that once the courts and federal law had been reestablished in South Carolina, it might once again be possible to try rebels for treason in a regular court of law, with a jury trial. Of course, the problem remained that the judges and juries would obey local law and would carry out local legislation on slavery. Congress had not yet determined to overturn state laws permitting property in human beings. At the same time, depending on how one interpreted the Second Confiscation Act, any slave putatively freed by the confiscation laws would have to bring a suit in order to prove that her or his former owner had indeed been a rebel. Section two of the law (the section requiring judicial proceedings, recently added by New Hampshire senator Daniel Clark) provided that the accused had to be convicted of the crime of treason before his property could be confiscated, although the sections referring to slaves (eight and nine) did not specify whether they were to be considered "ordinary property" for the purposes of confiscation. If they were, then they would have to bring suit in order to ensure their freedom. Presumably these suits would be heard on a case-by-case basis, which—had President Lincoln not issued the Emancipation Proclamation later that year—would not only have made it nearly impossible for the slaves of traitors to gain their freedom, but would also have threatened to congest southern courts for years to come.[9]

The Second Confiscation Act tried to redefine the crime of treason so that the federal judges could inflict a lesser penalty than execution on the convicted traitor. The problem with enacting a lesser penalty for a lesser crime was that it would be extremely difficult to define precisely what such a crime would consist of; that is, how did one define treason that did not merit the extremest punishment? The Second Confiscation Act provided that any slaveowner wishing the return of his fugitive slaves had to take an oath of loyalty, but did not permit Army officers to assess the loyalty or disloyalty of the alleged rebel. In any event, Congress had already passed a law in March forbidding officers to return fugitive slaves. Further, the redefinition of treason was based on vague and changeable ideas like "loyalty," which were almost impossible to define accurately and equally difficult to prove in a court of law. A trial held in the district where the crime was committed (as guaranteed by the Sixth Amendment) would probably not convict an accused traitor. New York Republican congressman James R. Sheffield demanded, "how are you going to convict traitors before a jury of traitors?" How would it be possible for any judge to define the limits of disloyalty? Democratic senator James A. McDougall pointed out that "loyalty" was not a precise legal term. It had to be obvious that the question of loyalty would be determined by "the caprice, proclivities, or inclination of whoever may be the judge in the case." When legislators undertook to "limit a man's right," he felt, "we should use such terms as would give a definite, fixed limit in exact and understood form of words." Loyalty was difficult to prove, even after the individual in question had taken an oath declaring his or her allegiance to the Constitution and the government. Washington, D.C., slaveholders who wished to be compensated for slaves freed by the April 1862 law first had to swear to their past loyalty. Within a few months, jurors, U.S. office-holders, and

9. Ibid., 942.

all persons contracting with the government would also have to take an "iron-clad" oath, swearing that they had never participated in or supported the rebellion. Some Army officers, especially those commanding regiments in the border states, also demanded that residents take a loyalty oath before being able to buy food, vote in local elections, hold office, or receive protection for their private property. Moreover, Army officers were able to exercise a great deal of control and discretion over the wording of the oaths.[10]

In the meantime, like their constituents, many members of Congress—both Republicans and Democrats—were growing tired of the gasconades occasioned by the confiscation debates. The opponents to confiscation thought that the law was nothing but an empty proclamation, and frequently called it by such epithets as *brutum fulmen,* or mere bravado. *Brutum fulmen* was simply a law that "fulminated noisily," or threatened and blustered but ultimately could not be executed. Jacob Collamer recognized that if the confiscation law were to function as an effective weapon against the enemy, it had to be enforced quickly. Since the law was mainly prospective, its military effectiveness was clearly limited. He declared that any law whose "present utility comes from its being speedily *executed,* but which purports now to emancipate slaves beyond our military lines, is mere bravado." Pronunciamientos, he said, were unbecoming "real sovereignty." He claimed that the American people were sick of, and the world was laughing at, "the amazing courage of Congress," those swaggering heroes, who wore "daggers in their mouths," and who

> Dash and vapor
> Less on the field of battle than on paper.

Cowan agreed that the confiscation bill was "little more than bravado." Valiant proclamations notwithstanding, no confiscation could ensue until the Army could actually seize the property and enforce the penalty. It stood to reason that when the federal government and the Union Army were "in a condition to do that, neither proclamation nor law of Congress nor resolution will be necessary." Confiscation, he disingenuously argued, would be "as well accomplished without them as with them, and, in any event, they would be meaningless and inoperative." Once again conservatives were arguing against their traditional

10. Burton and Green, "Defining Disloyalty," 215–21; *Cong. Globe,* 37th Cong., 2nd sess., 502, Appendix, 66; Hyman, *Era of the Oath,* 22–4, 36–7.

position: first, that the rule of law would in itself guarantee the survival of republic, and second, that traditional federalism (the separation of the legislative from the executive) would ensure that no one agency would overstep its
bounds. In their anticonfiscation speeches, however, men such as Collamer and
Cowan assumed nearly opposite viewpoints. Both men appeared to be arguing
(however insincerely) that the federal government and Union armies ought to
be able to carry out punitive actions without congressional legislation, and that
in the face of military might, such legislation was actually unnecessary. They
also appeared to be hinting that legislative actions were of little more value and
force than "pronunciamientos," and that projected difficulties in enforcing the
law (a rather pragmatic position for conservatives) invalidated the law itself.
Later, of course, their objections about the ineffectiveness of confiscation legislation would also be leveled at Lincoln's Emancipation Proclamation, in which
they would be joined by the radicals.[11]

A further paradox was the radical Republicans' desire to reform southern
society from the ground up, and, at the same time, to recreate a unified country. One way to accomplish this would be to repopulate confiscated southern
lands with northern migrants or former Union soldiers. A few radicals, such as
Thaddeus Stevens and George Julian in Congress, and black abolitionists, such
as Frederick Douglass and Francis Cardozo, would eventually propose settling
the confiscated lands with freed slaves, but such extreme ideas were hardly popular anywhere else in the North. The future of the freed slaves would not be
settled by confiscation legislation, whose primary purpose was to disable the
southern economy and to destroy the slaves' status as property, not to realign
southern social institutions. The 37th Congress had used antislavery legislation
to attack the institution in areas where Congress held nominal control (such as
the territories or Washington, D.C.), but Republicans who attempted to extend
the reach of the Second Confiscation Act to protect the liberty and civil rights
of the freed people were continually stymied by the moderates of their own
party.[12]

Ultimately, the 37th Congress was unwilling to enact legislation that interfered radically with southern society or with land ownership. When a government confiscates land from an enemy citizen, that land must stay where it is;

11. *Cong. Globe*, 37th Cong., 2nd sess., 935; 1138.
12. Cox, *Lincoln and Black Freedom*.

unlike crops, livestock, or money, land cannot be moved. Therefore, the conquering government (if it confiscates the land of the vanquished foe) must take responsibility for a wholesale reformation of the defeated society's economic and social arrangements, since leaving the land there and populating it with victorious soldiers or freed slaves would destroy the existing society. Although a few of the most radical members of Congress contemplated the possible redistribution of southern land, such ideas were simply too extreme to be seriously entertained by the majority. Moreover, land reform that included the redistribution of land to former slaves found no favor among the northern public. While many northerners—Republicans and War Democrats alike—might have considered the confiscation of slave labor a matter of military necessity, few of them were willing to contemplate the notion of setting the confiscated slaves immediately and unconditionally free and settling them on land formerly owned by white southerners. The radicalism of immediate emancipation was more than enough to occupy the minds and pens of white northerners—land reform on a grand scale went too far for the majority of them. Many northerners were willing to contemplate the reformation of constitutional guarantees of property in slave labor; they were not willing to revise the notion of the protection of private property rights to such a far-reaching degree.[13]

Moreover, moderate politicians took a wider view of the potential long-term impact of punitive measures than their radical colleagues or the home front. Edgar Cowan begged his fellow senators to consider the possible consequences of such a sweeping redistribution of property. Who would buy the confiscated plantations? And what kind of neighborhood could possibly exist between the former owner or his heirs and the new owners? Cowan shuddered when he tried to envision the "delights of this society." The dispossessed families would never forget the forfeiture of their homes. The memory of the loss, he predicted, would "sit continually by the hearthstone of that family a hideous specter, deathless for ages, prompting to revenge and inciting to rebellion. Sir, your thrifty purchasers will not like incumbrances such as these hanging over your forfeited estates." In fact, such arguments presaged the problem of maintaining federal control once the war was over. A massive military presence would have been required to enforce various statutes meant to reconstruct the

---

13. For land reform ideas during and after the Civil War, see Foner, *Politics and Ideology*, especially chapter 7, "Thaddeus Stevens, Confiscation and Reconstruction," 128–49.

states according to the Republican vision. Vermont senator Jacob Collamer demanded to know what his Republican friends "would . . . give for a farm in Tennessee or Georgia, with the people swarming around you unhoused, people believing themselves to be owners who were outlawed and deprived of their property by you? Why, sir, it would require two regiments to take care of every plantation. [Laughter.] No man would give a dollar for such a title." [14]

Despite the many practical problems, there was a continual tendency on the part of anticonfiscation men to exaggerate the sweeping nature of the confiscation bill. The confiscation bill that finally emerged was neither sweeping nor enforceable. John Sherman's list of persons (president, vice president, military and political leaders of the Confederacy) liable under the law was explicitly meant to target only upper-class southerners, who could not be reached by the law because they were behind enemy lines. Moreover, the law could not operate upon anyone not enumerated wherever courts were in session. If the bill passed with all these safeguards and provisions in place, it was in the highest degree unlikely that there would ever be any wholesale confiscation of property in the South. Orville H. Browning thought the Second Confiscation Act would excite the "ridicule of the world," and asked Lincoln to veto the law. But he did recognize one thing that appeared to escape his radical opponents: that it would be simply impossible to execute the law without "marching an army into the enemy's country, and by the strong hand of arms." Lyman Trumbull also vehemently denied that the confiscation bill was sweeping. As far as he was concerned, the entire law had been "grossly, or perhaps deliberately" misunderstood by its critics. "So far from striking at all the property of each and every citizen in the seceded States, it would not probably reach the property of one in ten of the *rebels*, and in no case would touch the property of a loyal citizen." In this he was probably not being strictly honest; if the law had not been hobbled by its own internal inconsistencies, it might have affected the lives and property of a large majority of southerners. Further, Trumbull reminded his opponents that the law only reached property, not persons, and the rebels still had time to avoid confiscation if they laid down their arms. Trumbull thought that the law would probably only affect those who abandoned their property. He was right. This was partly due to the fact that the law was so poorly constructed, and partly because President Lincoln would later steadfastly refuse to enforce it. By 1866, less

14. *Cong. Globe,* 37th Cong., 2nd sess., 1051, 1811.

than $2 million in property had been confiscated from rebels, and most of that was returned under President Andrew Johnson's amnesty proclamation. Southern slaveholders would also have counted the loss of their capital investment in human beings, which some historians have calculated at the value of $3 billion. By the end of the Civil War, the Union Army had gained control over the territory of the former Confederacy. Although there had been widespread forage, plunder, destruction, and outright theft of rebel land and crops, ironically very little private nonhuman property was legally confiscated. It was impossible to gain title of confiscated lands without court proceedings. Edward Bates consistently refused to give any specific instructions to district attorneys, and President Lincoln, always hoping for a reunion, was uninterested in any sweeping confiscation of southern property.[15]

After amending the conference committee's report on the confiscation bill to include confiscation as punishment for treason, authorization for the enlistment of black men, and a colonization provision, the House of Representatives adopted the measure on July 11 by a vote of 84–42. This bill was considerably stronger than the earlier select committee bill because it allowed *in rem* proceedings in all cases, not just the narrowly restricted ones listed in the previous measure. The new bill also reinstated the earlier language from the Senate bill (Trumbull's S. 151 bill), which emancipated the slaves of all persons aiding the rebellion after the passage of the law. After passing the House, the conference committee report was sent to the Senate on July 12, where it also passed, 27–12.[16]

In the end, partly because of constitutional issues and partly because Democrats failed to carry their opposition to emancipation, the 37th Congress created a law that barely confiscated any "ordinary" property, although it did make it easier to liberate slaves. However, most of the slaves liberated under the Second Confiscation Act were freed only after having "confiscated" themselves, because the law granted the U.S. Army the right not to return fugitive slaves. Therefore, the slaves first had to flee from bondage—assuming they did not have to bring suit in court—before they could be considered legally emancipated. The law did not protect the slaves in their newfound liberty, whether

15. See David Herbert Donald, Jean H. Baker, and Michael F. Holt's discussion of the problem of the loss of capital investment in slaves in *Civil War and Reconstruction*, 502; *Cong. Globe*, 37th Cong., 2nd sess., 1858, 1558.

16. *Cong. Globe*, 37th Cong., 2nd sess., 3266–7. For votes on the final version of the Second Confiscation Act, see Appendix 2.

gained as a result of the Confiscation Acts or by their own actions. In part for this reason, and because they recognized that the law would be nearly impossible to enforce, radical Republicans were disgusted with the final version. Zachariah Chandler said that the bill was not "worth one stiver," and called it "utterly worthless." But most of the members of the 37th Congress found that they could keep the Constitution alive, obey their own oaths to support and protect it, and take the poisonous center—slavery—out of the founding document without destroying the country. Their fundamental belief in the possibility of republican government was vindicated by writing a confiscation law that would be difficult to enforce. In the end, private property rights did not suffer the extreme penalties of war; but no one could predict with any certainty that Fifth Amendment protections of the right of due process would survive the passage of punitive wartime legislation.[17]

Recalling the sweltering days of July 1862, journalist Benjamin Perley Poore wrote in his memoirs that "Independence Day . . . was not joyously celebrated at Washington." The rip-roaring military parades of last year no longer seemed appropriate, now that the capital's hospitals were crowded with the wounded and dying. General McClellan finally had been defeated on the Peninsula and was taking shelter on a gunboat on the James River. On July 1, President Lincoln called up another three hundred thousand volunteers, but the nation was growing desperate over the defeats of Fair Oaks (May 31–June 1) and the Seven Days Campaign (June 26–July 2). On July 12, the president invited border state congressmen to a meeting at the White House, urging them to vote favorably on the compensated emancipation bill. Once again they refused to listen to him, reiterating all of the objections they had voiced during the confiscation debates. Observing all this, New Yorker George Templeton Strong wrote in his diary on July 14, 1862, that "we are in the depths just now, permeated by disgust, saturated with gloomy thinking." On the other hand, he had been reading in the newspapers that Congress was about to pass a stronger Confiscation Act, and was heartened that "the government seems waking up to the duty of dealing more vigorously with rebellion by acts of emancipation and confiscation."[18]

---

17. A stiver is an archaic name for a small coin, worth about one English penny.
18. Poore, *Perley's Reminiscences,* 2:128; Strong, *Diary,* entry dated July 14, 1861.

The following afternoon, on July 15, 1862, the 37th Congress passed the Second Confiscation Act. Some northern newspapers commented briefly on the event, agreeing with Strong that the government at last seemed to be interested in waging a real war. Others contented themselves with the bare announcement, refusing to commit themselves one way or another. But many papers pointed out that the law was simply impractical. There seemed to be little point in a "foolish bill" that confiscated property "which we have not in possession," or emancipated slaves "before we are in occupation of the territory where the slaves are to be found." On the whole, there appeared to be a general consensus that the law would amount to little, since it was necessary to "catch the hare" before one could cook him. However, most Republican papers were mildly optimistic about the law. The *New York Times* thought there was no doubt that Abraham Lincoln would promptly approve it, and commented that no one could claim the Confiscation Act was unnecessarily severe. Indeed, the *Times* found it "exceedingly lenient," since it would probably not affect "the great mass of those at the South who have been forced into the Southern army, or otherwise involved in the rebellion without their own agency." [19]

President Lincoln refused at first to sign the bill because he considered it to be unconstitutional. The Constitution forbade the absolute forfeiture of real estate, even as punishment for treason, because this permanently deprived the traitor's descendants of real estate belonging to their family. The Constitution only permitted the confiscation of property for the lifetime of the traitor. Lincoln did finally approve the law, but sent a veto message to Congress explaining his position. He asked Congress to include an explanatory resolution, or risk a presidential veto. Amid loud protests from radicals, who were outraged at this executive coercion, and repeated demands from conservatives to resubmit the bill as it was originally passed (thus ensuring the veto), Congress appended an explanatory addendum to the Second Confiscation Act, which specifically addressed Lincoln's objections; the addendum explained that no property would be confiscated beyond the traitor's "natural life." The president signed the bill on July 17, 1862. On that day he also approved the Militia Act, which provided for the employment of "persons of African descent" in "any military or naval service for which they may be found competent." Perhaps

19. *New York Herald,* May 27, July 16, 1862; *New York Times,* July 15, 1862.

more important, this law also explicitly provided for the permanent freedom of all such persons, together with their families.[20]

Predictably, home front reaction to Lincoln's handling of the confiscation bill depended upon the political stripe of the beholder. Although few private citizens wrote to their representatives in Washington about the bill or Lincoln's modification, there was some editorializing about it in the press. Newspapers like the Democratic *New York Herald* hailed Lincoln's modification as a "bold and patriotic" move. The *Philadelphia Inquirer* declared that Lincoln had shown his "sterling conservatism," and the *New York Times* called the explanatory addendum an "obvious dictate of justice no less than of humanity." The *Times* also thought that the president had now "fairly broken loose from both factions—the Abolitionists and Pro-Slaveryites," and hoped he would continue to "keep them all aloof from his counsels in future."[21]

The confiscation bill itself, however, came in for some severe strictures because the more thoughtful critics realized that Congress had passed a law that would be nearly impossible to enforce, and because it appeared to do nothing more than permanently free the slaves, rather than confiscate southern real estate and crops. This was not what northern voters had had in mind when they were urging Congress to pass stringent confiscation laws, or to facilitate severe war measures. A Massachusetts paper, the *Springfield Daily Republican,* claimed that the Second Confiscation Act was "practically an emancipation bill, and nothing else." There seemed to be little point in confiscating property "for the lifetime only of a traitor, which is all the Constitution allows, and by due process of law." Indeed, the bill was likely to amount to little. The *Republican* predicted accurately that any attempt to put it in force would be made "in but few cases, those of the leaders or millionaires of the rebellion, but the emancipation of their slaves is made absolute." The paper thought that wholesale emancipation would occur "just as fast as we get control of the slave states." Further, the bill was probably still unconstitutional, even with Lincoln's amendments added to it, because it did not distinguish carefully enough between the property of loyal Unionists in the South and that belonging to rebels. It did not matter that the law had been enacted in a state of war. Once the various confiscation cases

20. Shapiro, *Confiscation of Confederate Property in the North,* 36–41.

21. *New York Herald,* July 17, 1862; *New York Times,* July 17, 1862; *Philadelphia Inquirer,* July 18, 1862.

were heard in the local courts, most or all of them would be swiftly overturned. According to the *Republican*, "[m]embers of Congress may consider the Constitution set aside by the emergency, but the courts will not so regard it."[22]

If some on the northern home front were pleased with the law, it was probably because they simply misunderstood what the act was supposed to accomplish, and took it to be much more sweeping than it was in reality. A week after the act was passed, loyal Unionists in New York held a "Grand Union Square meeting," complete with stirring speeches and much applause. In an editorial entitled "The True Policy of Punishment," the *New York Times* reported that "all demands for the most unsparing punishment of the rebels, and for the most vigorous measures toward them" had met with great applause. This was especially true of speeches demanding "universal confiscation of real estate, . . . the wasting of rebel fields and harvests, the armed occupation of their houses, and the appropriation of all property." Clearly, in celebrating the recently passed confiscation law, the audience had not bothered to familiarize itself with its legal limitations, which would make the "appropriation of all property" extremely unlikely.[23]

Regardless of his reputation for "sterling conservatism," Lincoln lost no time solidifying the strength of the new confiscation law. On July 25, 1862, the president issued a proclamation aimed to "suppress insurrection." Lincoln warned all rebels to "cease participating in, aiding, countenancing, or abetting the existing rebellion . . . against the government." If they refused to return to their proper allegiance to the United States, they would suffer the penalties of the Second Confiscation Act. As had occurred on several previous occasions when the president took matters into his own hands (such as the Frémont and Hunter situations), home front response to the president's action was positive. This shift in attitudes is especially striking because in this case Lincoln was making a decisive move against slavery, rather than palliating an Army officer's emancipation schemes. In fact, the *New York Times* declared (somewhat optimistically) that the "historian who shall record the progress of the present war will have no trouble in determining the theory on which it was conducted in the United States."[24]

22. *Springfield* (Mass.) *Daily Republican*, July 19, 1862.
23. *New York Times*, July 25, 1862.
24. Basler, *Collected Works*, 7:341; *New York Times*, July 28, 1862.

There was little adverse reaction to Lincoln's proclamation, even though the northern public and press had declared itself heartily sick of such edicts in the past. Perhaps a proclamation coming from the chief executive carried more weight than one coming from an Army officer, especially since the president was now using an official pronouncement as an instrument of war. The *Philadelphia Inquirer* rejoiced that the nation was at last beginning to unsheathe the sword, and declared that hitherto, it was "only the Rebels who have been waging *war.*" Prior to Lincoln's proclamation, the "brawny fists of our Northern freemen [had] been muffled in boxers' gloves, our swords . . . but the fencer's foils, and our cartridges . . . but blanks." The *Inquirer* appeared to be implying that until the passage of the confiscation law, the instruments of war had been ineffective in achieving the aims of war. Indeed, until now, the Army and the administration had been "models of fraternal forbearance, patterns of courtesy, and paragons of chivalry," but this was now evidently to end. One Chicago physician foresaw in Lincoln's proclamation the "beginning of the end" of the war, and firmly believed that peace was now nearly "conquered."[25]

When conservative newspapers criticized the president's proclamation, they did so not because it contemplated taking enemy property but because it was likely to affect the property of loyal Unionists living in the South. The *Louisville Daily Democrat* declared that its editors had never supported a "rose water policy . . . against the guilty in this rebellion." On the contrary, they did not think there was any punishment the rebels did not deserve. But injustice should have no part in the nation's political policy, and for that reason they were "utterly opposed to all confiscation bills, as they punish more of the innocent than of the guilty." The *Democrat's* editors did not explain, however, how it would be possible to use "severity" against the guilty without confiscating their property.[26]

On the whole, the northern public had few criticisms to make. Any action was better than continual delay and indecision, and so long as decisive action came from a president who had shown himself to be unfailingly moderate in his handling of various crises, even conservative citizens were willing to accept his more stringent moves. At the end of the month the *Philadelphia Inquirer* published an editorial entitled "Popular Approval of the Policy of Action." The *In-*

25. *Philadelphia Inquirer*, July 24, 25, 1862; John O. Edwards to John Sherman, Sherman Papers, LOC, August 6, 1862.

26. *Louisville Daily Democrat*, July 27, 1862.

quirer besought its readers to think carefully in judging the president's proclamation. The editor was persuaded that calm reflection would show it was neither "radical" nor "ultra," and declared that public opinion had now "settled down almost universally to a thorough approval of the present policy of the Government." Although it was probably true that "peculiar institutions may suffer," the *Inquirer* was now equally sure that "the Revolution of 1861 will end in the thorough prostration of the conspirators, in the supremacy of the Union, and in retributive justice upon the plotters of the causeless Rebellion." Although the Second Confiscation Act did, in the end, "cause the peculiar institution to suffer," it did not visit retributive justice on the rebels, nor did it reimburse the loyal for the depredations of the traitorous. Still, the public reaction to the Second Confiscation Act and to Lincoln's subsequent proclamation indicates a growing acceptance of emancipation as a military measure even among moderate northerners.[27]

According to historian James G. Randall, from 1862 to 1865 the federal courts handled a "considerable volume of business" in confiscation cases, but these court cases resulted in an insignificant amount of income to the U.S. Treasury. The department solicitor's report, dated December 27, 1867, showed that the modest total of $129,680.67 had been paid into the Treasury from confiscated Confederate property. These unimpressive results are entirely representative of the way the law was debated and enacted. Although on a local level there was a great deal of interest in identifying and confiscating the property of rebels, in the courts and officially there was almost no real effort to effect the transfer of property from private hands to the federal government. This is not to say that southerners lost no property during and after the Civil War. The Captured and Abandoned Property Act (1864), the Direct Tax Act (1862), and military operations on enemy soil resulted in widespread seizure of land, cotton, livestock, and, of course, the labor of slaves. But of a legal confiscation of property, carried out in a court of law, there was very little sign.[28]

Some of the reasons for this difficulty were evident in the way the law had come into being. Through debate and the committee process, Senator Trumbull's sweeping bill had become a patched-together compromise measure that

27. *Philadelphia Inquirer,* July 29, 1862.
28. Quoted in Randall, *Constitutional Problems,* 288–91.

neglected all the practical details of taking the rebels' private property and freeing slaves. Moreover, the fact that no one was assigned responsibility for confiscation or for adjudging the guilt of the owners meant that the details would have to be hammered out—and the law enforced—by federal courts and the attorney general, Edward Bates. It would quickly become apparent that both the attorney general and President Lincoln were reluctant to enforce the Second Confiscation Act. Indeed, throughout the war, the president would remain cautious in the treatment of enemy civilians, as he had been cautious in the matter of emancipating their slaves in the early years of the war. He had forced Generals Frémont and Hunter to rescind their emancipation edicts, and would continue to treat future proclamations of military confiscation in a similar manner.

Attorney General Edward Bates had been born in Virginia, had represented Missouri as congressman, and was a staunch conservative on the slavery question. He always took a hard line on the question of military against civil authority. Throughout the war, Bates was ever protective of southerners' private property and usually demanded the return of confiscated lands and cotton. Furthermore, until 1863 he thought military emancipation illegal because he considered that the Fugitive Slave Law was still in effect, even after the passage of the First Confiscation Act, because the law only applied to the slaves of owners in arms against the United States.[29]

On November 13, 1862, Bates received an order from President Lincoln charging him to work out the practical details of confiscation proceedings. This was necessary because the 37th Congress had neglected to include any provisions in the Second Confiscation Act indicating how the act was to be carried out, who would take responsibility for its enforcement, or who would judge the guilt or innocence of the owner of the property to be confiscated. Bates's careful memorandum, which he distributed to all district attorneys the following spring, made it clear that both the First and the Second Confiscation Acts operated at the same time, and that all procedures would take place in federal, not military courts. Confiscation, Bates was always careful to point out, was a civil, not a military matter.[30]

The procedure Bates outlined was fairly straightforward. First, some interested party had to file a libel against an owner, or against property. The libel

<hr>

29. Cain, *Lincoln's Attorney General,* 160.
30. Basler, *Collected Works,* "Order Concerning the Confiscation Act," 5:496.

would be filed against the owner, for example, if he were known to be an officer in the Confederate Army, or against property, if it were being used to prosecute the rebellion in some way. The owner would then be warned to appear at a hearing; if he or she did not appear, the hearing would be held *ex parte.* If the property was condemned, the U.S. Marshal was to sell the property at public auction, and the proceeds deposited in the Treasury. In theory, the process should have worked fairly smoothly. In practical terms, however, the attorney general was of little help to local officers, who plagued his office with requests for advice on how to proceed. In most cases, Bates simply declined to answer the requests for guidance, and refused to enforce local confiscation proceedings.

One of the most famous confiscation cases occurred in May 1864 and perfectly illustrated Bates's usual handling of such situations. General Lew Wallace, who was at that time in charge of the Middle Department at Baltimore, issued two orders confiscating the property of Maryland rebels. As always, the authorities in Washington learned of these orders by reading about them in the newspapers. Bates, always careful to guard the civil against the military authority, warned General Wallace that he was overstepping his power, and told him to rescind his proclamation. Wallace refused to withdraw his orders, claiming that since his interpretation of the Second Confiscation Act differed from Bates's, he had a right to proceed as planned. At this point Bates took Wallace's orders and his own correspondence to President Lincoln, and threatened to resign his office as attorney general if military officers were to be permitted to usurp his authority. Lincoln sent an order through Secretary Stanton to Wallace, demanding that he withdraw the confiscation orders. Although Wallace stubbornly refused to withdraw his orders, no further action was taken to confiscate the Maryland property.[31]

During the debates over the Second Confiscation Act, radical Republicans such as Indiana congressman George Julian and Pennsylvania congressman Thaddeus Stevens had suggested distributing confiscated lands to Union soldiers and to freed slaves after the war. But such ideas were doomed as soon as the Second Confiscation Act was passed. Abraham Lincoln's insistence on an explanatory addendum to the law, which provided that property would not be forfeited beyond the lifetime of the traitor, made it clear that the land would remain in white owners' hands. There would be no redistribution of southern

31. Cain, *Lincoln's Attorney General,* 294–5.

wealth to the former slaves. There had been a few experiments along those lines early in the war, but none of them survived what one historian has called "middle-class Republican attitudes toward property ownership."[32]

As early as 1861, some abandoned plantations had been turned over to military commanders, who recruited the labor of the recently freed slaves for the cultivation of cash crops, mostly cotton. The most notable (and temporarily most successful) such effort was on the Sea Islands off the coast of South Carolina. When General Thomas W. Sherman took command of the Sea Islands in 1861, he opened the deserted plantations to black settlement in forty-acre allotments. There also were similar experiments on Louisiana sugar plantations in 1862, under General Benjamin F. Butler and later General Nathaniel Banks, and in the Mississippi Valley in 1863 under General Lorenzo Thomas. The freedmen worked under terrible conditions on these plantations, often suffering from starvation, overwork, and ill-treatment from Army commanders. They enjoyed little personal freedom, because officers and soldiers forcibly kept them at work, and the black southerners were compelled to grow staple crops, rather than food for the subsistence of their families, as they would have preferred. Indeed, the manner in which these plantations were managed presaged the postwar treatment of freed people.[33]

In September 1865, Thaddeus Stevens made a famous speech to the Republican Convention in Lancaster, Pennsylvania, in which he outlined his plan on Reconstruction. He believed that the planter aristocracy could not be destroyed, nor southern society fully reformed, until the large landholding tracts were broken up and distributed to loyal white and freed black people. But less than a month later, President Andrew Johnson forced the head of the Freedmen's Bureau, General Oliver Otis Howard, to deliver a heartbreaking message to the freed people then working on the Sea Island plantations. Howard had to tell them that they had no legal title to the land, and that if they wished to continue living and working there, they would have to make the best terms they could with the white owners. Over the next year and a half, Johnson would write an astonishing number of pardons to former rebels, about thirteen thousand in all. All of these pardons included restoration of the traitors' lands and,

32. Foner, *Politics and Ideology*, 149.

33. Foner, *Reconstruction*, 58–60; Rose, *Rehearsal for Reconstruction*, especially chapter 7; Donald et al., *Civil War and Reconstruction*, 504.

naturally, the expulsion of black families. In the end, about four thousand families retained some small property holdings, but the majority became sharecroppers. In 1866, when Senator Lyman Trumbull introduced a bill extending the life of the Freedmen's Bureau, Stevens once again tried to broach his radical land redistribution program. He introduced a substitute measure to Trumbull's bill that confiscated and redistributed the lands of convicted traitors to loyal white people and to freed slaves. The Republicans, who still maintained a majority in both houses, overwhelmingly defeated the substitute, 126–37, thus proving that even the many radical social changes brought about by the Civil War had not prepared Americans to overturn private property rights.[34]

The Confiscation Acts accomplished few of the ends demanded by the militant northern home front—they did not bring southern wealth into the Treasury, they did not materially aid the war effort, and they did not lead to the punishment of the southern rebels. Nor did these laws maintain control over the labor and lives of the freed slaves. The two Confiscation Acts did, however, pave the way in the northern public mind for President Lincoln to issue his Preliminary Emancipation Proclamation, and did give that proclamation a force and a power that Americans had hitherto disdained in verbal pronouncements. None of the politicians (both moderate Republicans and Democrats) who tried to treat enslaved southerners like "ordinary property" admitted explicitly that such ideas were both reactionary and untenable, but the arguments for and against the confiscation of slave labor made it clear that while there might still be some purpose to debating the property rights of rebellious citizens, there was no longer any rationale for debating the property status of slaves. This remained true in spite of the fact that radical Republicans had utterly failed, in the face of conservative and moderate opposition, in their attempt to guarantee the freedom of confiscated slaves. Radical Republicans were able, in a small way, to seize the property rights of slave labor from rebellious southerners and grant it, unequivocally, to the freed slaves themselves. The most important aspect of the laws was not the legislative product, but the debates surrounding them.

The political debates showed that the moderates of both parties were the most powerful element in Congress, and that they could force their radical (and conservative) brethren to meet in the center. This revealed that the spirit of

---

34. For the failure of the 38th Congress to enact land distribution measures, see Cox, "The Promise of Land for the Freedmen," 413–40.

compromise in Congress was still very much alive during the war, even though it sometimes resulted in unworkable and ineffective legislation. The coalitions that emerged during the first two years of the war would later enact a series of moderate Reconstruction policies, especially during the years of Andrew Johnson's administration. In the meantime, the political debates showed that while politicians took their oaths to uphold the Constitution seriously, they were growing increasingly more willing to question or reform the nation's founding document. The senators and congressmen insisted on a moral interpretation of constitutionally guaranteed civil rights and liberties, and they also asserted that a moral consensus over such an interpretation would now take precedence over individual property rights.

In the first two years of the war, the confused, angry, often irrational demands expressed by the home front washed up against this moderate center in Congress, where their ideas were turned into an unworkable but ultimately safe compromise. The moderate Republicans and War Democrats listened to the public's ideas, worked with them, and transformed them. In the end the political leaders had to hammer out a compromise that would keep the Constitution strong and whole and at the same time eradicate its fundamental contradiction. The compromise was a warning against future rebellions as well as a retreat from tyrannical measures. But the confiscation laws were a moderate and weak compromise in another way: although they helped to destroy the belief that human beings were property, these laws also failed to protect the rights and liberties of the freed slaves. Moderates expended their willingness to transform American society on laying the groundwork for the Thirteenth Amendment, and on extending the reach of the federal government over rebellious citizens. It would take a presidential proclamation to confirm the end of property status of slaves (at least in the minds of many white northerners) and the Reconstruction Amendments to enshrine their status as persons in the Constitution.[35]

35. Hyman and Wiecek, *Equal Justice Under Law,* 251.

Appendix 1

Final Votes on and Text of the First Confiscation Act

In the Senate

24 IN FAVOR

Henry B. Anthony, Rep., R.I.

Kinsley Bingham, Rep., Mich.

Orville H. Browning, Rep., Ill.

Daniel Clark, Rep., N.H.

Jacob Collamer, Rep., Vt.

James Dixon, Rep., Conn.

James R. Doolittle, Rep., Wisc.

William P. Fessenden, Rep., Maine

Solomon Foot, Rep., Vt.

Lafayette S. Foster, Rep., Conn.

James Grimes, Rep., Iowa

John P. Hale, Rep., N.H.

Ira Harris, Rep., N.Y.

Preston King, Rep., N.Y.

Henry Lane, Rep., Ind.

James Lane, Rep., Kans.

James A. McDougall, Dem., Calif.

John S. Sherman, Rep., Ohio

James F. Simmons, Rep., R.I.

Charles Sumner, Rep., Mass.

John C. Ten Eyck, Rep., N.J.

Lyman Trumbull, Rep., Ill.

Benjamin F. Wade, Rep., Ohio

Henry Wilson, Rep., Mass.

11 AGAINST

John C. Breckinridge, Dem., Ky.

Jesse D. Bright, Dem., Ind.

John S. Carlile, Un., Va.

Edgar Cowan, Rep., Pa.

Waldo P. Johnson, Dem., Mo.

Willard Saulsbury, Dem., Del.

Milton S. Latham, Dem., Calif.

James A. Pearce, Dem., Md.

Trusten Polk, Dem., Mo.

Lazarus Powell, Dem., Ky.

Henry M. Rice, Dem., Minn.

FINAL VOTES ON THE FIRST CONFISCATION ACT

In the House of Representatives

60 IN FAVOR

Cyrus Aldrich, Rep., Minn.

John B. Alley, Rep., Mass.

Isaac Arnold, Rep., Ill.

James M. Ashley, Rep., Ohio

Elijah Babbitt, Rep., Pa.

Portus Baxter, Rep., Vt.

Fernando C. Beaman, Rep., Mich.

John A. Bingham, Rep., Ohio

Francis P. Blair Jr., Rep., Mo.

Samuel S. Blair, Rep., Pa.

Harrison G. O. Blake, Rep., Ohio

James Buffington, Rep., Mass.

Jacob P. Chamberlain, Rep., N.Y.

Ambrose W. Clark, Rep., N.Y.

Schuyler Colfax, Rep., Ind.

Frederick A. Conkling, Rep., N.Y.

John Covode, Rep., Pa.

Robert Holland Duell, Rep., N.Y.

Thomas M. Edwards, Rep., N.H.

Thomas D. Eliot, Rep., Mass.

Reuben E. Fenton, Rep., N.Y.

Samuel C. Fessenden, Rep., Maine

Richard Franchot, Rep., N.Y.

Augustus Frank, Rep., N.Y.

Bradley F. Granger, Rep., Mich.

John A. Gurley, Rep., Ohio

Luther Hanchett, Rep., Wisc.

Richard A. Harrison, Un., Ohio

John Hutchins, Rep., Ohio

George W. Julian, Rep., Ind.

William D. Kelley, Rep., Pa.

Francis W. Kellogg, Rep., Mich.

William Kellogg, Rep., Ill.

William E. Lansing, Rep., N.Y.

Dwight Loomis, Rep., N.Y.

Owen Lovejoy, Rep., Ohio

James B. McKean, Rep., N.Y.

William Mitchell, Rep., Ind.

Justin S. Morrill, Rep., Vt.

Abram B. Olin, Rep., N.Y.

Albert G. Potter, Rep., Ind.

Alexander H. Rice, Rep., Mass.

Edward H. Rollins, Rep., N.H.

Charles B. Sedgwick, Rep., N.Y.

William Paine Sheffield, Rep., R.I.

Samuel Shellabarger, Rep., Ohio

Socrates N. Sherman, Rep., N.Y.

Andrew Scott Sloan, Rep., Wisc.

Elbridge G. Spaulding, Rep., N.Y.

Thaddeus Stevens, Rep., Pa.

Benjamin F. Thomas, Rep., Mass.

Charles Russell Train, Rep., Mass.

Burt Van Horn, Rep., N.Y.

John P. Verree, Rep., Pa.

John W. Wallace, Rep., Pa.

Charles W. Walton, Rep., Maine

Eliakim P. Walton, Rep., Vt.

William A. Wheeler, Rep., N.Y.

Albert S. White, Rep., Ind.

William Windom, Rep., Minn.

48 AGAINST

William Allen, Dem., Ohio

Sydenham E. Ancona, Dem., Pa.

Joseph Bailey, Dem., Pa.

George H. Browne, Dem., R.I.

Henry C. Burnett, Dem., Ky.

Charles B. Calvert, Un., Md.

Samuel S. Cox, Dem., Ohio

James A. Cravens, Dem., Ind.

John W. Crisfield, Un., Md.

John J. Crittenden, Un., Ky.

Alexander Diven, Rep., N.Y.

George W. Dunlap, Un., Ky.

William McKee Dunn, Rep., Ind.

James E. English, Dem., Conn.

Philip B. Fouke, Dem., Ill.

Henry Grider, Un., Ky.

Edward Haight, Dem., N.Y.

James T. Hale, Rep., Pa.

Aaron Harding, Dem., Ky.

William S. Holman, Dem., Ind.

Valentine B. Horton, Rep., Ohio

James S. Jackson, Un., Ky.

Phillip Johnson, Dem., Pa.

John Law, Dem., Ill.

Henry May, Dem., Md.

Robert Mallory, Un., Ky.

John A. McClernand, Dem., Ill.

Edward McPherson, Rep., Pa.

John W. Menzies, Un., Ky.

James R. Morris, Dem., Ohio

Warren Noble, Dem., Ohio

Elijah H. Norton, Dem., Mo.

Moses F. Odell, Dem., N.Y.

George H. Pendleton, Dem., Ohio

Albert G. Porter, Rep., Ind.

John W. Reid, Dem., Mo.

James C. Robinson, Dem., Ill.

James S. Rollins, Un., Mo.

George K. Shiel, Dem., Oreg.

Edward H. Smith, Dem., N.Y.

John B. Steele, Dem., N.Y.

John L. N. Stratton, Rep., N.J.

Francis Thomas, Un., Md.

Clement Vallandigham, Dem.,
Ohio

Daniel N. Voorhees, Dem., Ind.

William S. Wadsworth, Un., Ky.

Edwin H. Webster, Un., Md.

Charles A. Wickliffe, Un., Ky.

THE FIRST CONFISCATION ACT, AUGUST 6, 1861

Be it enacted by the Senate and House of Representatives of the United States of America in Congress assembled, That if, during the present or any future insurrection against the Government of the United States, after the President of the United States shall have declared by proclamation, that the laws of the United States are opposed, and the execution thereof obstructed, by combinations too powerful to be suppressed by the ordinary course of judicial proceedings, or by the power vested in marshals by law, any person or persons, his, her or their agent, attorney or employee, shall purchase or acquire, sell or give, any property of whatsoever kind or description, with intent to use or employ the same, or suffer the same to be used or employed, in aiding, abetting or promoting such insurrection or resistance to the laws, or any person or persons engaged therein; or if any person or persons, being the owner or owners of any such property, shall knowingly use or employ, or consent to the use or employment of the same as aforesaid, all such property is hereby declared to be lawful subject of prize and capture wherever found; and it shall be the duty of the President of the United States to cause the same to be seized, confiscated and condemned.

Sec. 2. *And be it further enacted,* That such prizes and capture shall be condemned in the District or Circuit Court of the United States having jurisdiction of the amount, or in admiralty in any district in which the same may be seized, or into which they may be taken and proceedings first instituted.

Sec. 3. *And be it further enacted,* That the Attorney General, or any District Attorney of the United States in which said property may at the time be, may institute the proceedings of condemnation, and in such case they shall be wholly for the benefit of the United States; or any person may file an information with such attorney, in which case the proceedings shall be for the use of such informer and the United States in equal parts.

Sec. 4. *And be it further enacted,* That whenever any person claiming to be entitled to the service or labor of any other person, under the laws of any State, shall employ such person in aiding or promoting any insurrection, or in resisting the laws of the United States, or shall permit him to be so employed, he shall forfeit all right to such service or labor, and the person whose labor or service is thus claimed shall be thenceforth discharged therefrom, any law to the contrary notwithstanding.

Appendix 2

Final Votes on and Text of the Second Confiscation Act

In the Senate

28 IN FAVOR

Henry B. Anthony, Rep., R.I.
Daniel Clark, Rep., N.H.
Jacob Collamer, Rep., Vt.
Edgar Cowan, Rep., Pa.
James Dixon, Rep., Conn.
James R. Doolittle, Rep., Wisc.
William P. Fessenden, Rep., Maine
Solomon Foot, Rep., Vt.
Lafayette Foster, Rep., Conn.
James W. Grimes, Rep., Iowa
John P. Hale, Rep., N.H.
James Harlan, Rep., Iowa
Ira Harris, Rep., N.Y.
Timothy O. Howe, Rep., Wisc.

Preston King, Rep., N.Y.
Henry S. Lane, Rep., Ind.
James H. Lane, Rep., Kans.
Lot M. Morrill, Rep., Maine
Samuel C. Pomeroy, Rep., Kans.
John Sherman, Rep., Ohio
James F. Simmons, Rep., R.I.
Charles Sumner, Rep., Mass.
John C. Ten Eyck, Rep., N.J.
Lyman Trumbull, Rep., Ill.
Benjamin F. Wade, Rep., Ohio
Morton S. Wilkinson, Rep., Minn.
Waitman T. Willey, Un., Va.
David Wilmot, Rep., Pa.

13 AGAINST

James A. Bayard, Dem., Del.
Orville H. Browning, Rep., Ill.
John S. Carlile, Un., Va.
Zachariah Chandler, Rep., Mich.
Garrett Davis, Un., Ky.
John B. Henderson, Dem., Mo.
Jacob M. Howard, Rep., Mich.

James W. Nesmith, Dem., Oreg.
James A. Pearce, Dem., Md.
Lazarus W. Powell, Dem., Ky.
Benjamin Stark, Dem., Oreg.
Robert Wilson, Un., Mo.
Joseph A. Wright, Un., Ind.

Final Votes on the Second Confiscation Act

In the House of Representatives

82 IN FAVOR

Cyrus Aldrich, Rep., Minn.

John B. Alley, Rep., Mass.

Isaac N. Arnold, Rep., Ill.

James M. Ashley, Rep., Ohio

Elijah Babbitt, Rep., Pa.

Portus Baxter, Rep., Vt.

Fernando C. Beaman, Rep., Mich.

John A. Bingham, Rep., Ohio

Jacob B. Blair, Un., Va.

Samuel S. Blair, Rep., Pa.

Harrison G. O. Blake, Rep., Ohio

James Buffington, Rep., Mass.

James H. Campbell, Rep., Pa.

Samuel L. Casey, Un., Ky.

Ambrose W. Clark, Rep., N.Y.

Schuyler Colfax, Rep., Ind.

Frederick A. Conkling, Rep., N.Y.

Roscoe Conkling, Rep., N.Y.

John Covode, Rep., Pa.

William P. Cutler, Rep., Ohio

William M. Davis, Rep., Pa.

Henry L. Dawes, Rep., Mass.

Robert Holland Duell, Rep., N.Y.

William M. Dunn, Rep., Ind.

Thomas M. Edwards, Rep., N.H.

Thomas D. Eliot, Rep., Mass.

Alfred Ely, Rep., N.Y.

Reuben E. Fenton, Rep., N.Y.

Samuel C. Fessenden, Rep., Maine

George P. Fisher, Un., Del.

Augustus Frank, Rep., N.Y.

Daniel W. Gooch, Rep., Mass.

John N. Goodwin, Rep., Maine

John A. Gurley, Rep., Ohio

James T. Hale, Rep., Pa.

Samuel Hooper, Rep., Mass.

John Hutchins, Rep., Ohio

George W. Julian, Rep., Ind.

William D. Kelley, Rep., Pa.

Francis W. Kellogg, Rep., Mich.

William Kellogg, Rep., Ill.

William E. Lansing, Rep., N.Y.

Dwight Loomis, Rep., Conn.

Owen Lovejoy, Rep., Ill.

Frederick F. Low, Rep., Calif.

Horace Maynard, Un., Tenn.

Robert McKnight, Rep., Pa.

Edward McPherson, Rep., Pa.

William Mitchell, Rep., Ind.

James K. Moorhead, Rep., Pa.

Anson P. Morrill, Rep., Maine

Justin S. Morrill, Rep., Vt.

John T. Nixon, Rep., N.J.

John Patton, Rep., Pa.

Timothy G. Phelps, Rep., Calif.

Frederick A. Pike, Rep., Maine

Albert G. Porter, Rep., Ind.

John F. Potter, Rep., Wisc.

Alexander H. Rice, Rep., Mass.

John H. Rice, Rep., Maine

Albert G. Riddle, Rep., Ohio

Edward H. Rollins, Rep., N.H.

Aaron A. Sargent, Rep., Calif.

Charles B. Sedgwick, Rep., N.Y.

John P. C. Shanks, Rep., Ind.

Samuel Shellabarger, Rep., Ohio

Socrates N. Sherman, Rep., N.Y.

Thaddeus Stevens, Rep., Pa.

John L. N. Stratton, Rep., N.J.

Carey A. Trimble, Rep., Ohio

Rowland E. Trowbridge, Rep., Mich.

Burt Van Horn, Rep., N.Y.

John P. Verree, Rep., Pa.

William Wall, Rep., N.Y.

John W. Wallace, Rep., Pa.

Charles W. Walton, Rep., Maine

Elihu B. Washburne, Rep., Ill.

William A. Wheeler, Rep., N.Y.

Albert S. White, Rep., Ind.

James F. Wilson, Rep., Iowa

William Windom, Rep., Minn.

Samuel C. Worcester, Rep., Ohio

42 AGAINST

William Allen, Dem., Ohio

William J. Allen, Dem., Ill.

Sydenham E. Ancona, Dem., Pa.

Joseph Bailey, Dem., Pa.

Charles J. Biddle, Dem., Pa.

George H. Browne, Dem., R.I.

Andrew J. Clements, Un., Tenn.

George T. Cobb, Dem., N.J.

Samuel S. Cox, Dem., Ohio

John W. Crisfield, Un., Md.

John J. Crittenden, Un., Ky.

George W. Dunlap, Un., Ky.

Philip B. Fouke, Dem., Ill.

Bradley F. Granger, Rep., Mich.

Henry Grider, Un., Ky.

Edward Haight, Dem., N.Y.

William A. Hall, Dem., Mo.

Aaron Harding, Dem., Ky.

William S. Holman, Dem., Ind.

James E. Kerrigan, Dem., N.Y.

Anthony L. Knapp, Dem., Ill.

John Law, Dem., Ind.

Jesse Lazear, Dem., Pa.

William E. Lehman, Dem., Pa.

Robert Mallory, Un., Ky.

John W. Menzies, Un., Ky.

James R. Morris, Dem., Ohio

Robert H. Nugen, Dem., Ohio

Moses F. Odell, Dem., N.Y.

George H. Pendleton, Dem. Ohio

James C. Rollins, Dem., Ill.

Joseph E. Segar, Un., Va.

George K. Shiel, Dem., Oreg.

John B. Steele, Dem., N.Y.

William G. Steele, Dem., N.J.

John D. Stiles, Dem., Pa.

Benjamin F. Thomas, Rep., Mass.

Francis Thomas, Un., Md.

Elijah Ward, Dem., N.Y.

Edwin H. Webster, Un., Md.

Charles A. Wickliffe, Un., Ky.

Benjamin Wood, Dem., N.Y.

THE SECOND CONFISCATION ACT, JULY 17, 1862

An Act to suppress Insurrection, to punish Treason and Rebellion, to seize and confiscate the Property of Rebels, and for other Purposes.

Be it enacted by the Senate and House of Representatives of the United States of America in Congress assembled, That every person who shall hereafter commit the crime of treason against the United States, and shall be adjudged guilty thereof, shall suffer death, and all his slaves, if any, shall be declared and made free; or, at the discretion of the court, he shall be imprisoned for not less than five years and fined not less than ten thousand dollars, and all his slaves, if any, shall be declared and made free; said fine shall be levied and collected on any or all of the property, real and personal, excluding slaves, of which the said person so convicted was the owner at the time of committing the said crime, any sale or conveyance to the contrary notwithstanding.

2. *And be it further enacted,* That if any person shall hereafter incite, set on foot, assist, or engage in any rebellion or insurrection against the authority of the United States, or the laws thereof, or shall give aid or comfort thereto, or shall engage in, or give aid and comfort to, any such existing rebellion or insurrection, and be convicted thereof, such person shall be punished by imprisonment for a period not exceeding ten years, or by a fine not exceeding ten thousand dollars, and by the liberation of all his slaves, if any he have; or by both of said punishments, at the discretion of the court.

3. *And be it further enacted,* That every person guilty of either of the offences described in this act shall be forever incapable and disqualified to hold any office under the United States.

4. *And be it further enacted,* That this act shall not be construed in any way to affect or alter the prosecution, conviction, or punishment of any person or persons guilty of treason against the United States before the passage of this act, unless such person is convicted under this act.

5. *And be it further enacted,* That, to insure the speedy termination of the present rebellion, it shall be the duty of the President of the United States to cause the seizure of all the estate and property, money, stocks, credits, and effects of the persons hereinafter named in this section, and to apply and use the same and the proceeds thereof for the support of the army of the United States, that is to say:

First. Of any person hereafter acting as an officer of the army or navy of the rebels in arms against the government of the United States.

Secondly. Of any person hereafter acting as President, Vice-President, member of Congress, judge of any court, cabinet officer, foreign minister, commissioner or consul of the so-called confederate states of America.

Thirdly. Of any person acting as governor of a state, member of a convention or legislature, or judge of any court of any of the so-called confederate states of America.

Fourthly. Of any person who, having held an office of honor, trust, or profit in the United States, shall hereafter hold an office in the so-called confederate states of America.

Fifthly. Of any person hereafter holding any office or agency under the government of the so-called confederate states of America, or under any of the several states of the said confederacy, or the laws thereof, whether such office or agency be national, state, or municipal in its name or character: *Provided,* That the persons, thirdly, fourthly, and fifthly above described shall have accepted their appointment or election since the date of the pretended ordinance of secession of the state, or shall have taken an oath of allegiance to, or to support the constitution of the so-called confederate states.

Sixthly. Of any person who, owning property in any loyal State or Territory of the United States, or in the District of Columbia, shall hereafter assist and give aid and comfort to such rebellion; and all sales, transfers, or conveyances of any such property shall be null and void; and it shall be a sufficient bar to any suit brought by such person for the possession or the use of such property, or any of it, to allege and prove that he is one of the persons described in this section.

6. *And be it further enacted,* That if any person within any State or Territory of the United States, other than those named as aforesaid, after the passage of this act, being engaged in armed rebellion against the government of the United States, or aiding or abetting such rebellion, shall not, within sixty days after public warning and proclamation duly given and made by the President of the United States, cease to aid, countenance, and abet such rebellion, and return to his allegiance to the United States, all the estate and property, moneys, stocks, and credits of such person shall be liable to seizure as aforesaid, and it shall be the duty of the President to seize and use them as aforesaid or the proceeds thereof. And all sales, transfers, or conveyances, of any such property after the expiration of the said sixty days from the date of such warning and proclamation shall be null and void; and it shall be a sufficient bar to any suit brought by such person for the possession or the use of such property, or any of it, to allege and prove that he is one of the persons described in this section.

7. *And be it further enacted,* That to secure the condemnation and sale of any of such property, after the same shall have been seized, so that it may be made available for the purpose aforesaid, proceedings in rem shall be instituted in the name of the United States in any district court thereof, or in any territorial

court, or in the United States district court for the District of Columbia, within which the property above described, or any part thereof, may be found, or into which the same, if movable, may first be brought, which proceedings shall conform as nearly as may be to proceedings in admiralty or revenue cases, and if said property, whether real or personal, shall be found to have belonged to a person engaged in rebellion, or who has given aid or comfort thereto, the same shall be condemned as enemies' property and become the property of the United States, and may be disposed of as the court shall decree and the proceeds thereof paid into the treasury of the United States for the purposes aforesaid.

8. *And be it further enacted,* That the several courts aforesaid shall have power to make such orders, establish such forms of decree and sale, and direct such deeds and conveyances to be executed and delivered by the marshals thereof where real estate shall be the subject of sale, as shall fitly and efficiently effect the purposes of this act, and vest in the purchasers of such property good and valid titles thereto. And the said courts shall have power to allow such fees and charges of their officers as shall be reasonable and proper in the premises.

9. *And be it further enacted,* That all slaves of persons who shall hereafter be engaged in rebellion against the government of the United States, or who shall in any way give aid or comfort thereto, escaping from such persons and taking refuge within the lines of the army; and all slaves captured from such persons or deserted by them and coming under the control of the government of the United States; and all slaves of such person found on [*or*] being within any place occupied by rebel forces and afterwards occupied by the forces of the United States, shall be deemed captives of war, and shall be forever free of their servitude, and not again held as slaves.

10. *And be it further enacted,* That no slave escaping into any State, Territory, or the District of Columbia, from any other State, shall be delivered up, or in any way impeded or hindered of his liberty, except for crime, or some offence against the laws, unless the person claiming said fugitive shall first make oath that the person to whom the labor or service of such fugitive is alleged to be due is his lawful owner, and has not borne arms against the United States in the present rebellion, nor in any way given aid and comfort thereto; and no person engaged in the military or naval service of the United States shall, under any pretence whatever, assume to decide on the validity of the claim of any person to the service or labor of any other person, or surrender up any such person to the claimant, on pain of being dismissed from the service.

11. *And be it further enacted,* That the President of the United States is authorized to employ as many persons of African descent as he may deem necessary and proper for the suppression of this rebellion, and for this purpose he may organize and use them in such manner as he may judge best for the public welfare.

12. *And be it further enacted,* That the President of the United States is hereby authorized to make provision for the transportation, colonization, and settlement, in some tropical country beyond the limits of the United States, of such persons of the African race, made free by the provisions of this act, as may be willing to emigrate, having first obtained the consent of the government of said country to their protection and settlement within the same, with all the rights and privileges of freemen.

13. *And be it further enacted,* That the President is hereby authorized, at any time hereafter, by proclamation, to extend to persons who may have participated in the existing rebellion in any State or part thereof, pardon and amnesty, with such exceptions and at such time and on such conditions as he may deem expedient for the public welfare.

14. *And be it further enacted,* That the courts of the United States shall have full power to institute proceedings, make orders and decrees, issue process, and do all other things necessary to carry this act into effect.

Bibliography

A note on sources. To understand the political debates, I read the speeches for and against the confiscation laws printed in the *Congressional Globe.* Determining the public's contribution and response to these debates, and to the resultant controversial laws, was a little more difficult. For this study, I was particularly interested in the communication between constituents and their representatives in Washington, which led me to read all of the relevant manuscript letter archives in the Library of Congress Manuscripts Division. More than half of the manuscript collections that have survived from the Civil War era contain the correspondence between congressional Republicans and their constituents. Although many of the politicians received hostile mail, most of the letters came from Union citizens who were at least somewhat sympathetic to Republican war aims. For this reason, I supplemented the manuscript letters with newspapers, pamphlets, private diaries, printed speeches, and sermons from a wide range of political viewpoints and geographic regions. For example, in my search for additional home front sources, I read thirty-four newspapers from twelve states, including the District of Columbia and three of the border states. I determined the editors' political standpoint by ascertaining their endorsements during the 1860 presidential campaign, as well as their views on controversial issues, such as civil liberties and emancipation. Of course, it is difficult to judge how persuasive northern newspaper editorials were, but the fact that many northern letter-writers included clipped excerpts from local newspapers suggests that at least some readers found the arguments contained in them compelling. I also researched dozens of sermons preached by ministers from all areas of the North, as well as pamphlets privately published by members of both parties. Pamphlets and sermons pose another kind of problem: pamphlets are usually authored by persons holding strong opinions, and may not be representative of mainstream public opinion. And none of the ministers who preached the sermons consulted for this work proclaimed their political affiliations. Moreover, in the absence of public opinion polls, it would be impossible to make definitive statements about "northern public opinion" during the Civil War.

Taken together, however, the pamphlets, letters, sermons, diary entries, and other primary sources reveal the important concerns under debate on the northern home front. My research indicates, above all, a profound preoccupation among northerners with several difficult issues: private property rights, especially those of citizens in rebellion; contested state and federal property ownership during a civil war; the difficulty of distinguishing between human beings who belonged to someone else and human beings who had goals and a purpose of their own; and, finally, the treatment of rebellious citizens in the world's first constitutional democracy. I found that northern citizens were as deeply troubled by these issues as their representatives in Washington were; indeed, every northern newspaper carried extensive editorial opinions on all aspects of property confiscation and, more specifically, on the changing identity and future of enslaved persons.

Manuscripts

Manuscripts Division, Library of Congress, Washington, D.C.

James A. Bayard Papers.
Thomas F. Bayard Papers.
James G. Blaine Papers.
Blair Family Papers.
Breckinridge Family Papers.
Benjamin F. Butler Papers.
Zachariah Chandler Papers.
Salmon P. Chase Papers.
John Covode Papers.
John S. J. Creswell Papers.
John J. Crittenden Papers.
Caleb Cushing Papers.
Henry L. Dawes Papers.
James R. Doolitte Papers.
Ewing Family Papers.
William Pitt Fessenden Papers.
Hamilton Fish Papers.

George P. Fisher Papers.
John Wien Forney Papers.
Joshua R. Giddings–George W. Julian Correspondence.
Horace Greeley Papers.
Reverdy Johnson Papers.
Francis Lieber Papers.
Lincoln Manuscripts.
Logan Family Papers.
Edward McPherson Papers.
Justin S. Morrill Papers.
John Sherman Papers.
Thaddeus Stevens Papers.
Lyman Trumbull Papers.
Benjamin F. Wade Papers.
James T. Ward Manuscript Diary.
Elihu B. Washburne Papers.
Israel Washburn Papers.
Henry Wilson Papers.
Houghton Library, Harvard University, Cambridge, Mass.
Charles Sumner Papers.

NEWSPAPERS AND PERIODICALS

The Albany Atlas and Argus, 1860–1862.
Baltimore Sun, 1860–1862.
Boston Daily Evening Transcript, 1860–1862.
Buffalo Morning Express, 1861.
Chicago Tribune, 1860–1865.
Christian Examiner (Boston), 1860–1863.
Cincinnati Daily Enquirer, 1860–1862.
Cincinnati Daily Gazette, 1861–1862.
Cincinnati Daily Press, 1861–1862.
Cleveland Daily Plain Dealer, 1860–1862.
Columbus Crisis, 1861–1862.
Daily Illinois State Journal, 1861–1862.
Daily National Intelligencer (Washington, D.C.), 1860–1862.
Detroit Free Press, 1860–1862.
Frankfort (Ky.) *Daily Commonwealth,* 1860–1862.
Frank Leslie's Illustrated Newspaper, 1860–1865.

Harper's Weekly Magazine, 1860–1865.

Harrisburg (Pa.) *Sentinel*, 1861.

Louisville Daily Democrat, 1860–1862.

Louisville Journal, 1860–1862.

National Daily Intelligencer, 1860–1862.

Newark Daily Advertiser, 1861–1862.

New York Herald, 1860–1865.

New York Times, 1860–1865.

New York Tribune, 1860–1865.

New York World, 1860–1862.

North American Review, 1860–1865.

Paris (Maine) *Oxford Democrat*, 1861.

Philadelphia Inquirer, 1860–1862.

Princeton Review, 1862.

Racine (Wisc.) *Gazette*, 1861.

Springfield (Mass.) *Daily Republican*, 1860–1862.

Springfield (Ill.) *Daily Republican*, 1861–1862.

Springfield (Ill.) *Journal*, 1861–1862.

GOVERNMENT PUBLICATIONS

Chase, Salmon P. *Report of the Secretary of the Treasury.* Senate Executive Document 2, 37th Congress, 1st sess., serial 1112. Washington, D.C.: Government Printing Office, 1861.

———. *Report of the Secretary of the Treasury.* Senate Executive Document 2, 37th Congress, 2nd sess., serial 1121. Washington, D.C.: Government Printing Office, 1861.

Congressional Globe, 1860–1862.

PUBLISHED PRIMARY SOURCES: BOOKS

Basler, Roy P., ed. *Collected Works of Abraham Lincoln.* 9 vols. New Brunswick, N.J.: Rutgers Univ. Press, 1953.

Bates, Edward. *The Diary of Edward Bates, 1859–1866.* Edited by Howard K. Beale. In. American Historical Association, *Annual Report*, 1930, vol. 4. Washington, D.C.: Government Printing Office, 1933.

Beale, Howard K., ed. *Diary of Gideon Welles.* 3 vols. New York: Norton, 1960.

Beatty, John. *Memoirs of a Volunteer, 1861–1863.* Edited by Harvey S. Ford. Cincinnati: Wistach, Baldwin, 1879. Reprint, New York: Norton, 1946.

Blaine, James G. *Twenty Years of Congress: From Lincoln to Garfield.* 2 vols. Norwich, Conn.: Henry Bill Publishing, 1886.

Boutwell, George S. *Reminiscences of Sixty Years in Public Affairs.* 2 vols. New York: McClure, Phillip, 1902.

Brooks, Noah. *Washington in Lincoln's Time. A Memoir of the Civil War Era by the Newspaperman Who Knew Lincoln Best.* Edited by Herbert Mitgang. Athens: Univ. of Georgia Press, 1989.

Browning, Orville H. *The Diary of Orville Hickman Browning.* 2 vols. Edited by Theodore C. Pease and James G. Randall. Vol. 20 of *Collections of the Illinois State Historical Society.* Springfield: Illinois State Historical Library, 1925.

Burlingame, Michael, ed. *Dispatches from Lincoln's White House: The Anonymous Civil War Journalism of Presidential Secretary William O. Stoddard.* Lincoln: Univ. of Nebraska Press, 2002.

———, ed. *With Lincoln in the White House: Letters, Memoranda, and Other Writings of John G. Nicolay, 1860–1865.* Carbondale: Southern Illinois Univ. Press, 2000.

Burlingame, Michael, and John R. Turner Ettlinger, eds. *Inside Lincoln's White House: The Complete Civil War Diary of John Hay.* Carbondale: Southern Illinois Univ. Press, 1997.

Butler, Benjamin Franklin. *Butler's Book.* Boston: A. M. Thayer, 1892.

———. *Private and Official Correspondence of Gen. Benjamin F. Butler During the Civil War Period.* 5 vols. Privately issued, 1917.

Chase, Salmon P. *Diary and Correspondence of Salmon P. Chase.* In American Historical Association, *Annual Report,* 1902, vol. 2. Washington, D.C.: Government Printing Office, 1903.

Cox, Samuel S. *Eight Years in Congress, from 1857–1865. Memoir and Speeches.* New York: D. Appleton, 1865.

———. *Union—Disunion—Reunion: Three Decades of Federal Legislation, 1855–1885.* Providence, R.I.: J. A. and R. A. Reid, 1888.

Daly, Maria Lydig. *Diary of a Union Lady, 1861–1865.* Edited by Harold E. Hammond. New York: Funk and Wagnalls, 1962.

Dana, Charles A. *Recollections of the Civil War.* New York: D. Appleton, 1899.

Dennett, Tyler, ed. *Lincoln and the Civil War in the Diaries and Letters of John Hay.* New York: Da Capo, 1988.

Donald, David, ed. *Inside Lincoln's Cabinet: The Civil War Diaries of Salmon P. Chase.* New York: Longmans, Green, 1954.

Du Pont, Samuel Francis. *Samuel Francis Du Pont: A Selection from His Civil War Letters,* vol. 1. Edited by John D. Hayes. Ithaca: Cornell Univ. Press, 1969.

Fisher, Sidney George. *The Trial of Our Constitution.* 1862. Reprint, New York: Negro Univs. Press, 1969.

Fletcher, Calvin. *The Diary of Calvin Fletcher.* 12 vols. Edited by Gayle Thornbrough, Dorothy L. Riker, and Paula Corpuz. Indianapolis: Indiana Historical Society, 1980.

Ford, Worthington Chauncey, ed. *A Cycle of Adams Letters, 1861–1865.* Boston: Houghton Mifflin, 1920.

Freidel, Frank, ed. *Union Pamphlets of the Civil War, 1861–1865,* vols. 1 and 2. Cambridge, Mass.: Harvard Univ. Press, 1967.

Furry, William, ed. *The Preacher's Tale: The Civil War Journal of Rev. Francis Springer, Chaplain, U.S. Army of the Frontier.* Fayetteville: Univ. of Arkansas Press, 2001.

Graf, Leroy P., and Ralph W. Haskins, eds. *The Papers of Andrew Johnson.* Vol. 5, *1861–1862.* Knoxville: Univ. of Tennessee Press, 1979.

Hamilton, James A. *Reminiscences of James A. Hamilton; or, Men and Events, at Home and Abroad, During Three Quarters of a Century.* New York: Charles Scribner, 1869.

Hayes, Rutherford B. *Diary and Letters of Rutherford Birchard Hayes, Nineteenth President of the United States.* Edited by Charles Richard Williams. Columbus: Ohio State Archaeological Society, 1922.

Hochfield, George, ed. *The Great Secession Winter of 1860–61 and Other Essays by Henry Adams.* New York: Sagamore Press, 1958.

Julian, George W. *Political Recollections, 1840–1872.* Chicago: Jansen, McClurg, 1884.

———. *Speeches on Political Questions.* New York: Hurd and Houghton, 1872.

Lieber, Francis. *Miscellaneous Writings of Francis Lieber.* Edited by Daniel C. Gilman. 2 vols. Philadelphia: J. B. Lippincott, 1880.

Lowell, James Russell. *Political Essays.* Boston: Houghton Mifflin, 1890.

McClure, Alexander K. *Recollections of Half a Century.* Salem, Mass.: Salem Press, 1902.

McCullough, Hugh. *Men and Measures of Half a Century.* New York: Charles Scribner's Sons, 1900.

McPherson, Edward. *The Political History of the United States of America during the Great Rebellion.* Washington, D.C.: Philip and Solomons, 1865.

Nicolay, John G., and John Hay. *Abraham Lincoln: A History.* 10 vols. New York: Century, 1914.

———, eds. *Complete Works of Abraham Lincoln.* 12 vols. New York: Francis D. Tandy, 1905.

Palmer, Beverly Wilson, and Holly Byers Ochoa, eds. *The Selected Papers of Thaddeus Stevens.* Vol. 1, *January 1814–March 1865.* Pittsburgh: Univ. of Pittsburgh Press, 1997.

Poore, Benjamin Perley. *Perley's Reminiscences of Sixty Years in the National Metropolis.* 2 vols. Philadelphia: Hubbard Brothers, 1886.

Richardson, James D., ed. *A Compilation of the Messages and Papers of the Presidents.* 10 vols. Washington, D.C.: Government Printing Office, 1896–1903.

Russell, William Howard. *My Diary North and South*. Edited by Eugene H. Berwanger. New York: Knopf, 1988.

Sherman, John. *Recollections of Forty Years in the House, Senate and Cabinet*. 2 vols. Chicago: Werner Co., 1895.

Strong, George T. *The Diary of George Templeton Strong, 1835–1875*. 4 vols. Edited by Allan Nevins and Milton H. Thomas. New York: Macmillan, 1952.

Thayer, William R. *The Life and Letters of John Hay*. 2 vols. Boston: Houghton Mifflin, 1915.

Thorndike, Rachel Sherman, ed. *The Sherman Letters: Correspondence Between General Sherman and Senator Sherman from 1837 to 1891*. 1896. Reprint, New York: Da Capo Press, 1969.

Wilson, Henry. *History of the Rise and Fall of the Slave Power in America*. 3 vols. Boston: James R. Osgood, 1874.

Wister, Fanny Kemble, ed. *That I May Tell You: Journals and Letters of the Owen Wister Family*. Wayne, Pa.: Haverford House, 1979.

Published Primary Sources: Pamphlets and Sermons

Abbott, John S. C. *An Address Upon Our National Affairs, Delivered in Cheshire, Conn., on the National Fast, January 4th, 1861*. New York: Abbey and Abbot, 1861.

Anderson, S. J. P., D.D. *The Dangers and Duties of the Present Crisis! A Discourse: Delivered in the Union Church, St. Louis, January 4, 1861*. St. Louis: Schenck, 1861.

Anonymous. *The North and the South Misrepresented and Misjudged: or, A Candid View of the Present Difficulties and Danger, and their Causes and Remedy*. Philadelphia: n.p., 1861.

Anonymous. *On Political Economy. Read and Ponder*. N.p., [1862?].

Aughey, Samuel. *The Renovation of Politics: A Discourse Delivered in St. Paul's Evangelical Lutheran Church, Lionville, Chester County, Pa., On the Evening of January 4th, 1861*. West Chester: E. F. James, 1861.

Austro-Borealis. *A Platform for all Parties*. Baltimore: J. P. Des Forges, 1860.

Baird, Samuel J. *Southern Rights and Northern Duties in the Present Crisis. A Letter to Hon. William Pennington*. Philadelphia: n.p., 1861.

Bassett, George W. *A Discourse on the Wickedness and Folly of the Present War, delivered in the Court House at Ottawa, Illinois, On the Sabbath, August 11, 1861*. N.p., [1861].

Bellows, Henry W. *The Advantage of Testing Our Principles, Compensatory of the Evils of Serious Times. A Discourse on Sunday Morning, Feb. 17th, 1861, Before the Second Unitarian Society of Philadelphia*. Philadelphia: C. Sherman and Son, 1861.

————. *Church and State in America*. New York: Anson D. F. Randolph, 1861.

————. *Duty and Interest Identical in the Present Crisis. A Sermon Preached in All Souls' Church, New York, Sunday Morning, April 14th, 1861*. New York: Wynkoop, Hallenbeck and Thomas, 1861.

————. *The State and the Nation—Sacred to Christian Citizens. A Sermon Preached in All Souls' Church, New York, April 21, 1861*. New York: James Miller, 1861.

Blake, Charles F. *The Rightful Power of Congress to Confiscate and Emancipate. Reprinted from the Law Reporter, June 1862*. Boston: C. H. Crosby, 1862.

Burbank, [Caleb]. *Speech of Judge Burbank, in the Senate of California, February 27, 1861, on the Crittenden Compromise Resolutions*. Sacramento: J. Anthony, 1861.

Candee, George. *Plan for Conquering Treason. Letter to President Lincoln, By a Citizen of Kentucky*. Green Springs, Ohio: n.p., 1862.

Carroll, Anna Ella. *The Relation of the National Government to the Revolted Citizens Defined*. Washington, D.C.: Henry Polkinthorn, 1862.

————. *Reply to the Speech of Hon. J. C. Breckinridge, Delivered in the United States Senate, July 16th, 1861*. Washington, D.C.: Henry Polkinthorn, 1861.

————. *The War Powers of the General Government*. Washington, D.C.: Henry Polkinthorn, 1861.

Chase, Warren. *The American Crisis: or, Trial and Triumph of Democracy.* Boston: Bela Marsh, 1862.

Citizen. *A View of the War; its Causes and Probable Results.* New York: George Russell, 1861.

Clarke, James Freeman. *Secession, Concession, or Self-Possession: Which?* Boston: Walker, Wise, 1861.

Collins, William H. *Second Address to the People of Maryland.* Baltimore: James Young, 1861.

Daly, Charles P. *Are the Southern Privateersmen Pirates? A Letter to the Hon. Ira Harris, United States Senator.* New York: J. B. Kirker, 1862.

Davis, Henry Winter. *Address of Hon. Henry Winter Davis Delivered at Baltimore on Wednesday Evening, October 16, 1861, At the Request of A Large Number of Merchants, Mechanics, and Business Men Generally.* Baltimore: n.p., 1861.

Democratic Party, New York. *Proceedings of the Democratic State Convention, Held in Albany, January 31, and February 1, 1861.* Albany: Comstock and Cassidy, 1861.

Democratic State Central Committee, Indiana. *Facts for the People! Relating to the Present Crisis. By a Citizen of Indiana.* Indianapolis: Weekly State Sentinel, 1862.

Dodge, Robert. *A Book for every Soldier's Knapsack: Tracts for the War. Secession: The Remedy and Result.* New York: James Miller, 1861.

Dorr, Benjamin. *The American Vine. A Sermon Preached in Christ Church, Philadelphia, Friday, January 4, 1861, on Occasion of the National Fast, Recommended by the President of the United States, Because of the Dangers which Threaten the Union.* Philadelphia: Collins, 1861.

Drake, Charles D. *The Rebellion: Its Origin and Life in Slavery. Position and Policy of Missouri.* St. Louis: n.p., 1862.

Eddy, Zachary. *"Secession—Shall it be Peace or War?" A Fast Day Sermon Delivered in the First Church, Northampton, April 4, 1861.* Northampton, Mass.: Trumbull and Gere, 1861.

Elder, William. *Debt and Resources of the United States, and the Effect of Secession upon the Trade and Industry of the Loyal States.* Philadelphia: Ringwalt and Brown, 1863.

Eliot, Thomas D. *Address of Thomas D. Eliot, of the 1st Congressional District of Massachusetts, to his Constituents.* Washington, D.C.: Henry Polkinthorn, 1861.

Evans, Llewelyn J. *The Duty of the Christian Citizen; A Discourse Preached in Lane Seminary Church, March 10, 1861.* Cincinnati: Moore, Wilstach, Keys, 1861.

Ewer, F. C. *Discourse on the National Crisis, Delivered by the Rev. F. C. Ewer, At St. Ann's Church, New-York.* New York: George. F. Nesbitt, 1861.

Fouke, Philip B. *To the Voters of the Eighth Congressional District of the State of Illinois.* Washington, D.C.: n.p., 1861.

Gardner, Daniel. *A Treatise on the Law of the American Rebellion, and Our True Policy, Domestic and Foreign.* New York: John W. Amerman, 1862.

Goodale, M. S. *"Our Country's Peril and Our Duty." A Sermon, Preached in the Presbyterian Church, Amsterdam Village, April 28th, 1861.* Amsterdam, N.Y.: "Recorder" Office, 1861.

Holt, Joseph. *An Address by the Hon. Joseph Holt, To the People of Kentucky, Delivered at Louisville, July 13th, 1861.* New York: James G. Gregory, 1861.

———. *Letter from the Hon. Joseph Holt, upon the Policy of the Federal Government, the Impending Revolution, Its Objects, Its Probable Results if Successful, and the Duty of Kentucky in the Crisis.* Louisville: Bradley and Gilbert, 1861.

———. *Letters of the Hon. Joseph Holt, the Hon. Edward Everett, and Commodore Charles Stewart, on the Present Crisis.* Philadelphia: William S. and Alfred Martien, 1861.

Hugg, John H. *Compromise Will Not Save the Union.* New York: n.p., 1861.

Hunter, Robert. *Speech of Hon. R.M.T. Hunter, of Virginia, on the Forts and Arsenals of the United States, January 11, 1861.* N.p., 1861.

Kennedy, John P. *The Border States: Their Power and Duty in The Present Disordered Condition of the Country.* Philadelphia: J. B. Lippincott, 1861.

Laurie, Thomas. *Government is of God. A Sermon Preached in Dedham and West Roxbury, May 12, 1861.* Boston: S. O. Thayer, 1861.

Libertas. *The Power of the Commander-in-Chief to Declare Martial Law, and Decree Emancipation: As Shown from B. R. Curtis.* Boston: A. Williams, 1862.

Lord, William H. *A Sermon on the Causes and Remedy of the National Troubles, Preached at Montpelier, VT., April 4th, 1861.* Montpelier: E. P. Walton, 1861.

Love, Alfred H. *An Appeal in Vindication of Peace Principles, and Against Resistance by Force of Arms.* Philadelphia: Maas and Vogdes, 1862.

Mason, J. *To the Hon. Abraham Lincoln, President Elect of the United States.* New York: n.p., 1861.

May, John F. *The Sectional Difficulties. Opinions and Remedies.* Georgetown, n.p., 1861.

New Orleans Picayune. *Extracts from the Editorial Columns of the New Orleans Picayune. Read and Circulate.* New York: Clarke, 1861.

New York Chamber of Commerce. *Report of the Special Committee of the Chamber of Commerce of the State of New York, on the Confiscation of Cotton in the Southern States by the Government.* New York: John W. Amerman, 1865.

Nicholas, Samuel Smith. *Habeas Corpus, the Law of War, and Confiscation.* Louisville: Bradley and Gilbert, 1862.

Paine, Levi L. *Political Lessons of the Rebellion. A Sermon Delivered at Farmington, Connecticut, on Fast Day, April 18, 1862.* Farmington: Samuel S. Cowles, 1862.

Perham, Josiah. *General Perham's Platform: The Most Feasible Plan Yet Offered for Suppressing the Rebellion.* Boston: Alfred Mudge and Son, 1862.

Pickett, Charles Edward. *The Existing Revolution, its Causes and Results.* Sacramento: n.p., 1861.

Potter, Elisha R. *Speech of Hon. Elisha R. Potter, of South Kingstown: Upon the Resolution in Support of the Union, with an Additional Note.* Providence: Cooke and Danielson, 1861.

Sargent, Lucius Manlius. *Mr. Stillé's Pamphlet "How a Free People Conduct a Long War."* N.p., 1862.

Scoville, Joseph Alfred. *What Shall be Done with the Confiscated Negroes? The Question Discussed and a Policy Proposed in a Letter to Abraham Lincoln, Winfield Scott, Seward, Archbishop Hughes, John J. Crittenden, Daniel Holt, Daniel S. Dickinson, Horace Greeley, Henry Ward Beecher, General George B. McClellan, General John C. Frémont and all other patriots.* N.p., [1862?].

Sizer, Thomas J. *The Crisis: Its Rational. Part I.— Our National Force the Proper Remedy. Part II.—Restoration of Legitimate Authority the End and Object of the War.* Buffalo: Breed, Butler, 1862.

Sloane, J. R. W. *The Three Pillars of a Republic: An Address Before the Philo and Franklin Societies of Jefferson College, Canonsburg, Penn., Delivered at the Annual Commencement, Aug. 6, 1862, by Rev. J. R. W. Sloane, New York City.* New York: Phair, 1862.

Smith, Edward Delafield. *Brief Appeals for the Loyal Cause.* New York: John W. Amerman, 1863.

Sprague, William B. *Glorifying God in the Fires. A Discourse Delivered in the Second Presbyterian Church, Albany, November 28, 1861, the Day of the Annual Thanksgiving, in the State of New York.* Albany: C. Van Benthuysen, 1861.

Stevens, John Auston, Jr. *Proceedings at the Mass Meeting of Loyal Citizens, on Union Square, New-York, 15th Day of July, 1862.* New York: George F. Nesbitt, 1862.

Swain, Leonard. *Our Banners Set Up. A Sermon Preached at the Central Congregational Church, Providence, R.I., April 21, 1861.* Providence: Knowles, Anthony, 1861.

Thompson, Joseph Parrish. *The President's Fast; A Discourse upon Our National Crimes and Follies, Preached in the Broadway Tabernacle Church, January 4, 1861.* New York: Thomas Holman, 1861.

———. *The Test-Hour of Popular Liberty and Republican Government.* New Haven: Thomas J. Stafford, 1862.

Tousey, Sinclair. *A Business Man's Views of Public Matters.* New York: American News, 1865.

Victor, Orville. *The Comprehensive History of the Southern Rebellion and the War for the American Union*, vol. 1. New York: James D. Torrey, 1862.

Whiting, William. *The War Powers of the President, and the Legislative Powers of Congress in Relation to Rebellion, Treason, and Slavery*. Boston: J. L. Shorey, 1862.

Willard, Emma. *Via Media: A Peaceful and Permanent Settlement of the Slavery Question*. Washington, D.C.: C. H. Anderson, 1862.

Wilson, William. *A Nation Nonplussed: But Enlightened, Extricated and Victorious, by turning its Waiting Eyes upon God. A Sermon, Preached in the City of Xenia, on the National Day of Fasting, January 4, 1861*. Cincinnati: B. Frankland, 1861.

Wilson, William Dexter. *Attainder of Treason and Confiscation of the Property of Rebels: A Letter to the Hon. Samuel A. Foot, LL.D., on the Constitutional Restrictions Upon Attainder and Forfeiture for Treason Against the United States by William Dexter Wilson, with Judge Foot's Answer, in further Elucidation of the Subject*. Albany: Weed, Parsons, 1863.

Wright, Allen H. *One Year—A Retrospect. Review of the First Twelve Months of the Administration of Abraham Lincoln. Reprint of an Editorial in the San Francisco (Cal.) Herald and Mirror, March 4, 1862*. San Diego: n.p., 1925.

Published Secondary Sources: Books

Abbott, Richard H. *Cobbler in Congress: The Life of Henry Wilson, 1812–1875*. Lexington: Univ. Press of Kentucky, 1972.

———. *Cotton and Capital: Boston Businessmen and Antislavery Reform, 1854–1868*. Amherst: Univ. of Massachusetts Press, 1991.

Abzug, Robert H. *American Reform and the Religious Imagination*. New York: Oxford Univ. Press, 1994.

Altschuler, Glenn C., and Stuart M. Blumin. *Rude Republic: Americans and Their Politics in the Nineteenth Century*. Princeton: Princeton Univ. Press, 2000.

Ambrosius, Lloyd E., ed. *A Crisis of Republicanism: American Politics during the Civil War Era*. Lincoln: Univ. of Nebraska Press, 1990.

Anastaplo, George. *Abraham Lincoln: A Constitutional Biography*. Lanham, Md.: Rowman and Littlefield, 1999.

Ash, Stephen V. *When the Yankees Came: Conflict and Chaos in the Occupied South, 1861–1865*. Chapel Hill: Univ. of North Carolina Press, 1995.

Baker, Jean H. *Affairs of Party: The Political Culture of Northern Democrats in the Mid-Nineteenth Century*. Ithaca: Cornell Univ. Press, 1983.

Bartlett, Ruhl Jacob. *John C. Frémont and the Republican Party*. Columbus: Ohio State Univ. Press, 1930.

Beale, Howard K. *The Critical Year: A Study of Andrew Johnson and Reconstruction*. New York: Ungar, 1958.

Belz, Herman. *Abraham Lincoln, Constitutionalism, and Equal Rights in the Civil War Era*. New York: Fordham Univ. Press, 1998.

———. *Emancipation and Equal Rights: Politics and Constitutionalism in the Civil War Era*. New York: Norton, 1978.

———. *A New Birth of Freedom: The Republican Party and Freedmen's Rights, 1861–1866*. Fordham Univ. Press, 2000.

———. *Reconstructing the Union: Theory and Policy during the Civil War*. Ithaca: Cornell Univ. Press, 1969.

Benedict, Michael Les. *Civil Rights and Civil Liberties*. Washington, D.C.: American Historical Association, 1987.

———. *A Compromise of Principle: Congressional Republicans and Reconstruction, 1863–1869*. New York: Norton, 1974.

Bensel, Richard Franklin. *Yankee Leviathan: The Origins of Central State Authority in America, 1859–1877*. Cambridge: Cambridge Univ. Press, 1995.

Berlin, Ira P. *Freedom: A Documentary History of Emancipation, 1861–1867*. Ser. 1, vol. 1, *The Destruction of Slavery* (Cambridge: Cambridge Univ. Press, 1985.

Berlin, Ira, Barbara J. Fields, Steven F. Miller, Joseph P. Reidy, and Leslie S. Rowland. *Slaves No More: Three Essays on Emancipation and the Civil War.* New York: Cambridge Univ. Press, 1993.

Blight, David W., and Brooks D. Simpson. *Union and Emancipation: Essays on Politics and Race in the Civil War Era.* Kent, Ohio: Kent State Univ. Press, 1997.

Bogue, Allan G. *The Congressman's Civil War.* Cambridge, Eng., and New York: Cambridge Univ. Press, 1989.

————. *The Earnest Men: Republicans of the Civil War Senate.* Ithaca: Cornell Univ. Press, 1981.

Boritt, Gabor. *Lincoln and the Economics of the American Dream.* Urbana: Univ. of Illinois Press, 1994.

Bradley, Erwin Stanley. *The Triumph of Militant Republicanism: A Study of Pennsylvania and Presidential Politics, 1860–1872.* Philadelphia: Univ. of Pennsylvania Press, 1964.

Brodie, Fawn M. *Thaddeus Stevens: Scourge of the South.* New York: Norton, 1959.

Cain, Marvin R. *Lincoln's Attorney General: Edward Bates of Missouri.* Columbia: Univ. of Missouri Press, 1965.

Catton, Bruce. *The Coming Fury.* Garden City: Doubleday, 1961.

Chambers, William Nisbet, and Walter Dean Burnham, eds. *The American Party Systems: Stages of Political Development.* New York: Oxford Univ. Press, 1975.

Chesebrough, David B. *"God Ordained this War": Sermons on the Sectional Crisis, 1830–1865.* Columbia: Univ. of South Carolina Press, 1991.

Cike, Donald B., and John J. McDonough, eds. *Benjamin Brown French: Witness to the Young Republic, A Yankee's Journal, 1828–1879.* Hanover, N.H.: Univ. Press of New England, 1989.

Cole, Arthur Charles. *The Era of the Civil War, 1848–1870.* Chicago: Univ. of Illinois Press, 1919.

Cooling, Benjamin Franklin. *Symbol, Sword, and Shield: Defending Washington during the Civil War.* Shippensburg: White Mane, 1991.

Cox, LaWanda. *Lincoln and Black Freedom: A Study in Presidential Leadership.* Columbia: Univ. of South Carolina Press, 1981.

Curry, Leonard. *Blueprint for Modern America: Nonmilitary Legislation of the First Civil War Congress.* Nashville: Vanderbilt Univ. Press, 1968.

Detroit Post and Tribune. *Zachariah Chandler: An Outline Sketch of his Life and Public Services.* Detroit: Detroit Post and Tribune, 1880.

Dilla, Harriette M. *The Politics of Michigan, 1865–1878.* New York: Longmans, Green, 1912.

Donald, David Herbert. *Charles Sumner and the Coming of the Civil War.* New York: Knopf, 1960.

———. *Charles Sumner and the Rights of Man.* New York: Knopf, 1970.

———. *Liberty and Union.* Lexington: D. C. Heath, 1978.

———. *Lincoln.* London: Jonathan Cape, 1995.

Donald, David Herbert, Jean H. Baker, and Michael F. Holt. *The Civil War and Reconstruction.* New York: Norton, 2001.

Doughty, Robert A., and Ira D. Gruber. *The American Civil War: The Emergence of Total Warfare.* Lexington: D. C. Heath, 1996.

Du Bois, W. E. B. *Black Reconstruction.* New York: Harcourt, Brace, 1935.

Ely, James W., Jr. *The Guardian of Every Other Right: A Constitutional History of Property Rights.* New York: Oxford Univ. Press, 1992.

Fausold, Martin L., and Alan Shank, eds. *The Constitution and the American Presidency.* Albany: State Univ. of New York Press, 1991.

Fehrenbacher, Don E. *The Slaveholding Republic: An Account of the United States Government's Relations to Slavery.* New York: Oxford Univ. Press, 2001.

Fessenden, Francis. *Life and Public Services of William Pitt Fessenden.* Boston: Houghton Mifflin, 1907.

Finkelman, Paul. *An Imperfect Union: Slavery, Federalism, and Comity.* Chapel Hill: Univ. of North Carolina Press, 1981.

Floan, Howard R. *The South in Northern Eyes, 1831–1861.* Austin: Univ. of Texas Press, 1958.

Foner, Eric. *Free Soil, Free Labor, Free Men: The Ideology of the Republican Party Before the Civil War.* New York: Oxford Univ. Press, 1970.

———. *Politics and Ideology in the Age of the Civil War.* New York: Oxford Univ. Press, 1980.

———. *Reconstruction: America's Unfinished Revolution, 1863–1877.* New York: Harper and Row, 1988.

Foner, Philip S. *Business and Slavery: The New York Merchants and the Irrepressible Conflict.* Chapel Hill: Univ. of North Carolina Press, 1941.

———. *The Life and Writings of Frederick Douglass.* Vol. 3, *The Civil War: 1861–1865.* New York: International Publishers, 1952.

Förster, Stig, and Jörg Nagler, eds. *On the Road to Total War: The American Civil War and the German Wars of Unification, 1861–1871.* Cambridge: Cambridge Univ. Press, 1997.

Fox-Genovese, Elizabeth, and Eugene D. Genovese. *Fruits of Merchant Capital: Slavery and Bourgeois Property in the Rise and Expansion of Capitalism.* New York: Oxford Univ. Press, 1983.

Franklin, John Hope. *The Emancipation Proclamation.* Wheeling, Ill.: Harlan Davidson, 1995.

Franklin, John Hope, and Alfred A. Moss Jr. *From Slavery to Freedom: A History of African Americans.* New York: McGraw-Hill, 2000.

Fredrickson, George M. *The Inner Civil War: Northern Intellectuals and the Crisis of the Union.* New York: Harper and Row, 1965.

Freehling, William W. *The South vs. the South: How Anti-Confederate Southerners Shaped the Course of the Civil War.* New York: Oxford Univ. Press, 2001.

Friedman, Lawrence. *A History of American Law,* 2nd ed. New York: Simon and Schuster, 1985.

Gallagher, Gary W., ed. *The Richmond Campaign of 1862: The Peninsula and the Seven Days.* Chapel Hill: Univ. of North Carolina Press, 2000.

Gallman, J. Matthew. *Mastering Wartime: A Social History of Philadelphia during the Civil War.* New York: Cambridge Univ. Press, 1990.

———. *The North Fights the Civil War: The Home Front.* Chicago: Ivan R. Dee, 1994.

Gazley, John Gerow. *American Opinion of German Unification, 1848–1871.* New York: Columbia Univ. Press, 1926.

Gerteis, Louis S. *From Contraband to Freedman: Federal Policy toward Southern Blacks, 1861–1865.* Westport, Conn.: Greenwood, 1975.

Gienapp, William E. *Abraham Lincoln and Civil War America: A Biography.* New York: Oxford Univ. Press, 2002.

———. *The Origins of the Republican Party.* New York: Oxford Univ. Press, 1986.

Gillette, William. *Retreat from Reconstruction, 1869–1879.* Baton Rouge: Louisiana State Univ. Press, 1979.

Gossett, Thomas F. *Race: The History of an Idea in America.* Dallas: Southern Methodist Univ. Press, 1970.

Grant, Susan-Mary. *North Over South: Northern Nationalism and American Identity in the Antebellum Era.* Lawrence: Univ. Press of Kansas, 2000.

Greenberg, Kenneth S. *Masters and Statesmen: The Political Culture of American Slavery.* Baltimore: Johns Hopkins Univ. Press, 1985.

Greenberg, Martin H., and Charles G. Waugh. *The Price of Freedom: Slavery and the Civil War.* 2 vols. Nashville: Cumberland House, 2000.

Grimsley, Mark. *The Hard Hand of War: Union Military Policy toward Southern Civilians, 1861–1865.* New York: Cambridge Univ. Press, 1995.

Guelzo, Allen C. *Lincoln's Emancipation Proclamation: The End of Slavery in America.* New York: Simon and Schuster, 2004.

Gunderson, Robert Gray. *Old Gentlemen's Convention: The Washington Peace Conference, 1861.* Madison: Univ. of Wisconsin Press, 1961.

Hall, Kermit L. *The Magic Mirror: Law in American History.* New York: Oxford Univ. Press, 1989.

Harris, William C. *With Charity for All: Lincoln and the Restoration of the Union.* Lexington: Univ. Press of Kentucky, 1997.

Henig, Gerald S. *Henry Winter Davis: Antebellum and Civil War Congressman from Maryland.* New York: Twayne Publishers, 1973.

Hess, Earl J. *Liberty, Virtue, and Progress: Northerners and Their War for the Union.* New York: New York Univ. Press, 1988.

Hesseltine, William B. *Lincoln and the War Governors.* New York: Knopf, 1955.

Hilkey, Judy. *Character Is Capital: Success Manuals and Manhood in Gilded Age America.* Chapel Hill: Univ. of North Carolina Press, 1997.

Horwitz, Morton R. *The Transformation of American Law, 1780–1860.* Cambridge: Harvard Univ. Press, 1977.

Huston, James. *Calculating the Value of Union: Slavery, Property Rights, and the Economic Origins of the Civil War.* Chapel Hill: Univ. of North Carolina Press, 2003.

———. *Securing the Fruits of Labor: The American Concept of Wealth Distribution, 1765– 1900.* Baton Rouge: Louisiana State Univ. Press, 1998.

Hyman, Harold M. *Era of the Oath: Northern Loyalty Tests during the Civil War and Reconstruction.* New York: Octagon Books, 1978.

———. *A More Perfect Union: The Impact of the Civil War and Reconstruction on the Constitution.* New York: Knopf, 1973.

———. *Quiet Past and Stormy Present? War Powers in American History.* Washington, D.C.: American Historical Association, 1986.

———. *The Radical Republicans and Reconstruction, 1861–1870.* New York: Bobbs-Merrill, 1967.

———, ed. *New Frontiers of the American Reconstruction.* Urbana: Univ. of Illinois Press, 1966.

Hyman, Harold M., and William M. Wiecek. *Equal Justice Under Law: Constitutional Development, 1835–1875.* New York: Harper and Row, 1982.

Jaffa, Harry V. *A New Birth of Freedom: Abraham Lincoln and the Coming of the Civil War.* Lanham, Md.: Rowman and Littlefield, 2000.

Jellison, Charles A. *Fessenden of Maine, Civil War Senator.* New York: Syracuse Univ. Press, 1962.

Kammen, Michael. *A Machine That Would Go of Itself: The Constitution in American Culture.* New York: St. Martin's Press, 1994.

Kirwan, Albert D. *John J. Crittenden: The Struggle for the Union.* Lexington: Univ. of Kentucky Press, 1962.

Klement, Frank L. *Lincoln's Critics: The Copperheads of the North.* Shippensburg, Pa.: White Mane, 1999.

Klingaman, William K. *Abraham Lincoln and the Road to Emancipation, 1861–1865.* New York: Penguin Books, 2002.

Knapp, Charles Merriam. *New Jersey Politics during the Period of the Civil War and Reconstruction.* Geneva: W. F. Humphrey, 1924.

Knupfer, Peter B. *The Union As It Is: Constitutional Unionism and Sectional Compromise, 1787–1861.* Chapel Hill: Univ. of North Carolina Press, 1991.

Krug, Mark M. *Lyman Trumbull: Conservative Radical.* New York: A. S. Barnes, 1965.

Kyvig, David. *Explicit and Authentic Acts: Amending the U.S. Constitution, 1776–1995.* Lawrence: Univ. of Kansas Press, 1996.

Leech, Margaret. *Reveille in Washington, 1860–1865.* New York: Harper and Brothers, 1941.

Linden, Glenn M. *Politics or Principle: Congressional Voting on the Civil War Amendments and Pro-Negro Measures, 1838–69.* Seattle: Univ. of Washington Press, 1976.

Lofgren, Charles A. *"Government from Reflection and Choice": Constitutional Essays on War, Foreign Relations, and Federalism.* New York: Oxford Univ. Press, 1986.

Lucie, Patricia. *Freedom and Federalism, Congress and Courts, 1861–1866.* New York: Garland Publishing, 1986.

Magdol, Edward. *Owen Lovejoy: Abolitionist in Congress.* New Brunswick: Rutgers Univ. Press, 1967.

———. *A Right to the Land: Essays on the Freedmen's Community.* Westport, Conn.: Greenwood Press, 1977.

Maihafer, Harry H. *War of Words: Abraham Lincoln and the Civil War Press.* Washington, D.C.: Brassey's, 2001.

Maltz, Earl. *Civil Rights, the Constitution, and Congress, 1863–1869.* Lawrence: Univ. Press of Kansas, 1990.

McCrary, Peyton. *Abraham Lincoln and Reconstruction: The Louisiana Experiment.* Princeton: Princeton Univ. Press, 1978.

McKay, Ernest A. *The Civil War and New York City.* Syracuse: Syracuse Univ. Press, 1990.

McPherson, James M. *Abraham Lincoln and the Second American Revolution.* New York: Oxford Univ. Press, 1990.

———. *Battle Cry of Freedom: The Civil War Era.* New York: Oxford Univ. Press, 1988.

———. *Drawn with the Sword: Reflections on the American Civil War.* New York: Oxford Univ. Press, 1996.

———. *For Cause and Comrades: Why Men Fought in the Civil War.* New York: Oxford Univ. Press, 1997.

———. *The Struggle for Equality: Abolitionists and the Negro in the Civil War and Reconstruction.* Princeton: Princeton Univ. Press, 1964.

McPherson, James M., and William J. Cooper Jr., eds. *Writing the Civil War: The Quest to Understand.* Columbia: Univ. of South Carolina Press, 1998.

Meyer, Michael J., and William A. Parent. *The Constitution of Rights: Human Dignity and American Values.* Ithaca: Cornell Univ. Press, 1992.

Neely, Mark E., Jr. *The Fate of Liberty: Abraham Lincoln and Civil Liberties.* New York: Oxford Univ. Press, 1991.

Nevins, Allan. *Frémont: Pathmarker of the West.* New York: D. Appleton–Century, 1939.

———. *The War for the Union.* Vol. 1, *The Improvised War, 1861–1862.* New York: Charles Scribner's Sons, 1959.

———. *The War for the Union.* Vol. 2, *War Becomes Revolution, 1862–1863.* New York: Scribner, [1959–1971].

Nichols, Roy Franklin. *The Disruption of American Democracy.* New York: Collier, 1948.

Novak, William J. *The People's Welfare: Law and Regulation in Nineteenth-Century America.* Chapel Hill: Univ. of North Carolina Press, 1996.

Oates, Stephen R. *With Malice Toward None: The Life of Abraham Lincoln.* New York: Harper Collins, 1977.

O'Brien, Patrick. *The Economic Effects of the American Civil War.* Atlantic Highlands, N.J.: Humanities Press International, 1988.

O'Connor, Thomas H. *Lords of the Loom: The Cotton Whigs and the Coming of the Civil War.* New York: Scribner, 1968.

Paludan, Phillip S. *A Covenant with Death: The Constitution, Law, and Equality in the Civil War Era.* Urbana: Univ. of Illinois Press, 1975.

———. *"A People's Contest": The Union and Civil War, 1861–1865.* New York: Harper and Row, 1988.

————. *The Presidency of Abraham Lincoln.* Lawrence: Univ. Press of Kansas, 1994.

Parrish, William E. *Turbulent Partnership: Missouri and the Union, 1861–1865.* Columbia: Univ. of South Carolina Press, 1963.

Paul, Ellen Frankel. *Property Rights and Eminent Domain.* New Brunswick: Transaction Books, 1987.

Perkins, Howard Cecil, ed. *Northern Editorials on Secession.* New York: D. Appleton–Century, 1942.

Peterson, Merill, ed. *Democracy, Liberty and Property: The State Constitutional Conventions of the 1820's.* Indianapolis: Bobbs-Merrill, 1966.

Potter, David M. *Lincoln and His Party in the Secession Crisis.* New Haven: Yale Univ. Press, 1962.

Pryor, Sara. *Reminiscences of Peace and War.* New York: Macmillan, 1924, 112.

Randall, James Garfield. *The Confiscation of Property during the Civil War.* Ph.D. diss., University of Chicago, 1911.

————. *Constitutional Problems under Lincoln.* New York: D. Appleton, 1926.

Randall, James Garfield, and David Donald. *The Civil War and Reconstruction.* Lexington, Mass.: D. C. Heath, 1969.

Rawley, James A. *The Politics of Union: Northern Politics during the Civil War.* Hinsdale: Dryden, 1974.

————. *Turning Points of the Civil War.* Lincoln: Univ. of Nebraska Press, 1966.

Richards, Leonard L. *The Slave Power: The Free North and Southern Domination, 1780–1860.* Baton Rouge: Louisiana State Univ. Press, 2000.

Richardson, Heather Cox. *The Greatest Nation of the Earth: Republican Economic Policies during the Civil War.* Cambridge, Mass.: Harvard Univ. Press, 1997.

Richardson, James D., ed. *The Messages and Papers of Jefferson Davis and the Confederate Congress, Including Diplomatic Correspondence, 1861–1865.* New York: Chelsea House–R. Hector, 1966.

Robinson, William Morrison. *The Confederate Privateers.* 1928. Reprint, Columbia: Univ. of South Carolina Press, 1990.

Rose, Willie Lee. *Rehearsal for Reconstruction.* New York: Oxford Univ. Press, 1964.

Roske, Ralph J. *His Own Counsel: The Life and Times of Lyman Trumbull.* Reno: Univ. of Nevada Press, 1979.

Royster, Charles. *The Destructive War: William Tecumseh Sherman, Stonewall Jackson, and the Americans.* New York: Knopf, 1991.

Saum, Lewis O. *The Popular Mood of America, 1860–1890.* Lincoln: Univ. of Nebraska Press, 1990.

Shapiro, Henry D. *Confiscation of Confederate Property in the North.* Ithaca: Cornell Univ. Press, 1962.

Silber, Nina. *The Romance of Reunion: Northerners and the South, 1865–1900.* Chapel Hill: Univ. of North Carolina Press, 1993.

Silbey, Joel H. *The American Political Nation, 1838–1893.* Stanford: Stanford Univ. Press, 1991.

———. *A Respectable Minority: The Democratic Party in the Civil War Era, 1860–1868.* New York: Norton, 1977.

Simon, John Y., and Michael E. Stevens, eds. *New Perspectives on the Civil War: Myths and Realities of the National Conflict.* Madison, Wisc.: Madison House, 1998.

Simpson, Brooks D. *Let Us Have Peace: Ulysses S. Grant and the Politics of War and Reconstruction, 1861–1868.* Chapel Hill: Univ. of North Carolina Press, 1991.

Smith, Edward Conrad. *The Borderland in the Civil War.* New York: Macmillan, 1927.

Smith, Elbert. *The Presidency of James Buchanan*. Lawrence: Univ. Press of Kansas, 1975.

Stampp, Kenneth M. *And the War Came: The North and the Secession Crisis, 1860–1861*. Baton Rouge: Louisiana State Univ. Press, 1970.

————. *Indiana Politics during the Civil War*. Indianapolis: Indiana Historical Bureau, 1949.

————, ed. *The Causes of the Civil War*, 3rd. ed. New York: Simon and Schuster, 1991.

Stern, Gary M., and Morton H. Halperin, eds. *The U.S. Constitution and the Power to Go to War: Historical and Current Perspectives*. Westport: Greenwood Press, 1994.

Stewart, James Brewer. *Holy Warriors: The Abolitionists and American Slavery*. New York: Hill and Wang, 1996.

Sunstein, Cass R. *Constitutional Myth-Making: Lessons from the Dred Scott Case*. Chicago: The Law School of the University of Chicago, 1996.

Sutherland, Daniel E. *The Emergence of Total War*. Fort Worth: Ryan Place, 1996.

Symonds, Craig L. *Confederate Admiral: The Life and Wars of Franklin Buchanan*. Annapolis: U.S. Naval Institute Press, 1999.

Syrett, John D. *The Confiscation Acts: Efforts at Reconstruction during the Civil War*. Ph.D. diss., University of Wisconsin, 1971.

Tap, Bruce. *Over Lincoln's Shoulder: The Committee on the Conduct of the War*. Lawrence: Univ. Press of Kansas, 1998.

Thomas, Benjamin P. *Abraham Lincoln: A Biography*. New York: Modern Library, 1968.

Thomas, Benjamin P., and Harold M. Hyman. *Stanton: The Life and Times of Lincoln's Secretary of War*. New York: Knopf, 1962.

Thomas, John L., ed. *Abraham Lincoln and the American Political Tradition*. Amherst: Univ. of Massachusetts Press, 1986.

Tise, Larry E. *Proslavery: A History of the Defense of Slavery in America, 1701–1840.* Athens: Univ. of Georgia Press, 1987.

Trefousse, Hans L. *Benjamin Franklin Wade: Radical Republican from Ohio.* New York: Twayne Publishers, 1963.

————. *Lincoln's Decision for Emancipation.* Philadelphia: J. B. Lippincott, 1975.

————. *The Radical Republicans: Lincoln's Vanguard for Racial Justice.* New York: Knopf, 1969.

Vinovskis, Maris A. *Toward a Social History of the American Civil War: Explanatory Essays.* New York: Cambridge Univ. Press, 1990.

Vorenberg, Michael. *Final Freedom: The Civil War, the Abolition of Slavery, and the Thirteenth Amendment.* Cambridge: Cambridge Univ. Press, 2001.

Wang, Xi. *The Trial of Democracy: Black Suffrage and Northern Republicans, 1860–1910.* Athens: Univ. of Georgia Press, 1997.

Ware, Edith Ellen. *Political Opinion in Massachusetts during Civil War and Reconstruction.* New York: Columbia University, 1916. Reprint, New York: AMS Press, 1968.

White, Horace C. *The Life of Lyman Trumbull.* Boston: Houghton Mifflin, 1913.

Wiecek, William M. *The Sources of Anti-Slavery Constitutionalism in America, 1760–1848.* Ithaca: Cornell Univ. Press, 1977.

Williams, Frank J., and William D. Pederson, eds. *Abraham Lincoln, Contemporary: An American Legacy.* Campbell, Calif.: Savas Woodbury, 1995.

Williams, T. Harry. *Lincoln and the Radicals.* Madison: Univ. of Wisconsin Press, 1941.

Wormuth, Francis D., Edwin B. Firmage, and Francis P. Butler. *To Chain the Dog of War: The War Power of Congress in History and Law.* Dallas: Southern Methodist Univ. Press, 1986.

Yearns, W. Buck, ed. *The Confederate Governors.* Athens: Univ. of Georgia Press, 1985.

Published Secondary Sources: Articles

Atherton, Lewis E. "The Problem of Credit Rating in the Ante-Bellum South." *Journal of Southern History* 12 (November 1946): 534–56.

Benedict, Michael Les. "Preserving the Constitution: The Conservative Basis of Radical Reconstruction." *Journal of American History* 61 (June 1974): 65–90.

Bestor, Arthur. "The American Civil War as a Constitutional Crisis." *American Historical Review* 69 (January 1964): 327–52.

Burton, Shirley, and Kellee Green. "Defining Disloyalty: Treason, Espionage, and Sedition Prosecutions, 1861–1946." *Prologue* 21 (fall 1989): 215–21.

Cox, LaWanda. "Lincoln and Black Freedom." In *The Price of Freedom: Slavery and the Civil War,* vol. 2, *The Preservation of Liberty,* edited by Martin H. Greenberg and Charles G. Waugh. Nashville: Cumberland House, 2000.

Farrar, Timothy. "The Adequacy of the Constitution." *New Englander* 21 (January 1862): 51–74.

Foner, Eric. "The Meaning of Freedom in the Age of Emancipation." *Journal of American History* 81 (September 1994): 435–60.

———. "Rights and the Constitution in Black Life during the Civil War and Reconstruction." *Journal of American History* 74 (December 1987): 863–83.

Gienapp, William E. "Abraham Lincoln and the Border States." *Journal of the Abraham Lincoln Association* 13 (1992): 13–46.

Harding, Vincent Gordon. "Wrestling Toward the Dawn: The Afro-American Freedom Movement and the Changing Constitution." *Journal of American History* 74 (December 1987): 718–39.

Kaczorowski, Robert J. "To Begin the Nation Anew: Congress, Citizenship, and Civil Rights after the Civil War." *American Historical Review* 92 (February 1987): 45–68.

McCrary, Peyton. "The Party of Revolution: Republican Ideas about Politics and Social Change, 1862–1867." *Civil War History* 30 (December 1984): 330–50.

Mowry, Duane. "A Statesman's Letters of the Civil War Period." *Journal of the Illinois State Historical Society* 2 (July 1909): 43–9.

Paludan, Phillip S. "The American Civil War Considered as a Crisis in Law and Order." *American Historical Review* 77 (October 1972): 1013–34.

Shortreed, Margaret. "The Antislavery Radicals: From Crusade to Revolution." *Past and Present* 16 (November 1959): 65–87.

Volpe, Vernon. "The Frémonts and Emancipation in Missouri." *Historian* 56 (winter 1994): 339–54.

Index